# GODWRESTLING
# ROUND 2

# GODWRESTLING ROUND 2

## ANCIENT WISDOM, FUTURE PATHS

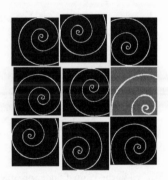

### ARTHUR WASKOW

JEWISH LIGHTS PUBLISHING

Woodstock, Vermont

Library of Congress Cataloging-in-Publication Data
Waskow, Arthur I.
Godwrestling—round 2 : ancient wisdom, future paths / Arthur Waskow.
p.   cm.
1. Jewish way of life. 2. Judaism and social problems. 3. Ethics, Jewish.
4. Bible. O.T.—Criticism, interpretation, etc. I. Title
BM723.W33 1995 95-24935
296.1'406—dc20 CIP r95


First Edition
10 9 8 7 6 5 4 3 2 1


ISBN 1-879045-45-1 (hardcover)
ISBN 1-879045-72-9 (paperback)

Manufactured in the United States of America
Book and cover designed by Glenn Suokko




Published by Jewish Lights Publishing
A Division of LongHill Partners Inc.
P.O. Box 237
Sunset Farm Offices, Rte. 4
Woodstock, Vermont 05091
Tel: (802) 457-4000   Fax: (802) 457-4004

For my brother Howard,
who taught me how to wrestle
and how to write about it,
and then invited me to join with him
in turning our wrestle to a dance.

And for Max and Esther Ticktin
who for a generation
have been my beloved friends and teachers
and for two generations
have loved and taught the Jewish people.

# CONTENTS

# GATEWAY TO THE SPIRAL

The Wrestle began for me before I knew it was a wrestle, before I had the language to describe it. It began just minutes before Passover in April, 1968. I was 34 years old, had grown up in a Jewish neighborhood in Baltimore with a strong sense that community, neighborhood itself, was warmly Jewish; that freedom and justice were profoundly, hotly Jewish—and that Jewish religion was boring boiler-plate. Except for celebrating the Passover Seder, which brought family, community, freedom, and justice into the same room, I had long ago abandoned the rhythms of Jewish religion.

And then on April 4, 1968, Martin Luther King was murdered.

I was not just a spectator to his passionate life and death. I had spent nine years in Washington working day and night against racial injustice and the Vietnam War—behind a typewriter on Capitol Hill and at the microphone on countless college campuses, sitting in unbearably hot back rooms of Convention Hall in Atlantic City in 1964 when Dr. King came hobbling on a broken leg to beg support for the Mississippi Freedom Democratic Party, marching in 1967 at the Pentagon against the Vietnam War, cruising D.C. streets in a sound truck (with my four-year-old son perched next to me), to turn out votes for Bobby Kennedy in 1968.

On the evening of April 3, Dr. King spoke to a crowd in Memphis: "I am standing on the mountaintop, looking into the Promised Land. I may not reach there, but the people will." Echoes of Moses. By the next night, he was dead.

By noon the next day, Washington, my city, was ablaze. Touch and go it was, whether 18th Street—four houses from my door—would join the flames. Just barely, our neighborhood's interracial ties held fast.

By April 6, there was a curfew. Thousands of Blacks were being herded into jail for breaking it. No whites, of course; the police did not care whether whites were on the streets. My white friends and I tried to turn their blindness to good use: For days we brought food, medicine, doctors from the suburbs into the schools and churches of burnt-out downtown Washington.

And then came the afternoon of April 12. That night, Passover would begin. We would gather—my wife and I , our son, our daughter (just nine months old), with a few friends, for the usual ritual recitation of the Telling of our freedom. Some rollicking songs. Some solemn invocations. Some memories from Seders of the past, in the families where our fathers had chanted—some of them in Hebrew or Yiddish, some in English.

A bubble in time, a bubble isolated from the life, the power, the volcano of the streets. Perhaps, when the rituals were over and the kids had been initiated into the age-old ritual, had taken their first look into this age-old mirror in which Jews saw ourselves as a band of runaway slaves, we might put aside the ancient book and talk about the burning—truly, burning—issues of our lives.

## PHARAOH'S ARMY

So I walked home to help prepare to celebrate the Seder. On every block, detachments of the Army. On 18th Street, a Jeep with a machine gun pointing up my block.

Somewhere within me, deeper than my brain or breathing, my blood began to chant: "This is Pharaoh's army, and I am walking home to do the Seder."

> "This is
> Pharaoh's
> army,
> and I am walking home
> to do
> the Seder.
> This is
> Pharaoh's
> army..."

King's speech came back to me. "Standing on the mountaintop, looking into the Promised Land...." The songs we had sung in Atlantic City four years before with Fannie Lou Hamer, who had come from a Mississippi sharecropper's shack to confront the Democratic Party: "Go tell it on the mountain, let my people go!" "Must be the people that Moses led, let my people go!" The sermons I had heard Black preachers speak, half shouting, half chanting: "And on the wings of eagles I will bring you, from slavery, from bondage, yes!—from slavery, to be My people—yes, my beloved people."

Yes, this *is* Pharaoh's army, and I am walking home to do the Seder.

Not again, not ever again, a bubble in time. Not again, not ever again, a ritual recitation before the real life, the real meal, the real conversation.

For on that night, the Haggadah itself, the Telling of our slavery and our freedom, became the real conversation about our real life. The ritual foods, the bitterness of the bitter herb, the pressed-down bread of everyone's oppression, the wine of joy in struggle, became the real meal.

For the first time, we paused in the midst of the Telling itself, to connect the streets with the Seder. For the first time, we noticed the passage that says, "In every generation, one rises up to become an oppressor"; the passage that says, "In every generation, every human being is obligated to say, we ourselves, not our forebears only, go forth from slavery to freedom."

In every generation. Including our own. Always before, we had chanted these passages and gone right on. Tonight we paused. Who and what is our oppressor? How and when shall we go forth to freedom?

To my astonishment, these questions burned like a volcano within me, erupting like the volcano in my city. Why did I care to make this connection? Why was this ancient tale having such an effect on me? How could I respond?

## WHAT'S A MIDRASH?

During the next six months, over and over when I faced some crisis in the world, some element of the Jewish story erupted inside me—often in my forebrain only dimly understood, yet with such volcanic power in my heart and belly that I could not turn away. In the fall, I found myself preparing for the next Passover by writing a Haggadah of my own, a script for our own family Seder. I hoped it would deliberately make happen in the future what had already happened, with no deliberation, in the midst of turmoil. I dug out my old Haggadah, the one I had been given when I turned 13, the one with Saul Raskin's luscious drawings of the maidens who saved Moses from the river, the one that stirred my body each spring, those teen-age years. Into its archaic English renderings of Exodus and Psalms, I intertwined passages from King and Thoreau, Ginsberg and Gandhi, the Warsaw

Ghetto and a Russian rabbi named Tamaret—wove them all into a new Telling of the tale of freedom. Where the old Haggadah had a silly argument about how many plagues had really afflicted Egypt, I substituted a serious quandary: Were blood and death a necessary part of liberation, or could the nonviolence of King and Gandhi bring a deeper transformation?

I had written half a dozen books—on military strategy, disarmament, race relations, American politics—but this was different: This book was writing me. I had no idea whether it made any sense to do this; I knew only that I could not stop. When I had finished, I called around to find a Washington rabbi who might be sympathetic. I asked him to read my draft: Was this a crazed obsession or a good idea?

Two days later, he called me: "I love it, Waskow. You've taken the story into our own hands, as the rabbis said God wanted the fleeing slaves themselves to do. Do you know that midrash? The one where God refuses to split the Red Sea until the Jews have gone into the water, up to their noses?"

"What's a midrash?" said I.

"Oho!" said he, and even over the phone I could feel the excitement rise. "The rabbis would take the ancient text, and read it in new ways. On this one, where the Torah says the people 'went into the sea on the dry land,' the rabbis ask, 'Which was it? How could it be both sea and dry land?' And they answer that the people went in while it was still sea; only then did it become dry land.

"You see?—the people had to act. The rabbis took the text into their own hands because they wanted the people to take history into their own hands. The text at first glance seems to leave the act to God; but the rabbis reread this oddity of text to mean the people acted.

"That's midrash. Want to read some?"

So I borrowed a volume of this "midrash," and I fell in love. A whole new language that my heart had searched for all these years, a whole new language I had never known existed. A language of transformation-through-renewal, a language that drew on an ancient language to make it deeply new. A language of serious play that could, with a wink, turn reality in a new direction and claim it was simply uncovering a meaning that was already there. A language of puns, serious and funny puns that took as cosmic teaching the clang of words and phrases with each other.

And this, the rabbi taught me, was what my new Haggadah was already: A midrash on the ancient text that turned it in a new direction. What neither he nor I expected was that as I was reinterpreting the text, the text was reinterpreting me. Turning me in a new direction, making a new me that was a midrash on the old "I."

## OTHERS ON THE PATH

It was not only my engagement with the Jewish text, with all the Jewish texts, that "rewrote" me. It was also my engagement with other Jews who were rewriting themselves, my engagement with communities that came together in the very process of wrestling with these texts.

("Wrestling." Notice that word? Along this path there surfaced what for me had been the dimmest of memories: *"Yisrael"* (in English, "Israel"), the very name of our community, meant "Godwrestler"—a name won in pain and wounding long ago. For now, we can leave this discovery, this uncovering, within parentheses. Soon enough, as I tell this story, it will leap into its bright and central place.)

For indeed, it turned out that others were entering this process, stirred by events in their own lives as I had been stirred by the streets of Washington. Stirred, some of them, by their needs for community, and the chilliness of conventional Jewish life. Stirred, some others of them, by their own spiritual yearnings, and the flatness of conventional Jewish life. Stirred, still others, by their hopes and fears for the State of Israel, which had stood on the edge of deeply dangerous waters in 1967, and crossed in triumph. Stirred, some who had never been welcomed into the hidden places of Jewish thought and practice, by the joy and triumph they saw as Blacks refused to melt into America, and instead unfurled the hidden flags of their own culture. Stirred, still others—mostly women—by the possibility of reshaping the Judaism that had always ignored their needs and their perceptions. Stirred, still others who already had deep knowledge of hidden Jewish wisdom, by the unexpected feeling that those riches could give new meaning to their lives.

Because I was not alone, because there were others for me to meet upon my journey, my journey became possible. As we discovered each other, we granted each other the truths of our own different stories, ultimately the truth that we could share a journey of many different journeys. We discovered how astonishingly rich were the Judaisms—plural—we had barely known, and how our forebears also had walked many different paths. And we discovered how astonishingly nourishing were the new Judaisms we ourselves could shape as we intertwined our own lives with each other and with the lives of our forebears.

From 1968 to 1972, my life turned in a new direction, one I would never have imagined. I had been a writer before this transformation; I continued to be one afterward, but with a difference. Before I had written mostly at a distance: History and political theory, occasionally a report from my own life-experience in the decade of upheaval. Now what I wanted to write came straight from my own life. There was theology in it, and Jewish history, and ritual, and politics, and family life, and communal sharing—all of it flowing from my new life-experience. From my experience with the Seder of 1968, I wrote the Haggadah that eventually was called "The Freedom Seder."

But the process did not end there; it simply began. Looking back, I can see that the Freedom Seder was the moment and the act through which I truly became a bar mitzvah: With it, I entered the gates of Jewish life; with it, I became an adult, shaping my own life. Given who I was, it was the only gate I could have taken: One I had to build myself. And by the same token, looking back, I can see how it was the entry gate that a newcomer would build: Clumsy, intuitive, marked by a blunder here and a blemish there, yet powerfully attractive to others who connected with its impulsive energy. The kind of gate that would be built by someone who had jumped onto his first bike and joyfully ridden it almost into a ravine before learning, barely in time, how to put on the brakes.

For me, the very desire to learn how to steer, how to brake, came only from the joy of the moving. If someone had insisted that I wait to create until I knew how to steer and to brake, I would have shrugged and moved on. Plenty of people did try to say that, but I was also able to find a community of searchers, for whom learning came out of the searching.

By 1971, that community in Washington had coalesced into a band of seekers, wrestlers, dancers that called itself "Fabrangen," from the Yiddish for "bringing together." By 1978, I was ready to do again what I had done with "The Freedom Seder"—bring that process to a wider community by writing about it. That writing became a book called *Godwrestling*, rooted essentially in the first several years of Fabrangen's life.

This process has now been the living center of my life for a quarter century. I have moved to a different city, taught and learned in different schools, prayed in different gatherings from other prayerbooks I have helped to write myself. Out of my wrestling have come other books. I have learned to understand Jewish time and Jewish thought as a spiral: Neither a straight line that must go always forward, even into a precipice, nor a circle that must remain forever stuck in repeating past experience. Instead, a spiral, which curves always backward in order to curve forward.

What makes time and life into a spiral instead of a straight line or an endless circle is setting aside time for reflection, rest, renewal. That renewal-time—Shabbat, the Sabbath—is the curve that moves the spiral onward. So is the sabbatical year the Bible calls us toward. So is every moment when we pause to catch our breath, to absorb what we have just done before we go forward to do more. All these let us re-view where we have been, so that we can go forward.

The wrestle with Torah, the process of midrash, I understand now as a spiral, in which we go back again and again in order to go forward. We draw on ancient wisdom to create new wisdom. What went before we turn and turn like a kaleidoscope; with every turn, there appears new beauty, new patterns, new complexity, new simplicity.

## REFLECTION AND RENEWAL

So at this moment it seems wise to make my own small spiral in this great spiral dance. This book is both old and new: It includes much of the Godwrestling that went before, it reflects on that Godwrestling, and it continues the process. What I could in those days share only from a thin slice of my life, I can now share from a greater chunk of it.

So in this old/new book, I have done four things: In some places, I have simply kept what I wrote almost twenty years ago. In some places, I have reworked what I wrote then, in the light of all my experience since. In some places, I have added passages, chapters, that are altogether new. They arise from discoveries in life and Torah that have come to me through the process of Godwrestling since the book *Godwrestling* was first published.

Above all, I have reframed the whole enterprise. I understand what I was doing then in a way I could not have until I had lived through much more of my new Jewish life. When I first wrote *Godwrestling,* I had glimmers of a great transformation in Judaism and the Jewish people that was just beginning. Now that process is much clearer, and I can see much more of where in that process I was, we were.

But reframing our Jewish self-renewal is only part of the reframing I have lived through. Twenty years ago, my children were children. Now they are adults, rethinking their own lives, and they have taught me to reexamine what I thought was going on between us when I wrote about them in the first *Godwrestling.*

So I have curved back to my work of then, but not in a flat and simple circle of endless repetition. Instead, I have curved back in a spiral, where I can see where I have been from a vantage point that is on a different plane—and yet is part of the same curve. My own miniature version of the spiral that for centuries, millennia, has been the shape of Jewish time.

Let us begin that spiral journey by leaping upon the bicycle of youth—the one through which I learned to brake and steer, to make a spiral rather than crash into a precipice.

Let us begin with wrestling, with "*Yisrael*," with "*yisra-El*," the one whose name became "Godwrestler." How and why did that become his name? How and why did that become our name?

# PART I

# BROTHERS' WAR / BROTHERS' PEACE

# CHAPTER 1

# FROM HEEL TO GODWRESTLER: JACOB AND ESAU

Opposites to unify:

Sealed into a tiny cabin above a dry canal in Western Maryland. Sealed in by falling snow and a broken ankle, sealed in to talk with my brother Howard in depth for the first time ever, to sleep in the same bed with him for the first time...since we were children? Ever? To remember how his body felt when we wrestled, to discover we loved each other.

And nine months later, a crisp fall day in Oregon, when I sneered at something he said, when he looked at me—face flat and ugly—and said someday he might have to kill me after all.

Hard opposites to unify.

When I struggled for words to say how hard it was, the words that came were from an ancient story as well as from my childhood living with my brother. A story that had taken on new life for me in the process of wrestling in a community that was new for me, with a text about wrestling that was old for everyone but new for me. The medium and the message met; small wonder that the metaphor that came to me was—

*I wrestled again with my brother last week,*
*First time since I was twelve and Grandma stopped us:*
*"She won't even let us fight!" we yelled, embracing,*
*But she said talking was nicer.*
*Wrestling feels a lot like making love.*

*Why did Jacob wrestle with God,*
*why did the others talk?*

*God surely enjoyed that all-night fling with Jacob:*
*Told him he'd won,*
*Renamed him and us the "Godwrestler,"*
*Even left him a limp to be sure he'd remember it all.*
*But ever since, we've talked—*
*we've only talked.*
*Did something peculiar happen that night?*
*Did somebody say next day we shouldn't wrestle? Who?*

*We should wrestle again our Companion sometime soon.*
*Wrestling feels a lot like making love.*

*But Esau struggled*
*to his feet*
*from his own Wrestle,*
*And gasped across the river*
*to his brother:*
*It also*
*feels*
*a lot*
*like*
*making*
*war.*

When I wrote that poem, I thought it was just *about* wrestling. Now I realize that if its two stanzas had bodies instead of only voices, one of them would have the other in a half-nelson, and the other would be slippery-straining to break out. Two voices, struggling with each other, yet for one moment fused in an embrace.

Hearing those voices as my own and Howard's, Jacob's and Esau's, each voice an echo of the other, taught me both the Torah of the scroll and the Torah of my unrolling life. Studying Esau and Jacob taught me Howard and Arthur. Studying Arthur and Howard taught me Jacob and Esau.

The voices came together in my hearing because I came upon the story of Jacob and Esau while I was struggling with my brother. So I came to that story with a question of my own: What does it mean to discover only as a grownup how to have a brother and how to be a brother? What did it mean for Esau and for Jacob—for my brother and for me—to discover only as grownups how different and how alike we were? How parts of us were enemies and parts were loving friends? How we had been held apart all our lives?

What did it mean to learn only as grownups how to touch and be touched—not only each other but anyone else as well? How to feel and be felt, how to fight and make love? And how inevitable it was that we could learn all this only as grownups. And how disastrous.

How inevitable it was that we had visited upon us the failings of our family—just as the Torah said, to even the third and fourth generations. And what disasters they had bred.

Inevitable, and disastrous. That was one link to Jacob and Esau, for the sense of inevitability and disaster pervaded my reading of the story of these brothers. Not my reading alone, for as I wrestled with my brother I was also meeting Jacob and Esau in a special way: I was learning to grapple with Torah in the midst of a community of Jews.

## WRESTLING WITH TORAH

How our community wrestled was as important as what we wrestled with. For us, this "Torah" was not "Bible," not a bound and boundaried book. It was a process. Not Law, as it is also sometimes translated, but a word from the world of archery: Pointing, *Aiming*. God's *Aiming* toward a faithful path of life.

And what was this "Fabrangen" in Washington that came to wrestle with the Holy Scroll? By leaving out one "r," we gave a seriocomic twist to the Yiddish word *farbrangen*, The Rebbe of a Hassidic community made a *farbrangen* by bringing his followers together to learn his Torah. But we had no single Rebbe to gather round. All of us were rebbes, all of us taught each other. The missing "r" stood for the missing "Rebbe."

When we gathered, in our center we saw not a human Rebbe but...what? You might say we saw the Nothing that is also Everything, the invisible Holy One. Or you might say, we saw each other—in our infinite variety, the visible face of the Infinite One. Or you might say we saw both: They are the same. To wrestle with each other was to wrestle with the Infinite.

In Fabrangen, people came together around the effort, the hope—sometimes bright, sometimes flickering—to walk a contemporary path that would draw from Jewish tradition in new ways. A path of life to reconnect what have become the separated areas of our lives: Work, leisure, politics, sex, family life. To infuse them all with awe and celebration, rather than limiting such feelings to "religion."

What this meant was that Fabrangeners gathered to make our hollow Friday evening and Saturday morning into Holy Shabbat. We sat in a loose and flowing circle, women, men, and children scattered as we chose, some of us on cushions on the floor and some of us in chairs. We wore loose and casual clothing, comfortable and colorful.

Our prayer shawls with their knotted fringes ranged from formal black-and-white to rainbow prints and stripes. We sang and chanted, danced and prayed, ate together, read and talked together. We talked especially about the regular weekly portion from the Five Books of Moses, the passage that each Shabbat is traditionally assigned as part of the yearly reading cycle.

We read the portion together—some of it in Hebrew, all of it in English. Then we talked about it. Some of us drew on rabbinic commentaries, on recent Jewish philosophy and modern Bible criticism, on the insights of mystics of the East and West, on history and archaeology—all in trying to understand what we are reading. But mostly we drew on our own lives:

What can Torah, this arrowed Aiming, teach us? What verse, what passage, sings to us with absolute truth as it wings its way toward the bull's eye? What passage makes us angry, or frightened, or incredulous? Why? Is there a truth we do not want to hear in these specific teachings, or are they no longer truthful teachings for our generation? Even if we find their surface meaning no longer an Aiming we can share, can we see a deeper level of the story?

Sometimes we got tense and angry with each other: Crucial issues of our lives were at stake. But we tried to believe—and act—as if there could be multiple truths in Torah, truths heard differently by different people. Some of us heard Torah as the revealed voice of God at Sinai. Some of us would not talk of God at all and heard Torah as the distilled wisdom of the Jewish people over the centuries. Some of us heard it as the same conversation between God and the Jews that we ourselves were engaged in—a conversation in which some of the sayings were wise beyond price, some were clumsy or stupid, some the jokes that enliven and relax a conversation when it gets too heavy. And all of it was learning, God's learning as well as ours. And some of us felt it even more than we heard it—felt it as a wrestle, not a conversation.

We tried not to let Shabbat become a ghetto-in-time, a restricted moment of "religion" with no impact on the remainder of our lives. We made up rowdy costumes and drank a dozen different kinds of schnapps together on Purim. We went on picnics. We studied Talmud, Isaiah, Buber, Marcuse. We learned to knit a yarmulke unique: Upon my head or yours, it spoke to others and to Heaven the colors and the patterns of our selves. We learned to sculpt a menorah for the candles that would shine into the dark time of the year, and we learned to let them shine within the darkness of our own mysterious searching. When we were working, eating, making love, seeing a movie, casting a vote, walking in a demonstration, giving to charity, we tried to link those actions with what we learned on Shabbat. We met new friends, got married, had children. We got divorced.

We who did not live in a neighborhood in space became a "neighborhood in time"—gathering from our homes in sprawling Washington so we could be neighbors for each other.

And we reached beyond our little neighborhood, outside our city. Three times a year, we went off together for a long weekend to meet with other *havurot*—the fellowships like ours, few and scattered in those days from Boston southward. We wrote and called and sometimes visited people like us in fellowships like ours, in Chicago, Los Angeles, Jerusalem, Berkeley.

We wanted no professional rabbi or charismatic rebbe—no single leader. The leadership of our prayer services rotated, and we tried to teach each other how to do it better. We experimented. We were clumsy. Sometimes people in the "center" of our circles of community got fed up and disappeared. Sometimes people on the margins discovered themselves and became central. Sometimes people with a special interest created a new grouping and spent most of their time in it. We were never quite sure how many members we had.

We wrestled with each other. And we wrestled with Torah and all of Jewish tradition. It was in the midst of that communal wrestling that I met both the critical moment of my lifelong struggle with my brother Howard, and the Torah story that is the very model of a lifelong struggle between brothers. From our wrestlings in Fabrangen we made new sense of the struggles of Jacob and Esau—and I made new sense of my struggle with Howard.

## WRESTLING WITH MY BROTHER

It began when one Fabrangener insisted on making a connection between Jacob's famous wrestle with God and the very beginning of the story, when Jacob and Esau begin to wrestle with each other even before they are born. They struggle so furiously in the womb that their mother, Rebekah, screams at God a question that in its own shape and grammar is at war with itself:
*"If this,*
*what for—*
*I!"*
And God explains that this is all necessary, that the two children within her must struggle and the younger must win. But God leaves Isaac ignorant of the future; only Rebekah is burdened with the knowledge of how their lives must be. At the very moment of birth, Jacob—his name means "the Heel" in both its English senses—grabs at Esau's

23

heel to drag him back, but fails and so is born second.

As they grow older they keep on struggling over the rights of the first-born. Left on his own, with no message from God, Isaac grows ever fonder of Esau. One Fabrangener suggested that perhaps Isaac is simply playing out another inevitability from his own past: Maybe Esau reminds him of his own lost brother, rough and rowdy Ishmael.

So the struggle deepens, not only brother against brother but also mother against father. The inevitable comes to pass—and proves disastrous. Rebekah teaches the cunning of her family—the cunning of her brother Laban—to her second, weaker son. So Jacob defeats the rougher, plainer Esau with his words—when if he'd wrestled in the body, he'd have lost. On Rebekah's advice, Jacob finally proves himself a heel by cheating his brother and lying to his father in order to win the first-born's blessing. Rebekah wins what God has told her must be won.

But at what cost! Her sons estranged and ready to kill each other, her husband furious, her family shattered. How can she bear it?

Why does she bear it? Having borne the boys, how can she bear their war against each other?

This is where Fabrangen choked on the story. As one of us said, why doesn't she scream again? It's one thing for her to scheme to bring to pass what God has said must come to pass, but when it takes lies and cheating, when it comes to the edge of murder, when Jacob has to flee the household, why doesn't she even scream? Do you only get one scream a lifetime?

For us, the question hung there until Jacob had spent his 20 years in exile. We realized the exile was an education, but we were looking for more than an education—for a scream. So we learned, but were not satisfied, when one of us pointed out the grim humor of Jacob's weddings to Leah and Rachel. He told us to listen hard to Laban, listen to his actions...until we could almost hear him muttering to himself:

*"You lied to your father about who was the first-born son? Then I'll lie to you about who is the first-born daughter. You won what you wanted because of your father's weak eyes? Then you'll win what you don't want—Leah, who has weak eyes. You learned that trickery from your mother Rebekah? You forget that she grew up here; she learned it all from me....And I'll teach you twice as much."*

We learned still more, but were still not satisfied, when another Fabrangener pointed out that the two sisters struggle over who is to have more children, their own version of the struggle for the rights of the first-born. "Listen to the text," he bursts out; "their struggle is so tense that Rachel says, *'With Godlike wrestlings have I wrestled with*

24

*my sister, and have prevailed.'* I never noticed it before. It's parallel to what's coming, parallel to the Godwrestle language, parallel to what Jacob does, and this one comes first! It's as if Rachel taught him how to do it!"

We began to see all this as a kind of karma. Jacob's future is mirroring his past. Not just Laban and Rachel but all of life are teaching him. God is teaching him. He is gathering the cosmic harvest: "What you sow, that shall you reap." But we were still waiting for the scream, waiting still for Jacob's education to go somewhere. We were learning from his story, but where would we go with our learning?

## WRESTLING WITH GOD

The moment of transformation comes when Jacob realizes he must face Esau again. Jacob had fled from his home because he thought Esau might kill him. Now he begins returning home, and word reaches him that Esau, at the head of a powerful troop, is on the way to meet him.

This moment connects their wrestle in the womb with the night of wrestling God. Jacob is frightened for his life, his wealth, and his family. He sends ahead to offer gifts to Esau, but he spends the night alone on the edge of the river Jabbok. The river's name is his own turned inside out.

Alone though he is, he wrestles all night with "a man" who then tells him he has wrestled "with God and with men" and has prevailed. ("Prevailed" is the translation used in almost every English version. But the Hebrew *"yacholti"* means "you have been able," "you have coped." More accurate for one who wrestles God and walks away in pain, with a permanent limp.)

The Person he wrestles renames him "Israel," "Godwrestler," but will tell Jacob no name to call him by. And Jacob calls the name of the place God's Face, because there he had seen God face to face.

Then Jacob crosses the river. Esau meets him, kisses and hugs him. And Jacob exclaims that seeing Esau's face is like seeing the face of God.

A Fabrangener leaped to point out the connection: If Esau's face is like God's, then God's face—the Wrestler's face—must have been like Esau's. It is hard to escape the feeling that in some sense Jacob wrestled that night with Esau. As Rachel had Godstruggled with her sister, so Jacob learned to Godwrestle with his brother. He had wrestled again with Esau as he had wrestled all his life, but this time in a new way.

Now he wrestled not to conquer Esau, but to conquer his own fear and hatred of Esau. That itself was a new beginning, but even that wasn't enough. He wrestled with more than Esau: "With God and with men," says his wrestling partner.

Then another Fabrangener added: It says he wrestled "men." If one was Esau, who was the other? The second "man" he wrestled with must have been himself. At last he was able to stand in Esau's shoes, to turn from his fear of what Esau might do to him and confront what he had already done to Esau. At last he could wrestle with his own guilt.

But there was more: What did it mean to wrestle with God? It meant that at last Rebekah's stifled scream could find a voice. Jacob passed through his own fear and his own guilt to ask the ultimate question:

Why does it need to be this way?

Why do I need to cheat my brother, to make my own way in the world? Why are we pitted against each other? I ought to win the first-born's blessing: God told my mother so. And I ought to be a decent, loving person. Then why must I give up one to get the other? Why couldn't Esau and I work it out together?

To become who I must become, why must I stop being the kind of person I ought to be?

These questions were Jacob's wrestle with God. With them, Jacob recognized that in some ways we are radically different from each other, inescapably and at our very roots turned toward different and incompatible desires. With that question, he faced the granite fact: In some ways human beings are pitted against each other—if not for love or money then for the honor, the prestige, the power of being "first-born." (There can only be one "first-born." I am a first-born. I should know.)

Only when Jacob struggled against that piece of Things-As-They-Must-Be, only when he knew it was, indeed, God and not mere human wants and wishes he was wrestling with, could he turn the war against his brother into love. Recognizing that the war of brothers was rooted in the granite of the universe made it possible for him to turn that conflict into embraces.

And Esau? I am Esau, too, the older brother. It seems to me he wrestled too, that night, on his own side of the river; wrestled not against fear of revenge and guilt over winning, for he had been the loser—but against his own hatred of the victor and his own shame at losing. And wrestled against the God whom he, too, realized as the source of his hatred and shame, the source of the defeat that led to hatred and shame, the source of the head-on collision that led to defeat.

Once the brothers stood face to face with the granite face of Things-

As-They-Must-Be, they could have fallen on their faces, turned their own faces into granite. They could have bowed down to the idol of ruthless competition, of "nature red in tooth and claw."

Or they could have turned away in depression and despair, to a world empty of hope.

They did neither. Instead, they wrestled.

From wrestling, they learned that the tiniest shift of attitude or tension could turn a stranglehold into a hug; that pressing of the flesh was always half an inch from making love. By learning that with the Person who had sometimes his brother's face, sometimes his own, and sometimes God's, Jacob learned how to turn warfare into love.

Through the wrestle, Jacob learned that God is not only Necessity but also Possibility and Desire. Since both Necessity and Possibility are deeply rooted in the universe, the one can be turned into the other. From entering the very depths of inevitability, he gained freedom. From entering the depths of enmity, he learned love.

From this teaching, this Torah, I learned that I could turn the old inevitable struggles with my brother into newness, into freedom, into love—but only if I were willing to wrestle not only Howard but myself and God. From this teaching, this Torah, I learned to face the inevitable. From this teaching, this Torah, I learned that my brother and I had been driven into enmity by the weight of generations. We could face each other ready to do murder because our parents had acted...so...and so. And they had done this because their parents had acted...so...and so.

There was no way to reach backward in time to remake our childhoods and our parents' childhoods. There was only a way to hear our estrangement in the present, to know it, to take it in. And to decide, each of us, whether each "I" wanted to transform it. To decide whether each "I" would risk a wrestle. Whether the joy of that moment when we had been able to wrestle lovingly along the C&O Canal in Western Maryland was worth the pain, the wounds we might have to carry away from wrestling with ourselves, with each other, and with God.

I decided to try. So did Howard. I keep deciding to try, I keep on trying. My brother-wrestle did not just end with one great outburst of embracing. I keep remembering that Jacob, even after embracing Esau, arranged to live apart from him. We keep on wrestling: It doesn't end.

Indeed, through the twenty years since we first talked above the dry canal, my brother and have gone through several turns of a spiral: Wrestling our way to a new place of connection, then going through a time of pause or even partial withdrawal, and then renewing our wrestle on a deeper and more intimate level. Ultimately we came to the point in which our trust outweighed our fear enough for us to write a book together—*Becoming Brothers*—in which we told our two stories, side by side and intertwined like wrestlers making love at last.

To get to that point, we went through many versions of the "brother stories" of the Book of Genesis. To me, our lives felt sometimes like the collapse of Cain's and Abel's aborted wrestle into murder; sometimes, like the reconnection of the brothers Ishmael and Isaac at their father's tomb; sometimes, like the morning after the Godwrestle or like the backward blessing of Jacob's first grandchildren.

I say that "to me" our struggles felt like those. To me, and just to me—because these were not the metaphors that spoke to Howard. For me, it was in Fabrangen that I learned the archetypal stories that made sense of our lives together. These stories became part of my wrestle with my brother. But his wrestle was from another place, across the river.

I wish—how I wish!—there had been one Torah tale that told in rich detail the story of one whole-hearted reconciliation. If we had been able to draw on one such story, my brother and I—and all of us, for millennia past and yet to come—might more easily have been able to write that tale into our own lives. For these Torah tales have been a sort of repertory for our living theater—a stock of plays, of well-known plots and characters, from which all of us have chosen parts and sometimes whole life-dramas to enact. So I wish some tale of sibling reconciliation had been easier to find on file in the stock of Torah repertory.

Why was it not? Perhaps the Torah wanted to leave open space, forcing us to write these healing chapters of the story, in our own lives.

From all my wrestles I keep learning. Learning that to wrestle with God or with my brother, with others or even with myself, is over and over to ask about Things-As-They-Must-Be and Things-As-They-Ought-to-Be, Necessity versus Desire. To ask that question not as an academic riddle but as a life demand. Can I change? Can my brother? Can the fight between us? Can what is old and inevitable about us and what is free and new about us both be true?

The question about Must and Ought lies at the heart of Torah.

The God who escapes our slippery grasp from one mode to the other is the God of Torah.

It would be easy if Must and Ought were utterly separate: If there were two basic principles in the universe, struggling against each other. But to assert that the two are ultimately One!—as the Torah asserts. To name as One the God who sponsors Rebekah's battle cunning and the God who sponsors her mothering love!

With such a God, what can a fully human being do—but wrestle?

Jacob's Godwrestling frees him from his lifelong necessity to wrestle Esau. It frees him next morning to be the brother he ought to be. It lets him turn his deadly headlock on his brother into a hug, and then a kiss.

Wrestling is itself the synthesis of making love and making war. To wrestle with God is to make in human action and on the human level the same unification of the same opposites that God unifies. It is a way of bringing to visibility that paradoxical Image of God which is stamped deep within us.

For to wrestle with God is also to wrestle with human beings— ourselves and others. It is to face polarities and unify them. Not only to face the polarities of Same and Other when we face each other, but also within ourselves to face the polarities of fear and guilt, of love and anger—and to unify them.

Perhaps it is no mere accident that a friend of mine heard the poem near the head of this chapter as what he called "the first Jewish poem that says God is gay." Not because I was indeed celebrating an act of physical sex between brothers, or men, but because I was trying to say that within each of us are all those polarities that conventionally have been assigned either to men or to women: Love and anger, gentleness and toughness, fear and guilt, the touching that arouses and the touch that kills. By convention, we have said a man and woman can connect these "opposites." So can two men who touch through wrestling; so can two women (like Rachel and Leah in their sister-wrestle); so, all the more, can a human being wrestling God.

There may be many ways to unify, if only for a moment, the polarities within us and between us. My brother learned it without Torah, without Jacob and Esau to teach him—through his own wrestle, in a different way, on the other side of the river. But my learning was from Torah.

## CHANGING TORAH, CHANGING OUR SELVES

No, my learning was not from Torah but from *wrestling* with Torah. For not only the content of what I learned, but *how* I learned these teachings was itself a Godwrestling. Not at night, like Jacob, but on every Shabbat morning, Fabrangen wrestled God, and each other, and ourselves.

We did not bow down to the tradition, but we did not turn away from it either. We wrestled it: Fighting it and making love to it at the same time. Bringing our lives to grapple, sweating, with its Teachings.

When we touch the Torah with our lives, both our lives and the Torah come alive. We change our lives. We change the way we act in politics, in sex, in our families, at work, in eating, when we celebrate, when we mourn. What we are doing is what the people Israel is all about: "Israel," the Godwrestler.

Touching the Torah gives it new life because the Torah resulted from such touchings in the first place. When Jacob wrestled, it was "with men and God" at once—distinguishable, but not separable.

From that wrestling flew fiery drops of sweat; they fell into place as the letters of the Torah.

For the Torah is struggle distilled into teaching. The new name that Jacob won in his wrestle was what we might today call a new theology, a label for his new way of apprehending God. His "theology" came not from academic study, but from throwing his whole soul and body into the most urgent struggle of his life.

Generations of Jews after Jacob have wrestled with themselves, with other people, and with God, and the sweat from their wrestlings too became the fiery letters on the parchment and the paper: Torah.

This book is itself a wrestle in several senses. For one thing, like the poem at the beginning of this chapter it is internally a wrestle of several voices: Midrash in the ancient fashion, autobiography in which my own life becomes midrash, modern theology and politics, story-telling of the new Jewish fellowships. But more deeply, retelling these stories of the struggles of my life itself involves me in a specific wrestle, one I need to share:

By telling stories about Fabrangen, I give Fabrangen a face. Yet even when I first told these stories, the face I gave Fabrangen was the one I saw, sitting in my own place within the circle. Others in the circle saw it differently. And now, twenty years later, the face in these stories is no longer my own face, and no longer Fabrangen's.

Because these stories are my stories, I remember the struggles and ideas that spoke most deeply to my gut and soul. Of necessity I leave out what others would remember because it spoke to them. If others in Fabrangen had written this book, it would have been just as true, but very different.

And now!—Fabrangen is no longer where I pray and study Torah. I am no longer the same person who sat in that circle, and the circle itself is no longer the same. The Torah we learned together there is no longer quite the same. All this has changed precisely because we wrestled together, danced together, looked at each other's faces and heard each other's words. In the very doing, each of us separately and all of us together and the great tale of the People Israel all changed.

What is the problem? Simply that for some people, my truth has falsified their understanding.

Indeed, when I first wrote these stories, some Fabrangeners, brothers and sisters whom I loved, were angry at my describing them, at my shaping their realities. They felt—as any community might feel—that just by describing them, I had become the younger brother come to steal their birthright. How do we preserve our collective process internally if one of us reaches outside to describe it?

Perhaps I could have avoided this problem by simply writing down the result of the process—my own learnings, my own conclusions, my own theology. I could have left Fabrangen to an honorable footnote. But that would have been unfaithful to my sense that my deepest learning was precisely the process of wrestling *in community*, not my own particular conclusions.

We will simply have to live with this dilemma for a while. Maybe someday we will understand from wrestling with it how to get beyond its collision of necessities to some new creative synthesis of participant and artist, wrestler and chronicler. But for now this is one of many struggles in which we are still straining our eyes in the dark before daybreak, straining to see....

Who is this God with Whom we wrestle? One whose Face is as easy and as hard to recognize as is my brother's. One whose Face is as easy and as hard to recognize as is my own, the face I have never seen, can never see except in a mirror image, backwards. One who wishes to be faced, who needs to be wrestled. One whose Self is not complete, not self-sufficient.

I have only begun to learn that Face, begun to learn it only from the struggles of my life. I welcome wrestling partners to this book. Together we may be able to begin to see the outlines of God's Face. And of each other's.

# CHAPTER 2

# FIRST-BORNS
# AND THEIR BROTHERS

In early fall there is a Shabbat called "In the Beginning," when we read the story of Creation and the Garden of Delight. The Fabrangen went away to a farm nestled in the hills of Pennsylvania where the fruit trees were ripening: Where else to celebrate the fruitfulness of Eden?

Four of us—Irene, who was then my wife; myself; and our children, David and Shoshana, then seven and four years old—had been living there throughout the summer. For us, indeed, it felt like Eden.

So we spent early Saturday morning reading the story of seven measured, rhythmic days, unfolding in Creation, and then the delightful story of the Garden. Several children listened as we talked, wandered out to play in the woods, wandered back unhurried, Eden-like. Our pleasure in the trees, the shrubs, the creek, the wind helped us ease ourselves into the world of Eden, where humans were at one with all around them, where pain and struggle were unknown, where even striving was unnecessary. The world of childhood, maybe.

But we also took great pleasure in our adult conversation, in our ability to teach and learn, to make distinctions, to misunderstand and yet strive to hear each other, to interpret.

As we read, the story darkened into trouble: The Tree of Knowledge, good and evil, Eden lost. The farm around us took on darker colors. As the Garden's fullness and delight gave way to sterner history in the Torah, so in the earth of that fall morning. The falling fruit, the ears of corn rotting into new seed for the earth, made even sharper our pain in being torn from Eden.

Most sharp of all: The story spoke, "Lest the earthlings take also from the Tree of Life, and eat, and live..." YHWH, the Breath of Life

Who breathes out as well as in, blew the human earthlings out of the Garden in a puff of wind.

## LOSING THE TREE OF LIFE

One of us exploded—Irene, perhaps because she had been longest at the farm and so longed most for Eden to be real. "How did it feel to them to write that down?" she asked. To write down that God expelled us all from Eden—and why? So that we could not eat from the Tree of Life. So that—having chosen the Knowledge of distinctions—we could not sustain the pulsing flow of Life.

How did it feel to them to realize that the penalty for being human is to feel separation, pain, exile, death? How could they love the very God they blamed for this? How could they calmly write this knowledge into Torah? Where is their rage, their own explosion?

And—how does it feel to us? Can we live without hot anger at the splitness of our world?—a life so split that flow itself is split into a billion molecules; a life in which the garden of delight must, moment after moment, be subdivided, analyzed into a billion structures....

Can we just read this Torah without anger, as its central Hero—God, the Creator—hammers home the painful truth of separation?

No, we could not. We let our anger surface; we wrestled with the God who made it impossible to eat of both the Tree of Knowledge and the Tree of Life. To be able to distinguish good from evil, false from true, female from male—all those distinctions whose knowing makes us human—means to forsake our flowing oneness in the world. For once the flow of life is reduced to moments, once it is contained within precision, distinction, separation, once the flow is interrupted, can we ever bring it back? No, not as it was. Once flow is interrupted, its essential quality—the undividedness of life—is lost to us.

The very interruption makes it impossible for us to forget the reality of interruptedness. We can't go back home again.

Not "back home." But maybe we can go "forward home," forward into some higher, deeper place that yet is home, the home not of our origin but of our destined destination? Can we make a spiral, turning to reach the level of a higher home, in which Flowing Life contains within itself the consciousness of Separation not excluded but transformed?

According to the mystics, that is what the Messianic Eden, higher Eden, ought to be. But on that fall morning, Fabrangen was looking deep into the winter of exile, not into some new and barely imaginable spring. Exhausted by our wrestle with the God of Must, we scattered to different private corners of the farm and of our selves.

34

Later in the day, we came once more together. When somebody pointed out that we hadn't finished the reading—we hadn't yet read of Cain and Abel—it felt like anticlimax. Reluctantly, we read the rest of the story.

## THE MISSING CONVERSATION

At first, worn a little dull by the intensity of our Shabbat so far, we talked almost casually about the deadly tale of brothers' battle. But I was still haunted by our morning's discovery of a new question to put to the Torah: How did it feel to those who wrote this down? And, I translated, how would it feel for us to write this down?

Suddenly the room we were in and the story we had read joined into the same moment of time. Here we were, cast out of Eden, down from the peaks of our early morning ecstasy, back from the fruitful farm to wrestle with each other. And there across the room were David and Shoshana, brother and sister, two of the children who had been playing with and near us. Translating Irene's question into our own lives, I asked, "How would it feel for us to have to write that David had killed Shoshana?"

There was a blink. Somebody answered, lethargic, not really hearing, puzzled: "You mean Cain and Abel? It's only about a death. It's true it was the first death, but we all have to get used to death."

"No," I said. "It's not just death; it's murder. And not just any murder: They were brothers. What if David killed Shoshana? How could we bear to write it? How could we understand it and explain it?"

Reluctantly—but who wouldn't be reluctant to face that story?—we turned our attention to Cain and Abel. The first event of normal human history is a war of brothers. And the Book of Genesis is almost woven of such stories. Just as the human race begins with a war of brothers, so does the Jewish people: Ishmael and Isaac, Esau and Jacob, Joseph and his brothers. Indeed, Genesis is unable to end until there is a peaceful pair of brothers: Ephraim and Manasseh. Only then can the Bible turn to other problems.

But why the murder in the first place? Why must humans turn to killing when they leave the Garden?

Abel and Cain bring offerings to God, the fruit of their labor in field and pasture. Abel's offering is accepted; Cain's is rejected.

Cain is angry. What else would you expect? But he says nothing.

God speaks the first word: "Why are you glowering?"

God waits. There is no answer. Instead Cain tries to turn his flaming face away, lest it betray his anger.

God tries again: "Why has your face fallen? If you intend good,

35

lift it up!"

Most of us had always thought these were rhetorical questions, and had located the real puzzle of the story in what Cain had done to make his sacrifice unworthy in the first place. But now, thinking of Cain and Abel as David and Shoshana, suddenly we could imagine ourselves as parents asking them these questions—not merely as a line of rhetoric but for real: "Why are you angry? Why have you turned your face away from me? Look at me! Talk to me! Answer me!"

In the tale of Cain and Abel, does God becomes a Parent, demanding that Cain face God directly and spit out his anger?

Cain still gives no answer. So God continues, "If you do not intend good, sin crouches at the door. Its urge is toward you, but you can rule over it."

Again, most of us had read this as a recollection of the past—remembering something Cain has already done for evil. But what if God is still addressing the future? Warning Cain once more to answer, face to face? Warning that to turn away will open the door to crouching evil?...

Cain does not answer to God.

Instead he speaks to Abel, to his brother.

And kills him.

Wait. Cain seems to speak to Abel, but the Torah text is very strange: "Cain said to his brother Abel..." *What?* What did Cain say? In most such passages of Torah, what follows these words is a quotation: A saying. Just above, the same words about God saying to Cain are followed by what God said.

But here there are no words, there is no quotation. Some contemporary translations leave an empty space. Three dots. A silence. No more can Cain speak to Abel than to God.

So the story continues, wordless, "So it was through their being in the fields that Cain rose up against his brother Abel and killed him."

Again with our own children vividly before our eyes, we could see the story in a new way. We could see them refusing to face our own parental challenge, failing to encounter us—and taking out their anger on each other, on someone weaker than an awesome parent.

## TRAGEDY AND TERROR

But why is the Parent so terrifying? Why did God reject Cain's sacrifice in the first place? And once Cain got angry, could there have been a better, gentler way for God to invite Cain into an encounter? Surely we can share Cain's initial anger at his Parent's favoritism. And even though we are filled with horror at Cain's twisting his anger against God into violence against Abel, we can still empathize with the fear that made him do that.

For by this point in the story, God the Parent looks not loving, but grim and awesome. The choice Adam and Eve made in the Garden has created a new reality of awe, terror, grimness. God has told Eve and Adam to choose a life of unknowing blissful childhood, and they have refused. Eve and Adam have chosen instead to leave childhood, even at the risk of death. For them and for their children, the Garden of Delight has disappeared. What replaces it is a life of toil, domination, alienation. They have been divorced from the blissful flow of Life; there is a chasm between them and God.

And this choice by Eve and Adam has not only entered into the lives of their children, but has—like even the most necessary choices of divorce—bitten cruelly deep. Eve and Adam have abolished blissful, unknowing childhood. Now there is scarcity. Not only material scarcity, but a scarcity of love and acceptance. Even God's fullness is damaged: Even God can only fully respond to just one brother.

Which brother? The easy choice would be the older one. The one who in every family already is bigger, stronger, when the younger sib arrives. The one who gives his parents their first assurance of a biological future. The one who in many social systems, including the Israelite law of inheritance, wins wealth and deference.

Yet God responds not to the older Cain, but to his younger brother, Abel. In a world of limited choices, God chooses to reverse what those who wrote the story knew was the "natural" order.

Amid these narrowed choices, God calls Cain to the most redemptive choice now left to him: Responsible adulthood, being ready to face God fully, being ready to acknowledge God's limits on the world. God calls Cain to face—Necessity. And then God demands that Cain challenge and encounter God, turn necessity into a free choice of love. God invites Cain into the encounter that we who have read ahead in the story know as the Wrestle that made Jacob into Yisrael.

This invitation comes from the grim and awesome God of Outside-Eden, who has no gentler choice to offer. It is only if Cain accepts the invitation that gentler choices will become available.

But Cain keeps sullen silence. He will not answer to God, he will not speak to his brother. He rejects adulthood. Perhaps he hears his parents' wistfulness for childish Eden; so he tries to choose what they gave up. Nostalgically, he tries to remain a child.

But there is now no bliss in childishness. To be childish now means to be sullen and resentful. To be sullen now means death.

At the risk of death, Eve and Adam had chosen to leave

childhood. The risk trembled in the balance: Would their children be able to move forward to adulthood and to life? Not yet: The risk they took is visited upon their children. The first death comes: Not, to be sure, upon their own bodies, but upon the body of their son. So Cain bequeaths to human history our long, long struggle to grow beyond the murder of each other.

We leave the House of Eden every day, when we decide that to be human means to know, to choose, to grow. But many of us have taken only the first step out of Eden: We still live in the House of Cain. Not enough, says God; we should grow up all the way. We should be ready to challenge God, to answer God, to wrestle God. That is the indispensable step toward adulthood.

If we fail to wrestle God, we will murder a brother; just as it is only when Jacob learns to wrestle God that it becomes possible for him to make friends with his brother. For we should not ignore what these stories teach about relationships among human beings, as well as between humans and God.

If we refuse to speak truth to power, we will speak lies or silence to the powerless—and do murder. If we refuse to see clearly, truthfully, the world our parents have bequeathed us, then we cannot make the world we want to make.

Be neither sullen nor nostalgic, says the Torah—for sullenness and nostalgia are the degenerate shapes of anger and of love. Better clear anger and clear love, with all their risks.

The story of Cain, Abel, and God (like the rest of the saga from Adam to Noah) is a story of total risk. God demands everything and risks everything. God demands that Cain take the risk of fully encountering not his brother, not his parents, not another human being made in God's image—but God's Own Self, unmediated, undiluted. When Cain turns away, the result is no mere exile, no lifelong enmity, but Abel's death. The Parent's gamble ends in total loss.

Demand all, risk all, lose all. And so it runs throughout the saga of the fathers and mothers of the human race: From Eden to the Flood and on to Babel, God's Own unmediated Self stands facing the whole of humankind.

It is as if this saga stands first in the Bible to teach the root truth, the "radical" truth of what is at stake in the world: *Everything is at stake.*

But the Bible then moves on to teach us that these ultimate issues enter human life—and God's life too—somewhat blurred. From the saga of the mothers and fathers of the human race, the Bible moves to a smaller arena, the saga of the mothers and fathers of the Jewish people.

Here again we hear the motif of the brothers' war. But here only a single people is at stake, not the whole human race—and this seems to open new possibilities. Here there are successive generations, so that the motif of the brothers' war can go through a series of variations. There is even one variation in which it is two sisters—Rachel and Leah—who struggle, as if to say: "Does it make a difference if the siblings are not men but women?"

In these stories of the Clan of Abraham, the risks are profound but not total. The conflicts are warlike, but not fatal. In each generation, the outcome is a reconciliation, until the brothers' war itself can be extinguished.

It is almost as if God learns from the mistakes and failures of the earlier saga and starts over to work things out another way. It is almost as if God says, "To redeem the world, I have tried putting My Whole Self into this encounter with the whole human race. The result has been not redemption but disaster after disaster. Now let me try working with a single people, and let My Presence take a subtler form."

## REACHING TOWARD RECONCILIATION

The hinge is Babel, where the unified human race suffers one last unified disaster: Its unity is shattered into a complex of peoples. Now it is possible for God to explore a number of different possibilities, to experiment and fail and experiment again. God learns. On the human side, there is after Babel the chance that a small people, unlike the whole human race, might respond to God coherently. From such a small model, others might learn the process.

So now we enter the saga of the children of Abraham. Generation after generation, there rises the issue of "first-bornness." It is settled differently from its settlement in the story of Cain and Abel. There God chooses the younger, but the older rejects that decision. So the conflict becomes irreconcilable, and the first-born "wins": He destroys his younger brother.

In the Abrahamic saga, generation after generation, God again chooses the later-borns. But in this saga, the first-borns a*gree* to lose. They lose some measure of material prosperity and spiritual redemption; but unlike Cain, they step aside.

By stepping back, they make it possible for the conflicts to be reconciled (and ultimately, for themselves to be blessed after all with prosperity and spiritual peace). Generation after generation, the stories end not with death but with a fragile peace in which the younger brother holds the limelight:

Of Abraham's sons, the Bible focuses on Isaac, not his older brother

39

Ishmael. But Ishmael is blessed as forefather of a people, and even achieves the twelve sons who symbolize successful peoplehood one generation before the line of Isaac does. What is more, the two brothers meet in love when their father dies.

Of Isaac's sons, the Bible focuses on Jacob, not his older brother Esau. But Esau survives with many flocks and followers to establish his own people in Edom. In this tale, also, the two brothers meet lovingly after decades of separation.

Of Jacob's sons, the Bible focuses on Joseph, second youngest of twelve brothers. He rises above them all and, after a story of fury, hatred, and separation, is reconciled with them.

And in that generation of the story the pattern begins to be broken, perhaps because the emergence of twelve brothers not only signals the existence of a people, but also relaxes the tension of two brothers struggling head-to-head against each other. Among twelve there can be allies, neutrals, peacemakers, change.

Joseph's two sons, Ephraim and Manasseh, embody resolution of the issue.

Jacob, their grandfather, insists on blessing them. Jacob, who had fooled his father into giving him the first-born's blessing, leaps across a generation to end the collision over first-bornness. Jacob, who has learned how to stop wrestling with his brother and wrestle with God instead, shows Manasseh and Ephraim how not to wrestle with each other.

Jacob affirms his own victory over his first-born brother by reversing the hands with which the blessings should be given. The right hand—the first-born's hand—he reaches out to Ephraim, the second-born. The left hand—the second-born's hand—he reaches out to bless Manasseh, the first-born.

But in the same moment, he dissolves the tension, for he blesses them simultaneously, with a single blessing. Lest they miss the point, he literally crosses his arms to bless them "backwards" and explicitly rejects Joseph's objection that he has it wrong. And he blesses them both in the same breath, saying "By you [a singular "you," each of them singularly at the same instant] shall Israel bless, saying, 'God make you as Ephraim and as Manasseh.'"

And indeed, Jewish tradition teaches to this day that children be blessed that they be as Ephraim and as Manasseh.

Why these two? Why not as Joseph the ruler over Egypt, or as Jacob who wrestled God, or as Abraham who went on the trackless journey? Because here, at last, are two brothers who share the same blessing, who do not have to suffer exile or separation or despair or death for the sake of battle with each other.

Now that you are at last twelve brothers, now that you are at last a people, says Jacob, your blessing as a people is to be like these two: Blessed in your loving friendship, in your ability to go beyond the brothers' war.

Why does this concern over the war between the first and second brothers permeate the Book of Genesis? Because with it, the Bible accomplishes a marvel of two-level teaching.

First it teaches that the first-born is not to dominate—almost certainly a teaching intended to reverse and resist a previous social politics in which the first-born won wealth, power, and blessing simply by virtue of birth.

And then it teaches that the second-born is not supposed to rule, either. What is supposed to happen is reconciliation, and finally the dissolution of the conflict itself.

But even the dissolution of the conflict must keep its memory alive. Otherwise the tugs of blood, fondness, charisma, power may revive and people may regress to letting the first-born rule again.

What a subtle teaching of how to end domination!

To a modern hearing, the brothers' war seems real enough—ask almost any brother, almost any sister. But it does not seem to be the sharpest struggle of our public lives. Perhaps substituting women for the second-borns in these stories and men for the first-borns would carry something like the same trumpet blast of liberation. Try it: The women who have for centuries been powerless win, time after time. Yet each time, there is a reconciliation.

Indeed, we might read this saga of the early brothers as precisely a tale about not only brothers but also about poor and rich, Black and white, female and male, Jew and gentile, gay and straight, ailing and healthy, speechless trees and the talkative human race. All the powerless of our society, in their relation with the powerful.

Read this way, the saga loses none of its power for talking about the uses of power in that smallest of societies, the family. It loses none of its energy for laying bare the agonies of those who literally are brothers or sisters—still, today, at war and struggling to make peace. But the saga gains power and energy if we hear it speak to every collision of the powerful and powerless in which we act and live.

It gains power and energy for change if we can identify ourselves with Isaac, Jacob, Joseph struggling to win free of the power their older brothers are born to—and then can identify ourselves with Ishmael, Esau, Judah struggling to win free of the humiliation and the weakness their younger brothers have put upon them. So just as Cain's murder of Abel is the first consequence of exile from Eden, the teaching of Ephraim and Manasseh is to be the key to reopen Eden. It is the

Cain-and-Abel story that must be overcome if the gates to reenter Eden are to open.

So the threads of Genesis lead us to this new beginning, beyond the brothers' war. By the end of Genesis, the family has learned its lesson. The band of brothers can become one model of how the human race as a whole might redeem the world.

## GRASPING POWER, SHATTERING POWER

Yet the Genesis model is not the only model of conflict in the Torah: There is Exodus as well. In Exodus, God makes Israel, the newest and poorest of the peoples, into God's own "honorary first-born." But the Older Brother, like Cain, refuses to step back. This time a God Who has grown in experience through the generations of Abraham will not permit the older, stronger brother to annihilate the younger, weaker brother.

So in Exodus, liberation cannot be achieved until the powerful have been shattered and the oppressed have departed, once and for all. There is no reconciliation with Pharaoh, not until the distant day that the Prophets prophesy: The day when the great empires, Egypt and Assyria, can live side by side in peace with little Israel. The Genesis model of reconciliation remains the great and generous model that overarches history. But in the meantime...there is Exodus.

And the Exodus model does not stand as a one-time event, alone in the biblical vision. Indeed, the Exodus model is one of the recurrent themes of the Torah. In this tale and the tale of Sodom and Gomorra, even the words the Torah uses are so similar as to signal us to listen:

In Exodus: *"The children of Israel sighed from the serfdom, and cried out so that their wailing rose to God from serfdom. And God heard their groaning, and remembered his covenant with Abraham, with Isaac, and with Jacob. And God saw the children of Israel, and God was intimate with them....And YHWH said, 'Seeing, I have seen the oppression of my people who are in Egypt and I have heard their moaning from the face of their taskmasters. So I know their pains, and I will go down to deliver them.'"*

In Genesis: *"The outcry of Sodom and Gomorra is very great, and their sin is extremely heavy. I will go down now, and I will see whether they are acting as it seems from the moans that come to me. If not, I will be intimate."*

Outcry, moans, seeing, hearing, "going down," "be intimate." (That last one is the verb, *"yodaya,"* which Hebrew uses for knowing a fact, making love, and cherishing God. It is so hard to find an equivalent in modern English that when the science-fiction writer Robert Heinlein wanted to convey the same meaning for his novel *Stranger in a Strange Land*, he had to use the Martian word *"grok."*)

These six identical words point to a similarity that otherwise we might not notice. But once we notice, we can look more deeply at the similarity: The society has turned corrupt and dreadful. Only a fraction are acting decently. In Egypt, it is the Israelites and a "mixed multitude" of others who leave the house of slavery and trudge the path to Sinai. In Sodom, it is Lot and his family who try to treat strangers decently and are attacked by the cities that hate all foreigners.

Once we recognize this pattern, we realize it goes back to the Flood—the whole world is corrupt except for Noah's family—and then forward to the Prophets' vision of the Land of Israel. For there even the Israelites themselves become corrupt. They are destroyed, and only a saving remnant who depart can return to redeem themselves and history and the Land.

This Exodus pattern has impressed itself on the minds of every people that has learned the Torah or its secularized analogues, like Marxism. It is the model for modern revolutions, national and social, where the saving remnant hopes to wipe out oppression and corruption, depart physically or politically from the oppressors and corrupters, and remake their country. The pattern has been so powerful that we pay little attention to the Genesis alternative: The war and peace of brothers.

We must remember: Exodus becomes a drama of destruction only because the powerful refuse to budge. The teaching of Exodus is that when joyful transformation is rejected, a grimmer transformation will follow. History will no longer allow Cain to win. What history welcomes is the model of the brothers' peace.

Today we need the model of the brothers even more urgently than through all previous history. For the world has grown too small for an easy Exodus, for a shattering of power that leaves the powerless with a place to go and make their own new society. Rare is the struggle today in which we want to destroy the oppressor and separate into a new society. Instead we need liberation-with-reconciliation. Not the gruesome grin of the powerless commanded to love their taskmasters, nor the gracious smile of the powerful who are glad to love their serfs. But the free laughter of wrestlers, in whom the grapple of liberation and the clasp of love are intertwined.

How many of us, women or men, want women to be freed from men by smashing men—and leaving them? How many of us, Black or white, want Blacks to be freed by smashing America—or leaving it?

Exodus may be the last resort in every struggle. If the stronger refuse to step aside, then like Pharaoh they may end on the ocean floor. But we should know that the door out is not the door in. Exodus is not the path to Eden.

# CHAPTER 3

# THE CLOUDY MIRROR: ISHMAEL AND ISAAC

During the summer of 1973 the Hillel House of a large university invited me to give the sermon for the first night of Rosh Hashanah. First I sweated over whether to do it at all: A one-man sermon to hundreds of passive students seemed utterly antithetical to the Fabrangen path of life. But I decided that I might be able to strike some sparks of Fabrangen's kind of Torah study and at least describe our path to people who had never heard of it and who might want to try it out.

For a while more, I sweated over what to talk about. Rosh Hashanah begins the ten days of *t'shuvah*, "turning" or repentance, that end with Yom Kippur and its sense of forgiveness and new beginnings. So I thought about a sermon on *t'shuvah*:

Maybe a community-wide *t'shuvah* about women-men relationships in Jewish life?

Or maybe I should draw on the reading for Yom Kippur of Jonah's mission to bring about the *t'shuvah* of that great city Nineveh, and so talk about the obligation of the Jewish community to call for a great American *t'shuvah*?

Or maybe this was the time to talk about a profound *t'shuvah* among Israelis, Jews, Palestinians, Arabs?

This last felt frightening. I had talked about it many times with Jews here and in Israel, and each encounter left me drenched with the sweat of love, worry, anger. So the thought of speaking to an issue so intense, on a night so intense, was frightening. But I couldn't get it out of my head.

I asked friends and the Hillel rabbi—What should I talk about?— And still I could not decide.

Finally, in a panic, only two days before Rosh Hashanah, I said to myself: I will let the sermon flow from the Torah reading for the first day of Rosh Hashanah. That is what the sermon traditionally was: A word about the Torah portion. So be it.

But I could not remember what the portion was. About the second day's reading I had no doubts: It was the Binding of Isaac for a sacrifice. But the first day was a blank. So I looked it up.

I was thunderstruck. The reading told how Abraham and Sarah, with God's approval, had forced Ishmael and Hagar to leave the family and go into the desert. Ishmael, says tradition, is the forebear of the Arab peoples. The one subject that had frightened me—Israelis and Palestinians, Arabs and Jews—seemed to flow directly from the reading. I had almost certainly "forgotten" what the reading was so I could avoid the question that frightened me. So it seemed as if the Torah had hunted me down, faced me with its question. I would have to deal with my fear and talk about Ishmael and his people.

But not by just referring to the Ishmael story as a hook to hang a political speech on. Rather, I felt obligated to grapple with the story, to try to hear its whole meaning.

## THE MANY KINDS OF LAUGHTER

The heart of the story is a struggle between two wives and two brothers. Abraham has taken his maidservant Hagar as a second wife, after his first wife Sarah has been childless for decades. With Hagar he has had a son, Ishmael. Tensions grow between the two women. Thirteen years later Sarah gives birth to Isaac.

As the boys grow up, Sarah sees trouble between them. She demands that Ishmael and Hagar be sent away. Abraham is concerned, but accedes when God endorses the demand.

Hagar and Ishmael wander in the desert, nearly die of thirst, cry out to God, and at the last moment are shown a well. They survive, and from Ishmael spring the twelve sons that for the Bible make not just a family but a peoplehood.

The readings for the second day of Rosh Hashanah complete the story of the brothers with a variation on the tale of Ishmael. Here too the father, in obedience to God, brings near death upon his beloved son. In the second story, God commands Abraham to bring Isaac as an offering to God; Abraham climbs Mount Moriah to obey by killing Isaac; and only at the last moment does God stay his hand and provide a ram for a substitute sacrifice.

The turning point of this terrifying tale of two wives, two sons, two brothers comes when Sarah demands that Ishmael leave. Why?

The text quotes her saying that Ishmael was doing something strange, *mitzachek* to Isaac her son. The word is usually translated as "making sport." The rabbis, clearly concerned over the seeming injustice of the expulsion, have cited the use of a similar word elsewhere in the Torah, and argued that it means Ishmael was engaged in idolatry, or violence, or sexual license.

But as I prepared my talk to the Hillel congregation, I recalled discussions of this passage at Fabrangen. To some of us, the form of *mitzachek* seemed much more important than attempting to extract a content from a different word used elsewhere. For *miTzaCheK* stems from the same root—*Tz-Ch-K*—as Isaac's name, *yiTzChaK*. The root means "to laugh": Isaac was the Laughing One, and Ishmael's *mitzachek* a different kind of laughter.

If Isaac was the essence of the joyful, triumphant laughter of Sarah and Abraham given a son in their old age, Ishmael responded with the hurt and mocking laughter of the displaced son. The laugher laughed at!

Suddenly it seemed that Ishmael was too much like Isaac for Sarah to bear: Alike, but unlike, as a steamy mirror reflects a clouded image. Sarah is struggling for her son's identity. She feels he cannot grow up to be himself if he is constantly with this other self, so like but so unlike. So she banishes that cloudy other "laugher."

But if the name of the one brother, his inwardness, is thus so importantly clouded by the behavior of the other, then what is the significance of Ishmael's name? Literally, the Hebrew *Yishma El* means "God heard," or "God will hear." The name is given first by God directly to the pregnant Hagar when God hears her sorrow over Sarah's harsh treatment of her. Then the name is confirmed in the desert when God hears the despairing cry of Ishmael and Hagar and offers them life and water.

But this name also has echoes in the other line of Abraham's seed; for at the formative moment of Jewish history, the moment of deepest suffering in Egypt, the people cried out and God *heard* their groaning and began the process of their deliverance from Egypt.

Again, so similar! The cry of despair rises from the exiles of the Land, both seeds of Abraham: The cry rises from the child of Hagar and from the children of Sarah. And the cry is heard.

## ESTRANGING OURSELVES

The outcries echo each other. Indeed, the echo starts even before Ishmael is born, in the very name of his mother Hagar. "Hagar" means "the sojourner," "the visitor," "the foreigner," "the stranger." When the Torah says we were "*gerim*," "strangers," in the Land of Egypt, it is from the same root. And Hagar is called "*Hagar ha'mitzria*," "Hagar the Egyptian," "the Egyptian Stranger." Over and over the Torah teaches us, "Love the stranger, for you were strangers in the Land of Egypt." Hagar the Egyptian was a stranger in *our* midst, we became strangers in *her* Egypt, and so we must learn to treat with love and equal justice the strangers in our land.

These commands of Torah about just and loving treatment of the stranger are repeated thirty-six times, more than any other precept. Why? It must have been a hard command to obey. Imagine: Just out of slavery, what would we feel? Very likely, that never again would we let any stranger gain the whip hand over us—and so we would subjugate all strangers in our land. No, says the Torah; you must learn precisely the opposite. You know the heart of the stranger, and so you must identify with the stranger—not with your own oppressors. Since this is a hard path to walk in the aftermath of slavery—or of Holocaust—the command must be repeated, over and over.

Thirty-six times! Twice *chai*, the word that means "life," the word whose letters add up to eighteen. Was this a quiet message?—For the sake of two lives, your own and the stranger's, you must follow this difficult path!

From this dialogue with Torah I learned two things: Compassion for Jews in the post-Holocaust generation who so strongly feel the impulse to rule over strangers who do endanger us; and commitment to strive toward the deeper wisdom of the Torah.

From these struggles to understand the ancient Torah text, my thoughts came back to my task in 1973, the Rosh Hashanah sermon. My thoughts came back to Palestinians and Jews: So like each other in so many ways, as Ishmael and Isaac were so much like each other!

Palestinians and Jews dreaming of the same land: Palestinians for decades, Jews for millennia.

Palestinians and Jews yearning to govern themselves in Jerusalem.

Palestinians crying out from refugee camps as we had cried out from ghettos—and in some places still do still cry out.

Palestinians crying out to be seen as a people, as Jews for centuries have cried out to be seen as a people.

And—most poignant, perhaps most similar of all—both peoples

refusing to hear each other's outcry. Said some Palestinians, "No Israel, so that Palestine can be born." Said some Israelis, "No Palestine, so that Israel can be safe."

My mind went back again to the banishment of Ishmael in the Torah. So like, and so unlike! Is there no other way to grow an identity but to banish what is like-and-unlike, thrust it out into the wilderness, almost to die? Ishmael grew up to be an archer, his hand against everyone, everyone's hand against him. And Isaac grew up to be a holy victim: Passive, a channel for the sparks of redemption rather than himself a striker of sparks. His most important life-acts were to go with Abraham to be bound for sacrifice; to take as a wife the woman chosen for him; and to be so blind as to be fooled by his son Jacob. Once Isaac and Ishmael had separated, these two who had been alike become most unlike. It is as if their father, the holy adventurer, was torn in two when his two sons split: One took his holiness, the other his boldness.

No surprise that the split identities make war upon each other: If you drive part of your own identity out to die, it will come back to threaten you, to kill you. Surely there must be another way to grow your own identity?

Maybe not. It was the Voice of God that confirmed Sarah's desire, told the troubled Abraham to send Ishmael away. The Voice of God, the God of Things-As-They-Must-Be. Maybe there was no alternative to banishment, maybe there would have been no People of Israel at all and no Arab peoples either, if Ishmael had stayed with Isaac. In other words, sometimes it takes a separation for identities to grow.

But does the separation have to be a threat of death? Must it be a dry and barren wilderness that Hagar and Ishmael go to? Must it be a sacrificial altar that Isaac is bound to? Can there not be a kind of separation that bears no threat of death but instead, like the separation of birthing, a promise of new life?

The Torah itself prophesies that Isaac and Ishmael will not always have to live in enmity and fear.

God prophesies to Hagar about Ishmael:

*A wild ass of a man shall he be.*
*[wandering as a nomad]*

That much is done.

*His hand against all,*
*hand of all against him.*

*[no longer just a wanderer*
*but an enemy]*

That much is done.

*In the face of all his brothers*
*he shall be present.*
*[no longer an enemy*
*but truly a brother]*

Not done. Not *yet.*

Not in 1973, when I gave my Rosh Hashanah talk; not even in the 1990s, though we have begun to take some steps along that journey.

## FACING EACH OTHER

When will it be possible for Ishmael and Isaac to wrestle God—the God-of-Things-As-They-Ought-to-Be—and on the morning after, rise from their wrestle to embrace each other, face each other, see each other not in a cloudy mirror but truly face to face?

An eerie thought. We read the tale of Ishmael on the first day of Rosh Hashanah. On the second day we read of Abraham's readiness at God's command to sacrifice his younger son. Why these two readings?

On those days we begin the days of *t'shuvah*, the turning and repentance that lead to Yom Kippur and our forgiveness. These two events are the two acts of Father Abraham's that we might think most need *t'shuvah*.

Is the message that we must somehow, someday, do *t'shuvah* for the banishment of Ishmael and the binding of Isaac—not condemn it in Abraham but turn ourselves to some other way of acting? And not just turn ourselves, but thereby help God turn, help Necessity turn, help the bedrock of the universe turn?

Another eerie thought. Look down the millennia: When have the children of Israel been able to choose from a place of power how to act toward the children of Ishmael? Not since Abraham—till now. During most of the periods when ancient Israel held power over others, the peoples nearby were Canaanites, Philistines, Babylonians, Romans, Greeks—not Arabs. In the Hellenistic-Roman period, Jews and Arabs were both subject peoples. And later, when Jews met Arabs in the Muslim era, it was the Arabs who were conquerors. Not until now have Jews ruled over Arabs. So now the story comes more alive than ever, almost as if it had been set there for us to search and learn from, as we move toward the end of days.

*"In the face of all his brothers he shall be present."* Is it then for our generation to do? Is it our generation's work to wrestle the God Who appears in the face of our brother Ishmael? Is it our generation's work to open up to the God-of-Things-As-They-Ought-to-Be?

How else could we deal with the Ishmael part of our identity than by driving it out into the wilderness? In the days of the Temple in Jerusalem, our people celebrated Yom Kippur by sacrificing one goat to God at the Temple and sending another goat out to wander in the desert with our own sins upon its head. One goat, you might say, for Isaac, sacrificed on the very rock of the Temple Mount where Isaac lay down to be sacrificed; and one goat sent out into the desert, as was Ishmael.

By Yom Kippur, God's Own Self is ready to do *t'shuvah*. God has learned in these ten days to say: "A goat, a goat. No human blood shed here, no human blood shed there. A goat, a goat."

And then the substitution moves to another level; for two thousand years now, instead of goats we have offered up our words of prayer and deeds of *t'shuvah*. The stories of the goats replace the goats themselves.

And what replaces the sending forth of sins?

Our people put our sins onto the head of the goat they drove out into the wilderness. But today we see another way to deal with sin: *"Ashamnu,"* we say on Yom Kippur, "We have sinned," each of us knocking at the door of our own heart to acknowledge the sin within. Not driven away, but owned as part of us, and thus confronted and changed.

The archer in ourselves, the wild wanderer within us, that part of us which lifts the hand of violence against everyone—how can we deal with that part of our identity?

The strategy of the Diaspora was to expel it, banish it, make the Jewish people into a holy people by forswearing all rage and fury. Isaac, the holy victim, became the model for the Jewish people. In reaction to the powerlessness of this Diaspora identity, Zionists demanded not only a state like all the nations, but that the Jewish people no more be a willing victim. The danger was that in rejecting Isaac as a model, the Jews might adopt that Ishmael whose fist was lifted against everyone. Might adopt the unholy joy of celebrating violence.

Could we neither banish Ishmael nor become Ishmael, but meet the Ishmael-part of our identity as our own, always to be confronted and transformed? Could we recognize that part of us which wants to destroy the Arabs, without succumbing to it? If we hear that fury in ourselves, could we see their fury as the brother of our own, and understand better how to end what drives us both to fury? Could see them as very like us, hear their cry for justice as we hear our own? Can we let our mutual tears wash away the triumph from our laughter, wash away the mockery from theirs, transform them both so their laugh and ours can join in joyful celebration?

Only then will God's final prophecy on Ishmael be fulfilled as have the preceding ones: "In the face of all his brothers he will be present," no longer an enemy but truly a brother. No longer will it be through a cloudy mirror that Isaac and Ishmael see each other, but face to face.

Could we learn from the stories of Ishmael and Isaac how to reunite our inner identities, to renew the inner wholeness that was Abraham? When Abraham dies, his sons join in burying him. Neither of them abandons his own identity; but once Abraham himself is missing, they are able to come together in peace. Perhaps they had always turned their fear of the father who endangered both their lives into fear and avoidance of each other; so once he is himself dead, they can bury with him their conflict with each other.

And with him dead, with the integrated holy adventurer gone, their own incompleteness becomes clear. The jagged broken edges of their own selves cry out for healing. By seeing each other face to face, they are able in a sense to create a larger Abraham.

Only after Ishmael and Isaac have joined to bury Abraham does God bless Isaac. Now that at last he can act on his own, he goes to live with Ishmael at *Be'er Lachai Ro'i*, the Well of the Living One Who Sees Me—the well that God had opened up for Ishmael and Hagar.

Most of this I said that Rosh Hashanah night in 1973. I ended by pointing to the prayer we say on Rosh Hashanah and, indeed, on any day: "Blessed be You, YHWH, Shield of Abraham," and asking that we say it knowing fully that Abraham had two families.

But even as I said that, I felt a deep dread that it might take something like the death of Abraham to bring our two peoples together. Some loss so deep that it would show us clearly in a mirror how broken is each of our identities—and would teach us how to drop the mirror and look at each other face to face.

My dread was confirmed just ten days later. During our prayers on Yom Kippur, Fabrangen heard, as millions of Jews around the world heard in the midst of their congregations and their prayers, that war had once more broken out. The years of looking past each other had brought one more harvest of death.

52

## GLANCING OR GAZING?

For years after the deaths of 1973, the peoples still looked past each other. Even when Egypt and Israel were both able to take the deaths of 1973 as a warrant to move forward awkwardly to end the war between them, most Israelis and most Palestinians still looked past each other. Among minorities in both communities, the process of looking clear-eyed at each other began. But most Palestinians were still unwilling to say that there was an authentic Israeli people, rightfully entitled to govern itself in part of the "Land of Palestine." Most Israelis and other Jews were still unwilling to say that there was a Palestinian people, entitled to govern itself in part of the "Land of Israel."

For twenty years more, the leaders of both peoples were unwilling to imagine that there might be a "Land of Abraham" in which his two descendant peoples are entitled to be present, face to face, each with its own identity and self, each with its own self-determination, each complementary to the other.

Those twenty years from 1973 to 1993 were painful for those Jews who saw their fears that a permanent war would weaken Israel confirmed, and their hopes for a healthier Israel thwarted. On the one hand, many of us were reviled and shunned by those for whom Third World insurgencies were sacred, a Jewish State was an anomaly, and ambiguities were demonic distractions from the path of Pure Justice. On the other hand, many of us were reviled, shunned, blacklisted, and fired by those for whom any Israeli government was the repository of all wisdom, Palestinian peoplehood was a lie, and ambiguities were demonic distractions from the path of True Judaism.

But for many of us, these twenty years were also a time of learning, of getting to know more deeply the inner recesses of the Jewish soul in all its hopes and fears, of probing deeper and deeper into the religious visions that are encoded in the Torah, of getting to know those Israelis, Jews, Palestinians, Arabs, Muslims who persisted in seeking peace because of their own deep faith in the God of Possibility, the God of Transformation.

Not till the eve of Rosh Hashanah in 1993, twenty years after the Yom Kippur War, did the Israeli and Palestinian leaders formally "see" and "recognize" each other, face to face. For many of us who were present to watch that famous handshake between Yitzchak Rabin and Yasser Arafat at the White House, the traditional *"Sheh'hekhianu"* blessing made utter sense: We were experiencing the God Who makes it possible for us to turn history around, the God Who had kept us alive and full of life, lifted us from despair, and brought us to this moment when past and future dropped away in the joy of being fully present. The God of Possibility and Transformation.

But for the leaders themselves, the ones who actually shook hands, that act and the difficult negotiations that followed were rooted not in the God of Possibility but in the reluctant, drag-heels attitude of doing only what was politically unavoidable, absolutely necessary: Obeying the God of "Must."

This attitude was profoundly vulnerable to the kind of impassioned religious commitment that led to the Purim Massacre of 1994 in the Tomb of Abraham at Hebron, carried out by a religiously committed Jew, and to the mass murders of Jews by Muslims in Afula, Tel Aviv, Buenos Aires, Jerusalem in 1994 and 1995. Over the years, I've come to feel more and more deeply that no peace grounded only in the God of "Must" will last; that only a peace that acknowledges and celebrates also the God of "Ought" and "Possibility" can respond without murder to the same deep religious and spiritual yearnings that became murderous in Hebron and Tel Aviv.

So long as Muslims and Jews tell their different versions of the story of Abraham and his two families in ways that assert only one people is truly entitled to the Land—so long will the peace process be weak, flabby, easily derailed. Even the "amended" version of this politics, a grudging acceptance of historical necessity—"We are really entitled to it all, but since we can't get rid of the usurpers we must make the best of it"—even that approach will find itself constantly on the defensive, always failing to satisfy the hopes of anyone.

## TWICE-PROMISED LAND

We do not need to be stuck in old ways of hearing the story. We can hear it in a different way—one that all the parties can affirm as true religion even if it gives a new turn to an ancient tale. True religion because it accords with our deepest contemporary needs, as well as with our ancient stories and symbols. Not so easy, of course, to convince whole peoples and faith-communities that an alternative reading of the story might fulfill even more of their yearnings than the older versions.

The new twist on the story is simple—and radical. It is to see that God—or Truth, or Inevitability, or History, or the Dialectic, or any deep force you want to name by any Name—promised the Land to *both* sets of Abraham's descendants.

Irony? Yes. God's jokes act themselves out in history, not in words alone. From this joke you could die laughing—and many people have. Perhaps the joke is exactly why Isaac/Yitzchak was "the one who laughs," and why Ishmael was *mitzachek*—laughing-with-a-twist.

Perhaps they got the joke, which is why they were able to be reconciled.

From the standpoint of the jealous and possessive traditions of Judaism, Christianity, and Islam, why on earth (or why in Heaven) might God have been so perverse and ironic as to promise the Land twice, to two different peoples?

Perhaps because the land that is called the Land of Israel, or the Holy Land, or the Land of Abraham, or Palestine, is intended to be a microcosm of the Earth, and Abraham's descendants are intended to be models for the human race.

And since the great round earth has no boundaries chiseled on it, since the many peoples of the human race must learn in their very distinctiveness to share it or wreck it, here we are: In macrocosm, one earth, many peoples; in microcosm, one land, two peoples. Two cousin peoples that must learn to share one land, one water table, one envelope of air, and yet be distinct and separate from each other.

I believe that this is indeed the story that Torah intended to tell, and that we will hear it, one way or the other. Those sharp and thorny letters that flame up from the Torah Scroll are beautiful on the parchment and enriching to the ear, but when we refuse to listen they turn into the sharpened knives and scorching fires of reality. If we refuse to hear them through our ears, we are forced to hear them through our skin, tearing and burning at our bones and flesh.

That is what the tradition meant when it said those letters are the atoms of the universe. The letters began as sweat from the Wrestle, distilled into teaching; if we are blind and deaf to the Teaching, it turns back into wrestling, sweat, and pain—to teach us that way. If we open our eyes and our ears to act, then not just the shape of the letters and the sound of the chant are beautiful, but so, too, are the shape and sound of human beings who then can pursue their lives in peace and joy.

How do we learn to read and hear the Torah before the letters fly off the scroll and turn into the swords and fires of a bitter history? What can unclog our ears, circumcise our hearts, pierce and dissolve the calluses that close us off from the teaching?

Only joining the Godwrestle, renewing the process of distilling Torah from the very pores of our own sweating wrestle with other human beings.

My own efforts to wrestle with the Ishmael story began from my fierce fears and hopes for modern Israel, my urgency to discover how Israel could live in peace, my efforts to talk with angry, fearful, and despairing Jews about what could be done. But as I wrestled with these questions, that still more intimate struggle of my life—my wrestle with my own brother—came to teach me about Ishmael, too.

## CALL ME ISHMAEL

Weeks after Yom Kippur, as the battles ended but the long, long war kept stretching on into the winter of 1974—as my dread and horror grew—I sent my younger brother my notes for my Rosh Hashanah sermon on what Isaac and Ishmael meant for the Jews and the Arabs, the Israelis and the Palestinians. I expected back some musings on the politics, or maybe his thoughts as a teacher of literature on how to read a text like Torah. Instead, I got only a note: "Dear Otts, Of course you realize you are Ishmael. Love, Howard."

What?! What craziness was this? I had realized nothing of the sort. I felt bewildered, but his statement hardly needed "proof." To be told by my younger brother that I was Ishmael was proof enough.

Still, I needed an explanation. So we talked. Talked about how he had been the "good" son, the one who behaved and laughed and made sense to the family, and I had been the angry son, the puzzling one, the one who stood on the edge of the family and kept everybody on edge, the one who was outcast, furious, mocking.

He told me stories of the past that I had never had the courage to dredge up. One story of how, when I was scarcely two, when my mother and grandmother kept a general store in the heart of poorest Baltimore, the baby doctor gave some stern advice: I might catch some dangerous disease from those poor people; I should be kept out of the store. So for months I stood behind the door, and cried and cried and cried.

Sent out.

Kept out.

When Howard told me that story, I smiled a little grimly: My grown-up version of Ishmael's mocking laugh. I couldn't cry. No doubt the tears had been used up when I was two. But the story shattered a wall, not the wall that had kept me out, but my own wall, the one that had kept out of my consciousness the knowledge of my own kept-outness. I began to understand why I had over and over positioned myself on the edges of the groups I had belonged to. Even when I passionately and lovingly plunged into my new-discovered Jewishness, I clung to that taste, that hint, of the outsider.

I began to realize how much of me is Ishmael, cast out into the desert. And then I heard his story, and Abraham's, and Isaac's, far more clearly. Maybe, for each of us, one way to hear the Teaching is to discover who in the Bible we "really" are: Sarah or Jonathan?

56

Jeremiah or Ahab? Naomi or Tamar? To discover our real name, or names. Maybe once we have a Place inside the story we can hear it better.

I learned that my own name—Abraham Isaac, the name I was given when I was eight days old—was incomplete. The third corner of the triangle, the name that got left out, the name that got written in invisible ink, the name that got called out in a cry of silence, was also me. Left out.

...What a blessing that my brother reached out to me and taught me not only that I was Ishmael, but that even as Ishmael I did not need to be outcast from him. Taught me how harsh and clear redemption needs to be, how reconciliation is anything but gentle. Only in the shadow of the death of Abraham....But it is possible. The old knots and prisons of the family bind, but not forever.

With my brother's help, I started testing the boundaries of Ishmaelness. I had been Ishmael almost all of my life; now I spent almost two years learning *how* to be Ishmael. Discovered what each gesture of the outcast was that I had known and used for decades. Learned what the uses of Ishmaelness were, as well as its dangers.

I did this with my brother and also with my people, the Jewish people: I worked out what it meant to love being Jewish but to stand just under the mezuzah in the doorway, one foot just barely inside the threshold and one halfway across it. I learned how my concern for Ishmael-the-Arab made me Ishmael-the-outcast in many Jewish eyes. And I learned how deeply Jewish it is to be the outsider, even to be the Jews' own outsider. I learned how deeply Jewish Ishmael was. It was as if the more I learned about being the outcast Ishmael, the more I understood about being the holy *nebbish* Isaac—and how being holy made even Isaac into an outsider in the world.

## LEARNING MY NAME

On the second anniversary of my Rosh Hashanah sermon, the Fabrangener who was leading our morning service asked me to say the blessings over a portion of the Torah reading. As is the custom, he asked my Hebrew name. I found myself completing the triangle of my name, telling him, "Avraham Yitzchak Yishmael"—Abraham Isaac Ishmael. He looked at me laughing, his face lit up with the joke. "That's not your name !" he said.

I laughed, too. What a theatrical gesture, changing my name like that! How ridiculous! And then I sat, trembling with uncertainty. Was this a joke, or did I mean it?

I meant it.

So I leaned over and told him, seriously this time, "I mean it. Call me up that way. That's my name now." He blinked, shrugged, called me up. As others heard my new name, there was one guffaw of laughter, and I turned red with fury: How dare they mock my serious life-turning?

And then I paused: It was like replaying the story. Like Sarah, I had laughed: Changing my name really was funny. And then, when someone else had dared to laugh at me, suddenly I could see nothing funny in the matter. So also Sarah, when Ishmael dared to laugh.

I said the blessings, then turned to hear the Torah portion. I had been so involved in deciding whether to rename myself that I had no idea where we were in the text. So it was a great shock in that moment to hear sentences about Sarah's laughter and the birth of Isaac. *Yishma El*, God heard and the Torah had spoken straight back to me.

I had chosen right, my name had been confirmed. And not with a reading about Ishmael—that would have been obvious and static. My choice had opened up the next birth, too. By making true and audible the Ishmael part of me, perhaps I had begun the process of giving birth to Isaac. Maybe now I could allow the Isaac part of me to come to life—the laughing one whose laughter is not a mockery but joyful: The holy one.

Abraham Isaac Ishmael. As if the sound waves of new life, beginning at the end of my name, were moving back through it…back toward the source, toward Abraham, toward the holy adventurer, toward wholeness.

Even so, for my brother and me it took another decade for us to achieve true reconnection. Another decade, and our mother's death. Like Ishmael and Isaac at their father's grave, we stood together when our mother died, stood together after a week of struggling to let her choose to die as she had chosen.

We stood together at the chasm of bitter rejection—or a new desire to touch each other. We chose to turn the wrestle into an embrace, a dance. We chose to meet each other's needs, and then to tell our stories to each other.

We told our different stories into a book together, a book of distinctive voices in a dance, a dialogue. We learned to listen as well as speak. We learned not to say, "I'm right; you're wrong." Not even to say, "You got it right; I must be wrong." Not even to say, "Let's weigh the memories of both of us and write the story we can both agree on."

Instead we learned to say, "So that's how you remember it? Amazing! So that's how you experienced it? Remarkable! How much a miracle that we have gotten to tell it to each other! How joyful that at last we are becoming brothers!"

We began the book in 1986; we finished in 1993. Even after six years of telling the stories to each other—six years, a tenth of our lives!—and making a larger story of their intertwining, we have different metaphors, different languages, to describe what we have done. My metaphors I draw—no great surprise—from images of Torah; my brother's, from the literatures and psychologies of the West.

As we finished writing, I remembered the three dots, the empty space, the unspoken words, in the Tale of Cain and Abel. "And Cain spoke to Abel..." But there was no speaking. And so the only alternative was murder.

Our book was the conversation Cain and Abel never had. It is what should have happened in the empty space between them. For us, our book. For someone else, patient sessions of psychotherapy, or prayers for healing in a circle round the Torah, or painful dialogues with political opponents, or...

All of them, the conversations, the wrestles, the dances, that are the only alternatives to murder.

And the Torah itself is such a conversation. There are those who can see it as sacred only if they hear in it a single Voice, the uniform voice of a One. But to my ears, what makes it sacred is precisely that it is a conversation, a weaving of the stories of many different wrestlers in our history. The priests got to tell their story, and the prophets; the kings and the guerrilla fighters; the thieves and the midwives, the nomads and the artisans, the poets and the landowners. Too few women, far far too few women: The glaring absence that has only begun in our own generation to be repaired and healed. But even with that gap in Revelation, those empty benches at the story-tellers' banquet, we have a growing Torah in which the outcry "*Sh'ma*!—Listen!" is what each story-teller says to all the others.

And they do. And we do.

# CHAPTER 4

# IN THE DARK: JOSEPH AND HIS BROTHERS

Each year as the days darken into winter, the cycle of Torah readings returns to the story of Joseph and his brothers. The rhythm of the seasons joins in the rhythm of the readings, to teach us that we are entering the dark side of the tradition.

And the story darkens us, every time we read it.

For the story of Joseph is one of ambition, envy, material power, slavery. Even darker: It is a story not only of slavery to men, but of slavery to fate; of determinism, not free will. And it is a tale of God's eclipse: Never does Joseph have a clear and unambiguous conversation with God as did Abraham, Isaac, Rebekah, and Jacob. Darkness reigns above and in his life.

To begin with, Joseph lives his life in a spiral of ambition. On two dimensions of the spiral, he moves forward to rule over those who had been his equals—and falls back when his equals take revenge. On its third dimension, he is always moving "upward"—in the scale of the community he seeks to dominate. He starts out small, in his own family. His very childhood seems to be a conspiracy between himself and his father to see him as his brothers' overseer—and even his brothers join in defining him that way. First Joseph reports to his father on his brothers' behavior. When he has some ambiguous dreams about his own power, his brothers and his father hasten to interpret the dreams as visions of his power over them. They teach him to think of himself as a boss or overseer. Then his father confirms the teaching by sending him to check on the brothers and report back. That is when they rebel and sell him into slavery. Some overseer!

But Joseph's training as a boss continues. On the second curve of the spiral, he starts as a slave in the household of Potiphar in Egypt.

But Potiphar soon appoints Joseph to oversee the house, subservient to Potiphar but in charge of everyone else. Although Joseph finds favor in his master's eyes, his master's wife casts her eyes upon him. She tried to seduce him.

It is easy to imagine that this was only a trick, never a real seduction: A desperate, furious effort to overthrow an upstart slave. It ended as it was supposed to, with Joseph in jail. Just as the brothers had sold him into slavery, so she sold him with lies into prison.

And there, for a third time, Joseph becomes an overseer: The prison's warden puts him in charge of all the other prisoners. The prison prospers, so much so that it becomes the preferred place to imprison Pharaoh's own high officers. Here Joseph interprets their dreams, but he is so unloved that even the butler whose return to the palace he predicts does not lift a finger to get him out of prison.

Finally Pharaoh himself, the father of his country, gives Joseph his chance to beome Grand Overseer. And Joseph, after years of suffering and fury, does not hesitate: He has been an outcast and a foreigner long enough. He wants to be a powerful Egyptian. So he and Pharaoh agree to make him Pharaoh's chief servant, who will turn all of Egypt's yeoman farmers into cringing servants of Pharaoh in exchange for saving them from famine. Indeed, Joseph volunteers to reduce all Egypt into one great prison-house, and Pharaoh triumphantly accepts.

What is the result? The people first harvest an abundance of grain, which they sell to Pharaoh's store-system. But when famine comes, they must year by year give Pharaoh first their money, their cattle, and finally their land itself, for bread to eat and seed to sow the land with. Step by step, Joseph reduces them to sharecroppers and all the land to Pharaoh's property. The role he had been practicing and learning all his life is fulfilled.

This time Joseph does the job so well that there no one can rebel and cast him into another slavery. Or so it seems until long after his death. When we turn to the early pages of Exodus and realize that the Jews have been flung into slavery by a Pharaoh who did not cherish Joseph, we may wonder whether the spiral has spun once again. Does the whole people suffer for Joseph's ambition?

For this is not ordinary ambition: It seems much darker.

## "I WANT TO BE A GERMAN"

Indeed, as the Fabrangen read the story, some of us reacted with horror. Here we were in Washington in the early 1970s, sharing an ethic of solidarity against tyrannical power—the kind of power that could kill many thousands of Americans and Vietnamese in an endless murderous war, that could haunt and disrupt the lives of those who worked for change by putting them on enemies lists.

If we had come to Torah with a hero, it was Moses, who holds princely power but joins with slaves to strike down an overseer. Yet here we face Joseph, who does the reverse: A prisoner, he becomes an overseer to tighten slavery. At every step, Joseph is appointed to his power by someone yet more powerful than he, and rules over those with whom he might have felt solidarity. His brothers, his fellow slaves in the house of Potiphar, his fellow prisoners, his fellow peasants in the land of Egypt—could he not have felt solidarity with all of them?

He didn't. As we Fabrangeners moved more deeply into the Torah story, someone muttered, "*Kapo!*" and a shudder ran through the room. In the Nazi death camps, *kapo* was the word for a Jew whom the Nazis chose to police other Jews. The word got under our skin like a venomous splinter. Someone stirred: I remember a terrifying poem that was written by a starving child in the Warsaw ghetto. This is how it goes:

*I want to eat.*
*I want to rob.*
*I want to kill.*
*I want to be a German.*

"Isn't that Joseph? So desperate not to be a prisoner that he wants to be a cop. So desperate not to be a Hebrew that he wants to be the second biggest Egyptian." Others half agreed. It seemed to be Joseph's need, his very life, to turn his victimization into the tool for victimizing others.

But another Fabrangener burst out: "Let's keep our concepts straight. The *kapos* were complicit in mass murder. And that poem says, 'I want to kill.' Joseph didn't kill. He did the opposite: He saved the lives of all of Egypt's people. Maybe he wanted to eat badly enough to rob others of their land; maybe he wanted to be free badly enough to become an Egyptian viceroy. But *kapo* is an uncompromising word. A *kapo* he's not."

Others joined a cautionary chorus. It is certainly true that Joseph's reading of Pharaoh's dream makes it possible to store up food against the years of famine. His new official power makes the possibility bear fruit, saving both Egypt and his own family, the bearers of Jewish peoplehood, from starvation. How can we ignore the Torah's jubilation at the rescue of Jacob's clan from famine? As Joseph himself says when he reveals himself to his brothers: Was it not God's doing that the brothers sold him into slavery, so that through this channel of the pit and slavery he would become Viceroy of Egypt and save their lives?

But others found this sense of inevitability the darkest aspect of the Joseph story: "Was this the only way to save the family? Wasn't Joseph free to choose another way?" For some of us, Joseph's sense of inevitability made it even clearer that he belongs on the dark side of the tradition. For in a tradition that usually looks toward free will, Joseph is a determinist. He predicts disaster, in a tradition that usually does not predict but prophesies disaster in the sense that a prophecy can be averted if the people change their ways.

Joseph's determinism is not just retroactive. He does not just tell his brothers afterwards that there could have been no other way. Joseph applies his determinism to the future, using it to shape the policy of Pharaoh. Joseph the determinist triumphs when he interprets Pharaoh's double dream: The dream of seven lean cows devouring seven fat cows and the dream of seven withered ears of grain devouring seven good ears.

First Joseph says he cannot interpret the dream; he must ask God. But he does not pause to pray, to ask God for guidance. He rushes ahead to say that the double dream is a proof that the future is fixed and certain. He says there *will—not* "might," but *will—be* seven years of plenty and seven years of famine. He shows Pharaoh how to alleviate the famine—not how to prevent it. His power flows from that moment. The centralization of Egypt under the king flows from that moment.

## THE POSSIBILITY OF POSSIBILITY

Could it have been different? Let us pierce between the lines to imagine what might have happened if Joseph had asked God for guidance, and God had answered. How might God have told him to deal with the danger of famine?

We have a hint: God's command of how to prevent famine in the Land of Israel. Each year, every landholding family must let the poor gather grain from the corners of the field. In the seventh year, the land must lie fallow and all debts must be forgiven. The seventh year? How instructive! Perhaps Pharaoh's dream should have been interpreted to say: There will be seven years of plenty. If you reap all seven years, there will follow seven years of famine. If you rest in the seventh year, you will have enough to eat. *If* .

What Joseph hears and what he creates is almost precisely the reverse of the process that God later commands for the Land of Israel.

Could that command have come earlier? Would God have made the Teaching available as soon as anyone asked?

Could that command have come in Egypt, *Mitzraiim*, the Land of

64

Narrow Straits, or only in the Land of Israel? What made Canaan into the "Land of Israel" was precisely that people wrestled there with God. The Teaching might have been available wherever anyone wrestled. Perhaps what made Egypt into the Narrow Place, unredeemed space and time, is that Joseph, the channel through which all Israel descended there, never spoke to God directly, never screamed or wrestled.

What Joseph teaches Pharaoh in Egypt is like a photographic negative of what God teaches Israel at Sinai—dark where Sinai is light, light where it is dark.

In the Teaching from Sinai, it is God who owns the land; in Joseph's practice, it is Pharaoh—who claimed godship for himself, who was a living idol. It is almost as if some dark vibration had said to Joseph, "God should own the land"—so darkly that he heard it as, "Pharaoh should own the land."

In the Teaching from Sinai, the priestly tribe of Levi is the one group of Israelites who are to hold no land at all. This checks the power they hold through the system of Temple sacrifice by making them materially dependent on the tithing of the other tribes. But in Joseph's practice, the only Egyptians other than Pharaoh who eventually still own land are the priests. Thus in Egypt the priests hold both spiritual and material power. It is almost as if some dark vibration had said to Joseph, "The priests are special"—but he heard it as, "The priests alone must keep their land."

The Teaching from Sinai prevents famine; Joseph's practice accepts famine and tries to limit its effects. The Teaching from Sinai decentralizes power into the families that share their gleanings and let their land lie fallow; Joseph's practice centralizes power into the hands of Pharaoh and his bureaucracy. The Teaching from Sinai frees the earth to make its own Shabbat, every seventh year; Joseph's practice enslaves the land itself to constant work. So all of Joseph's darkness and his sense of narrowness, unfreedom, congeals when he interprets Pharaoh's dream.

Joseph has no light from God. He does not feel free to call on God, although he wistfully remembers it is God who interprets dreams. Joseph believes that history is not free to change: It has been given. Perhaps even God is not free to change. And the people are not free to save themselves: They must become serfs to Pharaoh if they want to live.

Given no vision for a pathway of free choice, Joseph becomes a determinist, convinced there is no free will. It is precisely out of this spiritual experience and conviction that he creates a national policy that abolishes freedom for the Egyptians. They elevate Pharaoh to

Godhead and accept the yoke of an unchangeable history—even an unchangeable succession of famine and plenty in a remorseless rhythm, regardless of what human beings do.

This outlook is profoundly different from that teaching of the Torah that says: Whether we act on what the Sacred Teachings tell us is what determines whether the rains fall, the rivers run, our people eat in plenty—or the rains turn to poison, the rivers and the oceans flood, we starve. A teaching so important that it appears in our prayer books just after the *Sh'ma* itself, when we listen to ourselves proclaim, "Hear!—Our God is One!" What does God's unity proclaim? That the earth is one, we are entwined with rain and soil, we are free to make decisions about the earth that then have consequences in our own lives because we are indeed entwined with earth.

But this is not what Joseph heard. For him the absence of spiritual freedom, of personal psychological freedom, of political freedom, of freedom for the earth all mesh.

In Fabrangen, we sat silent for a while, gazing outside into the wintry darkness. One of us mused, "It's not only the measures to deal with famine that are like a dark version of the tradition. Joseph is like a dark version of Moses. Joseph precedes the people into Narrow Egypt. And then he brings them all in. Moses precedes them out, then leads them all out. Joseph goes from prison to the palace. Moses flees from the palace into exile. Joseph leads the people to material prosperity, but for hundreds of years in Egypt they hear nothing from God. Moses leads them out of the fleshpots of Egypt to Sinai and God's Self-revelation."

## TZADDIK IN THE DARK

One of us finally became impatient with the gloom outside and in. "Remember," he said, "the tradition insists that Joseph is a *tzaddik*, a righteous person. Not a *kapo*, not even an overseer, not even overly ambitious. A *tzaddik*. Is there anything we can learn from that?"

What evidence is there that Joseph is a *tzaddik*? First of all, the tradition fastens on one fact: He refuses Potiphar's wife. Despite all the attractions of sex—especially for a young man far from home and friends, a young man dazzled by sophisticated Egypt—despite all this, he refuses to commit adultery. Although God does not speak to him, he remembers what he has been taught about God's holy path of life.

Second, Joseph cares for his father and his family, even for the brothers who have wronged him. He was willing to plunge Egypt into serfdom, but he insists on raising his clan to prosperity. So his willingness to offer reconciliation may also make him something of a *tzaddik*.

But some of us were still wary. If Joseph is a *tzaddik*, he is a *tzaddik-in-the-dark*.

Indeed, we realize that his determinism runs deeper than his mental outlook on the world. We have been thinking about him as if he had again and again chosen the role of overseer. But there is a profound sense in which Joseph never chose this role. His life had worn this groove into his being the way a needle wears a groove into a phonograph record: Once a scratch appears, each circling of the needle digs it deeper, deeper. It is his father Jacob who first scratches this way of being on his life, by setting him above his older brothers.

Or did it begin even earlier? Was Jacob reenacting the family history in which his mother had chosen him to go beyond his older brother Esau, just as his father Isaac had been chosen by his father Abraham to go beyond his older brother Ishmael?

All these stories of supplanted older brothers we have seen as tales of freedom, reversals of the Fate that said an older brother was in charge. But perhaps at this point what began as an act of freedom, God's freedom opening up new possibilities to human beings, has worn a groove that is no longer free. Jacob invites his son Joseph not simply to go beyond his brothers, but to rule over them. He makes Joseph into his brothers' overseer even though no Voice of God has decreed this. He responds only to a dream, a dream seen only by another's eyes, spoken only by another's mouth. He might have paused to seek from his own inner Voice, the Voice of God, some meaning for this dream. It might have been a warning rather than a directive. But he let the scratch on his own life dictate what he heard in the dream that Joseph dreamed.

From then on, Joseph was a prisoner of fate. Indeed, long afterward he interpreted Pharaoh's dream without pausing for God to give a free interpretation, just as he had seen his father do with him. The process and the content, the medium and the message, fused. Joseph's father walked like an automaton down a path like the one Abraham and Isaac had walked with much more freedom; this automatic path led to domination, not transformation; and Joseph learned to think of himself as humble servant of an inscrutable fate, walking blindly through God's foreordained drama.

In Fabrangen, we faced our own family histories. Have they bound us inexorably to dramas of domination and submission? Is it true, as the Ten Commandments say, that the missteps of the parents control the lives of their offspring three, even four, generations into the future? How did my mother and father respond to the death of a parent when they were young? Did they pass that suffering on to me? What do my struggles with my brother communicate to my children? What can our families do to free ourselves from the tightness of the un-changing past?

Slowly we Fabrangeners realized: Maybe what is most important about Joseph is precisely that he is a *tzaddik* who has been left in the dark. It is true that he does not address God, but it is equally true that God never addresses him. God leaves him in the dark—speaks to him only through dreams, those visions of the dark, and mostly through other people's dreams at that.

Given no light to live by, Joseph tries to grasp the darkness, to walk firmly, not to stumble. He learns to turn the role of overseer, which might have degenerated into *kapo,* in the other direction—into the role of rescuer. Although he turns Egypt into a plantation, he does not turn it into a death camp. Indeed, he turns it into a plantation precisely so it does not turn into a death camp.

At the moment of his dark triumph as the Grand Overseer, Joseph is able to let go of that role in dealing with his brothers: He is able to turn toward them in real reconciliation. It is true that even this mo-ment burns with a kind of purple flame—for the brothers come down into Egypt, down into material wealth, down ultimately into slavery. And yet—and yet—if we are facing deepest winter, there may not be anything we can do but light a fire, however dark it burns.

With all these threads, the Joseph story weaves some darkness into Torah:

Inexorable necessity: Dark thread in God's gift of a world where choice is free.

Central power: Dark thread in God's gift of freedom in society.

Scarcity: Dark thread in God's gift of a world of plenty.

## THE DARKENING WORLD

As we watch, those threads darken more and more of the fabric until, as the Book of Genesis ends, even God goes into eclipse.

God disappears not only for Joseph, but for the whole clan and people. As Exodus begins, we realize that the Torah itself casts no light on hundreds of years of Israel's life in Egypt. Winter darkening outside our Fabrangen gathering-place, the Torah going dark inside the room.

As one of us pointed out, the fit between the cycle of the Torah reading and the cycle of the seasons is no accident. Winter always comes. Darkness always falls. Exile always overtakes us. How many of us have seen the Vision, heard the Voice? How many of us experi-ence the world as freedom and ourselves as free, for more than a moment of our lives? Or ever? So the story may be teaching us how to live in the dark. Even in the dark, it is possible to be a *tzaddik*. Even in the dark, one must strive to be a *tzaddik*.

For much of our lives, we find ourselves becoming small versions of an overseer.

In our families: Like Joseph, we often shape our relatives to meet the demands of some outside power other than ourselves.

In our jobs: Like Joseph, we often control our fellow workers to meet the requirements of the boss or the organization.

In society: Like Joseph, we calm our outraged anger in order to keep the institutions running. Or we meet some crisis by amassing more control than we had sought.

"Like Lenin, like Mao," said one Fabrangener. "They're Joseph. They tried to feed the people by centralizing all power in the state. Maybe we can no more write Mao and Lenin out of history than we can erase winter from the seasons."

Necessity and order. Obedience and order. We all demand it, we all coerce it. Even the most rebellious, even the most radical among us do it—sometimes. The issue is always: When? Do we let necessity overwhelm us? Do we let its moment expand to fill all life? Or do we limit necessity to but one of the four seasons, to but one of the four generations of the clan of Abraham? Do we simply turn passive when the winter darkens, or do we turn at Hanukkah to light the candles?

We hurry past the dark place in the Torah. As the days grow brighter, we greet the fire of the Burning Bush. Joseph takes us from prison to the palace; but Moses takes us from the palace to the Bush. And then to fiery Sinai.

Joseph reminds us to be a *tzaddik* when it's dark. But the sunlight brightens, springtime does appear, and we learn from Moses that God is free to change—and so are we.

# PART II

# MOTHERS, SISTERS, AND MESSIAH

# CHAPTER 5

# IN OUR IMAGE: EVE AND ADAM

Changing.

Maturing.

In every battle between brothers, there are dark years of conflict before the darkness itself teaches them how to make a peace of new maturity. As parents wrestle with the "raising" of their children, getting them to "rise" into maturity, as children mature into parenting, what is the path that makes this rising joyful? How can we make this path not an endless circle of repetition, each generation stuck in the mistakes of the one before, but a rising spiral of new light?

Perhaps the Torah's deepest tale of the spiral of the generations is not contained in a single specific story in the Torah, but the way we read the entire Torah as a great life-cycle telling. The moment when we see the Torah as a great whole, one Story, is one of the happiest of holy days—Simchat Torah, "the joy of the Teaching." That is when we complete the reading of the Torah with its tale of Moses' death and begin all over again by reading about the Seven Days of Creation. From the end of the story to the beginning, from the end of the life of the great teacher to the beginning of all life for everyone.

For centuries, Simchat Torah has been a day for adults to whirl and jump in seven dances with the Torah Scroll, a day for children to march in giddy, raggedy formation carrying flags emblazoned with the Torah and other Jewish symbols.

As Jewish renewal has spread over the last twenty years, Simchat Torah has taken on deeper meanings. Nowadays, many congregations are unfurling the whole grand Torah Scroll into one gigantic circle where the end can connect with the beginning—precisely to remind us that each ending is pregnant with new possibility, new life. Sometimes the congregants give words to a life-question they are facing, then choose at random a passage in the great parchment circle,

73

and interpret what they read as a response to their question. And nowadays the seven dances in a circle with the Torah may be planned to accord with seven different aspects of Divinity—what the Kabbalists called the *S'phirot*, the unfolding emanations of God. One mood, melody, rhythm for a dance of loving-kindness, another for strict boundaries, another....

But in the early 1970s, Simchat Torah was still largely a festival for children. I got ready to take my own children—eight and five years old—to Fabrangen, to dance and sing with the joy of the Torah. But I knew they'd never be able to hear and absorb the Seven Days of Creation in the whirl of the service, and I wanted them at least to have a feel for one of the deeper, grownup meanings of the festival. So I sat down ahead of time to read them the story of the Seven Days.

## WHEN A MAN BECOMES A MOTHER

By Day Five of the story they were jumping up and down. "When's God goin' to make people?" said David. "Soon...," I said, reciting the creation of the beasts and cattle; "Now!..." I said, reciting "Male and female created He them."

"I bet He makes the woman first!" shouted Shoshana. I stopped, disoriented. "Why?"

"Because the man would come out of the woman, of course!"

Of course. *Of course.* The man *would* come out of the woman. Even at five, Shoshana knew that.

So why is it written the other way around?

*Is* it written the other way around?

To ask these questions is to till the soil of Eden: To turn it and freshen it, to make it fertile with the fruit of knowledge—and perhaps of life. I have spent years turning that soil, using as my spade those questions that sprang from Shoshana's surprise. In Eden, who was the mother? Or is the better question, who mothered what?

To begin with: Who was Adam? Most of us have been taught to think that he was male and that the woman was created from his rib; but not all the rabbis who created what we call "Jewish tradition" thought so. The rabbis had to wrestle with a text (Gen. 1:26) that said, "And God said: 'Let us make Adam in Our image, after Our likeness; and let them have dominion...'"

Them? What "them"?

*Our* image, *our* likeness? What "Our"?

And the rabbis had to wrestle with a text (Gen. 1:27) that said, "And God created Adam in His image, in the image of God created He him; male and female created He them." What "him," what "them"?

And finally the rabbis had to wrestle with a text (Gen. 5:1-2) that said, "In the day that God created Adam, in the likeness of God made He him; male and female created He them, and called their name Adam, in the day when they were created." Called *their* name Adam?

There were several ways to explain these baffling shifts from "him" to "them" and back again, this frightening reference by God to "Our own image," as if God were plural—God forbid!

Some of the rabbis said these texts were simply summaries of the familiar story of the rib and Eve. This became the main line of interpretation. It came closest to expressing a sense of comfort with a world in which men were in charge and women were necessary—and pleasantly subordinate.

Some rabbis had a darker, nightmare vision. They imagined a woman created before Eve, created just like the male Adam from the earth, the "*Adamah*," and therefore equal to him. They imagined this woman, Lilith, "the night one," insisting on her equality, her freedom, and her sexual passion—"When we make love, why can't I be on top?"—until she terrified Adam, who thought he should be dominant. At that point Adam demanded God remove her and give him a new wife, Eve.

These rabbis were, of course, writing their own sense of the world—men belonged on top, literally and figuratively—into their image of Adam. But they felt some terror lest their rulership be challenged. They feared a free and passionate womanhood, and so they explained that the free and passionate Lilith became a demon, devourer of children, destroyer of men. And this dark fear colored hundreds of years of Jewish history—dark days and darker nights when men and women feared the furious energy that free and passionate women might set free.

But Rabbis Jeremiah ben Eleazar and Samuel ben Nachman, may they be remembered for a blessing to our generation, said that Adam was male and female in one person. Androgynous. These rabbis probably intuited that they themselves were emotionally and spiritually androgynous. Perhaps they even felt that women had enough power in their lives to say the society was "androgynous."

## IN OUR IMAGE?

Three different views: The rabbis disagreed and wrestled. What about the Torah text itself: What did it mean? To my own eyes, the androgynous interpretation is both the only way the world makes sense and the only way the text makes sense. To me, this text that one moment connects with God as "Our," in the next as "His"; one moment sees

Adam as "them," the next as "him"—to me, this sounds like a clumsy effort to describe what they could only intuit because there was no place to see it: A nondualistic duality, a unity of opposites, androgyny.

And the Torah even reveals how different this unified duality looks from God's standpoint and from our own. To the outside human observer, God looks utterly One: In His image, says the Torah. But from inside, God knows that the Unity contains all opposites: "In Our image," says God's own voice speaking about God's own Self.

Of this Androgynous One, why doesn't the Torah ever say that "She" was One? Here, I think, we bump up against the limits of the writers. Even if they too felt that Reality is "androgynous," that women and what they felt as "womanly" inside themselves had power, they were still men. These men who ruled biblical society and wrote almost all of Torah saw God in their own image—the Great Ruler, the Great Writer. To be Supernal Ruler and Writer meant therefore to be an "androgynous male," like them. To have imagined the Supernal Ruler/Writer as a Supernal Female (even androgynous) would have belied their own experience of who ruled and who wrote.

Still, we can hear the Torah story this way: God makes an androgynous Human in the image of an androgynous God. And then God decides it is not good for the Human to be alone. Perhaps it is the Human who thinks so first, learning from the procession of male and female beasts that march past to be named that it is not good to be alone. But if it is Adam who notices, it is God who must agree.

And God does agree. That is, the basic energy of the universe feels that unity as a given is not good. Perfection is not perfect. It is better to struggle toward unity than to own it from the start. Just as God needed there to be a world—just as God found it not good enough to be All in All, Utter Perfection Encompassing All, and therefore needed to withdraw from a space where the world could emerge—so, too, God knows that a human who encompasses everything is not the model human. God knows that a human being who is cast in the image of God needs an "*ezer k'negdo*,"—literally a "help opposite," often translated into English as "help meet," but perhaps best translated "counterpart."

So that each human might have a counterpart, the two sides of Adam, male and female, are separated. In this approach to the story, it is not a *rib* but a *side* (these are the same word in Hebrew, *tzela*, as Samuel ben Nachman pointed out) that is taken to make the woman; the other side becomes the man.

At this point in Eden, the similarity of the man and woman is most apparent. He greets her as "bone of my bones, flesh of my flesh." Their very names—*Isha* and *Ish*, Wo-man and Man—are emphasized to show how alike they are, how one came from the other. Both of them (and the text underlines the bothness) are naked. Naturally, they are not ashamed, since what they see in each other is alikeness.

## ANDROGYNOUS ADAM

First my children and I wrestled with this story and its possible meanings, then all of us in Fabrangen, and finally for many years all of us in the broader movement for Jewish renewal. I was moved to keep hearing our own generation's struggles reflected in this ancient debate, a debate that is not quite hidden in the Torah text, is more openly argued by the rabbis, and arises in full view among us.

Indeed, the ancient debate became an ironic element in one of our own generation's retellings of an archetypal tale: The story of Yentl, the woman who pretended to be a man so she could study Torah. Six years after the first edition of *Godwrestling* was published, Barbra Streisand made a film from Isaac Bashevis Singer's version of the Yentl story. Streisand inserted into the film something Singer did not have: An explicit reference to the rabbis' debate. In Streisand's film, Yentl is studying Torah with her good male comrade. He refers dismissively to Eve, generic Woman: "Only a rib," he says.

"No," says Yentl, flashing fire: "A side! Yes, a side!"

When I first saw *Yentl*, that moment stunned me. What had been so esoteric just six years before, suddenly appearing in a major film! That moment made sharply clear to me that what we had been talking about as deep spiritual needs—the need both to study the ancient wisdom and to recast it in new forms—were needs not just of a tiny circle of Jews but of huge circles of the human race.

Why did Streisand add this scene? Filming *Yentl*, she decided, required that she herself experience Torah study. So she studied with several rabbis who introduced her to the "side/rib" debate among the ancient rabbis, and she turned it into the key to her version of Yentl. What is it to be a woman, a human, *Isha, Adam*? Are we bone of each other's bone, able to learn the deepest Torah with and from each other—or profoundly alien?

For Streisand was not Bashevis Singer; she was a feminist, and the rabbis she consulted had themselves helped shape—and themselves been deeply reshaped —by a movement for Jewish renewal that was feminist. That the ancient "side/rib" debate came alive for them was because they were committed to Jewish renewal in a way no Jews had pursued it for centuries.

So let us turn back to what we might learn from the Torah's text. If separating the androgynous Human into man and woman is what the story actually tells, why have we been saddled for so long with the notion that the man came first, and only then the woman? Because after they are divided, the text continues to call the man "Adam." It calls the woman "woman" and later "Chava, Mother of Life." It never calls her "Adam." Unconsciously, we work backwards in the story: If in the later passages the male is Adam, then in the earlier passages Adam must be the male. How can we square this with the androgynous interpretation?

The hinge of this question is the moment when Adam becomes two people. Here I come back to Shoshana's question. For here the Teaching tells us that the woman came out from the man—not the other way around, as we know from our own lives and from all history. In Eden, the man becomes the mother.

Hearing myself say "From all history..." I realize that Eden is not about history. Eden is about the world that should be, could be, not the world that was and is. It is from Eden that we enter history, but Eden itself is not a part of what we call our history.

Eden is where a man discovers that his counterpart's "name will be called Woman," but he does not name her. Her name is hers already, from God or from herself. He does not control her essence. Eden is where humans are free and loving; where they can serve their cousin the earth in joy, not in sweat; where they name the animals but do not eat them; where there is no murder. In such a world, the world as it should be, a man can give birth to a child. Like every other sense in which Eden runs contrary to our daily lives and to all history, there is this one: A man can be a mother.

## MOTHERING CHILDREN, MOTHERING HISTORY

This is no put-down of woman, no male-chauvinist usurpation of her role of motherhood. This is a wistful reaching beyond rigid roles, toward the world in which men also could give birth. A joyful teaching that men are to reach toward that great joy: "And therefore shall a man leave his father and his mother and shall cleave to his woman, and they shall be one flesh." This is no mere anthropological note that the man shall leave the family of his birth and join the family of his wife. More deeply, it says that within every man there is a woman waiting to be brought forth; a man shall transcend the rigid categories of "fatherhood" and "motherhood" and shall cling to this woman within, and they shall be one flesh just as Adam before the division was one flesh, androgynous. Even now that we are divided into male and female, men and women are still androgynous—and should be aware of their androgyny, and celebrate it. The man shall be ready to become a mother.

And the woman? In Eden, in the Garden of Delight, the world as it should be and could be, the woman could do what she "cannot" do, is not allowed to do, is repressed from memory if she does do, in the history we know: The woman could mother all of history. For it is the woman who makes trouble, starts history, by eating the fruit of the Tree of Knowing Good and Evil.

The man could give birth to a human being; the woman could give birth to history. Both of them are mothers, each in the very way that our daily lives teach us is impossible. The Torah comes to teach us to know a different possibility.

But for millennia we have been told that the woman's trouble-making was a sin, and for that sin all women have been punished.

Not so. Not so. The story does not tell us that eating from the tree was a sin. Elsewhere it is specified that disobedience of God's will is a sin, but not here. Indeed, the Snake and the Earth are accursed, but not Man and Woman. The story tells us only that eating from the tree led to the hard and painful history we know and grow in. Before we accept the conventional view that eating from the Tree of Knowing was evil, the "Fall of Man, " we must look at the alternatives. What else could Adam and Eve have done?

## LEARNING GOOD AND EVIL

The wisest comment I have heard on the choices Eve and Adam had came—once again—from my children. We were spending August in a small New Hampshire town, sharing a house with others from our extended family of the *havurot*. One Shabbat morning we were munching apples, waiting for the service to get started, and reading a boring children's version of Creation.

David, who then was ten years old, said, "I knew they would have to eat. The only way to find out what is 'good' is to do something bad. If you never do anything bad, you never understand how to be good. If you never do anything bad, you just *are*. You are not good and not bad. You just *are*. "

"What's wrong with that?" I said. "Why shouldn't they just be? That's what God wanted."

David shook his head. "There's only one kind of people who just are, and don't know anything about being good or bad. That's babies. Who would want to be a baby all his life?"

"But if you were a baby all your life, if you didn't grow up, you wouldn't get old. I guess you wouldn't die."

But David insisted, "It isn't worth it. It's boring to be a baby all your life. I'd rather learn how to be good and bad and get old and die."

"That's what the snake said."

"He was right. He said knowing good and evil was being like God. That's right, too."

"But look how it all turned out!"

"So it's just like now: People have to work hard, it hurts to have babies, all that stuff. So what? Would you rather be a baby all your life, so somebody would feed you all the time?"

"But God told them not to eat!"

"Yeah, but look how God makes such a thing about a Tree: They should be sure not to eat from it and all that. Any kid would eat from it after that. It's almost like God teased them into eating. Maybe God wanted them to eat from it—but also wanted them to think it was bad to eat, so then they'd have to think about being good and bad."

"You're stretching it. God sure acts angry about their eating."

"Well, OK. Maybe God didn't want them to eat. But I'd still eat, if I was them. What if I did everything you told me, *all the time*? That's like being a baby too. That's boring. If that's what God wanted, God was wrong."

It all sounds sensible to me. Adam and Eve in Eden were like children. So children are the best people to comment on the story. And most children, I have found out, do want to grow up.

But of course if growing up is valuable, it makes sense to explore Eden as a grownup, too. (Was the snake a grownup? Maybe even a teacher, accursed for the classic crime of corrupting the young?) As a grownup I have kept thinking about what "knowing good and evil" means, and what the Tree of Life is all about. And I think that in our generation, when women *are* mothering history and men *are* becoming part of the birthing process and beginning to mother children, there are new ways of growing up that grownups can learn from the story of the Garden.

First of all, it is valuable to keep in mind that in Hebrew, "knowing good and evil" means "knowing" not in an objective, academic sense, but in the sense of deep and intimate understanding of what is Other from one's self. For "*da'at*," knowing, is used in Hebrew for making love and relating to God, as well as for absorbing "facts."

Thus the Tree of "Knowing Good and Evil" is ready to teach both the existence of Otherness and the ability to reach out across the void toward the Other. Indeed, when Martin Buber examines the uses of the phrase "good and evil" elsewhere in the Bible, he suggests that "knowing good and evil" means knowing/feeling/reaching not just toward ethical opposites, but toward all the opposites of the world. It means relating to a world made up of opposites, of I's and Thou's, by turning them into a loving I-Thou relationship.

Reconnecting what is distinct and separate is different from being part of an undifferentiated flow of life, from living in the shade of the Tree of undivided Life.

Buber doesn't mention one piece of the Eden text that tends to bear him out: Immediately upon eating of the Tree of Knowing Good and Evil, Adam and Eve realize they are naked and clothe themselves. Why? If the fruit of the tree was ethical knowledge, then suddenly Adam and Eve realized...what? That simply being naked together in the Garden was unethical? That seems unreasonable. Is "being na-ked" the Torah's code for having sexual relations, and now Adam and Eve see that sex between them is unethical? Then why does the Torah say openly, without code words, that they "knew" each other after they left Eden, and that Eve conceived?

In an era when many of us are wrestling with the issues of sexual ethics and also find value in wrestling with the Torah, these are im-portant questions. For centuries, this story has been construed in a way that imbues our sexuality with shame. But the people of Israel in biblical times do not seem to have been haunted by shame over their sexual energy. If the Eden story is not teaching us to be ashamed of sex, what is its point?

If we pursue Buber's line of thought, then the sudden shock of nakedness makes more sense. Before Adam and Eve ate from the tree, they had been most impressed by their bodies' likeness to each other: Bone of my bones, flesh of my flesh. After eating from the tree that teaches how to know distinctions, they would have been most im-pressed by their unlikeness. Just as they now felt the collision between good and evil, so they now felt the contrast between male and female. I imagine them so fascinated and shaken by the constant sense of their bodies' differences from each other that they need to cover those dif-ferences with clothes.

The making of these clothes—the first human act of technology—is itself a recognition that "Eden," the expression of undivided life, has already begun to slip away. There is work that must be done: Fig leaves, part of the flowing, undivided world, must be made into an object. "I" meets "It."

Small wonder that Adam now feels not his likeness to God but his unlikeness—and so hides from God's voice. For *everything* is now separate, divided, dialectical. The knowledge is painful and frightening.

81

# INTEGRATING OPPOSITES

Understanding "knowing good and evil" in this way can help us get beyond the shame and guilt about sexuality that underlie some of the Jewish and even more of the Christian outlook on the relationship of women and men. For it is clear that issues of male-and-female and of good-and-bad both run through the Eden story. Their intertwining has, in the past, been taken to mean that sexuality is evil and the beginning of sexuality is the defining moment of "the Fall." The eleventh-century Jewish commentator Rashi, long before Freud, even saw the snake as a symbol of sexual potency and danger.

Since Eve listens to the snake and convinces Adam to eat from the forbidden tree, it is easy to identify the woman with sexual temptation and with the dangerous attractions of the flesh. Many men found it attractive to read the text in this manner anyway, since they ruled over women and needed to justify their lordship. But it is not enough to accept that the text says what centuries of distortion have said it says—and then to shrug it off. Rather we are obligated, now that we begin to see the world from something other than a male-tyrannical position, to wrestle with the text again to see if it means something else, from which we can learn anew.

We cannot exclude either sexuality or ethics from the story; it is clear that both are involved. If we see the major event of Eden as the discovery of splitness—good from evil, female from male, God from human, even the Tree of Life from the Tree of Knowing Good and Evil—then we can more deeply understand the sexual issues: The goal of humankind is not to lift up male over female, chastity over sexuality, or the spirit over the flesh; it is not to lift up God over human, good over evil, Life over Knowing, or the other way around. It is to make all one flesh, to reach toward wholeness.

Looking at sex this way, looking at each other naked as Eve and Adam did, we are shocked to realize that we are not "one flesh." Instead, we have to *become* one flesh. Our desire for each other is proof that we are separate from each other. What will we do to reunite our selves? We are struck not with shame over our desire but with shame over our difficulty in doing what would really make us again one flesh: Sex, yes, and more than sex.

The Garden teaches that we fail most deeply in our sexual ethics not when we have sex (as official Judaism and Christianity have mostly insisted) but when we "have alienation," treat some authentic part of ourselves as alien. When we exile women, exile men, exile womanliness, exile manliness, exile sexuality and earthiness from our lives. And our deepest ethical failing about good-and-evil is not simply doing something wrong, but pretending to exile all wrongness from our own selves: Projecting it elsewhere, onto someone else.

Still, God must be disobeyed before humanity can be reconciled with God (just as Jacob must prevail over God before God can bless him). Man and woman must be separated before they can come together as one flesh. We must struggle with evil to do what is truly good. Experiencing wholeness requires experiencing splitness.

## GROWING UP FROM EDEN

As the kabbalists say, the Tree of Life and the Tree of Knowing Good and Evil were *one* tree; but Eve and Adam could not experience them as one tree. If they had, history would have achieved its goal from its very beginning. But not until childlike human beings had grown up enough to experience separation and alienation could they desire wholeness and search toward it.

The history we live in is still the history of alienation. God sends us out; the Garden disappears; and we begin the history in which humans battle nature and sweat to win a living from the earth; in which men rule over women and define their identities; in which we are exiled from our land; in which we kill each other.

Ought we to take as commandments the statements of the Torah that "You shall eat bread in the sweat of your brow" and "Your husband shall rule over you"? Did God command us to walk the path of life forever in such alienation?

I view these statements as honest, accurate descriptions of the direction that our path would have to take. Through them God says, "This is what it will be like for you to grow up." But the path continues ahead of us, beyond the dry plateau of alienation, and we need not get stuck there.

Only institutions that sought to defend and entrench the rule of men over women would have taken "Your husband shall rule over you" as a positive and permanent command. Only institutions that sought to justify and prolong the toil of some people in the service of others would have taken "You shall eat bread in the sweat of your brow" as a positive and permanent command. Like the other conditions of life outside Eden, these were the facts of life. We are invited to live through them and learn from them so we can move beyond them.

The path is a spiral path. We begin at a place of unconscious unity, then move to a place of conscious separation and alienation, and finally we are invited to curve once more upon the spiral, to a place of higher, conscious unity.

Our goal is to reunite the Tree of Knowing Good and Evil with the

Tree of Life. Our goal is to recreate at a higher, more conscious level that nondualistic duality, that unity of opposites, which was embodied in the original Adam. Our goal is to rediscover what it means to wrestle—not casting conflict out from love nor love from conflict, but fusing both into one process.

These are momentary glimpses toward a deeper vision. It is hard to describe what they might mean in our daily lives, which is exactly where they must become real. If they have been the glimpses of our mystics only, then we must build a democratic mysticism, in which these glimpses become the daily practice of us all.

Let me share one glimpse that might become a practice: Ecology teaches us both that there is a seamless web of life, constantly shimmering and flowing through the planet, and that this web is made up of countless specific threads and networks, each fitting in a unique and different niche. The web as a whole is the Tree of Life; distinguishing its parts is the Tree of Knowledge. We cannot have the one without the other.

Ecologists also teach that we humans are, in one sense, simply part of the seamless web of life upon this planet. Yet they also say, and they themselves are proof of it, that we are a specific and very special part of the web: The one part that is *conscious* of the whole web and of our part in it and of all the niches and distinctions that make up the web.

We create the science of ecology, which is the Knowing of the Tree of Life. At the same moment, we can flow in the Tree and we can describe its parts. Can we build a life-path that treats ourselves and the world this way?

And in the other areas that define our exile from the Garden: Can we reunite our man and woman into one androgynous flesh? Can we reunite our warfare and our love into a process for carrying on a peaceful conflict? Can we reunite our drudgery and our leisure into a kind of restful work?

These questions are signposts along the path of growing up.

# CHAPTER 6

# DO NOT STIR UP LOVE
# UNTIL IT PLEASE

When I was twelve, preparing for my boilerplate bar mitzvah ceremony, I discovered at the back of a traditional prayerbook a few astonishing passages in a section called the Song of Songs. The passages were descriptions of a woman's and a man's naked bodies, each by someone who enjoyed looking at them and celebrated how beautiful they were.

The passages enthralled me. I was too excited by them to wonder more than vaguely what they were doing in the prayerbook. Caught in that boring process of preparing to chant a Torah portion I didn't understand, I was in no mood to question any moments of pleasure that came my way. Anyhow, whom could I ask? Ask grownups such a question, and they'd probably make sure I never saw the Song of Songs again.

After that first randy year or so around my bar mitzvah time, my body may have remembered the Song, but the rest of me forgot. I did not meet the Song again until Passover 1973, in the midst of Fabrangen. Then it came to me not as a secret adolescent pleasure, but as a grownup joy to be shared as part of a community.

As Fabrangen sang and danced and studied its way through the first few years, we gathered the energy to add more and more elements of ancient practice—renewed in our own peculiar way. We learned that traditionally, each Passover there is a special reading of the Song of Songs in the synagogue. It is usually a hurried, almost surreptitious chanting by the older men. It certainly wasn't advertised: Who knows what the 13- and 14-year-olds might think? Or do!

But, of course, we did things in a different way. So in the spring of 1973, the women and men of Fabrangen gathered in the house of one member-family to sit in a circle on the floor, munch fruit and matzah, and fulfill the *mitzvah* of reading the Song of Songs together.

For this particular study session, Max Ticktin had volunteered to lead us. He was a rabbi, the former long-time director of Hillel houses at several great Midwestern universities, and had recently come to Washington as a national Hillel administrator. But we soon learned he was much more than that. He and his wife Esther and another rabbinic couple in Chicago had founded a group similar to ours. They thought it natural to join Fabrangen when they arrived in Washington, although the rest of us thought it astonishing.

They became models for us in at least two ways—especially models for how to ask new questions, not necessarily how to live specific new answers.

First, they were in the midst of remaking their marriage, aiming toward a partnership of equals whose life-concerns and passions overlapped, but were not identical. For many of us, caught in the upheavals of the women's movement with few clues about how to live in ways unlike our parents, they seemed to be just a step or two ahead.

Second, they were exploring how Jews who were steeped in Jewish tradition and Jews who were not could learn from each other with dignity, freedom, and growing wisdom. On this question, they realized, our *havurah* experience might be a step or two ahead.

Without their playing the roles of "Rebbetzin" or "Rabbi," without our playing the roles of subservient, adoring, or resentful congregants, they began gently and creatively to make their profound knowledge of the Jewish tradition—religious and secular, Hebrew and Yiddish, in Israel and Diaspora—available to us, and we made our hopes and hesitations clear to them. They did not scoff at our efforts to go beyond the domination of Jewish religious life by rabbis who were treated—and acted—like Official Jews on behalf of everyone else. Instead they affirmed our efforts toward participation and inclusion, not only in words but in their willingness to share without controlling. We quickly learned to love them, and to learn from them without the shadow of fear, anger, and projected mystery that surrounds and isolates many rabbis.

## THE FLOW OF WORDS AND MUSIC

As we Fabrangeners settled into place that Pesach evening, we found a pile of photocopied versions of the Song of Songs in English, marked in an unexpected way: Was a man or a woman speaking, in each passage? Max had drawn on an early draft of a new translation by the poet Marcia Falk, and his own sense of the Hebrew text, to mark who was speaking at any given moment in the Song. Our copies looked like the text of a play: Superimposed on the Jewish Publication Society's translation of the Song into English were stage directions heading different passages of poetry: Some for "Man," some for "Woman," some for "Chorus."

As we settled down, our conversation hushed to all the soft "shsh" sounds: "*Shir HaShirim, asher liShlomo* ...The Song of Songs, which is for Solomon":

*Oh, give me of the kisses of your mouth,*
*For your love is more delightful than wine.*

And, about twenty-five minutes later,

*"Hurry, my beloved,*
*Swift as a gazelle or a young stag,*
*To the hills of spices!"*

None of us had ever before read *Shir HaShirim* as a conversation among its persons, let alone one so full of erotic playfulness and innuendo, so full of tastes and smells, so full of longing looks between the lovers.

When the reading finished, there were a few minutes of warm and thoughtful quiet. Suddenly a woman burst out: "A woman wrote that! It's different from every other book in the Bible."

"You mean because the woman is fully equal here and chooses her own life? Because she is the one who searches for her lover, takes the initiative, reaches out? Like Eve?"

"That's part of it, but it's not just that. It's what she's like. There may not have been a single other woman mystic in all of Jewish history, but whoever wrote this was!"

Laughter and pleased nods from a few other women. Startled looks from most of the men, and then: "What in it makes you feel that way?"

Slowly, we began to unravel the text together. Images of flow and spontaneity: A cloud of goats scudding across Mount Gilead...the turtledove...dreams...the appearance/disappearance of the lovers...deep breaths of spice...

Over and over, a refrain, "Do not stir up love until it please."

Finally, from a man this time: "I think I see....It feels like a whole different form of spiritual life, a whole different way of being Jewish from the rest of the Bible, and the rabbis. They never say, 'Until it please.' They always know by the clock and the calendar exactly when to start and when to stop. What time of the day, what day of the month. Exactly. Let's reread what she has to say about the men in her life, her brothers and the rest."

One woman, smiling: "My brothers told me to guard the vineyard, but I didn't guard my vineyard."

Another, her amusement gathering: "My brothers told me that when I grow up, they will adorn me like a wall, like a door, with bronze and gold. But I told them that when I grow up my breasts will be my adornment. I don't need all their artificial ornaments."

Still another, laughing: "And as for Solomon, in the midst of this lovely springtime the poor man marches up to the city with a chariot of bronze and a retinue of sixty guards. Think of it: Guards to show his glory, when all around are smells and birds and flowers."

And finally, a man in a troubled voice: "And when she goes out at night to find her lover, the guardsmen beat her up."

A chorus: "Of course."

A pause. "Guarding. Guarded. Feeling guarded. The rabbis are always guarding. They want to feel anchored, especially anchored in time. The Talmud begins, 'From what time may one recite the evening Sh'ma?' The Song of Songs doesn't seem to worry about structure, about anchoring. Even about time..."

Several of us put it together: Shir HaShirim is a criticism, gentle but clear, of the whole "male" mode of guarding: The focus on calendars and clocks, on regularity and structure, that informs most of Jewish tradition. Do not stir up love until it please. We find ourselves using the words "floating," "flowing," again and again.

Another pause. Someone asks, "What are the traditional commentaries like?"

"They assert it's all a one-to-one allegory: The love of Israel for God. And they take it all so point-for-point—like, her two breasts are Moses and Aaron." (Laughter throughout the room.)

"In every other volume of classical Midrash that I've read, the rabbis open the text to spontaneity and freedom. In this one, they clamp down, as if this text already felt so open, they couldn't bear to open it up further and had to close it down instead."

"That allegory business feels wrong. Seems to me the Song is not just using one drama—the love story—to talk about another one, God and humanity. It's about three relationships all at once—a man and a woman, human beings and nature, God and human beings. You can't separate them, they flow into each other. At least when you relate this way, they do: Be free and flowing with the springtime, and you reach God; be free and flowing with each other, and you reach God."

"I'd go even further. There's no reaching God here. God is in the process. The book doesn't name God. The Song and Esther are the only parts of the whole Bible that never mention God. Seems to me that *Shir HaShirim* says if you're free and flowing with each other and the springtime, you are with God already. You don't have to wrestle God, to meet God face to face or all the rest. You're there!"

"Even the style of the book is about flow and spontaneity. You know, there's this old argument whether the whole thing is one connected story or simply a collection of different love poems. Feels to me it's partly both: The story is loose, not tightly plotted, pieces are left only lightly linked, sometimes just by an echo in the phrasing. But there are connections, it's not just an anthology. Is there a plot? Now you see it, now you don't. It's up to us to bring it all together. We have to finish making the story. Maybe we can make it different every time."

## THE FLOW OF SPIRIT

Another pause as people drink this in. Nods. Then: "Why are we supposed to read this on Passover anyway?"

"Well, presumably because of the Spring imagery and so on. But now I have a different sense of it. We read the Haggadah and tell the story of the redemption from Egypt to teach ourselves how to achieve the great redemption, how to bring Messiah. So maybe we have to read this too, because the Haggadah is not enough?

"The Haggadah is perhaps the best statement of the male mode of liberation. It's not just that Moses leads the Exodus while a woman leads the Song of Songs. It's deeper—the Haggadah keeps asking about what time of day, what day of the month, we should study the Exodus. The clock and calendar again. So maybe we can't bring Messiah unless we unify the male and female modes? Maybe we have to read *Shir HaShirim* and the Haggadah together in order to learn how to do it?"

"You must mean, to read it the way we've been reading it right now. Jews have read it for thousands of years, but not this way. Not women and men together as a statement about women and men and nature and God, together. It almost seems to me we couldn't have read it this way before the Holocaust, before the most terrible assault on Jewish bodies...That's when we rediscovered our bodies and re-covered the body of the land."

"So *now* we might learn how to bring Messiah?"

Silence again. There is a tradition that when ten are together, in deep community, the *Shekhinah*—God's Presence in the world, God's female aspect—enters the room. The silence deepens. We can feel the *Shekhinah* among us... *Sheh'hekhianu, vekimanu, vehigiyanu lazman hazeh*. Blessed be the One who has kept us alive, lifted us up, and brought us to this season.

# AWAKENING THE SONG

Afterwards I realized that, at least at the conscious level, it is mostly the women's movement that has helped us read *Shir HaShirim* in new ways—more than Jews' reconnection with the land or their bodily suffering in the Holocaust. And especially those parts of the women's movement that have taken a "wrestling" kind of posture, an androgynous kind of shape. For wrestling is androgyny-in-motion. Just as wrestling slips from fighting to making love and back again, so androgyny slips from duality to unity and back again.

What was "wrestling" about our encounter with *Shir HaShirim*? Our way of talking and the interpretation we developed neither treated women and men as identical, interchangeable units, nor separated them as utterly different. Instead, we moved back and forth from difference to interwovenness—just as, in the yin/yang symbol, there is a pulse of yang in the heart of yin and in the heart of yang a pulse of yin.

To say "women and men are both androgynous" is not to say "we are all simply human and there are no differences"—for the very word "androgynous" means "manly/womanly." It unifies opposites. It says there *are* differences between "manliness" and "womanliness," but also that all men are manly/womanly and all women are manly/womanly.

But there was a deeper sense in which the wrestling metaphor applied: Our spiritual experience of reading *Shir HaShirim* together was the fruit of a sometimes bitter social and political struggle, the feminist struggle. Wrestling with each other and wrestling God had fused into one process, as it had for Jacob.

To begin with, it was the energy level of women in motion that had opened the door to a new understanding of *Shir HaShirim*. The women had begun to wrestle with the text. In the very act of fighting against the ancient male interpretations of it, they had lovingly clasped it to themselves. In this Godwrestle they prevailed.

By accepting that "defeat," the men made reconciliation possible. The struggles of years had opened up the men, sometimes gently and sometimes forcibly. Their openness affirmed and enriched the new understanding.

Thus the men completed the androgynous process. They made what might have been only the alienated feelings of half a broken community into the understanding of a reunified whole.

The longer I reflected on our new approaches to the Song, the more I wondered what it really meant to say that the Haggadah or the Exodus is liberation in a male mode. "Male" overtones flash across my memory, but they feel like mere stereotypes of the way men actually live. Was I falling into the very stereotypes that Eden and *Shir HaShirim* teach us to discard?

For example, I remember one of the children at the Fabrangen Cheder, our co-op school where parents taught the children: Scared by hearing how Sinai quaked and smoked, thundered and flashed before the Ten Commandments, he blurted out: "It's like Daddy when he tells me something important. He yells and shakes me so I'll remember."

"Just Daddy? What about Mommy?"

"No, Mommy picks me up in her lap and tells me softly that it's really important. God was really a 'daddy' at Sinai."

So it is male to thunder and to shake? And because it is male, God is male? Or at least was male at Sinai? How do we discard this set of labels?

First, we could say that shaking is not essentially male. It is we who have made it male. It is certainly one aspect of human interchange, and indeed of the way the universe seems to act toward humans: Earthquakes, flood, drought, death. But what makes this aspect "male"? It is the attribute of unaccountable power; and males have taken power, without being held accountable, during most of history. So perhaps it was the reality of unaccountable male power on earth that shaped the image of God as an unaccountable male in Heaven. And once that male-God image had been fixed in human minds, it reinforced the assumption that men, not women, should hold power in society.

Now we may understand why we inherit certain "female" images of God—but only a certain few. For example, there is the story of manna, which God gave before the thundering at Sinai. The manna came in a double portion on Friday, and on Shabbat no manna fell. So God taught the people the rhythms of Shabbat for the first time not in thundering commands, but through quiet behavior modification. They learned not shaken in Nature's furious arms, but fed at Nature's breast. If God was "Daddy" at Sinai, God when giving manna was a "Mommy."

But for humans to be fed or left unfed at Nature's breast is still to be controlled. Still to be shaped by unaccountable power. The manna comes when it is sent; no human gets to decide. Mommy may be quieter than Daddy, but still she rules. The "father" and the "mother" roles have much in common.

Indeed, the image of God in Eden is precisely that of Parent: Birthing, feeding, commanding, rebuking the children-become-adolescents who are human. God as Parent/Mother/Father.

Not so in Song of Songs. The new Garden is one of male and female, yes; but there is no Parent and there are no children. No one gives orders; no one obeys them. Rather, there are grownups and lovers. God is gone: The Name is literally not mentioned. Even if we follow the rabbinic allegory that sees the lovers of the Song as God and Israel, then still the relationship is that of grownups, lovers, not of children facing Parent.

## EDEN ONCE AGAIN

The Song of Songs is Eden for adults. It is a profoundly "adult" story in which not only is sexuality clear and central, but human beings are not subject to unaccountable power. The Tree of Knowing Good and Evil is subsumed into the Tree of Life. The link that appears in Eden between the onset of sexuality and the emergence of human freedom is fulfilled in *Shir HaShirim.*

The Song is the prophecy of Eden fulfilled: A man shall leave his mother and his father and cleave to his woman, and they shall be one flesh.

When we can leave the Mother God and the Father God behind us, when we no longer need the unaccountably powerful Parent, we can reunite man and woman into one flesh.

When we can leave behind the Mother God and the Father God, we shall be able to know God as Lover.

But how do we transpose these thoughts and feelings into everyday practice?

One possibility is that we rework in practice, not only in thought, the relationship of the "sexual" with the "spiritual." The rabbis felt the spiritual charge in the Song of Songs, but could open themselves to it only by denying its sexuality. By saying that the whole Song is an allegory of love between God and Israel, they affirmed their own erotic relationship with Torah study, while turning away from more physical eros. When they voted to treat the Song as Holy Writ, part of the Bible, they simultaneously forbade it to be sung in taverns. Maybe they feared that it might easily degenerate into a bawdy "torch song," with no spiritual qualities. Today, can we affirm both aspects of the Song? Indeed, can we see them as one truth?

Thinking about this question, I recall one Friday evening at a farm in Pennsylvania in the summer of 1972. Some Fabrangeners and other Jewish-renewal seekers from around the country had gathered with the hope of creating a religiously rooted kibbutz. As we studied, farmed, and prayed together, we realized that in some ways our lives were like those of the small band of Kabbalists in the tiny town of Safed in northern Israel.

In the sixteenth century, they had created the ceremony of *Kabbalat Shabbat* to welcome the Shabbat Queen when she arrived each Friday night. The men immersed themselves in the ritual "ocean" of the mikveh. Then they changed into white robes to greet the Shabbat, and walked from the mikveh to the hilltops above the Sea of Galilee. As part of the service, they chanted the Song of Songs.

We decided to do as they had done. So we began the Shabbat service with a purifying mikveh. A dozen of us—men, women, children— joined hands in a circle in the creek, chanted the mikveh prayers, went deep beneath the water, let our bodies float to the surface, moving almost as fluid as the water. Rose to laugh, sing, pray, immerse again. Three times, as prescribed by tradition; and then another four, from ecstasy.

Seven immersions, the World in seven days. Almost a water-dance. The erotic energy was high and spiritually directed among us, as well as between us and the universe. Singing, we walked up the hill to greet the sundown and Shabbat from the highest point on the farm. We felt alive to the sexual energies within us, using them not for physical expression but toward more fully knowing God.

Singing six psalms and *L'kha Dodi*— "Come, my beloved, to greet the Shabbat Bride." Laughing as the children greeted butterflies. Coming back to the farmhouse for a Shabbat meal of cheese, nuts-and-raisins-in-cinnamon, wine. Staying sexually/spiritually alive through the evening service. Then, those among us who were coupled separating from the community, feeling the traditional *mitzvah* of making love on Friday night as a far more deeply holy act than ever before.

In the twenty years and more since then, I have not seen any of our communities attempt to carry out *Kabbalat Shabbat* this way. Perhaps we felt that without a kibbutz-like community where people know and profoundly trust each other, the risks would be too great. Perhaps it felt too hard to keep the energy focused on the path of making-love-to-all-the-Universe. Perhaps we lacked the courage to work out in careful practice how to shape that path. Surely we can all name the dangers that beset that path; yet once at least, we learned to walk the path and avert those dangers. To me it seems that we drew most authentically that evening on the highest, deepest meaning of the Song. So it is important that we learn how to transform that meaning into a practice that is healing and constructive.

Another effort: On a number of occasions, I have taken part in readings of the Song that try to go beyond an academic seminar or the speedy mumble often heard in a traditional synagogue on Friday night. Sometimes there are low lights, candles, incense, flowers, and fruits and nuts to share. Sometimes the community sits not locked in pews and rows where they cannot see each others' faces, but in an informal curve or circle.

Then a couple who have read the Song before may read it aloud in English dialogue. Often nowadays they will use Marcia Falk's translation with its division into the voices of a man, a woman, the chorus of the Daughters of Jerusalem. And with its richly sensual transmission of the sensual Hebrew imagery of taste and touch and smell. Often the reading is interspersed with songs in Hebrew and in English that have been written to the verses of the Song.

Sometimes my wife and I initiate the reading. We have encouraged others to pick up the dialogue: Two men, two women, a man and woman. The configuration rarely makes much difference to the atmosphere. Sometimes I have seen the reading done, verse by verse or poem by poem, by people going 'round the circle in the room. This is sometimes less powerful, but perhaps only because these readers are usually less intimate with *Shir HaShirim* than readers who have prepared ahead of time.

When the last verses are read, the last "*Dodi li*" sung or hummed, the community shares its thoughts and feelings as we did that Passover night in Fabrangen.

I have seen or heard about such readings of the Song in a community of elders in their 70s, in a group of adolescents, in a group of gay men, among lesbians, among the members of a conventional suburban family synagogue, among young single urban Jews. I have never seen this kind of reading fail to elicit a thoughtful, gentle, yet impassioned opening of the spirit among the people in the room.

Still another way of learning from the Song: How can we synthesize its sense of flowing time with the clockiness of Talmud?

Nothing could be more essentially a calendrical act than the traditional ceremony of Counting the Omer—literally and numerically, night by night simply counting off the forty-nine days from the second night of Passover to the eve of Shavuot, the festival of the Revelation on Mount Sinai. When Fabrangen prepared for Passover in 1974, we discussed how dry and rigid the Omer ceremony felt to us, especially as we remembered what *Shir HaShirim* had said to us the previous year. We recalled that in the days when the Temple stood, the Omer (originally a measure of grain) had been counted by waving sheaves of barley, celebrating the return from winter to spring as well as the ascent from Egypt to Sinai. We realized that because the Omer had been severed from the earthy symbols of new life, few of us had ever bothered to do the counting.

So we decided to revive the Omer by suffusing its calendric style with the teachings of *Shir HaShirim*. For the seven weeks of the Omer we chanted, in our homes and families, one chapter a week of *Shir HaShirim* (and the eighth on Shavuot itself). Each week, we looked at, smelled, and touched a new cluster of flowers. Each week, we met a new person, in flesh and blood or in a book. And thus, by reaching out to Torah, nature, and a human being, we reached out to God— spontaneously, flowingly, not against the calendar but with the calendar transmuted.

All three of these suggestions are ways to bring the Song or its unique atmosphere into prayer and ceremony. Can we also bring the Song into our ethics? In the years since that transformative Passover reading, I have wrestled more and more with the two issues that are central to *Shir HaShirim*, and I have watched the broader Jewish community wrestle with them more and more. These issues, which emerged from Eden, are now coming to an historic crisis: relations between "*adam*" and "*adamah*," the earth and its human earthlings; and the relations between men and women, both sexual and political.

## THE SONG AND ITS ETHIC

I deeply believe that the Song of Songs is Eden for a grown-up human race. And I believe the time for growing up is *now*.

Why? When the humans entered Eden, God said to them, "*Be fruitful and multiply, fill up the earth and subdue it.*" When the humans left Eden, these imperatives continued. They had to be addressed under conditions of strife and pain: Warfare between human beings and the earth, pain in birthing children, domination of men over women, sexual desire tainted with anxiety.

These commands were, in fact, the imperatives that have governed all human history. *But in our generation they have been carried out.*

The human race has not only been fruitful and multiplied but has indeed filled up the earth and subdued it to the point where we could destroy the fabric of life. We are already destroying more species than have died since long before we ourselves came into being — since the Great Meteor some sixty-five million years ago killed the dinosaurs and transformed the web of life.

The era that in our tradition began at Eden is over. Now what?

Now comes Eden for grownups: Now comes the Song of Songs.

Now comes a sexual ethic rooted not in fear, shame, dominance, and the need to multiply, but in a loving dance, as in the Song.

Now comes a way of relating to the earth rooted not in sweaty battling to make it barely feed us, but in a loving dance, as in the Song.

## ENTERING THE GARDEN

When the rabbis were arguing over what ought to be regarded as part of the Biblical canon, some felt *Shir HaShirim* should not. It was too sexy, too earthy, and it did not even mention God. But Rabbi Akiba said, "All the Writings are holy, but the Song of Songs is the Holy of Holies."

Akiba may have felt the same auras that we at Fabrangen felt from *Shir HaShirim*. He said that the day on which the Song was created was equally sacred with the day on which all else had its creation. He taught that the Song was the love story of God and the People of Israel, and he may have felt that to know God as lover was to live in Eden as a grownup. To these records of his teachings, let me add a fantasy—a midrash—about Akiba:

There is a story that Akiba and three other great rabbis had a powerful mystical experience of "going into Pardes"—the garden, the orchard, Paradise. We do not know what they saw there. But one went mad, one died, and one plucked up the Root of Being and denied there was a Judge or Justice in the world. Only Akiba, says the Talmud, came forth unharmed.

What was this Pardes? In my fantasy, they walked into the garden of *Shir HaShirim*. There they found goats and flowers, sexuality and love. They did not see the God of Sinai or of Eden; they did not hear the Name of God at all. They knew this was the ultimate experience.

One decided there was nothing that life or death could offer better than this Garden, and died in joyful bliss.

One went mad because this moment seemed utterly contradictory to Torah, and yet he knew for certain both were true.

One gave up God and Torah because this seemed more real.

Only Akiba knew that this *was* Torah: Highest Torah, Torah fulfilled, Torah for adults.

*Only* Akiba, and he came out unharmed. Scorched just enough to say the Song was holiest of all, like the Dark Beauty who says at the beginning of the Song that the sun has scorched her with its gazing.

Akiba—scorched enough to be the only one of the rabbis to proclaim the coming of Messiah. For once you have visited the Garden of the Song, how can you not believe Messiah has come?

CHAPTER 7

# MOTHERS OF MESSIAH

The Garden of Eden and the garden of the Song of Songs represent the beginning and the goal of human history: The given paradise of childhood and the worked-for paradise of full adulthood. Eve in her Garden and the woman of the Song are free, confident, and assertive. Should we read about these free women as simply fantasies who stand outside of history? Or should we see their stories as critiques of the "normal" human history that began after Eden—the history in which women are not free? Do their stories call us to transform this "normal" history?

The Bible speaks of free women who live not beyond normal time, but in the give-and-take of history. Indeed, there is one family lineage in the Bible whose story seems to have been deliberately shaped to celebrate several extraordinary and unconventional women.

This cluster of women is brought together by the Book of Ruth. Traditionally, the marriage of Ruth and Boaz is regarded as the key linkage that leads toward the birth of David—shepherd, guerrilla, lover, king, and poet—and therefore to his descendant, Messiah who is yet to come.

Ruth, a foreign woman and the childless widow of an Israelite, chooses to become an Israelite out of love for her mother-in-law Naomi. She arrives in Bethlehem with no land and therefore no livelihood. She gleans the forgotten grain in the barley fields of her distant kinsman Boaz, visits and attracts him one night on the threshing floor, where she wins his body, his heart, and his hand in a version of the "redeemer" marriage. (The brother of a man who died childless, and by extension his more distant relative if there was no brother, was obligated as a "redeemer" to raise offspring in the dead man's name by marrying his widow.) Thus from a landless, penniless, husbandless, childless immigrant Ruth remakes herself into a prosperous woman, the great-grandmother of the glorious King David.

Ruth herself is remarkable: A free woman who takes the shaping of her life into her own hands. But it is even more remarkable to realize that in the past of her own family and in the family of Boaz stood women who had been caught in situations analogous to Ruth's and who had acted with similar daring and independence to fulfill their visions of themselves.

The Book of Ruth ends with a triumphant genealogy of Boaz, as if to say, "Now that you know the story of Ruth and Boaz, guess who they really are!" The genealogy is most unusual in that it not only looks forward, where the climax is David, but also looks backward, to someone named Peretz. Who is this Peretz? He is born out of a strange tale in Genesis: The remarkable story of Tamar and Judah, which the Bible inserts in the midst of the Joseph saga.

Judah, one of Joseph's brothers, leaves the family and marries a Canaanite who bears him three sons. The oldest son marries a Canaanite woman, Tamar; but that son dies before they have a child. In accord with the rules of "redeemer" marriage, Tamar is married to Judah's second son. But this son also dies. Judah, frightened that some kind of doom is emanating from Tamar, refuses to marry his third son to her.

So Tamar dresses up as a whore, entices Judah himself to sleep with her, and becomes pregnant by him. When he realizes what she has done and why, he exclaims, "She is more righteous than I!" Tamar gives birth to twins, one of whom is Peretz. According to the Book of Ruth, Peretz becomes the great-great-great-great-grandfather of Boaz.

And in Ruth's own family there is a similar story of a strange liaison. Ruth is a Moabite—a descendant of Moab. And who is Moab? The son of Lot by one of Lot's own daughters. The Torah tells how Lot and his daughters flee the destruction of Sodom and Gomorra. Frightened and exhausted, they come to a cave in the mountains and live there. The daughters believe that the whole world has been destroyed, and with it all the men whom they might marry. Left childless widows, they are entitled to a levirate marriage. But with whom? With, they think, the only man alive—their father Lot.

So they get Lot drunk, sleep with him, and one of them gives birth to Moab, Ruth's ancestor.

The author of the Book of Ruth knitted these two tales together by intertwining the lives of Ruth and Boaz. So this tale becomes a third in the series of stories of assertive women who seek through unconventional means to accomplish the levirate marriage that is their due. How unconventional is Ruth? During the night she sleeps at Boaz' feet on the threshing floor to assert her claim or her desire, she "uncovers his feet," a phrase the Bible hints is a euphemism for initiating sex. And Boaz responds. We can almost hear the old family story of Lot and his daughter glimmering in Ruth's head—and the old family story of Judah and his daughter-in-law Tamar glimmering in Boaz's.

Why should David of all people, harbinger of the Messiah who will redeem all history, be the fruit of such a family tree? He is the offspring of three women who are not Israelites and who, in seeking the "redeemer" of levirate marriage, themselves become redeemers. These women redeem into righteousness what would otherwise have been the starkest violations of the legal code; they act with utter vigor and determination to decide their own futures and their family's destiny.

It is as if the Bible is suggesting that the authentic line of descent from the free primordial woman of the Garden to the free transformative woman of the Song must run through these three ancestresses of David. If Messiah is to redeem the whole world, then Jews and non-Jews must contribute to Messiah's inheritance. If (as our reading of the Eden story says) Messiah is to end the subjugation of women, then women who are free and self-determining must contribute to Messiah's inheritance. If Messiah is to make evil work for good, then the experience of such a redemption must enter Messiah's inheritance.

For Messiah to be made possible, what is most frightening to the tradition must be lifted into consciousness, confronted—and redeemed. And the redemptive process cannot wait until the end of days: It must start happening along the way. The worst nightmares of the Jewish men who rule and write the tradition seem to be assertive womanhood, idolatry, and unbridled sexuality. But even these nightmares must be faced—and so the story of Ruth performs a kind of collective psychotherapy.

Not that idolatry or incest or whoredom should be celebrated to make Messiah come; nor should they be celebrated afterward. What at first glance seem shatterings of Torah are redeemed in these stories, transformed into something else. So it is not the Ruth who is a Moabite idolator but the Ruth who says "Your God will be my God" who becomes the great-grandmother of David. So it is not prostitution that gives birth to Peretz, but what might have looked like prostitution until the claim of levirate marriage is asserted. When Judah says that Tamar "is more righteous than I," he becomes a redeemer not only in the legal sense of the levirate but also in the ethical-mystical sense, the Messianic sense: Judah has redeemed Tamar's action for the good.

But this is no one-way street. She has also redeemed his action for the good. She has made Judah become righteous through the very agency of his unrighteousness. Indeed, Tamar's redeeming act provides the opportunity, the impulse, and the need for Judah to become a redeemer.

So, too, with Song of Songs: It redeems, and it stirs us to redeem. Some modern scholars have said that *Shir HaShirim* is similar to Canaanite fertility songs; yet it breathes of holiness. What might have been seen as the Godless carnal poems of a fertility rite, or as idolatry and sexuality joined in the unholiest of unions, Akiba hears instead as the holy songs of a loving God. The Song that in our own days might have been seen as a throwback to ancient paganism is heard instead as a hymn to flow, to the noblest fusion of the spirit in the flesh.

But the very fact that we and Akiba can hear it this way is stirred up in us only by the holiness and wholeness of the Song. The Song redeems the unbound sexuality and the deafness to God's name that are within us. It turns these seeds of horror to good growth. And this then stirs us to redeem the Song.

A fantasy: I think of Ruth. A Moabite. A woman. I imagine Ruth bringing *Shir HaShirim* from the hills of Moab. I imagine her singing that song to Boaz that night on the threshing floor. I imagine that song becoming the dowry she brought to the Jewish people, the dowry we needed to make Messiah possible, brought by the *woman* we needed to make Messiah possible. And I imagine this dowry being handed down the generations to David's son Solomon: *"Shir HaShirim asher li-Shlomo,"* "The Song of Songs which is *for* Solomon."

A teaching, a reminder, to Solomon—Shlomo, the *"Shalom-*one." the first heir of the House of David. Maybe he might have been Messiah and brought *Shalom* to the world? Maybe he failed to hear the Song, and instead became entranced with chariots and palanquins and men of war? Maybe when Solomon failed to hear the Song, its teaching was handed still further down the generations, to the seed of Shlomo in us all?

How do we receive this message? What does it mean to us to hear from such extraordinary women as Ruth, Tamar, and Lot's nameless daughter, these "mothers" of Messiah? What does it mean for their assertiveness and vigor to have been channeled into motherhood? If the tradition seems to focus all their hopes and dreams not on what they themselves can do, but on their children and their children's children, how does this feel to us? If their way of overcoming passivity and subjugation is to become mothers, how does that feel to us? By emphasizing motherhood so strongly, does it pose the danger of narrowing the rich possibilities of a woman's life into that one role?

## MOTHERS AND MATRIARCHS

The Bible does not define motherhood as the be-all and end-all of a woman's life. Miriam and Deborah, for example, have no children. Even for those women whose motherhood is central to identity, the Bible hints that motherhood is sacred only when it becomes the arena of struggle and transcendence of roles. Let us look especially at motherhood among the Matriarchs, the four women who are considered the mothers of the Jewish people. For all of them, motherhood is presented not as the easy, "natural" event that a simple-minded sexism would have it be, but as an arena for struggle.

Each Matriarch has trouble giving birth. Sarah is barren. Rebekah first is barren and then goes through agonies in pregnancy. Leah and Rachel fight a tense and jealous battle over giving birth. Though Leah births seven children, she never feels a sense of ease about it. And for the barren Rachel, it becomes *naphtulai Elohim*, "Godstrugglings," to try to have children.

Indeed, the main difference between the four Matriarchs and the three handmaidens who became the Patriarchs' wives (Hagar, Bilhah, and Zilpah) is that the handmaidens become wives to ease the begetting of heirs, and do indeed find the process much easier. It is as if the defining characteristic of the Matriarchs is that they have trouble bearing children.

The result is that the Mothers of the tradition also struggle with nature and with history, although most do so in a sphere different from the one assigned to men. (Not so Rebekah; we will return to her.) It is not possible to birth the Jewish people without agony and struggle, without reaching to God. Perhaps the Torah is rejecting the fertility myths of Mother Goddesses and fecund women, the myth that motherhood is simple, earthy, and unencumbered with the difficult problems of society.

To get a sense of how important this outlook is, imagine the picture of women and men that we would have if in our great stories men alone wrestled with nature and history, work and celebration, while women in a simple, cowlike, painless way gave birth to children.

Even the separate spheres of Patriarchs and Matriarchs are not kept quite distinct. Abraham puts much of his energy—his doubts, his fears, his Godwrestlings—into begetting children, just as the Matriarchs put their energy into birthing children. So parenthood, the Torah makes clear, is not for women only.

And Rebekah shows that women can take part in the spheres that might be thought reserved for men—talking with God, coping with other peoples about conflicting rights to wells and flocks, managing inheritance and blessing. In these arenas, Rebekah firmly asserts her will. It is she who decides to leave her home to marry Isaac; it is she, not Isaac, who hears God's word about her children; it is she who plots and plans to secure the first-born's blessing for Jacob. The contrast with the quiet, meditative Isaac could not be greater. She comes far closer in her generation to the boldness of Abraham.

## MOTHERING MOSES

Turning and turning over in my head the tales of these struggling mothers, I remember one of the strangest motherhood stories in the Bible: The tale of Zipporah, Moses' wife and the mother of his sons, on the road from Midian to Egypt.

God has just commanded Moses to return and liberate the Israelites from Egypt. God's final words order Moses to tell Pharaoh that the people of Israel are God's first-born and that God has demanded, "Let My son go, that he may serve Me. But you have refused to let him go. Here, I will kill your son, your first-born."

With hardly a transition, the story says that on the road at the lodging place, "YHWH sought to kill him." Who is this "him"? Moses? The Moses who only a sentence before has been sent to Egypt as the liberator? Or perhaps, in a strange carryover from God's threat to Pharaoh, as if the one sentence, "I will kill your son, your first-born," belongs in both stories, God threatens to kill Moses' first-born?

Zipporah responds by taking a flint to circumcise her son and throws his foreskin at "his foot." Whose foot? The foot of…Moses? Of God? Of her son? The pronouns are unclear.

"For a bridegroom of blood are you to me," she says; and God let be whoever had been about to die. Then she repeats, "A bridegroom of blood for the circumcision."

The midrashic tradition assumes that God is threatening to kill Moses for having failed to circumcise his son; that Zipporah does it for him; and that Moses is the "bridegroom of blood." Maybe. Or maybe God is demanding that the boy be killed as a sacrifice, as God once demanded that Isaac be sacrificed. Maybe Zipporah uses the foreskin as Abraham used the ram, as a ransom and a substitute for his son's life. Or maybe Moses is threatened with death because *he* is uncircumcised, and when the text says Zipporah circumcised "her son" it means she made Moses "her son" by saving his life, giving him life—and then greets him, standing bloody before her, as her "bridegroom of blood."

Or maybe the story is deliberately leaving the pronouns unclear and the story uncertain?

In any case, the issues remain: Why this sudden attack on Moses' just-created mission? Why is it Zipporah who acts, not Moses? Why is it the mother who carries out this circumcision that all tradition says is a father's obligation? Notice that the Torah says "her son"—at this moment *hers*, for at this moment Moses is not acting like a father. Even if it is Moses who lacks the circumcision, we remember that when Abraham was in that same situation, he performed the circumcision on himself. Is that what makes him archetypally our father—*Avraham Avinu*—while Moses is only our teacher—*Moshe Rabbenu*?

One possible interpretation of the story arises for me from the experiences of Fabrangen and other *havurot* in making fresh the old meanings of Judaism. Some Jews accuse the movement toward Jewish renewal of shattering tradition even while pretending to renew it. They accuse us of forging an entirely new religion. Sometimes we ourselves are not sure what the boundary is. In fact, it is easy to imagine Moses walking on the edges: Where is the boundary?

So from this life-experience of ours I can imagine Zipporah, speaking to Moses after he returns from the Burning Bush, ready to set out for Egypt: "We are returning to your people? Then we should circumcise Gershom, don't you think? They won't be happy if we show up without..."

Moses, the Bush still burning in his eyes, is a little grandiloquent: "You don't understand. That's the old covenant, the one with Abraham. I was told God's Name anew. It all starts over now. We will have the Pesach lamb to sacrifice instead; our first-born are redeemed from circumcision just as they are from sacrificial death."

Zipporah: Troubled, frowning, silent...until the explosive God-fury suddenly threatens her son. Then she explodes into action, slashes with the flint she takes to Gershom, and turns to Moses, shaking in the aftermath of fear and fury: "Don't you see? You said the Covenant of Abraham was over...so God started back at the beginning. He wanted your son for an offering. But this time I was ready...You would have been my bridegroom steeped in blood!"

Then she turns back to God, exhausted, emptied out, calling Him as well a "bloody Bridegroom."

Such a scenario stirs in me ideas about old and new in religious growth, about the differences between restoring a tradition and renewing it, between renewing it and inventing something wholly new. But it also stirs deeper feelings about fatherhood and motherhood.

The social psychologist David Bakan, applying Freudian method to the Bible, has pointed to the inverse of Freud's Oedipus complex, in which the son wishes to kill the father. Bakan suggests that both circumcision and the Passover lamb (and also the one-time ram that

Abraham found on Mount Moriah) are ransoms against the father's ancient tendency to kill his offspring. Especially a son, who seems most like him; especially the first-born, who shocks and tests his previously worked-out equilibrium.

These rituals, Bakan says, are part of the Torah's overall effort to "motherize" men—to induce among men a sense of communion strong enough to prevent murder.

Certainly I have felt that tide of fury in myself. The more my children grew into new people—were not just an extension of my self—the more I have felt the tug of fatherhood fulfilled against fatherhood frustrated. On the one hand, I have felt joy at truly fathering—that is, at creating new and independent life. On the other hand, I have felt pride that what I have fathered is growing in the directions I desired.

Indeed, the tug-of-war inside me is even more complicated than that. The less like me my children are, the less they feel like "mine." The more like me they are, the less it feels as if I have created someone new. So the two feelings work with and against each other. When they are most at odds, I feel most fury.

Jewish tradition says that all children have three parents: Father, mother, and God. That is a way to celebrate the newness, the unpredictability of every child. In each child, there is something that did not come from either parent but from the world's inexhaustible storehouse of freedom: That is, from God. But there is also what both parents give.

If Bakan is right, circumcision and the Passover lamb are both efforts to say, "It's all right. Despite the tension of these tugs inside me, I will *not* kill you!" They are also efforts to say that the reason for such gentleness is God. It is God Who sternly commands not to murder; it is God who sweetly gives newness and freedom.

That is what Zipporah understood. That is what the mothers had to teach. That is what even Moshe Rabbenu, Moses our Teacher, had to learn.

So what Zipporah taught was not to cast aside the old *bris* of circumcision for the new covenant of Passing-over the Israelite first-born. It would not be enough to ransom first-borns with a lamb each year; it would also have to be done when a boy was born. The cycle of the seasons and the cycle of the generations must be connected.

She taught Moses: The old ritual, from Abraham our Father, must join with the new. You cannot be a good teacher, *Rabbenu*, of anything new, unless you have remembered what it means to be a good father, *Avinu*, who bears something old.

The Torah insists with utter vigor that every man who brings a lamb for the Passover sacrifice be circumcised. It does not think to specify this for Shabbat or the other holy days, nor even for the priestly celebrants of Temple sacrifice. It is as if Passover, with its echoes of the first-born of Egypt dead, the first-born of Israel redeemed, the lamb sacrificed as a ransom, is the one moment when people might think circumcision is irrelevant. God's warning is like Zipporah's action.

So my thoughts on fatherhood come back to motherhood, to Zipporah teaching me. This was as far as the story took me until one Shavuot (the festival of the Giving of the Torah) when Fabrangen decided to wrestle with the issue of women's consciousness in prayer and whether it was different from a man's. I found an experimental prayerbook done by women at Brown University, which began with a blessing on the occasion of menstruation. It celebrated menstruation as an offering of blood to God, a substitute for the blood offerings at the Temple, a substitute so powerful that when Messiah comes we will not need to renew the Temple sacrifices because through the temple of our bodies we already send our blood to God.

Most of the women of Fabrangen felt this view of menstruation was unduly romantic. To them, their monthly blood felt more painful, more cramping than a joyful offering to God. But it occurred to me to turn the blessing around: If menstruation can be seen as a substitute for the sacrifices, then the sacrifices might have been a substitute for menstruation.

Imagine: The men of ancient Israel, conscious that between the women and the universe there was a holy bond of blood. And not only blood, but pain. Somehow by giving up their blood and pain in the rhythmic round of the months, women could touch the rhythms of the world. But men could not. What could men do?

Men then should offer their own blood and pain...and do it with their fatherhood as women did it with their motherhood. And thus: The covenant of circumcision! Once in his lifetime, a man could give his pain and blood to God, touch the Life-giving One to his own organ of giving life. But once a life could hardly make a rhythm. So the rhythm of the sacrifices, in which surrogate pain and surrogate blood are offered to God, becomes the entryway for men to the rhythm of the world.

Of course there are differences between menstruation and circumcision. One is that circumcision must be done deliberately, while the menstrual flow comes from the body's unconscious calendar. If men deliberately chose to imitate menstruation, they were trying, in a sense, to unite the God of history with the God of nature. They were asserting that the decisions of human beings as part of society carry out the same will of the same God that women's bodies carry out by the rhythm of nature. But if men were trying to see God in history, maybe they risked seeing God only in history, ignoring the rhythm of nature.

Maybe this enriches our understanding of why Zipporah knew what needed to be done on the road from Midian to Egypt. Maybe Moses—exalted and still dazed by the light of the Bush that told him God was about to enter history in a new way—maybe Moses was ready to forget the God of nature. And maybe Zipporah, daughter of Jethro the priest, knew from her own experience that offering blood to God was necessary. Maybe she knew that even animal sacrifice could not wholly replace the need to offer blood from one's own body. Maybe while Moses was still dazzled, she was more conscious of her body and the body of her son. So conscious of her body that she could say to Moses, "Every bride comes to her husband a bride of blood; and we must make certain that every bridegroom comes to his wife a bridegroom of blood. My body remembers to menstruate; yours must not forget to do the *bris.*"

Does this mean that men are bound to the God of history, the God of conscious time, the God of the calendar and clock, while women are outside the calendar and clock, rooted in nature?

No. This story says precisely that both women and men must act in history, and both must live in biology. For me, its fullest meaning comes from what began as a puzzle, the strange line, "I will kill your first-born." This line is written once when it should be written twice. It seems to belong in two different stories. It signals the link between two stories and a linkage between men and women.

In the first story, "I will kill your first-born" refers to history, to Pharaoh's unwillingness to recognize Israel as God's first-born. In the second story, it is about biology, about circumcision and the blood of birthing. By giving us a single line that belongs in both these stories, the Torah teaches that these stories are inextricably intertwined. One of the stories begins with a man, Moses at the Bush; the other with a woman, Zipporah at the lodging place. By this one verse they are intertwined into one story: An androgynous story that both men and women must learn, an androgynous story of history and biology intertwined, of women and men intertwined.

Realizing this, I feel with a rush of excitement that this strange "Siamese twin" of a story, two stories united by a single vital organ, appears at the crucial hinge of the Exodus story to underline a truth for us: The Exodus itself is a story in which two worlds are intertwined—the worlds of history and biology. Two stories are intertwined: The story of spring and rebirth, and the story of freedom and history. They become one story: The story of God's first-born, Israel transformed.

This way of understanding the Exodus is newborn in our generation. We will examine it more closely in a chapter of its own. But before we do that, we need to acknowledge that Zipporah's daring on the road to Egypt stands with the daring of the mothers of Messiah—Ruth and Tamar and Lot's daughter. Indeed, by reminding Moses of biology, she made herself a mother of Messiah in a non-biological sense, an historical sense. For if she had not acted, Moses' mission to free the people and the people's mission to be freed would have been aborted.

By saving Moses' life, Zipporah became the mother of the covenant. She midwifed Sinai, which is the most nearly Messianic moment we have yet been able to achieve.

CHAPTER 8

# GIVING BIRTH TO FREEDOM

Seven years or so into my communal wrestling with God and Torah, I found myself in an utterly different atmosphere. A long long table in a New York conference room. Formal chairs. Neatly arranged passages of Torah. Twelve men and one woman: No casual gathering of Shabbat davveners, but a carefully chosen band of midrash-makers from several different fellowships around the country.

Someone had actually gotten a grant and chosen the people, to test out an idea full of holy chutzpah: Could we, in our own generation, create a commentary to the Torah that could stand alongside the great collections of midrash from the past?

Until then, most of us had felt that we were walking this journey simply because we ourselves needed this kind of community, we ourselves enjoyed this kind of thought. Few of us had ever asked whether we could transmit this path to future generations as Hillel and Rashi and Rambam had given their paths to their future—to us.

As I looked around the table, I wondered: What did it mean for us to have been so carefully selected? In several early *havurot*, this was no big deal: They had formal memberships, applications, even blackballs. But for me it was new. In my own Fabrangen, the doors were open. Anyone could walk in, pick up a copy of the Torah text, and join our wrestle.

After all, that was exactly what I had done: Walked into the Jewish people, picked up a copy of the Passover Haggadah, added a few sentences here and there and crossed out some others, and joined the wrestle that I did not even know was called a wrestle. Inside Fabrangen, that felt fine. But here? Maybe it needed to be this way for our specific purpose; but it still felt weird.

And why was there just one woman present? That too felt weird. This too, I realized, stemmed from running a gauntlet of credibility

111

and credentials. At that point in history, how many women could pass the tests of official Full-of-Knowledge Jew?

## WALKING VERSE BY VERSE

The one woman present was Lynn Gottlieb. She had wanted to enter the Conservative rabbinical seminary, but it had refused to admit women. She had kept on studying, and was prepared—if they kept refusing—not to wait forever but to seek ordination by an independent committee of rabbis. (That, in fact, is ultimately what happened.)

As we settled into place, casting uneasy glances at each other, our chairman proposed that we test ourselves in the classic way: We would pick a passage of Torah, go through it verse by verse, and say our say upon each verse. We had two days. Then we could decide whether the results were rich enough for us to do a new "Rashi," the twelfth-century rabbi who was the most respected commentator/collector of verse-by-verse midrash.

The passage we chose was the first portion of Exodus, which tells how the tiny Israelite community that entered Egypt had flourished and multiplied; how a new Pharaoh had reduced them to forced labor; how they had kept multiplying anyway until a newer, yet more frightened Pharaoh had decided to wipe them out as a people.

To do this, the Pharaoh had ordered midwives to kill all Israelite males as they were born. But the midwives, "fearing God," let the children live. When Pharaoh realized that male babies were still thriving, he called the midwives before him to explain. They answered that the Israelite women were so "life-animated" that "like animals" they gave birth quickly, before the midwives could arrive. (A Hebrew version of the "animal-animated" pun is an important item in the Torah text.)

We began moving one verse at a time around the table, the excitement building as we played with the richness of the Torah. Each phrase, each word, was lovingly caressed. Lynn, I noticed, was silent; the men fell easily into filling all the space. An hour, two hours, went by; we had just barely reached verse 10.

Suddenly Lynn said, "Look! I've just noticed, down below, about the midwives..." The chairman quirked an eyebrow at her: "Sure, Lynn, we'll get there. Let's keep going as we agreed, in order." The conversation resumed, got even more excited, the wind of words hovered even longer on each phrase of text. Half an hour later, Lynn broke in again: "Yes, look, see what the story says about the midwives..."

Again the chairman, slightly exasperated this time: "Lynn, look, we'll be there soon."

Suddenly Lynn grinned, shook her long hair, and said, "The Hebrew women are so animated, full of life, they give birth *quickly*, before the midwife comes to them."

The rest of us laughed. We kept on with the text. But for me, Torah had just happened—Torah straight from God, Torah *mamash*, for real. The medium and the message, the form and the content, had just merged. The newborn fact of women learning, teaching, Torah had just found its voice.

And the voice—unbelievable!—was an ancient voice, a Voice straight from the Torah text. The Voice was brash, persistent, disobedient, jokey—just as the midwives had been. They had made a pun, a wordplay, to ensnare the king and free the people. Lynn had made a play upon the ancient words, quoting them as a comment on our most immediate present: A kind of pun on the ironies of life. Gently, gently, she had raised the question: Who is Pharaoh? And who seeks to give new birth?

## THE NARROW BIRTH CANAL

When at last we reached the midwife passage, Lynn pointed precisely to the theme of birth. Here, she said, is where the liberation started. Before Moses, before Miriam, here—these two women, maybe Israelites and maybe not, had asserted freedom by defending newborns. And later God says all Israel is God's first-born. Somewhere here, she said, is a new way of looking at the story: A story of the birthing of a people.

From this spark has grown a glowing metaphor, a midrash that now seems obvious and utterly apparent from the Torah text, but once was utterly unheard of. Listen to the text with "birthing" on your mind, and suddenly the pieces of the story come together in a new configuration. Many ears have joined to hear it, many voices have joined to speak it: A piece of insight here, a new connection there.

We can begin even with the words for Exodus. *Yetziat Mitzraiim*, says the Hebrew: Going forth from Egypt. What is "*Mitzraiim*"? It comes from the Hebrew root for "narrow place," and it bears the Hebrew ending for a duality: Two ears, *oznaiim*; two eyes, *eynaiim*; two feet, *raglaiim*. The Narrows: Caught between the devil and the deep blue sea, between Scylla and Charybdis, between a rock and a hard place. Probably at first this was the word for Egypt because it is a long thin country, really just a narrow strip of people on each side of the River Nile. And then a narrow-minded place in Israelite experience.

But now think "birth," and of Israel as God's first-born, and *Mitzraiim* becomes also the narrow birth canal. The splitting of the Red Sea becomes the breaking of the uterine waters. And the story takes on a whole new shape. It does not lose the old shape, the shape of political freedom, of rising up against tyranny, of the triumph of the God Who sides with the despised against a resplendent emperor who claims to be a god. The new shape, the new metaphor, enriches the old one. And in my experience—we will come to that in a moment—this metaphor also enriches and expands and transforms the community for which Torah is a collective family story.

Once you think "birth" and "newborn," moment after moment of the story takes on new meaning. Begin at the beginning. What enters Egypt at the beginning of the Book of Exodus is a tiny band of households, a nucleus, a cluster of cells. They sojourn in a broad and open space, a womb that is nourishing and spacious.

And then these nuclei grow with astonishing speed, like any fetus: They were fruitful, they swarmed, they multiplied, they grew strong beyond and beyond, the land was filled with them. This string of verbs echoes precisely the Torah's language of Creation: As the world itself was conceived with these verbs of overflowing growth, so was the people Israel. They grow not only in numbers but in self-awareness. They grow enough that they feel the nurturing space around them beginning to close in. They feel their lives, pregnant with possibility, begin to point toward a destination.

But there arose a new Pharaoh, who unlike the old one did not have an intimate and loving relationship ("*lo yada,*" the verb that means both "know" and "make love" in ancient Hebrew) with the Joseph whom an earlier Pharaoh had embraced. The loving relationship that had led to this conception is broken. From now on, the pregnancy is in trouble.

How does the story signal this trouble? Precisely by pointing to the birthing at a level that is both biological and political. Pharaoh orders the midwives Shifra and Puah to murder the Israelites' newborn baby boys. In history's first recorded act of nonviolent civil disobedience, they let the babies live. The text is ambiguous about whether these midwives are "the Hebrew midwives" or "the midwives *of* the Hebrews," one or both of whom may be Egyptian. For millennia, Torah commentators have argued over their national origin. (If they were Israelites, how could Pharaoh have possibly expected them to join in national suicide? If they were Egyptian, why did they refuse?)

The real point is that the text is deliberately ambiguous, deliberately invites millennia of debate, deliberately laughs at the terms of the debate."Why are you arguing?" says Torah. "It doesn't matter what their nation was. What matters is that they were women, and they revered God. What matters is that they were more than mothers, for they mothered hundreds of children into life. What matters is that they mothered a people, and mothered freedom into the world."

Perhaps they made up an "international feminist conspiracy." In any case, as we are soon to see, Miriam and Pharaoh's daughter do make themselves an international conspiracy of women to save the babies that Pharaoh wants to kill.

The Torah does not tell us that God appeared to Shifra and Puah in any transcendent or explosive way, as did the Burning Bush that Moses saw. How then did the women come to "revere God"? I think they saw God's Face in every mother's eyes, they felt God's Breath in every mother's panting, they heard God's Voice in every baby's outcry.

The midwives' tale ends by saying that since the midwives revered God, God made them "households." The rabbis have long debated what this means: Did the midwives became prosperous? But when the text says elsewhere in the Torah that God made *men* households, the rabbis understood this to mean that they were given wives. In this one case, they avoid that interpretation. But suppose Shifra and Puah were lesbians, and God gave them spouses—women—as their partners? Suppose Pharaoh knew they were lesbians, and—utterly misunderstanding what that meant—thought they would be willing to kill male babies, but not females?

The theme of birth continues. Moses is born not once but twice, for his sister and the Pharaoh's daughter give him a second birth from the waters of the Nile. After Moses withdraws from Egypt to learn what it means to hear the silence of the wilderness and to shepherd a wandering flock, he begets a child. Only then can he see the fire of the Burning Bush. This birth is echoed on Moses' journey back to Egypt, in the eerie story of his son's circumcision. As we have seen, at this very moment God proclaims the People Israel to be God's first-born.

## BIRTHING A PEOPLE

From then on, the theme of birth shifts from individuals to the people as a whole. For the sake of this "first-born" people, God is ready to kill every Egyptian first-born. To protect the first-born of this "first-born" people, God imitates the skipping, stumbling *"pesach"* dance of a newborn lamb by skipping over, "passing-over" the Israelite houses.

Indeed, so strong is this message about the newly "first-born" people that in the midst of the passage about the Exodus and the ch celebration that will recall it, the Torah twice interrupts itself (Exodus 13:1–2 and 13:11–13) to command that the people make holy and redeem their own first-born throughout all generations. Just as the circumcision of all sons is meant to recall the covenant of fruitfulness with Abraham, Sarah, and Hagar, so the redemption of all first-borns is meant to recall the covenant of freedom.

But this people is not, in the normal course of history, a "firstborn." It is far younger than Egypt and Babylon, far weaker, far poorer in money and cultural sophistication. Just as individuals—Isaac, Jacob, Joseph—have been turned into first-borns by the will of God, just as the powerless have moved to the center of the story, so now this is to happen at the level of an entire community and a public history. God turns normal history around.

In the case of Isaac, Ishmael stepped back to allow the transformation. In the case of Jacob, Esau at last stepped back. In the case of Joseph, the older brothers ultimately stepped back. But Pharaoh did not step back to honor God's desire for transformation. So what might have been the birth-pangs of a difficult but bearable labor became destructive plagues.

Finally the waters break, the People Israel crosses over, and with songs and dances led by Miriam and Moses, the biology of birth is confirmed and enriched in the politics of freedom.

For each birth brings into the world a being who is new and unpredictable, compounded partly of unavoidable heredity and partly of unprecedented possibility. Each birth is an act of freedom. And the birth of a whole people—especially a people made up of the despised and the enslaved who come forward to change history—makes for the birth of a new approach to life.

Indeed, the Torah teaches that what went forth from the narrow birth canal to freedom was not a "pure" ethnic stock of Abraham's descendants, but a "mixed multitude," an *erev rav*, what ethnic purists might call a "riffraff." The tradition adds that Pharaoh's daughter was among them, she who was named only *Bat-Pharaoh* when she "rebirthed" Moses from the river. When she reaches Sinai, she is herself reborn and takes on the name *Bat-yah*: The daughter of God, Daughter of the Breath of Life. Thus not only a new people, but a new kind of people has just been born.

When does this birthing happen? In the springtime, when lambs are being born and barley is sprouting. When the earth itself is giving birth, human history joins in.

Indeed, when the rabbis later wrestled with the shape of the Jewish calendar, they made one crucial decision because of the timing of the Exodus. In some ways, the Jewish calendar is rooted in the

* women reading Torah = different interpretations especially sections dealing w/women *

"moonths" of lunar time. Twelve moonths do not quite make up a solar year. So if only lunar time were counted, the Jewish months would soon be cycling their way through the year, a single one moving from spring to winter to fall to summer. That is what the lunar months do in the Muslim calendar.

No, the rabbis decided; the calendar must be corrected every few years by adding an extra month so that each month would stay in its accustomed place. Why did they come to this conclusion? Since the Torah says that the month of the Exodus will be "the month of Spring," the rabbis felt it necessary to keep the time of Pesach, when the birth of the people and of freedom would be celebrated, in the yearly time of the earth's rebirth.

## NEW WOMEN, NEW TORAH

What do we learn from this "rebirthing" metaphor of the Exodus, and to what changes—what new birth of ourselves—does this midrash call us?

For me, the most powerful answer to this question came in a revelation on a Shabbat morning in New Orleans. I had been invited to teach Torah at a synagogue there. It was the custom, I was told, to follow the sermon with an open discussion—usually rich and thoughtful, full not just of questions but of independent comments. I was visiting during the time of year when the Torah is retelling the story of liberation from *Mitzraiim*. So I focused my talk on the Exodus as a birth. As advertised, the discussion was lively and creative. After the service, a congregant told me how extraordinary the discussion had been, "But—I thought it was always this way?" I said, puzzled and embarrassed. "What was so special?"

"Oh," he said. "The women. They never join in. Today they did."

So not only did the seed of this midrash come from a woman, but the midrash itself invited women into Torah in a new way, even when it happened to be a man who midwifed it in their particular community.

It is not accidental that this new midrash arose for the first time in the first generation when women are studying Torah and men can be present in the birthing room. Always before in Jewish life, the two worlds were totally separate. Now the barriers have broken down.

The metaphors that women learn about themselves matter. The fact that I had been present and took a hand at the moment of my daughter's birth—that mattered when I heard Lynn Gottlieb speak of Torah.

This process creates a "virtuous circle": The more women help to shape new midrash and new ways of understanding Torah, the more they will enter not only into Torah study but into shaping all the elements of Jewish life.

There is a second powerful effect of seeing the Exodus as birthing. It brings to consciousness again the earthy element of the festival of spring. It reminds us that history and biology, human earthlings and the earth, are intertwined. It reminds us that in a generation when the very cycles of the web of life on earth are stumbling, damaged by the ways we humans have been working on our planet, we may need to reshape history to keep the cycles of future generations flowing. It is poignant to live in a generation when, for some species, birth itself has become problematic—when on the one hand human populations are exploding and on the other hand pollution of the earth and air and water has reduced male sperm counts and made many marriages infertile.

Living at such a time reconnects freedom and birth in a new dimension.

These two new learnings from the metaphor of Exodus as birth are connected. As women bring themselves into the process of Torah, the earth will bring itself into Torah as well. Those whom the male rabbinic and kabbalistic traditions saw as intertwined and Other—earthy women, feminine earth—may be intertwined in their return to the center of Jewish life.

What are the implications of seeing the Exodus in these new ways?

What does it mean for us to say those astounding words, "Mother Egypt"? How might it change our outlook on our lives to see *Mitzraiim* as not only the Tight Place squeezing the old life out of us, but the Narrow Canal through which we emerge to new life?

Can we integrate into our spiritual and political lives this learning: We move from the spacious womb that nourishes, to the womb that constricts, to the womb that insists on pushing us forward, to the open space beyond the womb—the open space that is again a new womb that at some point, as we grow, will become a constriction that pushes us forward yet again.

What does this mean for our Pesach celebrations of the Exodus?

We might decide to create another Seder with a new Haggadah, one that draws upon the metaphor of giving birth to freedom, to use perhaps on a different night from the more traditional Seder.

We might add new symbols to the Seder table: Egg in salt water, a symbol that now appears in many households but that the Haggadah never mentions; seeds and nuts; a pot of sprouting plants, perhaps from seeds planted for the New Year of Trees on Tu B'Shvat two months before. We might write new questions for these symbols. Some of us might even make ourselves into birth canals for each other, having each of us pass through a line of tightly woven bodies to be reborn and say who we have become.

In such a Seder, the Four Cups of wine might represent the four stages of a complete birthing: Conception, gestation, birth, maturation in adulthood when the parent becomes a friend and comrade.

Or instead of separating the birth motif into a separate Seder, we might treat birthing the next generation as the focus of one of the cups of wine, spring and the rebirth of the earth as another, freedom from Pharaoh as a third, and the redemptive liberation of our own selves as the fourth.

And we might draw on the rebirthings of our own era, the moments of new imagination—especially by women—that can deepen our experience of Pesach. We might read together Muriel Rukeyser's great poem "Akiba," for example. It is woven from many generations of journey into the wildernesses of new possibility, from the original Exodus to the searchings of the rabbi who kept the Song of Songs alive and died a free Jew at the hands of Rome, and on into our own day, our own journeys not *to* somewhere but into the very process of the journeying.

We could celebrate in new ways the Seventh Night and Day of Pesach, when, according to tradition, the children of the Godwrestlers came to the breaking of the waters. On this day we paused at the Sea, frightened by the surge and storm of utter change. Not until we plunged into its midst did the waters break, the Sea split. We crossed in fear and awe. Behind us, born at last, we turned to see the afterbirth, to see the waters redden with the blood of Pharaoh's army. Then at last, like newborns we breathed and bellowed, sang and danced. Miriam the Prophet and all the women celebrated their lifelong labor to give a new birth to the People Israel.

And today? We could gather at some place of Pharaonic power. We could carry Pesach into public space as we did long ago. We could challenge companies that poison the air and the sea, to give new life to dying species, new health to women of the future who otherwise would suffer from breast cancer, new wholeness to babies of the future who otherwise would wail in agony from birth defects. In public, like Miriam, we might dance in earthy ecstasy and clang our tribal drums and tambourines.

And we could celebrate in new ways the Eighth Night of Pesach. The number "eight" in our tradition symbolizes one beyond the seven of wholeness. It is always the *next* step, the *next* possibility, Messiah. We might make an Eighth-Night Seder in which the Song of Songs is the central teaching. The Song is Torah for the next era of human history, the era in which the earth will be so full of people that we see sex not as the mechanics of procreation but as the chariot of joy; in which we see our relationship with the earth not as sweat and toil in exchange for thorns and thistles, not as war, but as a playful, sensual nurturing of all the strands in the web of life.

It is now more than twenty-five years since the night of Pesach in 1968 when for me the barriers between the Seder and the street dissolved. I now see that night and the Freedom Seder that grew out of it as just the first stirrings of a rebirth in Jewish possibility. The Pesach that for shepherds was the festival of lambing and for farmers the festival of barley, for ancient Israel the great public gathering of millions to celebrate victory over Pharaoh, and for rabbinic Judaism the private family gatherings to affirm our freedom in the very nooks and crannies of hostile civilizations—that Pesach which was reborn and reborn again and again to honor every rebirth of our people—that Pesach is in its labor pains again.

For the Jewish people is once more experiencing its rebirth, and this time women and men will shape the birth together.

# PART III

# TURN, TURN, TURN

# CHAPTER 9

# SHATTERED WINEGLASS, ENDLESS RING

Two marriages:

One shattered, like the shards of shattered wineglass at the wedding.

The other renewed, with rings exchanged anew each Shabbat dinner.

Better to talk about one marriage at a time.

My first marriage, shattered: An ironic reminder of the shattered wineglass that itself is a reminder that the Temple is still broken, the world is still not whole. Intended to remind us even—and especially—at the moment of our greatest joy.

Why do we need to be reminded? Maybe because the joy of a wedding is so great that we might be swept away—forgetting war, injustice, poverty, despair. Maybe because no family should be founded without a commitment to remember and repair the shattered world.

And more important, because no family should be founded without a commitment to repair itself. Without knowing that the very act that completes the wedding, the very act that calls forth the shout of "*Mazel tov!*" from all assembled, is an act of breakage. That from its very first moment, the marriage needs repair. Repair cannot go outward only.

Today, no marriage begins without the knowledge that divorce is no longer extraordinary, that one-third and more of marriages end shattered. Thinking back to the baleful glittering fragments, I used to wonder: Should we have saved the broken glass itself? Once a year, a month, a week, should we have brought it out to contemplate, to tell each other what was broken in our household? To pluck from our skins and souls each sharp and cutting word, to heal each bleeding wound? To pour our energy into repairing?

A living, growing marriage would do it all the time, with or without the glass itself. If we simply kept the shattered glass in mind, we might have done better at our marriage than we did.

To our modern ears, such a ritual may sound artificial; new rituals embarrass us even more than the old ones do. We can treat old rituals as "cultural deposits," that give us roots whether they make "rational" sense or not. Even so, we often drop old ceremonies when we can't explain them to our "objective" selves. But since a new ritual does not soothe us like a familar habit, it has far less power to convince us. If we start with a bias against ritual itself, it is not easy to be moved by something new.

## BITTER WATERS

The Fabrangen once wrestled with a Torah passage about what ritual to do when a marriage goes bad. It seems to be a very specialized passage, and a rather nasty one at that, for it's about what to do when a husband who has no tangible evidence suspects his wife of adultery, and is filled with rage.

Once we started wrestling with it, the passage opened up some deeper, broader perspectives. Fear of adultery was not the central issue in my shattered marriage; it isn't the central issue in most break-ups; and yet the feelings—the rage, the fear, the hurt—are often not so different from those the Torah speaks about.

What the passage (Numbers 5) tells us is that if a husband becomes obsessed with jealousy and suspicion but has no evidence, he shall bring his wife to the priest. And he must bring an offering of barley flour with no pleasant oil or spices, an "offering of jealousy, an offering of memory for remembering evil."

The priest then has the suspected woman (who is called a *sotah*) swear an oath that if she has been faithful, no ill shall come upon her; but if she has been adulterous, her belly shall swell and her thigh fall away (evidently a semi-euphemism that her genitals shall suffer for their crime). The priest writes this curse—which twice includes the Name of God—upon a scroll, and blots the scroll in holy water in which he has put dust from the floor of the Holy Shrine or Temple. So the ink of the curse dissolves into the water—the ink that bears God's very name, the Name we are told never to erase, *that very Name* we blot out in this water, and it becomes "water of bitterness."

The priest then waves the barley flour before God, and burns a handful of it on the altar. Finally he gives the woman the "water of bitterness" to drink. If she is guiltless, she shall conceive seed—a sign that her genitals are healthy. If not, her belly shall swell, and she shall become a curse among her people.

The *sotah* passage provoked Fabrangen to a stormy Torah session. Almost every woman in the room, and many of the men, exploded in anger: "How come there's no obverse ritual for a husband suspected of adultery?"

"What did you expect? There's not even any acknowledgement that a husband *can* commit adultery against his wife. If he sleeps with some other woman, and she has a husband or a father, it's an assault on that man—not on his own wife. Only men have the right to feel outraged."

"Even if we could understand all that, how come the *sotah* ordeal puts such enormous pressure on the woman—and *only* her?"

"Right! How come the husband bears no burden for his jealousy, even if she's cleared by the ordeal?"

The air crackled with our anger, intensified by our caring for the Torah. How could we justify our caring so much for a text that was so sexist?

We realized that there were reasons deeply rooted in biblical society for the asymmetry. Most basically: Men wrote the rules. Secondarily: Perhaps men felt queasy and unsure about their fatherhood, while women had no doubts. We noted that even today, when modern science can determine the biological fact of paternity, there remains a distancing between father and child that we have not yet fathomed how to go beyond. Yet we quickly agreed that all this made no difference to our feeling toward the *sotah*; we could not bear the way in which the woman was demeaned. For us, the issue was whether the passage had something else to teach us.

One of us pointed out that the *sotah* ritual strangely resembled what Moses did after the people worshipped the golden calf: "He ground the calf to powder, strewed the golden powder on the water, and made them drink. Was God accusing them of adultery with another god? God had said He was a jealous God, but Moses wasn't sure what they were doing. He had no proof. Remember, Aaron helped them; so it might have been a way of worshipping God. So Moses made up a *sotah* ritual, and of course they failed. But maybe we should think about the *sotah* in a broader way. Someone suspected of idolatry, of whoring after idols—that's a *sotah*."

"But that's no way to deal with suspicion! It's utterly irrational. No trial, no evidence. Just the ordeal. Judaism is a rational, practical religion. This thing makes me jittery."

Someone else chimed in, "That's the point. There isn't any evidence. There isn't any way to settle it. There's jealousy, suspicion, and that's all. Look at the psychology of it: Suppose in a family or a community there's jealousy, suspicion, rumor. It doesn't have to be sexual jealousy, it doesn't even have to be between spouses or lovers. It can be friends. Some infuriating rumor or suspicion. No proof. No disproof. Just corrosion, and no rational way to end it. What would we do?"

"We'd try to cure the jealousy, wouldn't we? We'd tell the guy that if there is no evidence, he'd better try some therapy."

"But they weren't sure it was all in his head. It might be true. So they used this bitter water like we would a lie detector or truth serum. Same thing. It only works because people expect it to. Blotting out God's Name....Talk about power!"

"In this situation they figured that only the woman knew the truth. Since she believed in the efficacy of the curse, if she were guilty she really would collapse. And if she didn't, everybody knew she was really innocent, and that's the only thing that could end the suspicions."

At this point, a woman who had arrived late for services and had missed the early part of the Torah discussion interrupted: "I don't know how you can go on about this thing. It's the most sexist thing I ever heard of! Some things in the Torah I just wouldn't bother with."

The tension thermometer climbed about ten degrees. Another woman: "We talked about that already. Writing off the Torah is like idolatry. It's making feminism an idol!" Snapped the newcomer, "No, treating the Torah like every paragraph is holy, true, and righteous—*that's* idolatry!"

A tense, stunned silence. Our ethic was not to contradict each other, to build when possible from one midrash to another—and when we can't, to let the different learnings stand as dialectical. But now...

Still another woman: "Look! We just did it to each other! Suspicion without cause, hostility without evidence. Some of us suspecting the others of idolatry. Look, just look!"

A long pause. A different kind of silence: Receptive, alert, still tense but open. One of those moments when the Presence fills the room. Somebody finally laughed—a real laugh, not hysterical or sardonic but full of the richness of the moment. "Well, shall I get some water from the bathroom? Easy enough to make it bitter—and then we'll do the ceremony for each other!"

Everyone guffaws.

"I don't think we need to. Let's make our ceremony be that we can go on to the next line of Torah. Look! It says, 'When either a man or woman shall clearly utter a vow...' They must have had the same fight we did."

Again a guffaw, and the reading began anew.

## WATERS OF FORGIVENESS

As a result of this explosive experience, a few of us in Fabrangen asked whether some transformed version of the *sotah* ceremony might be useful to us. We experimented: Would it help two people who were angry at each other to watch each other write their own misdeeds on paper, using water-soluble ink? And then watch each other plunge this paper into a bowl of bitter water, and see the ink melt off the page into the water, see the misdeeds "dissolve"? And then forgivingly wash each other's hands in fresh water, affirming to each other their fresh start?

We created the ceremony. But we found few couples willing to use it. Too new, too weird, too demanding: How can two people agree to such a volatile ceremony precisely when they both are angriest, least likely to agree on doing anything? They have no priest, no *koheyn*, with the clout to insist. Seemingly a failure.

But then it came to us: *Slichot,* the service of forgiveness on the Saturday night before Rosh Hashanah. We are supposed to forgive each other, but the old "technology" to help us do that—mainly chanting prayers—no longer works, for most of us. Perhaps...?

So we carried this transformed version of the *sotah* "bitter waters" into a transformed version of *slichot,* Indeed, the community found the ritual useful. There were tears as we wrote our misdeeds, more tears as we watched each other write with commitment and resolve on our faces, songs of joy and laughter as we watched the ink dissolve into the water. And loving warmth washed over us as we poured fresh water on each other's hands. The whole community became a *koheyn.*

The rage of the original *sotah* conflict arose from converting love into fury. Our ceremony tried to convert fury back to love. Where did this explosive chemical equation get started?

The God of Torah is good at converting love to fury. One Shabbat—a special one in the middle of Sukkot—we were reading a Torah portion in which God shows surpassing love. Moses had asked to see God's very essence, but God explains that no one can see the face of God and live.

So God shelters Moses in the shadow of a hand and lets Moses see only a back: Attributes, not essence. These turn out to be Grace, Forgiveness, and especially Motherly Compassion. Then God lovingly promises to bring the People to the Land of Israel and begins to describe how they will thrive there.

But then a dark note enters the story. God mentions a great danger: Once the people are comfortable and secure, they will begin to follow strange gods. Fury and doom. Finally, the passage ends with a single line: "You shall not boil a kid in the milk of its mother."

One puzzled Fabrangener said this last line seemed very strange. Why would God now toss in a command about kosher food? It felt disjointed, out of place. Yet somehow appropriate...

Then she said, haltingly, that she felt a link between the verse of Torah and her own relationship to her mother...who would hurt her worst when she thought she was being most loving.

Slowly, delicately, we helped her unravel the thought.

Finally she said, "Put it this way: God has started out loving and gracious, then gets so hurt and upset that He boils over in fury. Only here, I guess, God is 'She'—like my own mother. Because finally Moses can't stand the fury any more. —It's wonderful how gentle and how firm he is!—He says to God: 'You shall not boil a kid in its mother's milk.'

"It's not God talking at all. It's Moses saying that a mother's love should not be converted to destruction. He's trying to get God to calm down!

"We've always thought the line was God's. But here it isn't. Moses knew the line already, from a couple of other places in the Torah. Moses is horrified when God gets angry, and reminds Her how to be a decent person: 'Please, God! You started out so full of life and nurture, offering us Your milk, so warm and overflowing. Please don't heat the milk to boiling, don't pour it on our heads!'"

I begin to see this as the dark side of the "wrestling" sense of God. Wrestling can turn a stranglehold into an embrace in the flick of a wrist; but we can also turn an embrace into a stranglehold. It's t'shuvah, turning, in reversed direction. The more intense and passionate the relationship, the more destructive will this overheating be. Between God and Israel, parents and children, husbands and wives—we keep boiling each other in our warmest love.

The danger is that we move from love to hurt to anger so quickly that we don't leave a moment for the hurt to register and be assuaged. We begin with milk at nursing temperature and leap to boiling. Sometimes I don't even take time to let myself realize that I'm feeling hurt— let alone tell my spouse, or friend, or lover—before I'm steaming. What I need is a...stumble, a tumble, a moment to catch my breath.

What am I saying? What have I just written? "A stumble, a tumble, time to catch my breath!" One of my strongest memories of hurt when I was young was racing down the street, turning to catch a football, running fulltilt into a parked car, falling over with all the breath knocked out of me. My breathing paralyzed for what felt like minutes.

Have I been trying all these years to cancel out those horrifying minutes? To leap from the moment of pain to the moment of fury, so that I don't need to sit there trying to catch my breath?

Remember: If I take "time out" after being hurt, I can rest and catch my breath. Exactly the meaning of *shavat va'yinafash*, what God did in order to make Shabbat. Exactly what I need: A few moments of Shabbat—yes, that's "time out."

The *sotah* passage also teaches me that it's important to take the time to confront, absorb, and lay to rest the cracks and breaks in a relationship. It's not just a tiny moment of Shabbat that I need; I also need a few minutes of Yom Kippur.

Yom Kippur ask us to bring to the surface whatever is unjust, untruthful, unpeaceful, unclear, unhopeful in our relationships with others, and then to recognize that God and the community are ready to forgive and lay to rest these failings. On Yom Kippur, we mourn the death of what is deadly. For on Yom Kippur we recognize that our deadly twists and turns have a vigor, vitality, and energy that are perversely attractive. Having seen this, we bury our deadly sins. We even wear shrouds and fast, to mourn their death. But in our mourning is a deeper joy, since we know that in burying them we give ourselves new life.

What we need to do in a marriage or a friendship is to do this "Yom Kippur" more often, and on a smaller scale, than we do Yom Kippur itself. We need to see how lively are our deadliest behaviors. And then we need to lay them to rest.

It is hard to confront and acknowledge the evil we have done. And even when one partner does this, it may be hard for the other to acknowledge it has happened.

Each failure justifies the other. And then Yom Kippur never happens. If either partner will not confront the "broken glass," and either will not bury the shards in order to start over, then there is no starting over. The sharpened edges of their anger multiply, the wounds and scars deepen, until one or both muster the right mixture of concern and courage, good sense and bravado, to act.

If it is not possible to bury the failings, it becomes necessary to bury the relationship.

## TEARING THE GETT

Even that final act of burial can become a moment of reconciliation—if we have enough courage and good will. Years ago, Irene Elkin (then Waskow) and I prepared to face each other, to exchange *gittin*—

statements of divorce—with each other. In accordance with ancient tradition, we would tear the *gittin* in a unique pattern—as a form of identification, the tradition says, to make sure that each such paper applies to one couple and to no other.

But also, it seems to me, this ripping was the final echo of the wineglass we had shattered at our wedding.

Along with these formal documents of divorce, we did something that was not part of the tradition, though it is growing in some parts of Jewish life. We exchanged our own letters of sorrow, anger, caring, guilt, repentance, perseverance, hope. Our truths. We needed to say that our marriage had itself become a failing, a missing-of-the-mark; and so, as individuals and as part of our communities, we had to start over.

Even in parting, there can be a kind of reconciliation and renewal. When the wrestle becomes only a tug of war, the last act of love—love for the God Who is forever One and forever unites even those who war upon each other—the last act of loving connection is giving away the connection.

Having suffered through the disintegration of a marriage and the difficulty of making and preserving friendships, I believe we need communal ritual and ceremony to help individuals do the constant work of reconciliation and renewal. The wedding's broken wineglass and the *sotah*'s bitter water, the taking breath of Shabbat and the fast of Yom Kippur, are all reminders of how hard it is to make and remake and again make peace. Hard enough with the help of these communal ceremonies; almost impossible, alone.

I know that I needed more help, pastoral and ritual, than the community knew how to give. Most of our communities no longer involve themselves in strengthening relationships and encouraging reconciliation. Ritual and pastoral aid has become too weak—and that may itself be one of the reasons that marriages and friendships are harder to preserve these days. Any new life-path that we can walk with reasonable happiness will have to include rituals of facing broken edges and repairing them.

Irene and I exchanged our *gittin* in 1978. In 1986 I married again. During the years between I had, for the first time in my life, walked a path of learning, experiment, confusion, and doubt about who I was in relationship with women. I came to realize how important that process was if I were ever to make a happy marriage.

I came close to concluding almost the opposite of the official code: That in our society there should be a requirement, an obligation, that everyone experience at least two serious emotional/erotic relationships with some partner before entering one that they define as a communal and legal commitment, such as marriage. (I say "such as marriage" because during those years I also concluded that two men or two women can also in fact, and should also in law, be able to enter into the same kind of commitment.)

I do not literally mean what I have just proposed as an absolute rule; for it is an even deeper truth that human beings are unique, their relationships are unique, and no one rule except Hillel's can apply absolutely, in all cases. (Hillel: "'Love your neighbor *as yourself*.' That means, do not do to your neighbor what you would not want your neighbor to do to you. This is the whole Torah: all else is explanation. Go and study.")

Meanwhile, I had experienced other major changes in my life, during those years between two marriages:

My mother had died.

I had entered a new curve in the spiral of reconnecting with my brother.

I had left the place where I had worked for 15 years and the city where I had lived for 23—practically my whole adult working life.

My children had grown up, and gone off to live in their own cities.

I had reshaped my entire life—my work, my job, my friends, my community, my political outlook and effort—around and through the process I had come to call Jewish renewal.

## UNVEILING THE 70 FACES

All that made a difference. Perhaps the greatest difference between who I was when my first and second marriages began was that the second time, I had not only a sense of who I was, but also a sense that there was such a thing as knowing who I was. I knew not only where I stood, and whither I was walking, but also I knew there was such a thing as choosing a direction for my life. I knew that in different relationships, I was a different person; that, indeed, the "in-betweenness" of the hyphen in I-Thou was as important as the "I." That the "Thou" changes the hyphen, and the hyphen changes the "I." And that I needed to know all that, and keep myself alert to the different versions of my self.

From the beginning, the context of my marriage to Phyllis Berman was different. Even what we did with our names conveyed that difference. We kept the names we had grown up with, and added as middle names the word "Ocean," echoing experiences of oceans we had loved together. In this way we asserted to ourselves and others that we were still who we had been, but with a difference: A difference defined by our relationship. Both of us became a midrash on our earlier selves.

Our preparations for marriage drew on—and transformed—traditional forms. Until our generation, most Jewish marriages were preceded by *tenna'im* or "conditions," a contract—often worked out by parents who had arranged the marriage of young partners—that set out commitments about the time of marriage, financial agreements, and other details. *Tenna'im* were ritually affirmed by the breaking of a plate, perhaps a symbol that an old life-situation was being broken so that a new household could begin. When marriages ceased to be arranged, most partners ceased doing *tenna'im*. "Engagements" took on Western accoutrements—an expensive ring to echo the wedding ring, perhaps legal prenuptial agreements between the partners.

What Phyllis and I did was to make *tenna'im* both an emotional and a contractual reality, about a year before we intended to be married. We chose a day that, according to tradition, is the anniversary of the day when Moses, infuriated by the golden calf, broke the tablets of the Ten Commandments at the foot of Sinai. How to reverse this evil omen? We decided to break tablets of the "anti-commandments." Each of us took a plate from our kitchen, and wrote on it the five things we often did that in our own judgment (we did not consult each other at this point) were most damaging to our relationship.

We also asked each other what had been the hardest things to agree on about our lives together: Where to live? Whether to be monogamous? How to share our incomes and our savings, and provide for the futures of our children? We put the answers to those questions—the thorniest, not the easiest—in our *tenna'im*, the written agreement between us that we were prepared to make public.

With our closest friends, we read the *tenna'im* aloud. As the climax of our ceremony, we read aloud the ten words of our own most shattering actions, from the plates on which we had written them. Then we shattered them.

And so our *tenna'im* became a double midrash: A reinterpretation of what the traditional *tenna'im* had been, and a reinterpretation of the broken tablets.

One year later, our wedding ceremony also drew on the midrashic process. Traditionally, because of the trick that Jacob's father-in-law played on him by passing off one sister as another, the covenant under the wedding canopy is preceded by a *kabbalat panim*, an unveiling of the bride for the "recognition of faces." We turned this into a process to recognize and accept all the faces we wore in every world and with each other. As we faced each other, our friends gathered around us to say aloud the different faces they had seen us wear, lest we be fooled by knowing only some of them: The face of joy. The face of anger. The sullen face. The frozen face. The blazing face. The face

132

of shame. The face of grief. The funny face. The thoughtful face. The studious face. The seventy faces that some say are worn by every human being.

And again, as with our *tenna'im* so in our *ketubah,* our written contract with each other to be read aloud at the wedding ceremony, we put not a formula but our reality. The unspeakable words, we spoke: Money. Living-space. Turf. Sex. Politics. Dispute. Divorce. Death.

Some people gasped. We breathed easy.

For we knew that when we said the truths of our commitment, our friends would hear and respond, our community would stand with us even if moments arose when we might flee what we had said.

We changed the words that went with exchanging rings. The traditional words meant that the man was acquiring a wife, with the ring as both symbol and price. We wanted to establish that between us there was a covenant, not an acquisition. So we used the covenant language from Noah and the Rainbow because it speaks of "raising up" rather than "cutting" a covenant, and we changed the formula that speaks of the "custom of Moses and Israel" to "the custom of the generations of Israel."

Without planning it ahead of time, we found that moment of the rings had become the moment that we wanted to repeat in our lives together. Traditionally, when Jews eat together they begin with a ceremonial washing and drying of hands, with a blessing of the One Who has taught us that "lifting the hands" is a way of connecting with holiness. Phyllis and I have followed this custom not at every meal, but only at those that are especially sacred to us: Each Friday evening dinner when we welcome Shabbat, the meals of holy festivals, and occasional other meals in special circumstances.

Traditionally, the washing was done with hands bare of any ornament or obstruction to the water's flow, even wedding rings. We felt reluctant to remove our rings, until we decided to make a special point of putting them back on again. How could we do this? By reciting to each other, every Shabbat, the affirmation that had united us: "Look! With this ring I make you holy to me, in accord with the custom of the generations of Israel.

*Every* Shabbat. When we are in the mood for songs and dances, and when we are bone-weary. When we are calm, and when we are frightened. When we are worried, and when we are bursting with a new idea. When we melt into each other's loving eyes, and when we can hardly bear to look at each other's red and angry faces.

*Every* Shabbat. When nothing feels more wonderful, and when nothing seems more stupid.

Giving the rings, receiving the rings, saying and hearing the words of covenant—these all change us, no matter what mind or mood we bring to the moment. Beneath any feeling, any thought, this small ritual reminds us that we are in this together, week and week out, year in and year out, no matter how ecstatic or how miserable we are.

Reminds us that every different thought and feeling is part of a rhythm, a pattern, a continuity.

A covenant.

# CHAPTER 10

# THE QUESTION IS THE ANSWER

Over and over, Passover after Passover, we heard the youngest chant the Four Questions, and then listened as the Four Sons walked out on stage before us.

Year by year, there were challenges. One year—now it seems so long ago!—the challenge came from the Daughter, Shoshana, who suddenly called God "She." Shock, giggles, hoots ran around the table, till finally my father the teacher, my father the union organizer, firmly said, "I asked her to take that part of the telling and do what she wanted with it. She's entitled!" Some of the men slowly said, "Why not, after all? Why not 'God/She'?" It was the "sons" around the table who had the greatest trouble; perhaps what they really minded was that they sensed it would never be "four sons" again.

Ever since, indeed, it's "the Four Children." Now we would be startled and ashamed to say anything else, and God has become sometimes "S/He," pronounced "Sh'hee," and sometimes "You," and perhaps most often "the Source," "the Wellspring," or "the Breath of Life." So quickly does the world change, and then seem eternal and traditional!

But some struggles go on, it seems, forever. Every year, out of their year-long hibernation in the closet with the Passover dishes came the Wise Child, the Wicked Child, the Innocent Child, and the One Who Does Not Relate by Asking. And every year we stopped at the second child:

"And the Wicked Child, what does s/he say?"

"S/he says, 'What is this service, this serfdom, this slavery [the Hebrew could mean all of these] to you?'"

"'To you,' not to him. And since s/he plucks up the Root of Being by removing himself from the community, you shall make her teeth stand on edge by answering—"

"This is what YHWH did for *me* when I came forth from the Land of Egypt."

"For me and not for him; had s/he been there, s/he would not have been redeemed."

## FOUR CHILDREN, FORTY QUESTIONS

Over and over, Passover after Passover. And every year, my brother and my son object. Talking with my brother nowadays, we can't even agree on what his objections were. As I remember it, he used to say, "But then I'm the wicked son because I question the service, I 'pluck up the Root of Being.' Do you really mean to rule me out? Do you really mean to call me wicked?"

The way he remembers—would you believe it!—it's me he thinks is the rebellious son, because I was the one who was always angry, always on the family's edge, always having my teeth set on edge. I was the one, he says, who broke with the tradition—the *family* tradition—by taking Torah as my central life. And he didn't want the family to read me out.

And besides, he says, he really thought I was being autocratic. It was our ancient wrestle in new form: I was defining the community in such a way as to exclude him. The way he saw the community, whether it was the family or our whole neighborhood, he felt included.

And my son? He said, "It doesn't matter who the wicked son is; I think we should reach out to him. The answer's wrong—it guarantees he won't show up again."

In vain I said, "But look at the Haggadah. The 'wicked son' does show up each year. We don't get rid of him and forget him; we confront him every year, so he must get invited back to the Seder every year. He's like the second question, like the Bitter Herb: He's bitter to taste but he's necessary to the telling."

In vain I said, "Setting his teeth on edge doesn't mean slapping his face. It just means pushing the matzah and the bitter into his mouth, past his clenched teeth, letting him taste oppression, reminding him that 'oppression' and 'community' are not just words."

In vain I said: "But the answer takes him seriously and answers him seriously, no fakery. If you cut yourself off from the community while it struggles for redemption, you just don't get redeemed. Even if the community is willing to carry you along to redemption, if you back out of the struggle you won't feel the redemption in your own life. You won't become new."

In vain I said: "Each of the four children is part of each of us. The wise one, the innocent one, the one who does not relate by asking questions, even the wicked one. They are all inside us."

My son and brother wouldn't give that answer to an aspect of our selves, any more than they would to someone else. They want the rebellious face to get a hug, to be welcomed home. They act as if they are the community and I have rejected them, so they are ruling me out. They force me to taste how it feels. They make me chew on my own answer. In finding my answer in vain, they force me to think again.

And so I say, "The wicked son isn't the bad guy! Look, these four kids fit with the order of the Four Questions. The wise child asks a long, detailed question—and she gets a superficial answer—details with no depth, no heart. She covers everything, but she's flat, like matzah. The wicked one asks a shorter, sharper question—and gets a serious, sharper answer, like the bitter herb of the Second Question. The innocent asks only two simple words, 'What's this?' and gets the real answer: God liberated us from slavery with an outstretched arm. She's so uncomplicated and the answer is so simple, so clear, so direct, that the answer slides right off her, she needs dipping twice (like the Third Question, "Why on this night do we dip twice?").

"And the last child asks nothing. This child waits. This child leans back, like the Question about leaning. For this child, the Hebrew for 'know'—'da'at'—means 'relate,' 'connect.' This one doesn't relate by asking in words but in some more loving, intimate, touching way. And this is the one to whom you 'open' up; you use the same words that you do with the wicked child, but you do it with a totally different tone.

"This child waits with an open heart, so you, too, open up. When the Haggadah says, 'You shall open up to him,' the word for 'you' is feminine. The only time it uses the feminine form. Maybe it means to open as a woman does when she gives birth. Give birth to this one!

"We're watching a progression, from verbal skills to silence. See, each of the questions gets shorter and shorter: First nine words, then four, then two, then none. Each questioner learns from the inadequacy of the previous question and answer; each learns to ask more by asking less. Until, finally, the last questioner keeps silent. Questions are good, but the ultimate question comes from God: To us, not from us."

The family listens. But they don't accept the answer. My brother answers me, "If he's not the bad guy, why is he called 'wicked'? From the moment you meet him he's rejected, even before we are told to rule him out. Your explanation doesn't have the force of the words in the Haggadah for a real child sitting here at table. It's too abstract, too grown-up. The earliest thing a real child learns here is that it's wicked to challenge God and the community."

"God knows he doesn't learn that if *you're* sitting at the table !" say I. But I know that most Jews like him are no longer sitting at the table. So the wrestle goes on. Every year that I play the teacher, I am forced to learn a new answer. If I keep on putting the questions, I will keep on getting no peace. I can escape only by keeping silent.

*That* I could do: I could place on others the burden of defending the text, explaining the text. I could keep silent, I could try to hear the question instead of asking it.

## THE LEARNING SPIRAL

Or I could learn from the interplay. Dancing just below the surface of the Seder is a theory of teaching and learning. It is a set of questions from the youngest person present that sets it all in motion: "Why is this night different from all other nights?"

Why do we dip parsley into salt water so early in the Seder, long before we eat any real food? We do it to make this night different from all others, just to stir a child into a puzzled question: "Why tonight do we dip twice?" We do what is strange so that a child will notice and ask why we do what is strange.

The logic is circular, but the learning is spiral. It rises. The elders teach the children what questions to ask, so that the elders may teach from the answers. If the children ask something else, that's fine; but if there is no asking, there can be no answering. If there is no answering, there can be no new questioning. The highest learning of all is to ask new questions or to hear new questions. Or maybe the highest learning—the Fourth Child—is to make your whole self into a question.

The Seder's theory of education is that one-way learning is barren; all real education is an interchange between generations. Even the old must learn; the tradition itself must change. What path would we have to take in order to create schools of such learning?

At Fabrangen we kept trying, testing, learning how to do this. Some memories, some moments:

*The Fabrangen "Sunday Cheder," Spring 1973:* I'm reading to the class of eight-to-ten-year-olds the story in which Moses kills the overseer. Two kids grunt. I stop, look up, ask how they feel about it.

"He shouldn't have killed him."

Another kid gets sore: "Come on! What else could he do?"

"Maybe he could just have broken the overseer's stick."

"But the army would come and kill Moses or the slave!"

"So why is it any more important for Moses or the slave to live than it is for the overseer?"

I intervene: Why did Moses butt in on the slave's side anyway?

One kid: "Because he was a Hebrew and so was the slave."

Another: "No! Because slavery was wrong!"

The kids look at each other, baffled. They sense there is something attractive about both answers, but they are not used to the notion that two opposites can both be true. I think to myself that maybe the most important, and most Jewish, thing I can teach them is that it is possible to believe two contradictory things at the same time.

And meanwhile I grin to myself: Even ten-year-olds pose the classic questions: Ethnic or ethic? Cultural identity or universal religious morality? Nonviolence or self-defense? Which one is Jewish?

So I think: Can I put forward still another possible answer?—The answer, Both! Can I suggest that maybe the Jews whom Moses knew already had a glimmer that to be a Jew meant to seek justice for everyone, so when Moses saw the overseer beating up a Jew he realized this was injustice imposed on someone who was already seeking justice? Was it the Jews who created Passover? Or was it Passover that created the Jews? Is that too abstract for the kids?

I leave it. Better they keep pursuing their own questions.

*Cheder two weeks later:* I'm reading about Moses at the Burning Bush. Why did he keep asking God to let him off from being the liberator?

"He was scared."

"No, Moses was brave; remember when he killed the overseer?"

"I wouldn't be scared, even if I had to fight a lion." (This from a kid named Ari, "Lion"!)

I intervene: The only lion-fighters I know are at the circus, and they take a chair and stick into the cage. Maybe they're brave, but they look scared, too.

"Moses was brave, but he wanted to keep a place open to sort of go inside himself for the scared part to be able to come out."

"Moses wanted to explain to God ahead of time about all the problems if he went back to Egypt. He wanted God to encourage him, then he could do it."

Finally, a general agreement: It's okay to be scared *and* brave at the same time.

*Cheder:* The kids decide to have a Seder of their own. One says being free means being able to jump and run, so the Seder has to be outside in a park, and they will get up when the Seder says the Jews are free, and play and run for a while.

*My own family Seder, after all of us have learned from Cheder:* At nine, David joins the discussion when we recite the ten plagues: "If God could free the Jews without killing any of their first-born, why did he have to kill all those Egyptian first-born? If he's God, why couldn't he do something else?"

*Cheder two years later*: Me: "Why did the Jews have to wander in the wilderness till everyone who had lived in Egypt died?"

One ten-year-old: "The only country the old ones knew was Egypt. If they had just gone straight to Israel, they would have made a country just like Egypt—with a Pharaoh and slaves and everything. God didn't want that."

Another ten-year-old: "Egypt was terrible. They hated it. If they had been the ones to cross the Jordan, they would have built a country with just one idea—to take revenge on Egypt. God didn't want that."

Me: Stunned and silent, thinking, "Two midrashim that belong in some new Talmud...just like that!"

I feel tears in my eyes as I jot down these notes. I think they're tears from my own childhood. My family had a solemn Seder, but I never challenged God or the Haggadah or the grownups. I don't remember a time or space I could use to develop my own values, Jewish or otherwise, with a sense that grownups might listen and even learn from me.

## PLANTING SEEDS

What struck the spark in me to join with others to start the Cheder? I think it was returning full-time to Washington in the fall of 1972, after fourteen months of moving back and forth from city to country. We were experimenting toward creating a *milchig*-eating, organic-farming, Torah-studying kibbutz in North America.

During that time, my family had felt like a tiny counterculture: Connected to nature, to Judaism, to physical work that grew our food, to knowledge that was directly tied to emotion and grew from experience and conversation, not from a lesson plan. Maybe, above all, it was a time in which David and Shoshana had Irene and me and Kibbutz Micah as their primary peergroup, rather than kids from homes with different values and life experience. (Only twenty years later do my kids point out to me that there were hardly any kids at all, that they felt themselves awash in a sea of grownups, that they lost the chance to make a wider circle of their own friends and to experience in their own lives the growth, the discovery, that we grownups were experiencing with each other.)

Then the kibbutz ended. Suddenly we were back in the midst of a normal year in more or less normal America, with children who at eight and five would be going to school full-time. How could we make certain that our values were not swamped?

I remember comparing Fabrangen to the Jewish neighborhood in Baltimore where I grew up, and thinking how fragile was our kind of *Yiddishkeit*. Thinking that the Park Heights neighborhood, despite all the inanities of its conventionalized Judaism, had probably still been a great deal stronger in comparison to the American superculture of the 1940s than our Jewish counterculture was vis-a-vis the American superculture of the 1970s.

Why were we so worried?

*Item:* TV. It's always there, and we don't get to choose it. Utterly different from books. When I was a kid, I spent hours almost every day exploring the branch library by myself, creating my own individual version of American culture. Once I chose a book, I made up much of what was in it: The way the people looked, how their voices sounded, what went on between the paragraphs. I could stop and dawdle, daydream, fill in the blanks. My mother would call up to tell them to send me home when it was dinnertime. We knew the librarians; they knew us.

*Item*: The supermarket. Back in Baltimore I knew the grocer, the kosher butcher, the baker, the creamer, the non-Jewish barber who had learned Yiddish from his customers, the candy-store man who really ran the betting joint, the *shokhet* with his squawking dying chickens. I knew them all by name, and they knew mine. We bought slaughtered chickens from the *shokhet* not because we kept kosher, but because everybody on our block got chickens there.

It's easy to make the list of lost community. The point is, from childhood on I had a self-confident sense of growing up outside the Great American Machine. How could our kids get that feeling?

First thought: Their school was certainly better for that than most of the public schools around. It was a community-controlled neighborhood public school that was somewhat resistant to American norms because it was 95 percent Black in population and mildly pro-Black-liberation in outlook. It responded to the neighborhood, especially to the people who organized and fought for it to be community-controlled—and that included us. It was loose enough to let the kids take off every other week from school so they could go to the country.

Still, we didn't like some of the ways the school departed from American norms. More physical roughness. From some teachers, a sense that white kids didn't belong in a Black community school. Harsher discipline.

And in some ways it was still pretty standard American. Competition between students. Fairly rigid male and female roles. Using knowledge as an instrument to get ahead, rather than a joy in itself or a guide to ethical life. These weren't our values. And of course there was no sense that even the school's best values were connected to being Jewish, that being community-controlled and rooted in a real community might be part of being Jewish.

So what then? A Jewish day school? The existing ones felt like a perversion of the Judaism I'd come to love. Same values about sex roles and competition as the school they already went to. Another Americanization school. I wouldn't go; why send my kids?

What of the counter-culture cooperative free schools? They called for the same kind of time and devotion I was lavishing on becoming Jewish, and I didn't have enough energy for both. Of course, the free schools weren't Jewish; so I'd have been cutting down the time I could devote to our Jewish journey, to achieve for the kids a school that has decent values but no Jewish context. Now there's an agony.

Setting aside more family time to explore Jewishness and our values? Fine, but this ran into two problems: I, who cared a great deal about integrating Judaism with my values, was not trained in the Jewish tradition and was painfully (though joyfully) having to learn Hebrew and how to deal creatively with texts. So I didn't feel fully competent to teach the process. And Irene, who was far more deeply trained in "Jewish skills," found her spiritual, ethical, and intellectual interests most fulfilled in other-than-Jewish arenas. So the two of us would impart somewhat different outlooks in very different ways. Learning how to hear each other's way of expressing the world was a fruitful and deepening struggle to go through—but very hard work as well, and work we ultimately failed at.

Given all this, I felt caught: Wanting desperately to accomplish something with the children that I felt incompetent to accomplish.

I turned, naturally, to Fabrangen. That wasn't easy, either. Most Fabrangeners were in their mid-twenties, single or loosely coupled or very recently married. Almost all were childless. They reacted to questions about raising kids with polite boredom or honest bafflement.

Fabrangen itself reflected adult time and attention span. It wasn't working too well for kids. Welcoming Shabbat, mostly with songs and dancing, was accessible to kids. But even Friday evening services often went on too long for kids and led to tears or tension.

Kids couldn't join in a grown-up study group in Hebrew. Did that mean they wouldn't learn Hebrew? Kids couldn't sit from 10 a.m. till 2 p.m. on Shabbat, davvening and then discussing Torah. Did that mean they'd never learn to study Torah? Or learn to *davven*?

It meant we had to work together with the few families in Fabrangen and reach out to like-minded families in Washington. We found a dozen families, with about eighteen kids between four and eleven years old, who were attracted, not annoyed, by the notion of nonchalance and amateur standing as the key characteristics of Cheder.

They were ready to help teach, and to meet every three weeks to plan the sessions. They took cheerfully to providing the kids an extraordinary range of experiences: One week, parents teaching how to make a mezuzah; another week, Rabbi Zalman Schachter—one of the deepest Jewish spiritual searchers—teaching the kids how to pray and meditate; a third week, a Fabrangener showing how to "dance" in the shapes of Hebrew letters.

The parents also recognized when nonchalance didn't seem to work—for example, in learning Hebrew—and moved toward more careful structure in such areas. And they enjoyed the older kids' self-confidence in such matters as organizing their own Seder.

Beneath all this lay a crucial decision: We wouldn't lay on the kids a Judaism we didn't want for ourselves. Our problem was the opposite: How to let kids in on the good stuff we liked so much, which we liked precisely because it was grownups' Judaism: Torah. Buber. The continuous creation of new *Halakhah*. Kabbalah. Prophetic politics.

We learned to do this in shorter time slots, hardly watered down. You like to dance and sing with Shlomo Carlebach? Take the kids. You want to create a "Festival of Trees and Life for Vietnam?" The kids can set up a booth of their own. You like arguing Torah? The kids can argue Torah too.

Many of us had turned away from Judaism because when we were twelve and even twenty-two, we had been peddled a Jewishness hardly satisfying to nine-year-olds. What we were trying to do was make available to nine-year-olds a Judaism that not only felt good to us at twenty-nine and thirty-six and fifty-one, but that the kids knew felt good to us. That was why we had to be the teachers: To make our Cheder into the opposite of dropping off the kids on Sunday morning.

Becoming teachers taught us to be students. Three years after the school began, it doubled in size as new parents heard of it by word of mouth, just as they were also hearing new Jewish stirrings in themselves. They came, saying it was for their kids' sake, but quickly realized that to teach the kids, they needed to study with each other. Soon we froze the school's membership at the twenty-seven families who belonged already, so the school could itself become a community.

## LIBERATING TIME

Sometimes the whole process felt like a struggle to liberate time. Guerrillas conventionally try to liberate space, territory. Abraham Joshua

Heschel taught that Jews care more about holy time than holy space. So Jewish guerrillas should learn how to liberate time—like turning Saturday into Shabbat.

That included two struggles to liberate some of my own time from the workplace into the home: One struggle against my own self-image, and another against the demands of my workplace. Neither was easy, and even twenty years later I have not fully won either battle.

The struggle to liberate time is also a struggle to find whole new ways of aggregating time. Maybe a Jewish summertime could be to the year as Shabbat is to the week? Maybe we could create a "Summer Cheder," a counterculture Jewish family "camp"?

It took until the mid-1990s for us to organize such a place and time, but at last it has begun: Elat Chayyim, a retreat center in the good old Catskills where adults can come for weeks of serious and joyful Jewish time: Time for Kabbalah and time for Martin Buber, time for Jewish feminism and time for meditation, time for "drushodrama" where we act out the missing pieces of a Torah story and time for writing poetry under a master's guidance, time for Jewish yoga and time for Jewish dance.

*Plus*, a kaleidoscope for Jewish youngsters who live near their parents but just one autonomous step away. Not being baby-sat but exploring for themselves: Giving *tzedakah* and carving a *tzedakah* box, learning to *davven* and learning to videotape the davvening so as to *davven* better.

I still have unresolved questions about helping kids grow in and through being Jewish: How do we open up spiritual experience for kids? Maybe by being quiet in the midst of nature, they can learn a sense of God-presence. Maybe by being silent in a community they can listen inward/upward. But silence seems hard for kids, anyway.

Or is the problem that we normally teach our kids to be "unsilent" and unquiet? Can davvening do even for kids what it does for many grownups—give them a sense of inner harmony and outer listening? Would davvening time for kids need to be shorter than it is for grownups, as it is for Torah study?

Several motifs of these notes and reports suggest where we need to look, test, and experience further.

One is that my strongest and best sense of how to be with David and Shoshana came from remembering how it felt to be a kid in Baltimore. Not a romantic version of that childhood, which contained misery and anxiety as well as joy. But a sense of what was missing as well as what was wonderful. The best teaching I did came from vivid memories of what I learned—and didn't—from those who taught me.

My teaching also felt best when I was most open to having the kids teach me. The Talmud says, "I learned much from my teachers, more from my comrades, but most of all from my students." Over and over, I am stunned to realize how accurate that is. Whether I am teaching Cheder kids or adults, I learn from teaching—if I let myself teach like someone who wants to learn. Feeling like a kid, feeling like a student, makes teaching most fruitful.

That was what the rabbis realized when they worked out the form of the Passover Seder. They had before them the Hellenistic "symposium"—a formal philosophic dinner with four cups of wine, where a sage like Socrates forced his students to answer difficult questions. By posing the questions, the sage got to predetermine the answers. That was all right, if he knew The Truth already.

But the rabbis were celebrating freedom, and they were living in an era when Judaism was in transformation. They did not know all the answers, and perhaps they had a glimmer that no one ever would. So they turned the questioning upside down. They asked the youngest to ask the Four Questions. They opened up the search, instead of shutting it down.

They affirmed that asking like a student is what makes for the richest teaching.

CHAPTER 11

# BETWEEN THE GENERATIONS: GOD'S LAUGHTER, ELIEZER'S TEARS

It is not easy to "feel like a kid," to experience what is going on inside your children or your students. Twenty years later, I have discovered that in their childhoods, my own kids felt cut off from other children in ways I had not imagined. They point it out to me now, sometimes in anger and sometimes in sadness: How at first, during my intense leap into this new Jewish framework for my life, I had taken them leaping with me; but there were few other children in the new community. Even the Cheder, they point out, was so small that the universe of children from whom to choose friends was tiny, tiny.

Only now are the Jewish-renewal communities bursting with children. Only now is the movement for Jewish renewal turning its attention toward growing the next generation with its own values, not in conventional Jewish schools.

When we were beginning, my grown-up children now tell me, they felt like Isaac, carried off to the mountaintop to fulfill his father's vision, carried up to the altar to please his father's God.

I remember a moment at the Cheder. We are doing "drushodrama" with the tale of Isaac's binding. I have asked the kids to take on the roles of the "personas" in the story: Not only Isaac and Abraham and Sarah, not only the two servant-boys at the foot of the mountain, but also the donkey and the ram and the flame of the burnt-offering. And God.

I ask them to act out the blank space in the story: God's messenger has intervened. Isaac is alive. The ram is dead. The offering is ablaze. Now what?

147

They begin the action. Abraham and Isaac are coming down the mountain. But Isaac is stumbling at every step.

I stop the action. "What's going on?" I ask.

Isaac looks withdrawn. He says, "It's true that he didn't kill me. But. But I feel broken."

The other children nod. To them, it seems a truthful midrash. To me, too. And I tell them that in the ancient midrash, the rabbis taught that Isaac, who was too blind in his old age to distinguish between Jacob and Esau, was blinded not by advancing age, but by the moment on the mountain. Some say he was blinded by the tears of the angels; some say by the flash of the knife above him.

So I tell them that long ago the rabbis, too, thought that Isaac would be hurt by this ordeal. I am happy they have figured it out themselves, I am happy I have been able to connect their reaction to that of the ancient tradition. They will not forget, I think to myself, that they are part of a great chain of thought, a spiral of Jewish learning and regrowth.

And I am right. They do not forget. Moments like this come again and again, and they learn not only to become Jews but also to become *mentshn*, full human beings with hearts and minds and spirits. It lasts as they keep growing.

But me! Whose eyes were blinded? Now, twenty years later, my children tell me that my eyes were almost always on the mountain, far away—not looking close to home, at them. That I was blind to them. They remind me of moments when they tried to tell me, through anger or through passivity—and when I didn't get it. Perhaps this moment of the Isaac drushodrama was just such a moment—and I didn't get it.

So now I find myself reframing with a new grief what had been my purely joyful understanding of this past. I've let in a story that overlaps with mine. A different story, from another angle of vision. The other story does not cancel mine, but changes it profoundly.

Why does it not cancel out my earlier version of the story? Because creating this movement of Jewish renewal, this vision for which precisely I turned my eyes to the faraway mountains, was also good for the kids. It gave them a way of growing roots in a culture far deeper than the one that grows from the mass American media. It gave them a way of growing roots in their own beings. When I looked to the mountains, I was seeing their future, caring for them. And yet, and yet...

Given who I was and what I knew, who I wasn't and what I didn't know, I could not see both the children of the future, the children of the mountains far away, and the children as they were at that very moment, stumbling down the mountainside.

Tears. Today, now, tears.

Only now can I see both visions, see them in tears. Only now, in the future of that moment. God's weeping angel is always from the future.

The weeping angel, the one whose tears made Isaac blind, was already crying at the self-blinded Abraham. Crying for the pain that Abraham would cause by turning his eyes away from the face before him. The Abraham who would not look into the face of Isaac bred the Isaac who could not see the face of Jacob, the face of Esau.

Who was God's messenger in tears? Now it seems to me it was, is, will be my future self. My helpless future self, helpless to change what happened twenty years ago, reaching back through time....

Who tries to speak in tears to Abraham, but cannot be heard through the thickened glass of time.

## SHAKING MOUNTAIN, QUAKING CHILD

What might have made it different when it happened? What might have made it possible both to act on the vision of the children of the future and stay present to the children of the present?

I would have to have been then the kind of father that I am only beginning to be now. When the Cheder began, we knew that we were reinventing womanhood and motherhood, but we only dimly realized that we were trying to reinvent fatherhood.

It takes time to do all this: Especially time away from regular work. Once we decide this is time well liberated, we should realize we are chopping at the root of the modern "career." Who will promote me, make me famous, multiply my power, for spending time reading Torah or learning to dance with a dozen kids? When the Cheder began, this was totally new territory for most men; most women knew how to focus on the family.

To make it possible for men to want to do this, we will have to change what the kids themselves taught us: "God was a father at Sinai, shaking and yelling and scaring us like that!" We will have to change the father who looks always to some infinitely distant mountaintop and shouts because the children will not listen.

We will have to change the "father" image that most Jews project onto God, which then God the Father reprojects into male character structure and role, so that it shapes our images of how to be a father, a mother, and a child. Back and forth, across millennia.

Some doctors think some brain-damaged kids may be that way because they were shaken in the early months by frustrated, furious parents, shaken before the brain case was well enough formed. Did God shake the People Yisrael too hard at Sinai and damage our communal brain in the shaking? Is that why, ever since, we have found it so hard to obey the Commandments?

Or to put it another way: When we tell the story of the thundering God and the golden calf and the shattered tablets at Sinai, are we reflecting and justifying a certain way of being parents in our day? If so, we must create new ways of being parents, of being children, of talking without shouting, shaking, screaming; and we must also strengthen our stories of a Parenting God Who does not shout and shake.

Here too we need to keep both eyes open: One eye on our vision of where we are going, one eye on the present. My own children tell me, twenty years later, that I was so committed to my vision of fathering them in a way that my father hadn't fathered me, that I leaped beyond my reality. So when my wife and I separated, I insisted on sharing the parenting even though I didn't know how to do it well. I couldn't cook their food they way they liked it, and worse: I didn't stop to see they didn't like it. Once more, I was not watching the real me and the real children in the present as closely as I was watching who I wanted to become. And again, as I hear this from them, I realize how the future intrudes to recast the past, to reframe and reshape our stories. Our children remake us.

The Talmud tells a story about God as a Parent who sorrows and rejoices in the freedom of the children, and about human beings as children who recast the story from the future, remaking God.

The story begins with a debate among the rabbis over an oven they called "serpentine," built with brick spirals. The rabbis voted that this oven was taboo. But Eliezer, who had the highest prestige, voted no. The others wound words and words and words around this question, like the snaky spiral of the oven itself. But Eliezer cut through this wordy spiral. He appealed to the earth to prove him right.

The earth responded. A carob tree uprooted itself; the other rabbis stood firm. A river turned backward; the other rabbis continued walking in the direction they had chosen. The walls of the House of Study began to lean; the other rabbis stood even straighter in their certainty. At each test, the rabbis insisted that they did not learn Torah from trees, or rivers, or the walls of sacred places—but only from talking Torah with each other.

Finally, Eliezer asked that Heaven speak. From Heaven came an Echo of the Holy Voice: "Why are you arguing with Eliezer? The sacred path of life is always where he guides you!"

But the rabbis refused to listen to this parental Voice. Instead, they quoted Torah to its Holy Author: "'It is not in Heaven,' You taught us, Holy One, 'but in our own hearts and mouths!'" And they challenged God even more deeply by quoting and transforming another verse of Torah: "Do not follow a majority to do evil, nor respond in a law-case so as to lean toward the majority." They ripped the last few words from context and faced God down: "Lean toward the majority!" they said.

Then they excommunicated Eliezer. Outraged on behalf of his beloved child, God brought a parent's wrath upon the earth: A third of the olives, the wheat, and the barley were destroyed. And a great storm threatened to drown the president of the Sanhedrin, Gamaliel, who had led in banning Eliezer.

Gamaliel calmed both God and the sea. Eliezer returned, shattered and humiliated, to his home and his wife, Ima Shalom, "Mother Peace," who was Gamaliel's sister. She watched Eliezer's suffering, and on every occasion when he sought in his agony to fall upon his face before the Holy One, she stopped him.

But one day she was busy giving bread to a beggar, and she came back to see Eliezer on his face, in profound prayer. "Arise," she shouted, "you have killed my brother!" Indeed, the shofar sounded: Gamaliel had died.

How did she know this? She knew that if Eliezer once fell from his high station to the lowly earth, once let his humiliation sweep fully over him, it would burn through every cautious gate of Heaven and consume the one who had ordered his humiliation.

## GOD'S DEFEAT, GOD'S VICTORY

Read to this point, the story seems to be a cautionary tale, warning against the chutzpah of the rabbis in refusing to obey their Parent's Voice.

But I have left out a sentence or two that the Talmud inserts in the midst of the original story, a passage from the future. Just after the rabbis twist to their own purposes the Torah verse about majorities, the Talmud inserts a tale about a later rabbi, Nathan. On his journeys one day he met Elijah, the prophet who entered Heaven without ever dying. "Elijah," asked Nathan, "What did God do on that day when the rabbis put the ban on Eliezer?" "Oh," said Elijah, "God smiled and said: 'My children have been victorious over me, my children have made me eternal.'"

In the Talmud's Aramaic, the sentence is simply repeated, in exactly the same words: "*Nitzchuni banai, nitzchuni banai.*" The Aramaic word for "victory," *netzach*, also means "eternity," and I believe the sentence is repeated so God can assert both meanings.

This interpolation transforms the meaning of the story. Indeed, many Jews have learned the story without ever hearing about the disasters, as if the story stopped with Elijah's report of God's laughter. But the story is far more complex than that. It is exactly about parents, children, the past, and the future.

In the story, God as Parent realizes that the parent does not lose, but wins when, for the first time, the children invoke the Parent's own teachings to claim their own authority to shape their lives. The Torah does not, in fact, enter the mouths and hearts of the people until they do this. And at this moment God—precisely by being defeated—becomes eternal.

Till then, it is a tenuous question: Does the teaching really matter? Does everything depend on the teacher's constant presence, the parent's constant presence, for the learning to be lived? Only by being "defeated" does the parent win, and thus become eternal: The parent can die, can disappear, but the task of teaching is complete. The children know everything they need to know, including—especially—how to learn what they do not yet know.

But this also is not the whole meaning of the story. For there is a cost, a terrible cost. This learning, on the part of child and parent, on the part of God and rabbi, has come through tragedy and loss. It is only in the reframing of the story several generations later that everyone can say the process has succeeded.

Nathan's report of Elijah's report of God's laughter is like my tears, years later, about what I failed to see was happening in my children's lives. Yet I have to take these tears another step. Somehow, in the very midst of the tears I feel about their loss, their anger, I have to summon up the joy of seeing them take their own lives into their own hands.

I have to join them in joyful laughter for the sake of their independence—and yet I must preserve the sense that my laughter is different from theirs. For they won their independence at the cost of suffering pain that I imposed on them. It would cheapen the victory we share for me to ignore the pain I did not share—indeed, the pain I caused, the pain that they may transcend but cannot forget.

When, I ask, did God cry for the pain of Eliezer, of Gamaliel, of the wheat and rice and olives and of those who starved because their food was stricken?

## WHEN SCHOOL IS FAMILY

In some ways, our Cheder and similar schools recapture the past as well as step into the future. Hasidic schools were, like ours, more closely tied to the families' values and experience than has been the norm in the professionalized schools run by synagogues, denominations, or communal federations. Hasidic schools had to begin like this, because the Hasidim were often minorities in the Jewish communities of Eastern Europe, and Hasidic families had to create their own schools if they were to instill their own kind of Judaism in their children. We set out on our own for similar reasons.

By doing so, we have recreated a relationship in which the school more closely approximates the home. What we give up, often, is the detailed Jewish knowledge and the more intensely Jewish life-practice of the professional Jewish teachers. What we gain is that Jewishness does not seem to the children to be something "out there," something artificial at the end of a rubber band that ultimately snaps you back to reality—a home much less Jewish than the school.

A parents' co-op, in fact, has the opposite effect: Since parents must do the teaching, they are constantly being stimulated to learn more. What the Seder creates for a night or two—a family turned into a school, where the generations learn from each other—the parents' co-op tries to do throughout the year.

The professionalization of Jewish education was absolutely necessary when the American Jewish community felt itself less and less capable of recreating Jewishness organically. But the Cheder may point toward a future in which the community feels more and more, not less and less, Jewish. If so, the community may feel that it can reclaim Jewish education from the professionals to whom it had handed over the job.

But this will not come easy. Since the Cheder was founded in 1973, some changes in America may have made the task even harder. While more men have moved toward the kind of parenting a Cheder needs, more women have adopted the old version of the "male" career, leaving little time for family or community. This has broken down old stereotypes of gender roles, but has not accomplished what we hoped: That more and more men and women would drop their internal barriers and limits, creating lives in which the flow of work and family was more fluid than either men or women had previously enjoyed.

Why has that been so hard to bring about? Because in the last twenty years or so, American society has actually made it harder to be fluid about time at work. Great advances in computer-driven "productivity" have not been channeled into letting men and women have more time to shape their own life-work and life-play, more time to raise children and enhearten neighborhoods and share the burdens of community. Instead, many people have been thrown out of jobs, out of families, out of neighborhoods—landing in the streets or in prison or in menial drudgery at minimum wages. Others have found themselves working much longer and much harder to keep their heads above water and their careers on track.

So it is harder to create a Cheder now than it was in 1973. If the Cheder is a good idea—for families, for communities, for the Jewish people—then action must be taken to make it possible. The Jewish community alone cannot make this happen, unless it helps change how America deals with broader questions of work, leisure, and income. For this new pattern of family Jewishness to become possible, we need to work with other communities to redefine not only what it means to be male and female, but the meaning of a job and a career. Although we cannot make such changes on our own, other communities face the same issues and have good reason to work along with us.

When we created the Cheder, we did not imagine that shifts in the structure of work would make it harder to follow our example. That lights up for us a broader truth: We need to think further ahead. What changes in society are likely to affect the Jewish people, and what might we do to shape such changes to strengthen, not weaken, our best version of ourselves?

## BETWEEN THE GENERATIONS

The model for how to do this well could be, of all things, the Four Questions and the Four Children of the Haggadah. For learning and planning must hear the next generation's questions as well as the last generation's wisdom. Not only in the family but in the centers of high learning, in the great think tanks of planners, in the radical councils of rebellion.

We should not think of "schools" and "future planning centers" as totally distinct places. We should try instead to make the Seder's intergenerational questioning and answering into a model for our sages all year long. Indeed, this very process of interchange between the generations is what made the sages of the Talmud into sages. The interchange went back more than one thousand years to wrestle with the text of Torah, and forward at least five hundred years as generation after generation of rabbis entered their wisdom into the pages of the Talmud. Often they would wrestle not in chronological sequence but leaping across the generations, with someone from five centuries later suddenly appearing in the midst of an earlier text. God's messenger, an angel from the future, bearing tears or laughter that the present could not bear to understand.

During the period of Roman conquest and the destruction of the Temple, the Jewish people advanced by retreating to a few small towns—Yavneh in Judaea, later Pumbeditha in Babylon. There the rabbis could teach their students and the students of their students and could learn new Torah from their questions. There they could replace the shattered stationary Temple with a portable process—wrestling with Torah.

The rabbis created the Talmudic process because they had suffered an earthquake in their lives.

So, too, has the Jewish people in recent generations. The impact of the modern world led to the Holocaust, to the creation of a Jewish state, and to the first fully free Diaspora Jewish communities in history. And though the Jewish people has suffered sharper traumas than most other peoples, the advent of the modern world has wrenched out of shape the lives of almost all of them.

So for the Jews and perhaps for other peoples, it is Yavneh and Pumbeditha that we must create—centers of living Torah where the questions back and forth between the generations are answered both on paper and in practice. But this time, Yavneh and Pumbeditha will be different. They will need to be in face to face communities, in new kinds of villages—and also on the Internet, spanning the earth.

I can speak already of a hint, a beginning. I now live in a Philadelphia neighborhood called Mount Airy. It is a neighborhood of the rich, the middle class, the working poor, and the desperate; a neighborhood of woods and creeks and grass and bursts of flowers; a neighborhood that astonished the city government by putting out its blue recycling cans in unprecedented numbers on the very first day the city would collect them; a neighborhood of devoted Christians, Black and white; of Jews who have become spiritually open to God, intellectually excited by Torah, and emotionally committed to each other; a neighborhood of celebratory street fairs and energetic local politics that reach across these lines of class and culture.

Within the Jewish strand in the fabric of Mount Airy, there is an amazing variety of writers and singers and artists and dancers and davveners, social workers and community organizers, teachers and students of Torah. Some use a traditional prayerbook; some use one or another moderate or radical revision of it; some *davven* with no prayer book at all. There are women who celebrate the New Moon and men who celebrate the moon's first growing quarter-phase. Some of us sing at the circumcision of a boy, and some refuse; some dance at the wedding of two women, and some won't. Many move back and forth among these sub-worlds, learning and growing and healing: Praying for a newborn who has a failing heart, washing the body of a neighbor who has died, standing vigil with a woman whose breast is about to be removed.

And over and over, in word and in practice, we wrestle with Torah, dance with Torah, learn old Torah, create new Torah. We renew Judaism and the Jewish people.

We have become extraordinary people, though we did not begin that way. We teach ourselves to become more extraordinary every time we look from face to face around a circle on Shabbat, saying quietly as we look into each face, "This is the face of God. And this is the face of God. And this. And this."

If we were not living face to face, I do not think this would be happening. And we know of other places where it is happening, also face to face: Berkeley-Oakland. Washington. In towns and suburbs ringing Boston: Cambridge, Somerville, Sudbury, Brookline. Eugene and Ashland, Oregon. On the Upper West Side of Manhattan, and in the Park Slope patch of Brooklyn. Here and there in Colorado and New Mexico. Miami. Rio de Janeiro. London. Basel. The Baka neighborhood in Jerusalem.

From the roots that have sprouted in some of those places have come branches that reach everywhere. The face to face neighbors of Mount Airy have created ALEPH: Alliance for Jewish Renewal, a network that reaches around the world with books and journals and e-mail and tapes of new songs and chants of prayer and celebration. As the face-to-face of Yavneh and the face-to-face of Pumbeditha reached across space and time to make the Talmud, so now the new villages of Jewish renewal reach out to find each other, learn from each other. On the Internet and face to face, the old and the young take time to converse and to change, to debate and to question, to proclaim and to doubt.

To sow the seeds of growth. From slavery You freed us with an outstretched arm: An arm, *zeroa*, outstretched to sow new *zera*, seed. Each question seeds new answers, and from each answer sprouts a host of questions.

# CHAPTER 12

# TO CATCH A BREATH

Through the narrow gateway of a Passover lit up by burning streets, in 1968 I caught a glimpse of Torah. In the Passover of 1985 I found a darker Torah, a gateway into death, yet also a gateway into a deeper meeting with my brother. A darkness through which I saw my life more clearly.

This is a story of my mother, a story that I share with her other son, my brother. It is, in fact, a story that we have told together. For the gate through which she walked to die opened, for us, a gateway into telling our different stories in a way that intertwined them. Through her death we became brothers, and through her death we came to write a book together about our lives together. We called it *Becoming Brothers* because it told what had kept us civil enemies throughout our lives and how we became brothers in more than our similar sets of DNA. Beloved brothers.

So the story I am about to tell is in some ways a lessening, a diminution, of the story that we told together—for the richest Torah is the story of our many stories. But the story is also my story alone, the story of my loneliness. Indeed, the first writing I did about it was alone. It was after that, that Howard and I worked together to retell the story.

For this book, I have done what once I could not have imagined doing; I have asked my brother to let me tell the story once more in my own way, my own words, some of them purely my own and some the words I had come to in dialogue with him. He said it felt a little strange to have words that I had written for our work together appear again, on their own. Yet he said "Yes." A very gentle wrestle, a very loving dance.

The story begins at the Seder of 1920, many many Seders before I was born. My mother's father, the grandfather for whom I am named,

came home for the last time to have Pesach dinner with the family—
the last meal they ever had together. Then he went back to a sanitarium, to cough out his lungs and die of tuberculosis.

For fifteen years and more, my grandmother punished God: She
refused to make a Seder full of joy in our Exodus from Egypt, the
Narrow Place, to honor the One Who turned her life into a narrow
space. When my parents insisted that the children had reached the
age where there must be a Seder, she sat with us, jaw set, eyes full of
tears. When we asked the famous questions of the evening, we did not
think—or did not dare—to ask the question that would have really
made a difference: "Why is this night different from all other nights?
On all other nights, Grandmom laughs or cries and tells old stories;
on this night, she sits silent."

"Tell it to your children on that night, saying..." But no one told the
story of her sadness. The family kept silent, and its silence constricted
the Tale of how we left the Narrow Place. It tightened the energy in a
way that made the Seder still more powerful.

But neither my grandmother's punishment of God nor my family's
silence at the Seder exorcised the demon. In 1945, still in her early
30s, my mother began to cough and cough and cough. In her teens
she had been a lively, laughing dodge ball champion, but from 1945
on, for 40 years, she could never once breathe easy.

## DON'T BREATHE A WORD

She would not go to a sanitarium: That meant to die. Fiercely, she
stayed home and lived apart. At the age of twelve, I learned to stand
in the doorway of a room I couldn't enter, to blow a kiss past bedsheets
I couldn't touch. She learned to lift a face that each week grew more
gaunt, a face we couldn't kiss.

One doctor said he didn't want her as a patient. What was the
point? She would be dead within the year.

Again, again, and again, she went away to hospitals. Once I came
to visit when every breath came as a gasp, when even an oxygen tent
could not relieve her from the endless gasping. She listened to my
groping efforts to make contact, nodded and whispered—correcting
my grammar. For she willed herself to be alive, to teach, to mother.

She willed herself to be well enough to come to synagogue when I,
and then my brother, became bar mitzvah. She willed herself to live
on one lung, when the doctors collapsed the other lung to halt the
spread of infection.

She willed herself into a remission, a cure. Then a relapse, remission again, and a cure. She willed herself to live until my brother and

I were graduated, until we married, until we had children. She lived, and she breathed. She hated rooms filled with people; they made it harder to breathe. She hated clothes that were tight; they made it harder for her to breathe. She hated an absentminded "Huh?" or "Could you repeat that?" for each extra sentence made it harder to breathe. And when she got a cold or the flu or bronchitis...she trembled.

But the rest of us? We got used to it. To the shortness of breath, and the shortness of temper, and the insistence on efficiency lest a single breath be wasted. We got used to it all, we forgot it all. We never spoke aloud the fears of childhood or of adolescence, for fear (redoubled) that if we breathed a word of them, they would depress and frighten my mother and take away her will to live. For fear that they—*we*—would kill her.

So the fears were breathed in—and never breathed out. Like carbon monoxide, they entered our blood and caught hold. The fear that she would die. The fear that she would never die, and bankrupt us. (My father held four jobs to pay the bills.) The fear that other people would find out she had TB. (In those days, it was shameful, or so she thought.) The fear that our anger would burst out and kill her. (How dare we be angry at her for getting sick?)

## WHEN ELIJAH COMES TO VISIT

One spring Friday night at Fabrangen, these fears finally came boiling out of my blood. We were getting ready for prayer just before the special Shabbat that ushers in Passover, when a "difficult" woman appeared in our midst. She could have been 32; she could have been 57. She was from Florida, had almost no money. She had heard there were jobs in New York. So she set out to find them. But her railroad-ticket money had run out in Washington.

Here she was. Could she stay in somebody's home? Until she could get on her way again?

I said yes. After all, on the eve of Shabbat, the verge of Passover, how could I say no? She might be Elijah the Prophet!—coming to share the Passover meal, coming to announce the coming of Messiah, coming in well-accustomed guise: The tired, the sick, the poor.

I said yes. And we began to chant our prayers.

But she didn't. She began to cough them. Deep, gut-wrenching coughs. Unending coughs.

My voice in the prayers began to falter and fail. I knew that cough. It was my mother's cough. My "Elijah" was coughing her lungs out. And I was about to take her home to stay with my wife, my children, myself? To cough at our Passover table?

159

My images turned inside out, upside down. Was she Elijah, come to my door, or the Angel of Death, come to smear blood on my doorpost? The thoughts I had never thought toward my mother boiled up inside me.

Terror. An ethical nightmare, and nightmares deeper than ethics.

I grasped for a solution: Stay overnight, and visit a doctor tomorrow. "No!" said "Elijah." "They said in Florida it was just a bad cold."

"No!" said my family and I. A visit to the doctor—or a ticket to New York, where we could give her the name of a social worker.

Very well, said Elijah. New York. Not a doctor.

So she set off for New York. And she did call our social-worker friend. But when the time came to meet—no "Elijah." No body, no cough, not a breath of a stir of a presence. Truly Elijah, come and gone. Bearing no name of Messiah; bearing only a harsh old message: Weigh what you owe to your own, what you owe to the stranger. Love the stranger as you love yourself: No more. No less.

Or maybe bearing Elijah's own message: Turn the hearts of the children to the parents and the hearts of the parents to the children. Turn my heart once more to my mother? Strip away the sheath of numbness, the forgotten cover that lay over the forgotten nightmare?

The next year, on the Friday night before Passover, I told the story to Fabrangen. In the middle of the tale, an old man walked into our room, then walked around the circle of people. He peered at our books, our backs, our faces. I finished the story. He walked out of the room, out of the building. He was Elijah, for sure, affirming "Elijah," for sure!

## THE BREATH IS ONE

But our hearts were hard to turn. What my mother knew best was to tough it out: If her lungs grew weaker, she could tow oxygen around in a cart. If the range of her life narrowed while her passion and curiosity for life burned still brighter, she could still pour her passion within the narrowing circle. If the world got slower and her breath still shorter, her temper could burn yet brighter.

And if I felt caught in the narrowing circle, burnt by the hotter temper, then I could do what I knew best to do: Thicken the numb sheath around my heart, look blandly at the cart of oxygen, accept her temper as a way of being.

But my heart could not keep silent. "Don't breathe a word!" said my history. But my heart would not stop sighing, in the voice Elijah heard in the midst of silent wilderness: Not thunder, not a whirlwind, but a still, small, whispering voice.

And then the whisper, barely murmuring, became for me the fullest voice of God. I am tempted to tell the story here, but I know I need to tell it somewhere else: When I explore with you the changes in the ways that I imagine and connect with God. So here let me tell the story only in a kind of whisper, just a hint. Ten years after my visit from Elijah, my Jewishness had grown from a passion into a lifepath, from a lifepath into a career, from a career into a deeper passion. Wrestling with Torah began to bring me into a murmuring conversation with the God Who dances in and out of the story.

One such time, I found myself looking at the Name God speaks at Sinai:

"YHWH." It is the Name that by tradition we are forbidden to pronounce.

Free yourself, I thought: Pronounce it.

With no vowels, it came out: "Yyyyhhhhwwwwhhhh."

It sounded like a breath. God's Name: The breath of life! No words, just the whispering, murmuring sound of a deep-drawn breath.

For years I took delight in this discovery. It changed the way I prayed, learned Torah, healed the world. Yet the heart of what had moved me I still had not discovered. I did not know it was my mother's breath I yearned for. For my mother to breathe easy once again, to draw once more a deep and even breath—that would be God for me. For each of us, I realized, the deepest Name of God arises from the depths of our own life.

How did I learn this? In my mother's dying.

In the midst of Passover, forty years late, she became in the same breath Elijah and the Messenger of Death: The herald of our freedom and the carrier of rest.

The family was regathering for Pesach, coming from across the continent. My mother prepared to welcome us as she always had, even though her lungs now left her always short of breath.

## TELLING THE TALE OF BONDAGE

But this time it didn't work. Once more, bronchitis; her doctors said she belonged once more in hospital. At first she would not go. Give up, with the family gathering once more for Pesach? Not yet, not this year. Next year, she told me when she called about the menu, I might have to do the family Seder. Once more, she tried to tough it out.

But this time...

I pause in that sentence, pause to catch my breath. Sitting here writing, I am short of breath. This story is hard work to tell.

This time...

The doctors insisted. By the time we all arrived in Baltimore, she was in the hospital. At first, it seemed just like the last time we had come to visit her in hospital, and the time before that. But my mother was in a different mood.

I came with Phyllis. We had recently decided when we were getting married, and we wanted to tell my mother. She smiled, then said she might not be able to make it. I was astounded, horrified. "But we can make arrangements for your oxygen!" She gave me her skeptic's glance and turned to talking details and plans, still teaching the grammar of how to manage life.

Plans for the Passover Seder. She had already negotiated with the hospital, to let a dozen people have the Seder in her room. "All the cooking," she breathed, gasped, "All the cooking...finished...except the knishes....Finish them....Bring the kneidlach...and the gefilte fish...and wine...."

And then, with almost no transition, plans for her death. Papers to sign. Where they were filed. What my father should do, where he should live.

And then: A kind of "testament" of clear-eyed love. Turning to Phyllis: "Arthur has a terrible temper. But at the core, he's good..." Handing over her loving knowledge of me to my lover, to draw on when the stores of our own love might dwindle.

That night, my brother Howard and his kids arrived. They found my mother full of life. The next morning, my father awoke early and fierce: "She hasn't called yet. Something's wrong. I'm calling her." He calls, and after rebuffs from the nurses finally reaches her. Says, "You sound bad." A single word, no breath wasted: "Yes." "Should I come?" "Yes."

We came. We didn't know it yet, but her lung muscles had begun to tire. Decades of pushing tons of air uphill had worn them out. But the muscles come back. She began to breathe again, but had no energy to talk. I gently rubbed her back, then stopped for a moment. She thought I had been troubled by an old scar; she hated the scars that were reminders of the pain, the defeats. She muttered ruefully, "Where they put in...the lucite balls...to hold my lung down." I said, "You have been a wonderful teacher of never giving up." She says, "I'm ready...to give up now."

My breath caught in my throat. Never had she hinted such a thing.

She told us to come back after lunch. No Seder. She was too tired. We must do our own, at home. But bring her a kneidel, a knish, a drop of wine, a sheet of matzah.

We returned after lunch. She was barely breathing. The muscles were played out. The doctors said she would die within hours if we did not authorize them to insert a respirator. The respirator, they said, would give her muscles time to recover and beat the bronchitis. My brother asked her what she wanted. No answer. We asked her, "Did you understand?" She muttered, "No. Repeat." We could not get through.

We were frightened: Once the respirator is in, no one will take it out; it will breathe her, she will not really live and breathe. We asked the floor doctor, again and again: If it does not work and we—my father, my brother and I—say to stop, will they stop? "Give us four days," he said. "And then? Will you stop?" "Yes," he says. Only later do we learn it is a lie.

So we said yes. They inserted the respirator. The oxygen reached her lungs, her blood, her brain. She reawakened, furious. No talk: The respirator made that impossible. Shook her head violently, no no no. Reached to disconnect the respirator. The doctors and nurses overpowered her. Held her arms. She turned one burning, pleading glance on my brother: Pleading, he is convinced, that he save her, free her from this narrow space, these bonds; free her to die. Sobbing, he whirled out of the room in despair and helplessness, pounded a pillow on the couch outside. The doctors give her "tranquilizers"—three times the normal dose, to knock her out.

We were distraught. Had we chosen wrong? She has always fiercely insisted on living. To her, this has meant organizing her own life. Had we conspired to deny her what to her meant living, in the guise of helping her to "live"?

She reawakened, now in the Intensive Care Unit. She needed to speak, but she who loved speech was speechless. She gestured toward her throat—mute, speechless, gagged. She tried again to disconnect the respirator. They tied down her arms. Oh, God, worse and worse!— she so much hated all restrictions on her movement!

She spelled out words into the palms of our hands, and we repeatedly failed to decipher them. It took thirty minutes before we thought of getting paper and pencil. "WRONG," she wrote. She would not give up the right to give up.

We went home to wrestle and rethink. My father was clear: Allow the chance that she will recover.

Even if this meant days of torture?

Yes.

All right: He had lived with her 55 years, it is he who would have to live without her. He was entitled. But how many days must she be tortured, if the respirator did not help her to live on her own? They said: Four days.

163

Again, the next morning: "WRONG." "Won't forgive." "Silly." "Stop."

I put it to her clearly: "If several days of this might get you back to where you were, is it okay? Will you take the chance, will you try?" A long long pause. Slowly, reluctantly, she nodded. "How long?" she scribbled. "They say four days." She wrote across the paper, "3 DAYS TOPS."

"That's why Dad decided to try," my brother said. She took my father's hand. Forgiven.

But the struggle was only beginning. "Promise," she wrote, her eyes blazing. "I promise," my father said.

And then, that morning, the hospital made it clear: The doctor on the floor was wrong. They cannot withdraw a respirator if the result will be immediate death. That would violate the law, the medical code of ethics, hospital policy. If they concluded that her problem was irreversible lung and muscle damage, they would remove her from Intensive Care, put her on a less efficient respirator, and stop monitoring her vital signs. They could not, would not, may not simply *stop*.

We were aghast. We had promised: "3 DAYS TOPS." And we might not be able to deliver on our promise.

We kept our vigil. Four times a day, for half an hour each time, we visited. I came with my kids and with Irene, my former wife. We stood around the bed together. My mother wrote, "Glad friends." Shoshana fumbled to interpret, finally said, "You're glad that Mom and Dad are friends?" She nodded. My daughter burst into tears. My mother wrote, "All," and underlined it.

Next day, Phyllis looked out the window, saying, "Here it's April 9, and snow is coming down." My mother wrote, "Mother." We all looked puzzled; my brother was frightened that she was asking how her own mother was feeling, frightened that she had forgotten: Grandmom had died just eight months before, at 97. She saw our questioning looks, wrote "Birthday." Oh! Today is her mother's birthday! Far from forgetting, she was more in touch with the family history than we were. My brother burst into tears.

And over and over, despite her agreement, she wrote, "How long?" "What day?" "Torture." "Silly." "Promise."

The doctors tried to "wean" her from the respirator, to reduce its breath-beats per minute to see if her lungs could work on their own. No. In fact, her breaths grew feebler. She was clearly failing. We talked with one of the doctors—an extraordinary woman, who acknowledged that the respirator was torture and acknowledged also that one doctor had spoken not-the-truth. She acknowledged the pain it gave us for her to carry out the ethic she believed she must carry out. Tears

164

in her eyes—the only doctor with tears in this whole story.

## TELLING THE TALE OF FREEDOM

We went home. It was clear to us all, and we said it to each other: She was dying. We saw that the doctors saw it. For the first time, we felt at peace, because we knew that she would have the peace she was ready for.

The morning of the fourth day dawned. It had been almost three days since the respirator was inserted. The doctors came to tell us that she had had an inexplicable sudden drop in blood pressure. Did we want to use heroic measures? No, we said. It was clear to us: She had said "3 DAYS TOPS," and even at the level deep beneath her mind, the level of her heart and blood, she was making sure that her decision would be carried out. She still ruled her life. And death.

The doctors came again. Although her blood pressure had picked up again, they finally accepted the truth: There was no reversing the decree, the disease. They could have forced my mother to stay alive, but they could not help her to become well. The respirator was not the temporary crutch they had hoped it would be.

So they proposed moving her and changing to the less efficient respirator. "How long do patients live that way?" we asked. "Up to a week," came the answer.

A week! Twice as long as my mother had already said was torture? Once more we took a deep breath, ready if necessary to make the hospital fulfill its earlier promise. But first we went to see her, each alone.

Howard told her that the doctors had concluded that she could not make it, that they were ready to move her out of Intensive Care. He did not specify how long it might take for her to die. She understood, she nodded, he said good-bye.

When I walked in, she was somewhere between sleep and coma. I told her I will forever see something of her intensity and passion in my daughter Shoshana. She brushed my hand so lightly I was not absolutely sure whether it was a conscious good-bye squeeze or an accident.

They moved her. Two hours later, she was dead. On the fifth day of Pesach, she had won her freedom.

I said, and I meant it, the hardest, the harshest, the curtest of all blessings, the one my grandmother would not say when God let her beloved husband die so young, so needed: "*Baruch dayan ha'emet.* Blessed is the true Judge."

My grandmother would not say it because she knew her husband's death was not true justice but a false and twisted judgment, and she would not lie. But I could say the blessing because I saw my mother's battle for her freedom. I knew that freeing her was truthful judgment.

This is the one blessing in which "YHWH," "Lord," "Yyyyhhhhwwwhhhh," the Breath of Life, does not appear. Of course.

The next morning, my brother and I faced a frightening precipice. For the past week we had worked together more closely, loved each other more deeply, heard each other more clearly, than ever in our lives. Now we had to create a funeral: We, whose religious lives and outlooks were so different; we, whose wrestle with each other was so bound up with our different senses of our mother and our father.

How to shape a funeral that would honor our mother's truth? That she would want it to be Jewish was clear. That she had no institutional connections—not even to a friendly rabbi or a once-a-year synagogue—was equally clear. I alone in my family had focused my life around Judaism. Did that make me the maven, the expert, even the "rabbi," for this moment? What would that do to my father or my brother?

Howard and I agreed that I would call Max Ticktin, my teacher, friend, and rabbi from Fabrangen. Max agreed to lead the service. But he had a suggestion: Perhaps Howard and I should each speak about what our mother had meant to us and to all the others she had touched. Better us than someone who had barely known her.

To me, that seemed perfect. I went back to Howard to propose it. "No," he said. "To you it's perfect because you know how to take what's intimate and make it public. That's how you write; that's how you speak. I can't do that. I would break down, just stand there weeping. It's too close, too intimate, for me to do.

"My closeness to her was different from yours," he went on. "Maybe you are more like her than I am. But I could talk with her. You couldn't. And she could talk with me. She *did* talk with me. I can't tell all that, and I can't talk without telling all that. So I can't talk."

For one murderous moment, a flash of hatred ran through me as I thought, "He's saying Honey loved him more than me!"

And then I had this conversation with myself:

"So what?"

"But if he says that, I ought to kill him."

"Really?"

"Well, at least I ought to hate him."

"Really?"

"Well, I do hate him!"

"Really?"

I looked for the murderous flash, to prove I hated him. But it was gone. The days of loving wrestle were still there. With a shiver of regret, almost nostalgia—"Where are you, Murder, now that I really need you?"—I turned back to my brother.

"I understand. If you can't do it, you can't. But I can, and it's what I know to do to give her honor. It's true that I can take what's intimate and say it in the world. Is that okay?"

After a long pause, he responded, "I'd feel diminished. It would look as if you were speaking for us all, as if your version were the truth. My truth of her would get left out. I know I'm choosing to leave it out, but I don't want yours there and mine not. So I wish you wouldn't speak."

"But that's not fair! That's not legitimate! You decide you won't speak, and then because you won't speak I shouldn't speak. Come on!"

"I know it's not 'legitimate.' But if you talk, I'll feel diminished."

I walked away in total pain. Pain for me, pain for him. A double bind.

To be who I fully am—in the moment out of my whole life when I most want to be my fullest self—means to speak aloud my love, my honor, my truth about my mother. But what honor would it be to my mother to make my brother feel terrible? What fulfillment of my self would it be to make my brother feel diminished? Back and forth, back and forth.

Would it be my responsibility if he made himself feel terrible? No! I thought, and for a moment I felt released. I could do what was mine to do; he would be responsible for feeling bad.

But it didn't matter. Did I want him to feel diminished? No! Did I want him to feel fully himself? Yes! Then must I take the positive steps to make that possible? Not for his sake but because I wanted it that way?—Yes, yes!— But what about my own fulfillment? Back and forth, back and forth.

I went to Phyllis. She suggested: "Ask Max to meet with all of us, to hear our stories of your mother and retell them—as our stories, not as his. It won't pretend to be a polished eulogy; it won't shimmer and flow. It will be real; it will have in it what you want to say and whatever Howard is able to say and whatever the rest of us say."

I went back to Howard. He listened, nodded. "That's fine, that's what I'd want." Me again: "But not what I want!" And for a few minutes we went through the whole thing again.

## THE TALE OF OPENING SPACE

All the while, my heart was hammering and knocking with a silent voice of its own: "You know what you're supposed to do. You're the older brother. You've been first. You even wrote about it—all that stuff about Ishmael and Isaac, and Esau and Jacob. You *know* what you're supposed to do. Give it up, give it up, give it up!" And me, in silence answering back, a voice not from my head or heart or lungs but even deeper: "I can't do it. All right, I know; but I can't do it. Why should I do it? No, don't tell me why; it doesn't matter; I can't do it. I can't."

And then an outburst, yelling at Howard. "It's not a compromise; it's not halfway, you understand? I don't want it; it's not what fits me. It fits you and not me, you understand? I don't want it, you under-stand?"

He looked at me quietly: "I understand."

And then the barrier between my two silent voices collapsed. Aloud I said: "Okay. Let's do it. Let's ask Max to collect our stories. I'll call him." And I felt solid. Not joy, not love, not sadness, not anger, not relief, not resignation. Solid. There was work to do; let's do it.

I went off to call the rabbi, asked the family to think of the stories they wanted to tell, and jotted down some of my own. Max said all right. The work was under way.

An hour later, my brother came to talk. "Would you do it? The way we said to have Max do it? Would you collect the stories and then tell them—not in your own voice but in all our voices? I'd like for you to do that."

And then I cried, and I remembered: Surrender, and space opens up. Maybe your brother will surrender back to you. (Maybe not.) Surrender, and the universe might surrender back. Surrender what you wanted: Some new path might open up. It might turn out you want the new path even more than the old one.

So that is what we did. I gathered stories, and I told them. I began with a story about my mother's love of pistachio ice cream, and I went on with stories of her passionate, curious love of all of us and all of life, and I ended with the story of her passionate love of Dad. Howard hugged me and said he felt his voice had been well spoken.

I had been the best that I could be, even better than my own best self, because the wrestle had forced me to hear the other selves as well and speak them.

"Two brothers," I said in my talk. "Two brothers from the same womb; so different. From the same womb, two different intertwining stories."

From that moment when we let our stories intertwine, when Howard heard my story and I his, there began our writing together the stories of our lives. From that moment came not only the book we made from the writing, but also a new and deeper story through the writing itself.

Thirty-one days later from that moment, I was scheduled to speak at a Mother's Day gathering. It was intended to celebrate the work of mothering the world by ending the threat that nuclear weapons pose to all children. It was near the day when the Torah says the Rainbow appeared, to celebrate the end of the Flood that had endangered all life, to celebrate the covenant between God and all that breathes upon the planet.

On every previous Mother's Day of my life, I had had a grandmother and a mother. Suddenly, I had neither. No one to call, no one to write, no one to feel mothered by.

But I had a gorgeous rainbow *tallis*, a prayer shawl big enough to cover my whole head and body with seven glorious curves of color arched across it. It was the *tallis* that my mother had sewed for me, for my fiftieth birthday.

So to begin my speaking I showed it to the crowd, explained who had made it and when she had died.

Then I put it around my shoulders, and I said the blessings:

*Blessed is the One Who frees those whose hands are tied down.*
*Blessed is the One Who sends Elijah, to turn the hearts of*
*    children and parents—to each other.*
*Blessed is the One Who mothers the world.*
*Blessed is the One Who is the Breath of Life.*

Then I covered my head with my mother's Rainbow *tallis*. I let the Breath of Life breathe into me. I listened to her breath: So calm and easy, so joyful in the brightness she had sewn for me. And then I began to speak about a future full of life.

# PART IV

# WHEN A PEOPLE WRESTLES GOD

# CHAPTER 13

# THE FEVER IN MY BONES

One night in early March of 1972, I came home from a Fabrangen meeting feeling far more exhausted than any meeting could have made me. As I fell into bed, I realized that my elbow was sore, with a red patch. A boil, I thought. I tried to fall asleep.

Four hours later, there was a red streak up my arm and my temperature was 105. I called my doctor. "That's blood poisoning," he said, his voice tense and brittle. "I'll call an all-night drugstore. Get hold of penicillin. Right now!"

For three days, I took huge doses of aspirin and penicillin. On the fourth night, I couldn't sleep at all. Every time I closed my eyes, a color movie began to unreel: Places I had been; people I had known. My life was truly running like a film before my eyes.

The film ran all the way into the present. Then a sequence from the future started. I watched myself give a sermon at a synagogue where I was due to speak in a week. And I listened to the discussion after my talk.

A question: "After your experience with the Freedom Seder, how do you feel about writing liturgies?"

My answer: "There is only one more that I would like to do: A memorial for the Holocaust and Hiroshima."

"Then why don't you write it?"

"I can't!"

And suddenly, not in the film of my future but in my most immediate present, my arm began to throb and burn as if some unimaginable heat from Hiroshima and Auschwitz were seething in it, trying to drip down through fingers that could not write it out.

And then: There welled up in me a total certainty, clear as a voice but without even the semblance of a sound, a total certainty in every vein and muscle, in every nerve and bone:

173

"If you, if anyone, can ever write the liturgy that brings their suffering to life, those very dead will live again. Their bones will join again, one to the other; their ashes will turn to flesh again; the breath of life will fill their lungs again."

Suddenly, sweat poured out from every inch of me, my arm stopped burning, I touched my forehead to find it cool. And I fell asleep.

A week later, my doctor told me that before penicillin, people died from blood poisoning. He said it used to take four days. At that burning moment on the fourth night, I would have been dying.

Two years later, I bumped into a passage of Jeremiah: "Your words burn like a fever in my bones. If I shut the doors of my mouth to keep Your word within me, turn all my strength toward keeping silent— still, I cannot stop my burning tongue."

I gasped. For an instant, my body flamed again, the words that had burned their way into my arm came back again.

I relived the quandary of that night: What could it possibly mean to write a liturgy for the Holocaust and Hiroshima? A real liturgy, not just a piece of paper but a "people's work," as the Greek of "liturgy" means.

No answers.

## TRIANGLE IN TIME

I told the story to a friend of mine. He arranged for me to have lunch with Elie Wiesel, who listened and said only: "If you keep telling the story, its heat will dissipate. If you want to do what you heard to do, keep the story within you."

No answers.

I found myself wrestling with a three-cornered pattern of disaster:

The Holocaust, the smoke and ashes of six million Jews.

Hiroshima, not for itself alone but as the deadly warning of an ever more deadly future, a world of universal holocaust where every city could become a crematorium without a chimney.

The burning of the Temple in Jerusalem, that moment which, in Jewish thought, became the moment of God's Own exile because the microcosm of God's world had been destroyed.

Each of these three points in time connects with the other two; together, they make up a triangle in time.

The first line of the triangle is the line between Hiroshima Day,

August 6, and the memorial day for the destruction of the Temple, Tisha B'Av, the Ninth of the month of Av, which always comes in late July or early August.

I was haunted by the timing. Sometimes the two dread days actually coincide. They did on the first anniversary of Hiroshima, and again on the fiftieth anniversary.

Even their precursors coincide. In Jewish tradition, exactly three weeks before Tisha B'Av falls the day on which the Babylonians breached the walls of Jerusalem. Then there was a pause of three weeks: You might almost say, a breath caught. Would the breached walls be turned into an occasion for embracing—let the walls between us fall and let us be friends!—or for destruction? The choice was for destruction.

Exactly three weeks before the bombing of Hiroshima, the very first atomic bomb was tested at Alamagordo. The walls of the atomic nucleus were breached. For three weeks, without knowing it, the world's breath was caught. Was there an alternative to bombing a city? Could a gesture of peace be made, perhaps a demonstration bombing to warn a nation that was already on the brink of collapse? No. The logic played itself out: Logic, uncontrolled by heart and spirit.

At the burning height of summer, when we might fear that the sun is scorching the world to death, we face these two warnings of the burning of the world.

Haunted by this timing, I have, year after year, tried to connect the dates. Several times, I have fasted from the one day to the other. Many times, I have added to the observance of each a little of the story of the other. There is, for example, a traditional wailing chant that is used to read aloud the Book of Lamentations on Tisha B'Av. From Rabbi Everett Gendler I learned the practice of using this soul-shaking chant to wail the laments of the children of Hiroshima—to wail them in Jewish communities on Tisha B'Av and in general communities on Hiroshima Day, explaining to each what is coming from the other.

The second line of the triangle is the one between the Holocaust and Hiroshima. They are certainly not identical, nowhere near it; but they echo and multiply each other:

Multiply modern dehumanizing propaganda times modern annihilating weaponry.

Multiply modern all-encompassing administrative technology times modern all-consuming physical technology.

Multiply the instantaneous destruction of a city times the twelve-year destruction of a people.

Multiply them, and you achieve the Doomsday System to incinerate the earth.

Multiply them, and you achieve distortions of the global weather system that can heat the prairies, melt the ice, kill the plankton, rip the weave of earthly life—and so create more human cancers, immune-system collapses, infertility, and swiftly mutating drug-resistant diseases.

The third line of the triangle, by connecting the Destruction of the Temples by Babylon and Rome with the Nazi Holocaust, connects two disasters of the Jewish people and two possibilities of its rebirth.

Tisha B'Av symbolizes how first the attractive aspect of Hellenism, with its new science and its new technologies of organization, weakened the intellectual and economic patterns of biblical Judaism, and how its destructive side then militarily shattered the biblical world. In an analogous way, Yom HaShoah symbolizes how first the attractive aspect of Modernity weakened the intellectual and economic world of Rabbinic Judaism, and then its destructive face physically shattered the Rabbinic world by carrying out the Holocaust.

Just as the destruction of the Temple confirmed that it was necessary to create the Talmud and Rabbinic Judaism, so the Holocaust confirms that we must create a renewed Judaism.

Such a Judaism will be shaped by the whole people—women as well as men, the Jewishly learned as well as those learned in other arenas, gay as well as heterosexual, converts as well as those born Jewish, those who live throughout the world as well as those who live in the Land of Israel. In short, it will be a "whole-earth, whole-people Judaism"—Holistic Judaism.

So our generation shares shattering and rebirth with the generation of Tisha B'Av. In that, we are alike.

In another way, however, we are profoundly different. The Rabbis taught that the destruction of the first and second Temples resulted from the sins of the Jewish people. We were in a responsible position, governing ourselves, and we acted irresponsibly. But few of us apply that way of thinking to the Holocaust. In Eastern Europe we did not govern ourselves, we were not allowed to be in a responsible position. A government in which Jews had never had much power or legitimacy became abominably destructive. Others, not ourselves, stood by irresponsibly. On Tisha B'Av, we assess and criticize ourselves. On Yom HaShoah, we assess and criticize the world.

Some Jews have said the Holocaust should be mourned on Tisha

B'Av. The wisdom of the folk has opposed collapsing the two into one. Precisely because I think the two situations were profoundly different, I think they need to be remembered at different times and in different ways. I think the folk is right.

## BETWEEN THE FIRES

In all three corners of the triangle, there are flames and fire. The fever that could consume the world. What dream, what healing potion of a life relived, could cool those fires?

In the saga of Abraham, the Torah tells an eerie story of two fires. Between those fires, the wandering Abram—not yet Abraham, not yet our forebear—experiences the Covenant that stills his doubts and fears.

Abram has come in spiritual agony, fearful that for him and Sarai there will be no next generation. At God's command, Abram places the divided bodies of several sacrificed animals in two rows. They flame up in a "smoking furnace." He stands between these fires, and there falls upon him a "thick darkness." He slips into a profound trance.

In it he becomes a partner in the covenant of the generations: He and Sarai will have seed, more numerous than the stars and the grains of sand, and they will live in the land bounded by the Jordan and the Sea.

God and Abram have created what from a much later perspective we can see is a kind of "Shabbat in space," rather than a Shabbat in time. The Shabbat in time that we know is also bounded by two fires: In one direction, the candles that begin Shabbat; in the other direction, the Havdalah candle that ends Shabbat. God and Abram kindle these two fires on each side of him, and Abram lives in the trance between them. What makes this space into a Shabbat-space is that in it, Abram experiences and accepts the Dark of Mystery.

Shabbat is the emblem and the practice of Mystery. In it we recognize that although we may think we know exactly what to do next and may feel driven to do it, in fact we do *not* know what comes next. For in life there is a mysterious element. And so on Shabbat we honor this truth by doing nothing, and celebrate the not-knowing with joy, not fear or anger. From our plunge into this mystery we learn new paths.

Abram lets the mysterious darkness come into himself. He rests— not merely pausing, but letting the Mystery absorb him. So there wells up in him the covenant that extends through time to future generations. Since this covenant includes the promise of a holy space—the

177

Land that is infused with Shabbat—he receives this "Shabbat" in space rather than in time.

How does this speak to the meaning of the Holocaust? *We* are the generation that stands between the fires—behind us the smoke and flame that rose from Auschwitz, before us the nightmare of a flood of fire and smoke that could turn our planet into Auschwitz. Before us is the nightmare of the Bomb, before us is the nightmare of global heating: The nightmares that one or another fire of our own kindling could consume us.

We come, like Abram, fearful that there may be no next generation.

What will transform the fire that lies before us?

What will turn it into a light that enlightens rather a blaze that consumes? What will make possible the covenant of generations yet to come?

The first teaching of this story is to see the Holocaust as both unique and not-unique: To see its fire reflected in a giant mirror that could dwarf even its unprecedented horror. To see ourselves living not *after* the fire, but *between* the fires. And to see a profound connection between them, not mere accident.

The second teaching of the story is to make this time between the fires into a time of Shabbat: A time of affirming and celebrating Mystery, a time of pausing from modernity and letting a new path emerge from the mysterious darkness.

What does it mean to experience and connect the two fires?

Both flame up from the dark sparks of modernity, struck on the granite face of History by the dark side of modernity. There are two ways to talk about this: One uses God-language; the other, History-language. Let us start with the second, the one that modern people are used to, and then see whether we learn something more from talking the language of God

Over the millennia, the human race learns and empowers itself. Learns to organize larger and larger societies, more and more complex patterns. Learns to make itself, and then learns it is remaking itself. It breaks away from the traditions of its past and decides that there are no mysteries to be celebrated, only ignorances to be conquered.

The human race creates modernity. It learns the workings of the planets, the stars, the Galapagos turtles, DNA, the proton, the id, the working class, the historical dialectic. It reconnects the two supercontinents. Abolishes smallpox. Sets foot on the moon, makes deserts bloom, births five billion people, brings down the hydrogen-fusion center of the stars to burn the surface of the earth.

Along the way, as a byproduct, it makes possible the Holocaust. Before modernity, there could be pogroms—but no Holocaust. Only a modern bureaucracy, only telephones and radios, only railroad trains, only Zyklon B could make an Auschwitz possible.

## BURSTS OF DIVINITY

But why were Jews the target of this runaway modernity? In the language of modernity, we can say that history put the Jews of Eastern Europe into the most vulnerable position possible when confronting a human race that was drunk on its new-made "modern" power. The Jews were a stateless people. A non-military people. A *prototype people.*

What is it Elie Wiesel says? That in the face of nuclear annihilation the whole earth is Jewish—like the Jews who faced the Holocaust.

Why is everyone like the Jews (say I)? Because now *we are all, like the Jews of Eastern Europe, stateless persons.* Because in the face of Planetary Auschwitz Camp I, each so-called nuclear super-power had no power to protect its people. It had only the power to build Planetary Auschwitz Camp II. To protect people who had become defenseless, stateless persons, it had only the power to make them yet more defenseless, still more stateless.

Not only does the H-bomb turn us all into stateless persons but so do the chemicals that decimate the ozone layer, the automobiles that choke the planet with carbon dioxide, and the deforestation that wipes out the trees that breathe in carbon dioxide and breathe out oxygen.

The holy Jewish people, the stateless people, the people who had only the Talmud for a Constitution and rabbis for police: They died the soonest. But they point the way for all of us—unless.

And that is the crucial question: "Unless" what?

We have been talking the language of modernity. This language is necessary, but not sufficient. If the Holocaust Past and the Holocaust Yet-to-Come are cancers of modernity, then some other language that encompasses and transcends modernity is necessary. I propose that this language is God-language. But not the old God-language. It is God in a new key, with a new Name. For the *old* God-language was itself transcended, reduced, relativized, by the leap of modernity.

The Hasidic Rebbe of Chernobyl gave us a hint, two hundred years ago. He taught that we must see the world as God. True, the God Who is the world is veiled in robes of God so as to appear to be material. But those robes are only a disguise for the truth: *Alz iz Gott. All is God.* Our job is to unwrap the veil to dis-cover that our history is God, our biology is God, our everything is God.

In this way of speaking, the Nazi Holocaust and the Bomb and other forms of technology gone berserk are byproducts of the Divinization of the most highly conscious part of this "everything"—the human race. The Holocaust and the Bomb and global warming are byproducts of a halfway step into the Chernobyler Rebbe's teachings—the half-step that treats only a certain limited sort of technological wisdom as Divine, and stops short of treating all life as aspects of God.

It was this half-step on the Chernobyler Rebbe's pathway that brought us the meltdown that shattered his town, Chernobyl. To the teaching that asserted, "All matter is Spirit, and should with joy be celebrated as Spirit," technology answered. "All matter is energy, and can be turned back into energy." And so the meltdown.

Even the Holocaust—it is all right to tremble as you read this, for I am trembling as I write it—even the Holocaust was an outburst of light. Those who say we cannot blame God for the Holocaust are only partly right: It was the overflow of God, the outbursting of light, the untrammeled, unboundaried outpouring of Divinity, that gave us Auschwitz and may yet consume the earth.

Catch your breath for a moment, pause with me to take a long, long view.

Start back, long before the Holocaust. Imagine the Infinite, Unutterable God Who stood outside the world, but let a spark of Godness flare up not *into* the world but *as* the very world itself. As the spark grew, flamed, it lit the first thin twigs of life and then of human consciousness.

Over millennia of slow human history, the spark became a glowing presence. It became not merely an aspect of God, but the knowledge, the *awareness*, that it was an aspect of God. God became Self-reflective. We learned to sense God, the Presence: Hovering among us, but not only among us. Dancing within us, but not only within us.

And then, in the burst of light that is the modern age, the coals burst into flame. Powers once felt to be Divine flowed into human beings: The power to make a revolution (it was God Who made the Exodus from Egypt). The power to destroy all species and to create new species. Flame by flame, the human race in the modern age incorporated into itself the powers that we once called Divine.

## CANARIES IN THE MINE

Now let us ask again in this God-language what we asked before in secular language: Why the Jews?

The God Who chose us from outside history at Sinai is still choosing us from inside history. We are God's canary-people: The people God sends down the mine shaft first, to test whether the air breathes revelation or is full of carbon monoxide. If we keel over....Now God knows, we all know: The air is indeed heavy with poison.

So: Was the Holocaust inevitable? Were the Nazis God's own Arm, in a paroxysm not of punishment—not "for our sins"— but of untrammeled power striking down its holy victim? Did God forget to put on *t'fillin* one morning and the unbound Arm of the Almighty...?

Wait a minute, you may be saying, *damn* your midrashic poetry. Are you saying the babies and the bubbes died because God was coming deeper into the world? How good can such a God be?

*Very* good, I say; but not totally good.

*Very* good, despite and because of the evidence of the Holocaust, because it was the surge of God-power to do good in the world that also made it possible to do such enormous bad. And *very* good because the teachings from God and about God taught—and still teach—how to prevent the Holocaust. And *very* good because the teachings left us free to choose.

But not *totally* good. For if God's Own Self were totally good, there never would have been a need for any aspect of God other than the Unutterable, the Unending. Pure Holiness would have been enough. Pure Infinite Holiness felt unsatisfying, incomplete, to the Holiness Itself—or there would never have been a world at all, never anything but clones of God, never an aspect of God wrapped in robes of God.

Auschwitz was not inevitable. But the Divine Insurge made it very hard to avoid. The looming Planetary Holocaust is not inevitable, but the Divine Insurge is making it very hard to avoid. Indeed, it is a little less hard to avoid because we have already experienced the Nazis. The fact that our "canary-people" keeled over is one of the weightier rocks that we can roll into the path of the juggernaut. Maybe the most we can hope to gain from Auschwitz is not perfect peace and security for the State of Israel, not the end of anti-Semitism as a Christian dogma, and not the Messiah, but just the minimum: Never again.

I do not mean Meir Kahane's "Never again the Jews." That is easy to refrain from doing. Why bother with the Jews again? Who needs to prove that *that* is possible? But *"never again, not the whole earth,"* now *that* remains to be proved. The Universal Auschwitz is an eternal monument still waiting to be erected by some Super-Hitler who will not even mind that no one will remain to be horrified by his monument. So "Never again" as a warning to prevent such a Super-Hitler may remain as the one usable product of the Holocaust.

I am not saying that God sent the Holocaust and murdered the

Jews *in order to* warn the planet. I say, instead, that God—and only God—made the Holocaust immensely possible. But God also made the Holocaust avoidable. And we humans made our choice.

If we can learn from the Holocaust not to destroy the earth, then we could have learned from the murder of Abel not to do the Holocaust.

Why did Abel die? Because, as we have seen, Cain could not bear to talk with him. Because they had not learned to pause and reflect on their experience, each to draw on his own reflection in his brother's eyes. They had not learned the connection between our knowledge of each other and our knowledge of the Mystery. Because they were caught in the aftermath of Eden: Work-work-work-work until you die. Exhaust yourself. That is the world that Martin Buber calls "I-It," in which everything is a thing, even your brother. It is Shabbat that makes possible "I-Thou." Shabbat comes into the world to reverse the curse of Eden.

From all this, the teaching is *to pause.* To make Shabbat. To put a loving limit on the unbridled God-energy bursting into the world. Just as God needed to pause after six days of Creation in order to seal the acts of making with a non-act of not-making, so, too, do we.

The modern era, with its works of production, must pause and make Shabbat if the very brilliance of its productivity is not to burn up the earth. It must celebrate Mystery instead of trying to conquer it. It must learn from Mystery that the dark is light enough; that it is joyful, not frightening.

Why is the celebration of Mystery crucial? It is not that Super-Hitler will necessarily come as Hitler came, with deadly, murderous intent. The idolatry of death may come this time not with deliberate intention, but by putting into place a potentially lethal system—and then insisting that we can keep it totally under control. *No* mistakes, *never* a mistake. *All* is known, *all* is controlled. The total rejection of Mystery.

We, the human race, have during our history painted a number of extraordinary pictures. The most recent, perhaps the most extraordinary, of these pictures was completed more than a generation ago, but we kept on painting the same canvas. In our very effort to make the painting still more beautiful, we have added brush-strokes that smear it. Hiroshima was a brush-stroke too many. The Holocaust was a hundred brush-strokes too many.

The painting is now marred and on the verge of ruination. We must take it off the easel. We must recognize that *we do not know* what to do next, we must celebrate that mystery, stop doing, make Shabbat, and find a clean canvas. *Then* we will hear the new teaching from within us. Only then will we uncover what to do. Only then will a new painting emerge from deep within us.

For we are the generation that stands between the fires.

## THE LITURGY AT LAST

As I heard and felt this over and over again, I began to see the liturgy that my fever had burned into my soul:

There are two parts. In the first, everyone stands between two rows of torches: Large candles, flaming almost out of control. Between these fires, which echo the very fires between which Abram stood to receive the Covenant, we all recite together:

*We are the generation*
*that stands*
*between the fires:*
*Behind us the flame and smoke*
*that rose from Auschwitz and from Hiroshima;*
*Before us the nightmare of a Flood of Fire,*
*The flame and smoke*
*that could consume all earth.*
*It is our task to make from fire*
*not an all-consuming blaze*
*But the light in which*
*we see each other fully.*
*All of us different,*
*All of us bearing*
*One Spark.*
*We light these fires*
*to see more clearly*
*that the earth and all*
*who live as part of it*
*are not for burning.*
*We light these fires*
*to see more clearly*
*the rainbow*
*in our many-colored faces.*
*Blessed is the One within the many.*
*Blessed are the many who make one.*

And then those present divide into two groups that turn to face each other: All who are thirteen and older on one side, all who are under thirteen facing them. First the elders and then the younger generation recite, in Hebrew and in English, the very last passage of the

183

last of the Prophets, Zechariah:

*Hinei, anokhi*
*sholai'akh lakhem*
*et Eliya haNavi,*
*lifnai ba'yom YHWH*
*hagadol v'ha'nora.*
*V'heyshiv lev avot al banim*
*v'lev banim al avotam,*
*pen avo v'hikayti*
*et ha'aretz khayrem.*

*Here! I will send you*
*Elijah the Prophet*
*Before the coming*
*of the great and terrible day*
*of YAHH, the Breath of Life.*
*And he shall turn the heart*
*Of parents to children*
*And the heart of children to their parents.*
*Lest I come and*
*Smite the earth*
*With utter destruction.*

When each of the two generations has recited this, they recite in unison the following:

*Here! I myself am coming*
*As Elijah the Prophet*
*Before the coming*
*of the great and terrible day*
*of YAHH, the Breath of Life.*
*And I shall turn the heart*
*Of parents to children*
*And the heart of children to their parents.*

If we see each other this clearly, we can make where we stand into a place of Shabbat. We can, like Abram, receive the Covenant of the Generations: There *will be* future generations, despite our deep dread that it will end with us. And the future generations of all humanity will live in the land that lies between the rivers and the ocean of space: All earth.

If we do *not* see the two fires in relation to each other, then the fire behind us will lose all meaning, and the one that is yet to come will consume us.

Between the fires is the place of thick darkness, of impenetrable mystery. Will we celebrate this Mystery and live? Or scorn it—and die?

# CHAPTER 14

# THE NIGHTMARE AND THE WRESTLE

What does it mean for the entire people "Yisrael" to wrestle God as Jacob did? Jacob won a path into the future by wrestling with the nightmare of his past; how does an entire people wrestle with such memories of nightmare?

For many grownups, a comforting memory is that of waking from a suffocating nightmare to be embraced by a loving parent and told a calming bedside story. On two occasions in its history, the Jewish people has felt itself rescued by God from a nightmare of misery and despair.

One of those moments became the Jews' central mythic experience of trust and hope and the Parent's love: The great journey of the Exodus. By walking the path of sacred festivals each year, we live again the comforting tale our Parent walked us through, from slavery to the spiral of the fruitful seasons, flocks and fields and orchards in the Land of Israel.

The other moment became the tale of Hanukkah, when hopelessness turned to victory and fear of darkness became the miracle of light.

But other nightmares did not end in loving arms. There were centuries of exile, nightmares of death; stories that bespoke not a confident nursing at God's breast but millennia of wailing to be welcomed at the table.

Such are the stories of the Temple destroyed, the Six Million murdered. Even the dark and bloody jokes of Purim bespeak the kind of laughter that is a cover story for the choked-back tears. How did the Jewish people transcend these woeful memories? How do we, today, wrestle with our collective nightmares?

It is Tisha B'Av, a blazing August night in Washington. Once again, we are in mourning: The Holy Temple has been burned, the people shattered. Already, by midnight, we are a little thirsty and a little grumpy, though it is only four hours into our twenty-four-hour fast from food and water, from washing, making love, wearing leather. Together we have wailed and chanted Eikhah, the Book of Lamentations on the first destruction of the Temple. We are sitting on the floor. The room is full of memorial candles. Our Holy Place has been destroyed, the whole People of Israel is in mourning. It is as if every family has had a death. Or as if the whole People has died, and we are our own ghosts sitting shiva for ourselves.

We in Fabrangen have tried hard for several years to experience Tisha B'Av in its depth, to grapple with the suffering.

One year we spent an entire night and day on the steps of the United States Capitol. As its Roman dome weighed us down, made us feel like grasshoppers in the Roman shadow, we handed out leaflets about the Vietnam War. "What the Roman Empire did to old Judaea, the American Empire is doing now to Vietnam…As Jews, we remember and protest…As then they sowed the land with salt so that no crops would grow there, our government now sows Vietnam with chemicals so that the forests will die…As Jews, we remember and protest."

Another year, we picketed on the steps of the Soviet Embassy, demanding freedom for Soviet Jews. Even on this solemn day, there was a dark humor in the moment. As we stood just outside the Embassy door, a Russian guard appeared.

"You go away," he shouted, "or I call police."

"Strange," I said, full of the 1960s rage against hypocrisy. "Strange that you socialists would call the capitalist police!"

"Makes no difference," he yelled. "This private property. You go or I call police!"

My mouth fell open. "This private property"? Now that was "emes"—truth, real truth, no truer truth.

The Russian guards called the American cops. When they arrived, we rang the Soviet doorbell in a panic, wanting to deliver our demand for freedom before we had to leave. The buzzer sounded; the door swung open. As we were about to walk in, a cop yelled: "Don't go! It's their territory, they could hold you forever." So I tossed our placards and letters on the floor, turned to leave. But the cop grabbed me. "You're under arrest!" he said. My mouth fell open again. "For what?" I asked. "Don't know," he said. "Wait here."

He went inside, where he had just warned us not to go. A minute later, he came out, triumphant. "Littering in a public place," he said, brandishing our placards. Off to jail.

Russians, Americans, Romans. All the same. Cops and armies. All the same. Tisha B'Av and the dark humor of Purim, not all the same but tangled up. Sometimes they kill you; sometimes they jail you; sometimes you win. Sometimes you need to wail; sometimes to make a shattering noise, guffaw and giggle. Sometimes the laughter is just a cover story for the unshed tears. Or screams of rage.

Another year, another Tisha B'Av. The regular citywide service seemed so perfunctory and staid that we decided to wear white shrouds and carry candles, stand in two rows outside the synagogue door so people would have to walk between us to go in. They shuddered, turned their eyes away. At least we had touched them with a shiver from the ashes. We made them see: This was about mass death.

## FOR OUR SINS?

But then came a year we had chosen to gather on our own. No effort to change the world or other Jews. Tonight we were together, alone, by ourselves, in our own space. We let ourselves experience Eikhah itself, with no adornments. "Alas, women eat their own fruit, their newborn babes."

"Oh, God!" says one of us. "What a horrifying metaphor!" Says someone else, "What makes you think it was a metaphor?" A long pause. The destruction of the Temple is no longer far away. It is like a holocaust, it was a holocaust. And yet the Book of Lamentations blames the Jews! "Our sins..." we say.

"Do we blame the Jews of Europe for the Holocaust?"

The question is met with a unanimous moan of horror. We put the question aside, not to bury it but to come back when we have lived with it a little.

We start reading the midrash on Eikhah. Seven hundred years after Eikhah was written, the rabbis face the second destruction of the Temple and express their thoughts and feelings as they comment on the Book of Lamentations about the first destruction.

One aspect of their thought is that once again they blame the Jewish people. The rabbis say that Roman wrath came down upon the people because some Jews went to Rome with lying stories about other Jews. So it was their "causeless hatred" for each other, the jealousy and strife where there should have been community, that ruined them.

So once more the question has surfaced. Once again we are struck silent, not because the history seems implausible, but because of the tone of its telling. Once again the oppressor is hardly blamed, once again it is the victims who are criticized.

Again the Holocaust rises in our throats. Do we blame the victims? No! Who could bear to blame those innocents? But then somebody says, "I blame them. Sheep to the slaughter. They didn't fight back. They let it happen. That's blame. "

The deeper this sinks in, the more agonized the faces. One of us whispers, "I used to believe that. When I was a kid, I wouldn't learn Yiddish because I thought those people were disgusting. So stupid, so weak. Now the more I know, the less I believe it. They weren't sheep. They resisted with guns, with prayers, with songs, with Yiddish. Whatever they had. Someday, somehow, we are going to have to rip that 'sheep to the slaughter' business out of our guts. It is the ultimate Jewish self-hatred."

Silence. You can see guts churning, faces twisting. At first, we thought we couldn't believe it was our fault, but now we know that some aspect of our selves can't help believing it. Can't help blaming ourselves.

Except that we *can* help it. The deepest victimization is that we, the victims, blame ourselves for being victims. Once we start staring that self-blame in the face, we begin to free ourselves from being victims.

Was the victim role what Tisha B'Av did to us? Was the religious tradition really to blame, as some Jews say, for the "exile" mentality, the victim role? For wasn't this the heart of the exile mentality, wasn't this the cancer we carried into Exile—that we were to blame for our own disasters, that the God we love is scourging us for our own good? Is there any way for us to blame our oppressors and still be faithful to the God of the tradition?

"No, it's not the same," says one of us. "When we say we brought the Temple down through our own causeless hatred, we are saying we were an active force. Self-destructive, but active. When we say about the Holocaust that we went like 'sheep to the slaughter,' that blames us for being what we were not—passive."

"Right," said somebody else. "When the Temples fell, the Jewish people ruled themselves. When the Holocaust came, we didn't. The tradition is telling us that if you fall into disaster when you had the power to act differently, then blame yourselves. Correct yourselves. At such a moment, self-pity will finish you off. Self-correction takes strength; self-correction will give you new strength.

"But if you fall into disaster when you have no power to shape your own destiny, you made no mistake, unless you surrendered your power willingly. If you have been stripped of your power, then blame the oppressors. For us, the psychology of the Book of Esther is right: Fury against Haman, no blaming ourselves."

There are a few nods around the circle. No chorus of acceptance, but a reluctant, troubled agreement. It's an opening crack in the wall, but hardly a path of delight.

Somebody else makes it still harder: "Wait, let's be clear. We can use Esther instead of Lamentations so long as we face backward to the Holocaust. But that's only part of our history. Now we have our own State, we have power again, we rule our own lives. So if you're right—the warnings of Eikhah speak to us too, especially now. The Holocaust wasn't our fault. But if Israel gets hurt, it's partly our fault, because we had the power to do something different. Of course, now that we have Eikhah to teach us, maybe we don't have to wait for disaster. Maybe we don't have to praise God for correcting us afterward. Maybe we can correct ourselves before the scourge falls." Some more nods. But still...

"That feels like a piece of an answer, but I want more. I'd like to learn more about how the rabbis responded. Remember, when Eikhah was put in the Bible everyone knew the exile had lasted only seventy years. Redemption had come. That might have made it easier to see Babylon as God's scourge—a temporary corrective. But when the rabbis collected the midrash, it had already been about two hundred years since Rome had destroyed the Temple and sowed salt on the land. There was no glimmer of redemption in sight. So the problem ran deeper."

Nods again. The room is tense. This is no academic matter, it affects how we feel about ourselves as Jews: *Why* be Jews? And as covenanters with God: *What* God? Even more, it affects how we feel about our most primordial selves, bodies intertwined with identities, selves linked to bodies that can be ripped away in ultimate pain. I know three women and two men—American-born, not refugees—who unexpectedly found themselves feeling like Holocaust victims when they had to have operations in hospitals. The machines that were to cure them looked like tools of torture. I know a woman who, when the police sealed off part of a protest demonstration against the Vietnam War, said at once, "They're taking us to the gas chambers."

To be vulnerable, to be a victim, to be physically invaded or physically controlled is to be on the edge of the Holocaust. Our bodies remember Auschwitz even when our minds do not.

## BIRTHING MESSIAH

Tense and shaky, we turn back to the midrash on Eikhah. A strange story leaps up at us from the midrash. A Jew is plowing his field when his ox begins to bellow. A passing Arab calls to him, "Unyoke your ox and mourn, Jew, for your Temple is destroyed." The Jew unyokes his ox and asks, "How do you know?" The Arab answers, "From the bellow of your ox."

The ox bellows again and the Arab says, "Hitch up your ox again, Jew, and celebrate; for the Messiah is born!" The Jew decides to find out whether all this is true and sets out to Jerusalem. When he arrives he learns that, indeed, the Temple has been destroyed. To test the other half of the prophecy, he makes some baby clothes and peddles them from door to door. One woman admires the clothes, but won't buy any. Instead she bewails her young son, who has been carried off.

"Carried off, ma'am?"

"Yes, he was born on the day the Temple was destroyed. Later he was carried away by a whirlwind."

So the Jew concludes that the Messiah had, indeed, been born on the day the Temple was destroyed, and hidden away till the time of his coming is decided. "But why," says he, "did I need to learn this from an Arab? For surely Isaiah tells us, 'Lebanon shall fall by a mighty one, And there shall come forth a shoot out of the stock of Jesse.' 'Lebanon' means the Temple made from Lebanon cedars, and the shoot from Jesse's stock is the Messiah out of King David's house—for Jesse was David's father. So I could have learned it from Isaiah."

A silence. So this is where the tradition begins that Messiah will be born on Tisha B'Av! From the moment of our worst despair will grow the moment of our highest hope.

"But notice that he *does* learn it from an Arab. From the Arab, from his own direct experience, and from the Bible. As if the Messiah won't come until we can learn all three ways: From our enemy the Arab, from our own lives, and from the tradition."

A murmur of agreement, then a growl. "But what does it teach us to *do*? It's all very well to say that our hope must grow from despair, but hope only makes a difference if we act on it."

As we kept reading, we reached a story that tells about action, a story whose energy stands our hair on end.

This midrash begins with the death march of the Jews from Jerusalem to Babylon. So terrible was the suffering, say the rabbis, that one by one the Patriarchs and Prophets rise up before God. Abraham, Isaac, Jacob, then Moses, and Jeremiah, then the Torah herself, and one by one the very letters of the alphabet. Each confronts God:

"You made a covenant with me for all of them! Now You have broken Your Word, broken the covenant. You have broken Your Law!"

One by one, they demand that God annul this punishment and renew the covenant with Israel.

To each, God says, "I am a jealous God, and you were whoring after strange gods. I'll have none of it. Stop piling up your dirges in My Face."

Finally, our mother Rachel arises. She says, "You're a jealous God? I understand. I was a jealous woman, jealous of my sister who was given to Jacob, although he was to be my husband. So jealous that I knew beforehand that my father was going to do that trick, and I gave Jacob signals he could use to tell whether it was me or Leah in the marriage bed. I was a very jealous woman.

"But, when the moment came, I couldn't go through with it. I realized how shamed my sister would be, how ruined her life would be, if Jacob threw her from her marriage bed.

"So I told her the signals. I even hid beneath the bed and spoke aloud in my sister's stead, so that Jacob would think it was me he had married. My jealousy had vanished, because I loved my sister.

"I was jealous of a real, flesh-and-blood sister, and You, God, are jealous of what? Empty idols, sticks and stones! For such a jealousy You will destroy Your people?"

Then, and only then, the *Rebbono Shel Olam* reversed His decree. Maybe at that moment, Her decree.

## THE REDEMPTION OF GOD

This midrash does not accept the Destruction as punishment for Israel's sins. This midrash stands on the barest edge of faith. When the rabbis wrote it, two hundred years or so after the destruction of the Second Temple, they were remembering that Rachel got what she demanded. The people were redeemed only seventy years after the first destruction. The rabbis were saying to God, "It was only seventy years the last time: Well? Well?"

At last we connect. Here is a post-Holocaust theology from the rabbis. It is one we can learn from. It does not deny God, nor does it submit to God. It is Rachel's Godwrestle. I remember—it is more than remembering, it bursts in on me—that Rachel has had her own Godwrestle with her sister. Maybe Rachel's wrestle was to turn her jealousy to love? Maybe when Rachel wrestles with her sister Leah in jealousy, her struggle becomes a Godwrestle precisely because she turns from jealousy to love? For it is precisely her love for Leah that becomes her ground from which to challenge God, dare God, threaten God.

When the rabbis describe Rachel's ultimate struggle with God, they say that the challenge begins with the Fathers. They say that even those building blocks of the universe, the letters of the Torah, challenge God. But the story lets not all the Fathers, but a mother and a sister win.

The challenge that transforms God does not cite the legal formula of the covenant, as the Fathers do. It is Rachel facing God with a human model of sisterly love. Can God live up to that model? Can God live up to the Image of God that is stamped upon Rachel? The midrash asserts that if we can challenge God in anger and with love, we can win redemption.

Why does this midrash speak so powerfully to us? Maybe because it comes directly from a sense of terrible suffering, unmediated by the calculation of sin or the calculation of Messiah. Maybe because Rachel's very body—the marriage bed and sexual union—are at stake, and this connects with our unconscious sense that our very bodies are still in danger from the Holocaust. Maybe because it honors a human challenge to a cruel God. Maybe because it sees a human model—Rachel's effort to make her love prevail over her jealousy—as the stimulus to God's change.

But even Mother Rachel is not quite enough for us. For we can see even deeper into the abyss than the rabbis. How deep is the abyss of exile? Those who edited the Book of Lamentations knew for sure the exile could be ended; indeed, *had* been ended, when Israel turned from its sinful path. The rabbis, six hundred years later, trembled that exile might never end. But in our day, the fear runs even deeper: That we could return from exile and yet carry exile with us.

For we *have* returned from exile and yet carried exile with us. In the afterglare of the Holocaust, the cries of the Jewish people rose to Heaven—and most of the world responded by permitting, encouraging, protecting the emergence of the state of Israel. We can almost hear the Jewish people pleading with God as Rachel pleaded: Walking God through Auschwitz and reminding God of every act of love and comradeship in the midst of nightmare, as Rachel reminded God how her sisterly love prevailed over jealousy. We can almost hear God's remorseful decree, granting that the tender shoots of early Jewish settlement in Palestine become the sturdy trunk of Israel.

But a generation later, we see not the coming of Messiah but a very human state. We see not a "Jewish state," but a state that is struggling to know what "Jewish" means. We see not redemption, but self-determination. Almost all Jews believe that self-determination is a good and useful responsibility for the Jewish people. Most Jews have acted as if self-determination were enough. But some of us keep searching for the next step forward a step beyond self-determination, a step toward redemption.

But maybe self-determination *is* enough. The line between victim and victor is so thin. Maybe all we can do is cross that line, not walk it. Maybe the state of Israel *is* the answer to the Holocaust: Not victimization, but victory.

Maybe the only answer to our sense of being vulnerable is to sheathe ourselves in toughness. Maybe out of the search for love, the search for redemption, comes only wounding and death.

"How can you believe in God, after the Holocaust? Of course if you keep on bothering with God, Rachel's stance is the only one that's decent. But why bother at all? What kind of loving God could have permitted the Holocaust? Especially a 'loving' God Who is supposed to have covenanted specially with the Jewish people! The Holocaust makes a mockery of the Torah. Maybe the rabbis who imagined Rachel could not imagine a world without God, but we can."

Slowly faces turn, bodies shift. One voice, slowly: "But how can we *not* believe in God, after the Holocaust? If there is no God, then what was evil about the Holocaust? If the Image of God is not in every human being, why is any human being of infinite worth, not just a tool or an object? Is there any difference between saying human beings must always be treated as ends, not means, and saying 'God'? Like it or not, we *need* a loving God, or some ultimate loving equivalent, to resist the Holocaust."

"But we're not talking about what we need or what we like, even to resist the Holocaust. We're talking about what's true, what's real. Is there anything basic in the universe that says that humans are of infinite worth, not to be debased?"

## CHOOSE!

The question stirs a story to my memory, a kind of Holocaust midrash in miniature. Moses our teacher asks God how generations after him will use the Torah. God shows him Akiba, teaching students with delightful, playful seriousness, interpreting for new/old paths of life even the crowns on the letters of the Torah, saying that his teachings are not really new but were already revealed to Moses who had brought the Torah long ago from God.

Moses then asks God what reward such delightful Torah teaching brings. God grimly shows him Akiba tortured to death by Roman soldiers, his flesh torn from his bones by red-hot metal combs. Moses gasps and questions, "This is the reward for loving Torah?" God answers, "Be silent, for such is my decree. Be silent, or I return the world to void and chaos."

We can hear this story telling us that God is infinitely potent, infinitely inscrutable, infinitely arrogant. Or we can hear it saying that even God stands on the knife-edge of despair. "I did not torture Akiba," says God. "You humans did. Would you have me prevent it? Then you are not free. But I created the world only, only, only, so that you would be free. Free from me. Free to face me. Free to debase me. If you challenge this, I can only return the world to chaos. Perhaps this is the better choice? Choose, Moses!"

And Moses, having challenged God, now chooses to be silent. Better Akiba's death than the world a wilderness empty of will, choice, meaning.

What is real and true about the universe is that any approach to good involves, requires, imposes, the risk of evil. The more radical the good, the more radical the evil that is risked. The world is on the knife-edge now, for good or evil. There can be a world of peace and justice, the world of Messiah—or universal torture, death, perhaps even the death of Earth herself. No wonder the Holocaust came now. The proof of a loving God is that we have the power to choose, the power to do radical evil. If we had no such power to choose, we would be tools of fate, and our lives would be empty of meaning.

Better the Holocaust—even the Holocaust—than a world of slaves to fate.

What does it mean to say that we are living on the knife-edge of all human history? In 1945, in *Paths in Utopia*, Martin Buber wrote:

> For the last three decades we have felt that we were living in the initial phases of the greatest crisis humanity has ever known. It grows increasingly clear to us that the tremendous happenings of the past years, too, can be understood only as symptoms of this crisis. It is not merely the crisis of one economic and social system being superseded by another, more or less ready to take its place; rather all systems, old and new, are equally involved in the crisis. What is in question, therefore, is nothing less than man's whole existence in the world.

Buber wrote this even before we had full knowledge of the Holocaust or Hiroshima; before we invented the H-bomb and the ICBM; before the Chinese Revolution transformed the lives of one-fourth the human race; before the manipulation of human genetics became possible; before the earth's population had grown by two billion in a single generation and promised to do so again; before we knew that we were poisoning the very air and oceans.

It is only from the knife-edge of despair that we can ask ourselves: Can we do Rachel's wrestle? Can we face God with a model of "sisterly" love? Can we turn history around before another, wider Holocaust? What would it mean for us to win like Rachel, to bring redemption, to birth Messiah?

We Fabrangeners found another challenging story in the midrash on Eikhah, this one calling to communal transformation. Perhaps it was the Rabbis' own response to the question, What does it mean to birth Messiah in the very moment that the Holy Temple vanishes? For this is their story of themselves:

Its hero is Yokhanan ben Zakkai, who headed the Sanhedrin while the Temple was being besieged by Roman troops under General Vespasian. The Temple had stores of food enough to last for years. But one group among the Jews, the Zealots, were not satisfied. They could not bear the thought of waiting for years while the Roman presence defiled the holy Land. They wanted to rush forth to fight; for surely God would come to the support of Jews who marched out against the idol-worshipping Roman armies!

But how to force more cautious Jews to force God's hand? Ah! Since the stores of food and water gave comfort to the cautious, the Zealots ordered all the stored food burnt.

## FROM THE COFFIN INTO LIFE

Yokhanan ben Zakkai bewailed this burning. Perhaps he knew the Torah of his people. Perhaps he knew that when the Israelites took the Holy Ark into battle in order to force God's Hand against the Philistines, God laughed—and the Ark was captured. Perhaps he recalled that Jeremiah shouted, "You call aloud, 'The Temple of the Lord, the Temple of the Lord,' and you think that God must intervene to save this building that you desecrate? Forget such empty mouthings!"

Yokhanan bemoans the burning food: "Woe!" He is overheard and hauled before a Zealot court-martial. For fear that this court will have him executed for lowering morale, he says that he had exclaimed not "Woe" in sorrow but "Wow!" in joy. This lie the rabbis thought so wise they applied to him the verse, "Wisdom preserves the life of him who has it."

Soon Yokhanan saw that with the food gone, the Jews were boiling straw to make a thin soup to keep from starving. Said he, "Can men who boil straw and drink its water withstand the armies of Vespasian? I must get out of here!"

But when he seeks to leave the Temple precincts, the Zealots warn him: Only the dead shall leave the city (for corpses were taboo in the Temple area).

So he has his students nail him in a coffin, and thus they smuggle him out.

He goes to meet Vespasian. Through midrashic understanding of

197

the Torah, he answers questions Vespasian puts to him, and hails him as Emperor before Vespasian himself learns that he has been newly elected by the Roman Senate. Vespasian offers him a gift.

"Spare our Holy Temple and its defenders," he says. But Vespasian answers, "Did the Romans send me these many thousand miles that I should abandon the siege of this city? Choose another gift."

So Yokhanan ben Zakkai secures Vespasian's permission to open an academy to teach new rabbis in the town of Yavneh. The Temple is destroyed, but through Yavneh, Torah survives.

How deep is this rabbinic tale of hope and warning! At every point, Yokhanan ben Zakkai chose as much life as possible, for himself and his people. He pretended to choose death in order to choose life, when the Zealots were pretending to live in such a way as to make their deaths inevitable. He was willing to wait out the Romans, looking like a coward, rather than to die in courageously attacking; he was willing to lie, to twist his words, rather than die in truth for subversion; he was willing to lie, to pretend to die, rather than die in truth of starvation. He did not want the Temple destroyed; but once it has been, he acts to make sure that Torah survives.

But this last is all he is able to accomplish. The Zealots have pulled the Temple down on their own heads. And the Temple that in their blindness they pull down is their own and God's—unlike the one blind Samson shattered.

This story speaks powerfully to us. Its parallels seem easy to follow: Zealotry in modern Israel may be disastrous, self-destructive. The boldest, shrillest patriots do not always serve their country well. Frightening people into hushing their dissent may deprive the nation of their wisdom. There is no holiness in daring God to do a miracle— no religious worth in putting ourselves into such extremities that only God can save us; for God is no idol to be so managed, and may not save us. Sometimes Jewish strength is like the strength of water, not of steel.

These are lessons at the political level, but also at the personal level. Surely they warn me against my tendency to throw myself in fury against what seems to me to be injustice or imprudence. Yokhanan ben Zakkai chose life at every level. He did not choose life for himself at the cost of death for the people; he did not choose death for himself in order to buy life for the people. He did not throw himself on the gears of the Jewish death-machine, just as he did not want the Jews to throw themselves on the gears of the Roman death-machine. He took risks, but he set limits on them.

## BURNING BRIDGES, BUILDING BRIDGES

So now *I* try to set some limits. I try to think to myself: Is there a chance of saving this particular holy place? If so, is caution or bold confrontation more likely to save it?

I'm never sure. Who could be sure? But now I try to ask myself.

It's never easy. After all, what if Yokhanan ben Zakkai had thrown his whole energy and good sense against the Zealots before they had burnt the stores of food, before they had made the Temple's fall inevitable? Could he have saved the Temple?

Maybe he tried, maybe he failed. The story doesn't tell us. Maybe the whole point of the story is to teach us how to act after the zealots, *our* zealots, whoever they are, have taken the irretrievable step. Where there is no hope, create new hope.

*Memo to myself*: Even if the zealot within me has abandoned prudence, and burnt the last bridge behind me, it is still possible to pull myself, my true self, together. To build a new bridge.

*Memo to myself*: This is for political behavior, but not only for political behavior. When, in loving someone, you have zealously marched forward to a chasm, before you jump into it, do you see where a new bridge can be built? *Seek it, seek it.*

Maybe building a new hope requires changing the focus of vision as radically as Yokhanan ben Zakkai did. At the very moment when most Jewish energy focused on defending the Temple and the offerings there to God, he began to imagine as a new center what had been important but not central to Judaism: The concentrated study of the Torah.

What Messiah was born on the day the Temple was destroyed? Yavneh. The rabbinic alternative.

How radical does Yavneh need to be?

Two final tales of Yohkanan ben Zakkai may teach us how to answer that question.

Shortly after the Temple was destroyed, there came a Rosh Hashanah that fell upon Shabbat. Jewish law was clear that except at the Temple, the sacred ram's horn—the shofar—could not be blown on Shabbat, even for the festival that was defined as the day of Shofar-blowing.

Except at the Holy Temple—and now there was no Holy Temple.

Yokhanan proclaimed that the community at Yavneh where the rabbis studied Torah was now, as it were, the Holy of Holies for the People Israel. So the shofar would be blown on Shabbat/Rosh Hashanah in Yavneh.

There was an uproar. The Sadducees, heirs and guardians of the priestly tradition, protested. The Temple was unique, the Offerings were a sacred path that only priests could understand. It was sad that the Temple was unavailable, but in God's Own time it would again be possible to blow the shofar. It was one thing for the rabbis of Yavneh to study Torah, another to bend it out of shape.

"I understand," said Yokhanan. "Yet there is no time to submit this issue to the Sanhedrin. So we will blow the shofar in Yavneh, and then gather the Sanhedrin to adjudicate."

Reluctantly, the Sadducees acquiesced. The shofar was blown, Rosh Hashanah ended.

They came to Yokhanan, demanding: "Now call together the Sanhedrin."

"To rule on what?" he said. "The shofar has already been blown in Yavneh on Shabbat."

Yokhanan had broken the content of the rules; now he also broke the rules of process, so urgent did he think it to establish the authority of Yavneh and the process of the rabbis.

And finally, Yokhanan lay upon his deathbed. He called his students to him. "I have had a terrifying dream," he said. "The messenger of death came to me. Since my years are long and full, that was not terrifying. But was he coming to take me to Paradise or Hell? I could not tell."

I hear a message that is powerful and poignant: There is no way of telling, no way of being certain. Yokhanan brought his whole strength to wrestling with Torah, wrestling with God. From the nightmare of the Temple shattered, he woke to face a God Who comforted the people with new tellings of the Torah, Who once again called the community to Wrestle.

So Yokhanan wrestled. He held back nothing; he walked fully the life-path of this Torah that emerged from his Godwrestle.

Yet from this Wrestle he was wounded, on this new life-path he walked limping. Limping even into death. Was his way a path into life? Or a covenant with death?

There was no way for him to know. He chose to act fully and to doubt deeply. He was able to live in the uncertainty. He stayed open in love to the possibility of his own error. Only hundreds of years later could the rabbis say with confidence that he had saved Torah and the Jewish people, that what he had taught was sacred. Perhaps its sacredness stemmed from the very fact that even when he acted most vigorously, he never claimed utter certainty.

CHAPTER 15

# ON THE FRINGES

One Shabbat morning during Fabrangen's second year, we had just begun the Torah reading. Suddenly a young woman who had been a member from the earliest days walked up to the Torah table, looked around the circle of our puzzled faces, took a deep breath, and said in a clear, calm voice, "I have a grievance that I need the community to address. I invoke the ancient right to interrupt the reading of the Torah to ask you to address my grievance."

We gasped. Some of us knew that in medieval Europe, there was exactly such a custom. But—a grievance? Inside our community? We were such friends; how could there be?

The person who had been about to read the Torah covered the Scroll, turned to the woman, and said, "All right. What is your grievance?"

"At our Shabbat-morning service three weeks ago," she said, "barely ten of us were present. Our davvening leader looked around and counted, and went forward with the prayers for which we need a minyan. But as most of you know, I was born into a Christian family. Although I have been living as a practicing Jew for several years, I have never taken part in any ceremony of conversion. I was one of the ten who was counted that Shabbat for a minyan.

"Just yesterday I learned that since that Shabbat, a number of you have been talking about whether I should have been counted. But you have all been too embarrassed to ask me to take part in that discussion. I have prayed here, studied Torah here, danced here. All of us have acted as if I were a Jew. *But—am I?*

"My grievance is simply that I have not been asked to join in this discussion. I am not embarrassed. I think the community needs to decide this question, and I can live with whatever we decide. But there needs to be a process, and I need to be part of it. So I ask you to begin."

So for the first time we publicly faced the question, "Who is a Jew?" For the rest of that Shabbat, and in special community meetings over the next few months, the Torah we discussed was the Torah of— "Who is a Jew? What is a Jew? When is a Jew?" Perhaps we should have realized that our interrupted Torah reading was a crystal of a larger truth—that over the next decades, Jews everywhere would have to pause from their accustomed rhythms to face that same question.

In our case, we decided that becoming a Jew was a process, with a beginning hidden in mystery and an end that was never completed, whether or not someone was born a Jew. But we also decided that someone not born a Jew who entered this process needed to cross a formal and explicit boundary to become a Jew. Immersion in the miniature ritual ocean of mikveh, we decided, was that boundary-marker— just as ancient Jewish tradition had determined.

We also decided that we, as a community of Israel, were fully competent to carry out a conversion: That is, to decide whether a non-Jew had gone far enough into the process of inner conversion for us to authorize her to enter the mikveh and come out a Jew. We prepared to hold a meeting of the whole community that could function as a *beit din* (rabbinical court of judgment) to make this determination. We scheduled a trip to the mikveh. And then our Jew-in-process faced us with a new dilemma: During the months of study, she had concluded that she wanted to enter the people Israel through Fabrangen's gateway—and also through the gateway of an Orthodox *beit din*.

What a conundrum! There is no way to convert twice: Once it's done, you're a Jew. To do it twice would delegitimate one of the ceremonies: Ours or the Orthodox rabbis'. What to do? Finally, we realized: The moment of conversion is the moment when the Jew-in-process says a blessing in the mikveh. Two different communities could authorize her to immerse herself; two different witnesses could witness. Yet the transformation would happen only once.

That is what we did. Our *beit din* did much more than ask some formulaic questions: We had a long, rich discussion of what it meant to be a Jew. What it meant for her; what it meant for the rest of us. By the time she was ready for the mikveh, each of us had become more fully Jewish than we had been before.

Even so, we did not see the implications of this experience in the larger world. Once we decided there were boundaries, we thought that what they were was clear enough: Anyone born to a Jewish mother or converted by any Jewish community was a Jew; others weren't.

Twenty years later, it is not so clear. There has been an enormous wave of intermarriages, and an enormous wave of conversions, the most since the days of Rome and the Talmud, when the Jewish people was rebirthing itself from the biblical to the Rabbinic form. Different Jewish groups are asserting different standards for conversion and for deciding whether particular individuals need a conversion ceremony or are already Jews.

And the boundaries of Jewish peoplehood have been softening in other ways as well. What about Buddhist Jews? Sufi Jews? Jews who celebrate with a Native American sweat lodge? Jews who believe that Jesus was the Messiah?

What are the boundaries of Jewish peoplehood? Who are part of the family and who are not? Is it a "family"? If so, in what sense?

Why is all this happening? Much of the agonized reappraisal has avoided saying out loud that the new intermarriage rates are rooted in the triumph of modernity. The Jewish people is not the only one profoundly affected by modernity, and we will better analyze our own situation if we keep that in mind.

Modernity has shown *all* those who walked the ancient life-paths, all the ancient communities and traditions, both ethnic and religious, that a "secular," "scientific" approach to the world has enormous power. Modernity has brought the various old spiritual traditions into much closer physical, intellectual, and emotional proximity with each other than before. The high fences between them have dissolved into semipermeable, uncertain, fuzzy boundaries. The boundaries are now more like fringes than like fences.

This has become true in three spheres of life:

First, the ideas mingle. Ancient traditions that used to be quite distinctive have all been listening to each other, absorbing bits of each other and of secularism—and have thus become more similar.

A poignant example: The Dalai Lama, head of a community of Tibetan Buddhists who are exiled from the homeland where they have lived for many centuries, asks to meet with Jews. Teach us, he says, how to keep a land-rooted religion alive in exile. And the Jews respond: Our people are searching for meditations, for spiritual "detachment." What, they ask, can you teach *us*?

One century ago, no such conversation would have been possible. The Dalai Lama was immured in Lhasa; his only teachers were other Buddhists. And most Jews would have viewed him as an idolator, proclaiming no god, bowing to the statue of a fat and laughing human.

Second, the peoples intermingle. The Jewish and Christian and Buddhist and Muslim and Native communities meet. Ghettos dissolve.

Third, actual membership in a tradition—the definitions of who belongs to, crosses over into, and actually lives with and rears children in the community/tradition itself—is far fuzzier than it used to be. *That* is intermarriage.

The first step in this process was secularization: Modernity itself was seen as an adequate, indeed powerful, life-path. Ethnicity and spirituality seemed impediments to personal and social progress. Many Jews welcomed this process.

## CHOOSING THE JEWISH PATH

But we are already seeing a "post-modern," "post-secular" realization that spirituality and community are necessary if personal wholeness and the earth's survival are both to be protected.

Still, this does not automatically mean that individuals return to the communal and spiritual forms of their childhoods. Now, when people search toward community and spirituality, they may find themselves *choosing* a form that fits their individual needs, rather than replicating that of their childhood because they know nothing else. Indeed, some may so deeply identify the childhood patterns as merely "childish" that they can be satisfied as adults only by some form that they discover as adults.

Thus, in North America, more and more people who are born into households of one or two Jewish parents will choose whether to shape a Jewish identity for themselves or walk some other life-path. More and more people who are not born to Jewish parents will also be choosing their futures—and an appreciable number of them will choose Judaism. Those from *both* kinds of family backgrounds who see themselves as having consciously chosen a Jewish identity will become a large part, perhaps a majority, of North American Jewry.

Under these conditions, therefore, many North American Jews—perhaps most—will experience the Jewish community and Judaism as a spiritual/religious community of choice rather than an ethnic community in which membership is defined chiefly by birth.

It has been two thousand years since we faced the question of how to shape such a Judaism. That was when Hellenism (like modernity today) broke down our own and other communities' boundaries. The result was not only many conversions, semi-conversions, and intermarriages, but the very remaking of what Judaism was. What had been the biblical pattern of getting in touch with God by bringing offerings of food from a single land to a single place in that land, became a pattern in which a people scattered across Europe and the Middle East touched God through words: Prayer, Torah-study, and midrash-making.

As then, so today. This dynamic requires Judaism to transform

204

itself. An ethnic community can survive by merely having children. For a spiritual/religious community to survive, it must not only survive but vivify: Give people a sense of new life. Only a Judaism that is open, risky, spiritually alive and inviting will continue to keep non-Orthodox Jews involved in Jewish community, and will attract non-Jews into the Jewish community.

# GOOD FRINGES MAKE GOOD NEIGHBORS

One useful metaphor for the new Judaism can be drawn from the tradition that on the corners of our individual garments we wear carefully tied fringes, *tzitzit*. What would it mean to draw on this tradition at the level of the entire community?

What are *tzitzit*? They are a specially tied and knotted set of fringes that many male Jews and some women once wore on all their garments, and more recently wear on the ceremonial prayer shawl. They seem abstract, but not only is there a tradition of the meaning of the numbers of turns and knots, but as a gestalt the *tzitzit* honor and celebrate the fact that between individuals within a community there must be not high hard fences but soft and fading boundaries. These fringes are a mixture of "my" cloth and "communal" air.

In biblical tradition, this was affirmed by assigning the produce of the corners of "my" field to the communal needs of the poor, the stranger, the orphan. The field was "mine" (under God's ultimate ownership), but its corners faded away into communal space. In the new pattern shaped by the rabbis, the fringes of "my" garment played this role. Just as the shared communal use of the corners of the field betokened God's share in my property, so the communal fringes of the garment betokened God's share in my identity. God's representative, in both cases, was the community. If individuals were not open to and connected with other individuals, there would be no community—and no divinity. *Tzitzit* Judaized this assertion of connectedness: Gave it a Jewish name, symbol, affirmation.

But while individuals had permeable boundaries with others in the same tradition, the community *as a whole* had high, strong fences in regard to other communities.

But now the fences between communities have become very leaky, fuzzy. There are in fact not fences but unclear boundaries between the Jewish people and other peoples, other societies. What do we do about it?

One option is to rebuild impenetrable fences. This is what the Hasidic and some other Orthodox communities try to do.

Another option is to leave the boundaries fuzzy. Until now, that has been the underlying assumption of the greater part of the American Jewish community. What is new is a deep sense of disquiet about this answer. But so far, there seems to have been an underlying assumption that there are only two possible options—sharp fences or fuzzy fringes. Back to the ghetto or a formless people.

But we might create a third option: Tying *tzitzit*. Recognizing that the boundaries *are* leaky, permeable, and turning that very permeability into a Jewishly affirmable fact. Some of us may view this permeability as a troublesome but valuable concomitant of moving out of the ghetto. Others may view it as a flaw or illness in the Jewish body politic, and so are reluctant to affirm the permeability in any way. But even on such a view, there may be Jewish ways of responding to the malaise. To use a physical analogy, we might say that Jewish experience recognizes that illnesses will come to the individual body and that some of these are in our present life-conditions inevitable and incurable. Our community does not then throw up its hands in despair. We develop a Jewish response, *bikkur cholim*, a whole Jewish pattern of how to respond to sickness, drawing on Jewish paths and symbols. Similarly, we need to respond Jewishly to the new fact of Jewish existence that the boundaries of our community are permeable.

We must create *tzitzit between communities*. In other words, we need to bring the permeability of our boundaries into the purview of the community. We need to "own" the fuzziness itself, give it a ritual form that is our own, Judaize it.

Making "*tzitzit*" at the communal level means developing conscious spiritual and communal language—conscious *Jewish* language—for being open to people who are the community's "collective *tzitzit*"—our collective fringes, part "us" and part universal. This is true in regard to intermarriage and also to the spheres of life we call "political" or "intellectual."

## SACRED KNOWING AND ACADEMIC KNOWLEDGE

For example, let us look at the role of Jewish Studies professors in secular universities. They are, so to speak, the *tzitzit* of the rabbinate. In this era, we must have Jewish guides and teachers not just inside the community but also on its fringes, bringing not Judaism itself but knowledge *about* Judaism not only to semi-universalized Jews but also to semi-universalized Christians, Buddhists, secularists, etc.

We have begun to "Judaize" this need by inventing the academic field of Jewish studies. But so far we have assumed that this new field of study will follow Western modes of knowledge, and we have not yet explored shaping the field itself so that in some limited ways, in a "fringe" sense, it can express Jewish ways of thought.

What would this mean? Suppose that the Jewish Studies discipline took seriously an intriguing fact about the Hebrew language that we have already noted: The Hebrew for "know" has a broader range of meaning than the same word in English. Look at these three uses of the word:

"And the Earthling [Adam] *knew* Life-giver [Chava, Eve] his wife, and she conceived."

"There arose a new king over Narrow Straits [*Mitzraiim*, Egypt] who did not *know* Joseph."

"For the earth shall be full of the *knowledge* of YHWH as the waters cover the sea."

When the classic English translations of the Bible were done (about 500 years ago), it did not seem peculiar to translate all three of these passages so that the Hebrew "*yada*" became "know." The clear-eyed emotional and spiritual intimacy that "*yada*" obviously meant in these three texts did not seem alien to the kind of knowledge that was learned in the universities of that day.

Today, after 500 years of modernity, the two seem quite distinct. "Knowledge" has become "objective," gained from standing back, from being standoffish. Facts are not only objective but objectified. And "making love" has become romantic, kissing with eyes closed or holding the partner so close that there is no way to take a clear-eyed look even if your eyes are open.

Both the couch and the classroom have lost a great deal from this divorce. Neither "romance" nor "objectivity" is the path to a whole truth. The way the Hebrew language uses "*yada*" teaches the value of reaching toward some form of knowledge that is beyond both romance and objectivity. It does this implicitly, in the very structure of the Hebrew tongue itself. One might almost say that any language in which the word for "know" and "make love" was the same was bound to have a creation myth in which God created the universe by speaking words.

Indeed, when those strange scholars the rabbis addressed explicitly the question of the relationship between knowledge and action, they came to a conclusion similar to that embedded in the word "*yada*":

R. Tarfon and the Elders were once reclining in the upper story of Nithza's house in Lydda [during the Hadrianic persecutions], when the question was raised before them: Is study greater, or practice? R. Tarfon answered, saying: Practice is greater. R. Akiba answered, saying: Study is greater, for it leads to practice. Then they all answered and said: Study is greater, for it leads to action. (*Kiddushin* 40b; Soncino transl.)

Does this raise any useful questions to those who carry on "Jewish Studies" within the university?

Perhaps not. The sages were, of course, talking not about the modern knowledge of a university but about the study and practice of Torah. And they were talking at a time when both Jewish study and Jewish practice were outlawed, and choosing which was "greater" posed life-and-death issues for individuals and for the Jewish people as a whole. So perhaps we should simply say that this discussion is irrelevant to the work of a modern Jewish-studies scholar. Its values may govern in a rabbinical seminary or a synagogue school, but not at the University of X.

But let us take a second look. Suppose we hear the sages talking not only about a "should," but more deeply about an "is." They are saying not, "Should we treat study as greater than practice?" but "Is study in fact greater than practice, since it leads to practice?" That is, will the ideas of our people spring inevitably from the material conditions of their lives, or can we shape their lives by shaping their ideas?

Most urgent: Will the Romans' destruction of the material basis for Jewish life in the land of Israel make inevitable the dissolution of Torah and the people, or is it possible to preserve the social fabric of the people by the learning and teaching of Torah?

First they asked, What is the nature of society and social change? And only then did they ask, What ought we to do?

Heard this way, the debate certainly speaks to the nature of the modern university, even before it speaks to the values of the modern scholar. For if it is addressing not only the structure and process of Jewish peoplehood and Torah but also the structure and process of any society and any ideology, then the conclusion of the sages—that study *is* greater than action because it *does* lead to action—suggests that the modern university has itself been shaped by a set of ideas, by an ideology.

If this is true, it might hint that all scholars should learn from this Jewish approach to Torah-study. But what about a narrower application of the principle? Should these ideas about intertwining knowing with doing have any special resonance for scholars of Jewish Studies in a modern university?

What might such a resonance be? Surely not that Jewish study should simply lead to Jewish practice—for one major difference between a Jewish Studies department and a rabbinical seminary is that the former welcomes students of all ethnic communities and all religious orientations, and does not attempt to get them to practice Judaism.

An imaginary scenario:

As every university seminar begins, there is a moment of quiet focusing, after which a six-month-old baby is gently handed from person to person round the circle of students and teachers in the room.

As each person holds the baby, s/he looks carefully into its eyes and says, "Everything that we do in this class we do in order that you can grow up to become at least as old as we are—and more healthy, more knowledgeable, and more compassionate. I will choose life so that you and the generation after you may live."

What are the origins of this image, and what its implications?

It is a midrash on a Torah passage and on *brit milah* (circumcision)—a midrash that draws not on the ethnic and religious specificities of *brit milah* but on its universal implications. The midrash-as-ceremony focuses not on the initiation of the child into the adult community, but on the adult community's self-aware guidance of itself into paths of life.

So first of all, simply because it is a midrash, it teaches a value that is deeply embedded in Jewish culture: The value of drawing on and transforming ancient texts, ancient practices. It teaches that the ancient wisdom is not to be ignored, not to be treated as a mere object of curiosity, yet also not to be worshipped as immutable.

Secondly, it asserts another value that is deeply embedded in Jewish culture: Studying history, literature, music, economics does matter. It matters to whether a child and a generation live or die, heal or divide, learn to "know" or only to cogitate.

Third, it affirms that the intellectual enterprise is simultaneously individual and communal.

If we used this kind of ceremony to highlight these values, we and our students might find ourselves asking new kinds of questions as we studied the past:

We might inquire not just what past Jews said or did, but what in their wisdom or unwisdom we can draw on.

We might study Buber through a conversation *with* him, not about him.

We might study a decision of the medieval Jewish communal Council of the Four Lands concerning allowable expenditures for weddings by *responding to* their decision, not just describing it.

We might study how Jews of the Talmudic period preserved their communal identity while transforming their culture, with the explicit intent of learning how Jews and other cultures today could do this.

This approach would treat Jewish Studies as a new kind of midrash on Jewish culture, one that would aim to become part of the fabric of Jewish culture and—here is what makes it a new kind of midrash—*part of the larger fabric of human culture as well.* This is new because in the past, most Jews expected that our enrichment and transformation of our own worldview would change only our own lives.

Two more examples of what it might mean to create *tzitzit* for Jewish culture as a whole:

Just as modernity has brought all the ancient traditions to bump up against and interpenetrate each other, so it has brought Adam and Adamah, the earth and us earthlings, bumping up against and interpenetrating each other in a profoundly new way. We have of course always interacted, but now, through modernity, we have created an ecological crisis. We can destroy life on earth, and in the process the web of life on earth can radically damage or destroy us.

How does the Jewish people make *tzitzit* for itself that reach outward to address this issue? What *Jewish* ways of being in the world would recognize our relationship to all of Earth, not just to the Land of Israel? Can we draw such *tzitzit* from the traditions of a rhythm between work and rest, doing and being, making and contemplating, which we express with Shabbat, the sabbatical year, and the Jubilee? All of them, according to previous Jewish tradition, apply only to the Jewish people (and the latter two only to the Land of Israel). But are there now "fringes" of this rhythm that we should carry outward to the rest of the human race and the whole of the earth, as a response to the eco-crisis? Should we be inventing *"tzitzit"* for Shabbat, sabbatical year, and Jubilee to share with the other peoples and the earth?

Similarly, could we create an *"eco-kashrut"* that would be something like *"tzitzit"* for the code of kosher food—Jewishly shaped "fringes" on *kashrut* that would apply earth-healing values not only to food but to other consumables, to money, to energy sources and uses?

# THE RAINBOW AND THE CHUPPAH

Finally, let us return to the issue of intermarriage.

In regard to at least one sphere of Jewish peoplehood, a working household in which Jewish culture is acted out from day to day, the intermarried make up the collective fringes on our collective peoplehood. But at this moment, these fringes are ragged, helter-skelter: We have put little conscious planning into shaping what relationship these households might have to the people as a whole.

By the logic suggested above, these fringes need to be made Jewish. We need to tie them into careful *tzitzit*. We need to set clear standards about what the spirals and knots of such new *tzitzit* must be—that is, what conditions would need to be fulfilled for an intermarriage to be affirmed by the community, and how the household would continue to connect.

These conditions might include standards about the household's observance of Jewish ceremonial time, its rearing of children, its connections with the local and worldwide Jewish community—and about a wedding ceremony that would not mimic traditional Jewish forms but would be rooted in relevant Jewish symbols. Only carefully shaping such communal standards and ceremonies could turn these fringes into *tzitzit*—a way of accepting and transforming, rather than being transformed by, the new marital realities.

Where in Jewish tradition might we look for such *tzitzit*? When the rabbis wanted to address issues of the human race as a whole, they turned to the Torah passage at the end of the story of the Flood. There God makes a covenant with all human beings and with all breathing life upon the planet. The rabbinic tradition developed this tale into a code of universal law that applied to all human beings, the "seven *mitzvot* of the children of Noah." Among these were the obligations to create law courts and to refrain from murder, idolatry, and incest.

For these reasons, more than a decade ago Rabbi Rebecca Alpert, Rabbi Linda Holtzman, and I created a wedding ceremony to be performed under Jewish auspices between a Jew and a non-Jew, if they intended to identify with the Jewish people and its tradition. This ceremony drew on the symbols of the Flood, the Rainbow, and the Children of Noah rather than on the traditional symbols of *kiddushin*—a Jewish wedding. Our notion was that *kiddushin* represented, so to speak, the broad expanse of the *tallit*; this marriage ceremony for the "Children of Noah" represented the *tzitzit* that the community might tie at the corners of its being.

We proposed that this ceremony be used only if the couple had

211

studied Judaism together before the marriage and affirmed both privately and publicly that they intended to bring Torah seriously into their household.

More important than the specific rituals and guidelines that we proposed, however, is whether there might be a process by which the Jewish community could come to a *communal* decision on this question.

If a broad spectrum of Jews were to conclude that this was a useful exploration, would it then make sense to work out a *B'nai Noach* ceremony that would not violate present understandings of Jewish law, and to work out guidelines for when, how, and for whom to use the ceremony?

Above all, is it possible for all of us to think about these questions with a prayerful suspension of certainties, with a hope that by together examining the issues we might best carry on the work of our Godwrestling people, our sacred Torah, and the Holy One Who does the deeds of creation?

Ancient teachings tell us that as we say the *Sh'ma*, the affirmation of God's Unity, we gather the *tzitzit* together from the four corners of our prayer shawls, and look at them with care and consciousness.

Why? Looking at the *tzitzit* is intended to remind us of all the *mitzvot*. In most traditional Jewish circles, the *mitzvot* have been thought of as "commandments" imposed by the God Who is a Commander, King, and Lord. From this standpoint, the *Sh'ma* is the ultimate assertion of God's Lordship, and its recitation is therefore a powerful and appropriate moment to focus on the *tzitzit*.

There is another way of looking at this looking. In some communities of Jewish renewal, there is a growing desire to imagine God not chiefly as a Commander above us but as the Weave of Connections within and among us. If we think of God this way, how can we understood the *mitzvot* ?

In several Semitic languages—including, occasionally, in Hebrew—the verb that is at the root of *mitzvot* may mean "connect" in place of or in addition to "command" (for "command" is only a special way of connecting). From this perspective, it becomes attractive to think of the *mitzvot* as connections. Whatever actions make stronger connections among the different aspects of the One are *mitzvot*.

Suddenly we can see that the *tzitzit* visually echo the *mitzvot*—for the *tzitzit* are indeed connective. Looking at the *tzitzit* reminds us that the boundaries between us are not sharp, reminds us that we need to make connections between us and among us.

The *tzitzit* are, literally and visually, the Weave of Unity.

# CHAPTER 16

# THE SPIRAL OF THE TORAH

When I first wrote about Godwrestling, it seemed to be a dance of joy. A light with no alloy of darkness. Even the aspects of the Torah that seemed to me most dangerous—its subordination of women, its willingness to destroy whole peoples—seemed also possible to transcend.

I still believe that. Yet all these years later, I have a deeper sense of how great the pain and how deep the danger that some aspects of Torah carry. I see now that, like Jacob, we might leave this Wrestle with a wounded thigh. The same Hassidim who teach that the Torah is Divine Light also teach us that the only way to light is through darkness, that "There was evening, there was morning: One day." Creation begins in the dark of night; only then can it dawn. Streaks of dark remain forever in the One Day.

Since I wrote the first version of this book, I have twice experienced a moment of utter darkness in the weave of Torah's light.

The first came when my wife Phyllis Berman and I were leading a class on sexuality in the Torah, at a summer institute of *havurah* people. We asked people to read as overnight homework the story of Dina in Genesis.

Dina, the one daughter of Jacob who is named alongside his twelve sons, goes out to "visit the daughters of the land." She is raped by Sh'chem, one of the local Canaanite notables. He falls in love with her and asks to marry her. Jacob's sons insist that he and all his clansmen be circumcised first. Sh'chem and his followers agree. On the third day, when they are in the most pain from the operation, two of Jacob's sons fall upon them and kill them all.

In the entire story, Dina says not a word.

Phyllis and I asked the class to be prepared the next day to speak in Dina's name. We were ready for a "drushodrama" in which Dina would speak first and then others might play different parts.

Next day, when we asked for a volunteer to speak Dina's words, a man's hand shot up. I blinked and said, "That's fine, but before you give your voice to Dina, I'd like to have two women have their say."

There was a silence. Then a woman stood. She closed her eyes, then looked around the circle of our faces:

"Raped.

"I have been raped three times.

"Once by Sh'chem.

"Once by my brothers, who did not ask me what I thought before they did this killing.

"And once by the Torah, which will not let me speak. By the Torah, which is still raping me."

She began to cry, and sat down. There was a long, long silence. Finally, I said, "I asked for two women to speak in Dina's voice. Is another woman ready to speak now?" There was a longer, longer silence.

Then Phyllis said, "Is no one coming forward because you other women feel that Dina has truly spoken, that what we have already heard is really Dina's voice?"

All the women nodded. And Phyllis said, "Me too."

Raped by the Torah. Silenced by the Torah.

What can anyone say? What can any man say?

Ever since, I have tried to keep that moment of darkness alight in my consciousness whenever I have wrestled with Torah. Even as a newcomer and an outsider, even as one looked down on by those who have spent a lifetime learning the elaborate process of Torah study, I could find some version of myself in the various stories. But I was never silenced; I was never raped.

What would have to happen for women to feel at home in these stories?

Despite the darkness of that moment, I did see the light that sprang from it, just as the Hassidim said it would. For in the very same breath that our Dina was saying that the Torah rapes her, she was saying it by doing midrash on that very Torah. She was drawing on that same sacred text of sacred—rapist—Torah, to weave a new tale into that sacred—rapist—text.

A radical midrash. Perhaps the most radical imaginable midrash, for it utterly negated Torah at the very moment of affirming Torah. Affirmed *it* by negating it. Negated it *by* affirming it. The light could not be separated from the darkness. Smile away the dark discovery, and enlightenment would also vanish with it.

It was like running headlong into a Black Hole of utter emptiness, in the despairing hope that within the hole there is the birth of an entire universe, a billion galaxies.

Is there another Torah hidden within the one we have? Another Torah, to be found only by plunging deep into the terrifying darkness of the one we read?

The rabbis, I remember when I am just on the brink of despair—the rabbis found "another Torah" in the white fire between the letters of the written Torah: The other Torah that they called "Torah through the power of the mouth." (Most translators say "oral Torah," but notice how they lose precisely the power of the mouth.) The Rabbis said this Torah of the mouth only seemed like new Torah; it really came at Sinai, alongside the Torah of the power of the pen.

And we clever modernists, we think they fooled themselves. We smile with admiration at how successfully they did it, but most of us cannot bring ourselves to believe that the "oral Torah" came from Sinai. We think the Rabbis made it up—successfully.

Where does that leave us? Can we, historically sophisticated readers that we are, draw a new Torah from the silences within the old one, as they did? Or are we too smart to fool ourselves, as we think they fooled themselves? Are we too smart to be successful?

## DARK GOD, DARK TORAH

Back to the Torah that comes in the dark. Aside from Dina's silent Torah, my other moment of terror and despair came on a spring morning in 1994.

I had just awakened from a pleasant sleep after celebrating the raucous, rowdy, hilarious, spring-fever Purim festival the night before. Purim is intertwined with the Scroll of Esther, in which a pompous king and a wicked prime minister are ultimately outwitted by a wise Jewish courtier and a courageous Jewish queen.

At one level, the story is about a genocidal threat aimed at the Jews. By echoing an earlier genocidal threat from the tribe of Amalek, the story turns the danger into an archetype. To this threat the Jews respond with diplomatic wisdom and, ultimately, a delicious revenge.

At another level, the story is a joke: What you intend to do to me, that's what happens to you. So, the wicked Haman would hang the Jews? He ends up swinging from his own gallows. So, the pompous king refuses to take orders from a woman? He ends by doing exactly what his Queen tells him to do.

When I say the Scroll of Esther and the Purim festival are "intertwined," I am choosing my words with care. In the official version of Jewish history and ritual, the story of Queen Esther led to the celebration of Purim. Today, most scholars think it went the other way: A

215

ribald festival of early spring was justified by a jokey novelet: The Scroll of Esther. All agree that the two are intertwined.

From the easy laughter of a Purim evening—reading the Scroll of Esther with its scathing humor aimed at kings and ministers; rattling my noisemaker at every mention of the name of wicked "Haman"; joining in the bawdy plays called "Purimspiels" that poked fun at rabbis, Torah, Jews, at God's Own Self for choosing to be absent from this book—from all this, I woke to hear the radio:

Some religious Jew named "Baruch" ("Blessed") had walked with a machine gun into the Cave of Machpelah in Hebron, the Tomb of Abraham and Sarah, and there had murdered thirty of his cousins, the children of Abraham's other family, who were praying prostrate on their faces.

From behind.

At prayer.

For the sake of God.

Yes, for God he killed them, for the God to whom they were at the very same moment praying. Killed them because it was Purim, the moment when we are to remember to blot out the name of Amalek, the archetypal murderer who had assaulted us from the rear, killed us when we were helpless.

He turned his gun into a midrash.

The Talmud says that on Purim, we are to get just drunk enough to not know the difference between "Blessed Mordechai" and "Cursed Haman." Between *Baruch*, "Blessed," and *Aror*, "Cursed." For Purim is the day of inversions, inside-outs, of turning the world upside-down. Hilarity and grotesquerie.

This man had become so drunk on blood that he could no longer tell the difference in his own identity between *Baruch*, Blessed, and *Aror*, Cursed; between becoming the murderer Haman and becoming the healer Mordechai.

And he had made his gun into a midrash. A brilliant midrash.

I lay in bed, drowning out this new name of Amalek as it came pouring from the radio, saying, shouting, screaming, wailing, "No no no no no no *no*."

Twenty-five years of joyful prayer and midrash, shattered with one gun and thirty lives. Twenty-five years of hope and anger, grief and loneliness, rolling the spiral of the Scroll, walking the spiral of the festivals, learning the Hebrew puns that point the path to Torah meaning.

No no no no no no *no*

The Black Hole of Torah, sucking in all light, all meaning.

At last I got out of bed. I called my children, my friends, my teachers, my students. We began to weave a counter-midrash, a weave of tears and healing, not of blood and bullets. For it to have power may take years, decades, centuries in which it grows from seed to sprout to Tree of Life.

## THE AMALEK WITHIN

But we began. On the very day of Bloody Purim, we began. We said to each other, *We will have to understand "Amalek," the archetype of genocidal hatred, in a new way.* For the Purim story does not stand alone. Jewish tradition connects it with a story from the Exodus and Wilderness: A nation named Amalek attacked the Jews from the rear, killing the women and children who had been placed there for safety. The Torah teaches that Jews must forever remember to blot out the memory of Amalek. Haman. Torquemada. Hitler. They are all Amalek.

Of course, after the Nazi Holocaust—the Holocaust from which no Esther saved the Jews—this archetypal myth of disaster bit home with intense cruelty and fear. Suddenly, Jews for whom the Amalek story had become somewhat quiescent, became attuned to it.

And then came the long, complex, and deadly struggle between the national movements and hopes of the Jewish and the Palestinian peoples. In that struggle, some Palestinians became terrorists. Some Palestinians called publicly for the State of Israel to be shattered. So for some Jews, all Palestinians become Amalek. We must "blot out" their memory.

What does it mean to blot out their memory? To Baruch/Aror Goldstein, it meant murder. He had guns and police protection; he had power. He could make the fantasy come true.

But "blotting out the memory of Amalek" must come to mean something other than murder. The key to a deeper spiritual understanding is to see that a spark of Amalek may arise not only in outsiders and enemies, but also in ourselves.

Within days of the Purim massacre, two women who had been deeply engaged in the struggle to create a feminist Judaism pointed toward new meanings for Amalek.

Barbara Breitman, drawing on her own experience as a psychotherapist, asked us to look carefully at the key command. It has two parts, she pointed out: First, "Remember what Amalek did to you." Then, "When your God brings you safely into the land, you shall blot out the memory of Amalek."

First, she said, the victim must fully recover the memories of victimization and abuse. Then, when we are no longer weak and powerless, when we are "safe in a good land," we must no longer be obsessed

217

with Amalek. For it is exactly an unrealistic and obsessive fear that will drive us to desperate acts—indeed, into acting like Amalek.

Rabbi Tirzah Firestone pointed out that Amalek was a descendant of Esau—that grandson of Abraham who was cheated from the birthright and the blessing that would have let him follow in Abraham's footsteps. Amalek, she suggests, is part of our own family, the residue of rage that sprang from Esau's grief and anger. Amalek is always a possibility within us, as well as within others. The Torah is teaching that even as we face the danger of an Amalek without, we must also blot out the urge to Amalek within ourselves, by turning that urge toward compassion.

These teachings showed us where to begin. Then we said to each other:

We will have to read the Scroll of Esther in a new way. In its last passage, we chant verses of triumph when the Jews kill 75,000 of their enemies. So long as we understood the whole Scroll to be a fable, we could live with this bloody denouement as the angry fantasy of a powerless people: Just once, they could destroy not only those who seek to kill them but *everyone* who ever sneered at them.

What does it mean to reread the Scroll? At the first level, literally to chant it in a different way. We must take the verses of destruction and read them in the wailing chant of Lamentations that is traditional for the verses that describe our fear of our own destruction.

But "rereading" must go on at other levels, too. What shall we do when some people think the story must be acted out? What spiritual and ethical dangers do we run when we are powerful but pretend to be still powerless?

We were powerless for a long time. Indeed, the last time we found a new Torah hidden in the white fire of the Scroll, it was precisely a Torah for living powerless, landless, bodiless, yet skilled with words. So one of the new elements that demands we search again for new Torah hidden within the old is precisely the reemergence of a Jewish people—in Israel and in many communities throughout the world—that can have a say in the politics of life. Count up the coinage of a political power that has no precedent in Jewish history: One of the dozen strongest military forces on the planet; a strong political presence, greater than our number by proportion, in the world's one superpower; enough clout in what was the Soviet Union to challenge its might with nonviolent courage and make the first cracks in its Goliath armor; half a dozen prosperous communities in prosperous countries scattered round the globe. We face a new Jewish reality, and so we need to create a new Judaism.

## RENEWING THE FAST OF ESTHER

We will have to understand Purim in a new way, and yet an old way, rooted in the Fast of Esther that Jews used to observe during the daylight hours just before Purim. They fasted in memory of the fast that Esther undertook as she wrestled with her fear of Amalek. We too must fast to face the danger of Amalek—the Amalek that comes from within and without, that crouches in every human being and in each people. In a year when Muslims had murdered Jews in the name of God just as a Jew had murdered Muslims, we could see that Amalek lurked in every people.

So we began to see there was a profound wisdom in the rabbis' prescription of the Fast of Esther. All fasts require self-control. On the eve of the very festival when the rabbis taught us to loosen self-control, they also taught us to remember it. They knew that hilarious playfulness is one necessary step on the spiritual path, when the distinctions between Blessed and Accursed must collapse. But perhaps they glimpsed the danger that when the clear and solid boundaries collapse, a flood of blood might be released. So they gave us first a day to confront this "shadow" within Purim.

There is an old rabbinic pun. Occasionally, in Hebrew, the Day of Atonement is called Yom HaKippurim. Someday, the Rabbis said, Yom HaKippurim would be like the Day of Lots, a Yom Ha K'Purim, a day like Purim. When Messiah comes, they said, the day when we need to atone for our sins would dissolve into a day like Purim, a day beyond sin because all sin would be transcended. Of all the holy days, they said, only Purim would still be celebrated after Messiah comes.

But the equation is also true in reverse. There must be an element of Yom Kippur in Purim, and that element is the Fast of Esther.

The Fast of Esther could become a time for us to meet with other communities and face our nightmares about each other. In our neighborhood of Jewish renewal in Philadelphia, one year after the Purim Massacre in Hebron, on the evening before the Fast of Esther was to begin at daybreak, Jews, Christians, and Muslims gathered to look at the nightmarish teachings of each of our traditions and to examine how to move beyond them. Then we sang our different chants for each other, read the Psalms that delight all three traditions, fed each other bread and the fruit of the vine and touched each others' foreheads with the oil of anointing.

Then we went home to sleep, to wake, to fast in memory of Esther.

## THE PRESENCE OF AN ABSENCE

But for me, the night before the fast was haunted by the absence of the Holy Presence. In all the Scroll of Esther, the Name of God is never mentioned. Some people have argued that God is present in a hint of Mordechai's: He teaches Esther that if she will not act to save the Jews, their salvation will come from another place. A Place, say some: A hidden Name of the God Who is the Place of the world. But for others, it is the name of Esther, which in Hebrew echoes the words *"seter"* and *"nistar,"* the words for "hidden," that really tells the story. Just as Esther hides her Jewishness, so God hides in the story.

In the midst of restless dreams of emptiness, arising from the darkest place of massacre close to the end of the Scroll, I saw a not-vision and heard a not-voice:

*And then appeared Darkness,*
*Her Head wrapped in mourning,*
*Her tallit all black,*
*Her **Place** only Absence,*
*Nistar b'nistar:*
*Her Voice was a Silence:*
*"I came to defend you,*
*My people beloved;*
*I strengthened your hand*
*to beat back your foes;*
*But then you betrayed Me.*
*For your hand became frenzied,*
*You struck down the harmless,*
*You struck down My children*
*While they reached out to Me.*

*On the day of rejoicing*
*You hollowed My Name;*
*In My Own Tree of Life,*
*You hollowed out life,*
*left only a mocking*
*pretense of My Self.*

*And I see—yes, I see—*
*That in days still to come*
*Your deeds will give warrant*
*To a child of your children,*
*To murder your cousins,*

220

The children of Ishmael,
The children of Abraham,
In the Place of his grave,
On this day of rejoicing.

So My Name I withdraw—
Yes, My Name will be hidden,
Nistar b'nistar;

For I will not permit you
to call out from this Scroll
My Name on this day.

Yet I teach you that Purim,
Alone of the seasons,
Will continue beyond
the time of Messiah.

On the day that both families
of Abraham's offspring
turn away from their murders,
their murders of each other,
on that day will my Name
take its **Place** in the S croll.

On that day Purim
and Yom Ha'K'Purim
at last will be one.

On that day, at last,
This Purim will lead you
And light up your way
to the Days of Messiah.

On that day all the nations
will laugh and will dance,
will turn robes of power
into masquerade mirth;
will turn every gun
to a clackety grogger.

On that day will My Name
Take Its **Place** in the Scroll
In letters of Light.

I awoke to turn this Black Hole of the Torah, the Hidden God, into these words of a promise of new light. Then at last I felt free to celebrate Purim: To laugh and somersault, to turn the up side down; for then I knew that washing away the boundaries of rules would not bring on a flood of blood and murder.

## HEARING TORAH, WEAVING TORAH

In these two moments of darkness—not from them, but within them— I glimpse new Torah: From the first, a Torah that women are empowered to shape; from the second, a Torah in which the Jewish people is empowered in the world and so can create, must create, Torah for a people no longer slaves and outcasts.

A new Torah: Frightening words. How could we do this without coming out the other side as a new people, a different people, not the Jewish people?

We have done it before.

When the Rabbis shaped the Talmud and the Jewish people accepted it as a "macro-midrash," they told of a new Torah that was also old—the Torah of the power of the mouth, spoken at Sinai but never written on the parchment. What this "new Torah" accomplished for the Jewish people was putting great emphasis on certain parts of Torah that had been barely explored, while turning away from vast quantities of Torah as if they no longer mattered. Conquest of the Land, eradicating the peoples of idolatry, carving out the architecture of the Temple and the choreography of sacrifice, the seven-yearly rhythms of the restful land: All these were put aside. The rules that governed the seventh day of rest and the rules of kosher eating were much more fully explicated. Without erasing sacred texts, the community let what had come to seem irrelevant or abhorrent fade from vivid color to pale gray.

This new rabbinic Torah operated in thought the way a spiral operates in space: It curved back so that it could curve forward. By doing this in thought, it expanded the spiral of Jewish time from the small curves of week and "moonth" and year and Jubilee into the great spirals of eras and millennia.

Even in the earliest shaping of the Torah, there are some hints that Israelite culture was spiraling back-and-forward, making midrash on the pre-Torah spring festivals of shepherds and barley farmers to redefine itself through the great Torah epic of the Exodus from slavery and the Pesach festival that sealed it into memory.

We know much more about the transformation from biblical to rabbinic Judaism, and the rabbis' use of the great myth of Sinai's "oral

Torah" to make their own macro-midrash possible. It is not clear whether the rabbis themselves believed that myth. They told a story about Moses: Peering from Paradise into Akiba's classroom, he did not recognize a word of Akiba's Torah until Akiba said his Torah came straight from Moses' mouth. Then Moses "recognized" Akiba's Torah!

That story hints that some of the rabbis understood that the myth of oral Torah was true—and not true—at the same time. Perhaps the story was very sophisticated indeed, and intended to teach that the words, the content, of Akiba's teaching were totally new but that the process of the teaching was very old. In any case, many Jews accepted the truth of the notion of a double Torah, written and oral, that came from Sinai.

Could we again use that myth of oral Torah to explain why and how we are making what seems to be new Torah? Not in the same way. For us, it is neither authentic nor truthful to assert that the new decisions we are making about the content of a Sacred Path "really" came by word of mouth from Sinai. Yes, for many of us there is an archetypal truth in saying that the midrashic *process* of creating Torah is very ancient. So in that sense the process we are joining came "from Sinai." But for me, there also needs to be a sense of where the content comes from, and how our changing it is rooted in our own Jewish encounter with the Spirit: In Godwrestling, in being and doing Yisrael.

When I began to wrestle, I did not ask this question; I just enjoyed the wrestle. Even as I wrote the original version of this book, I took the process itself for granted. I felt deep joy in the way we worked with our lives and played in the Torah from Shabbat to Shabbat. But now, perhaps because I have lived this way for two decades, perhaps because those decades demanded that I keep my eyes open when the Torah turned dark, I have found it necessary to ask myself: What *is* this Torah that I wrestle with?

That question is essentially the question that I think Jacob faced. Can I turn my struggle with the Torah into a deeper Wrestle, as he turned his struggle with his brother into a deeper Wrestle?

Two experiences come to me of an opening, a birthing in my sense of Torah. The first was reading with delight the insights of a poet, historian, and theologian of Jewish renewal, Joel Rosenberg of the Boston *havurah*. Rosenberg took up the layers of thought about the Bible that have emerged in the last 150 years. First was the discovery of the German historical linguists that the text of Torah can be unraveled into several different documents: J, E, D, P they were named, each letter corresponding to an author: The one who liked to name

God *JHWH*, the one who liked to name God *Elohim*, the writer of Deuteronomy, and the *Priestly* author. The German scholars said there was also R, the Redactor or editor, who brought it all together.

There was intense argument in the Christian and Jewish worlds about whether to accept this "documentary hypothesis," and if so whether it shattered the faith and meaning of biblical religion. Then, in Germany between the world wars, the great Jewish theologian Franz Rosenzweig said (I am paraphrasing): "I too can see the different strands of the Torah literature. But I must add something else: This *R*, this Redactor, is also '*Rabbenu*,' 'our teacher'—as Moses is called '*Moshe Rabbenu*, Moses our teacher.' For the Redaction is what counts. The text we have that weaves all these different strands into a single Torah, this is what counts. This finished fabric is the Revelation with which our Jewish faith engages. Truthful history does not destroy that engagement." This outlook became the approach of many Conservative Jews.

And then in our own generation, along came Joel Rosenberg to carry this discussion to a new level. (Still paraphrasing:) "Yes," he said; "I agree with the documentary historians and with Rosenzweig as well. But I ask myself, why did the Great Redactor, our '*Rabbenu*,' not weave the fabric so well that we would not see a seam here, a tear there, a patch in many places?"

And Rosenberg answered, "Because the deepest revelation was the knowledge that there are many strands. Imagine if someone gives you a perfect shimmering robe, a faultless piece of pottery. What can you do but put it carefully on the shelf to be admired? But give me a shirt that's beautiful and slightly torn, colored a little oddly, and what I do is get to work. I make the shirt more beautiful; I get my hands into the process.

"That," said Rosenberg, "is the work of a God I'm glad to know. A Creator Who demands that I join in co-creating, a Torah-teacher Who insists that I join in teaching Torah. Writing Torah. Of course there are many voices in the Torah, and of course both God and the Redactor/*Rabbenu* want me to hear the many voices—not just one. The Infinite Voice speaks out in many voices—or It isn't Infinite."

For many years, this fed my mind and I thought I was satisfied. Then I found myself engaging in a process so similar to the one that Rosenberg described that I understood in the *kishkes*, not just the mind, what Torah was and is.

## VOICES IN THE FAMILY

This was, in fact, my experience with my brother, seen in a new light, felt at a new level. When we wrote our book together, we did not try to smooth it out into a single voice. Instead we heard in it at least five voices: My own and his own; mine-in-dialogue-with-his and his-in-dialogue-with-mine; and the voice of our editorship, the Redactor, the two of us when ultimately we had to be a single voice deciding together which of our several voices would get to appear at any moment. And what the order and the architecture of the book would be.

Our differences in voice were serious, even though we came from a single womb, a single house, a single economic depression and world war. Looking out from the same front porch at one same block of Cottage Avenue, we saw around us different worlds, and we told different stories.

Once I had done this, I heard Torah in a deeply different way. I welcomed the kingly voices along with every prophet, the ones who danced the God of drumming rhythm and the ones who shouted out the God of overturning, the cheats and murderers and gentle meditators, all of the family voices.

Not all. I missed the women, the converts, the voices of gay men. And the horrid children. The woodcutter who was stoned to death for breaking Shabbat—how did the family feel to him? And I missed some voices the stories barely mentioned: Mathematicians. Clowns.

These were the voices of my own generation. Once they were in the story, it would need a new Redactor.

And once the world quakes, we need a new Redactor. A new Talmud, as we did when the Mediterranean shook.

There are two ways to look at why we need to unearth "new Torah." One is to look at the big world, the great earthquake. The other way is to look at the people who are caught in the earthquake. Both are important.

From the standpoint of the big world, the world where there is no "standpoint" because there is nowhere firm to stand, the process I am suggesting is analogous to what Jews did during the seven centuries between 200 BCE and 500 CE, when they acted out and wrote down the Talmud. Just as Jews then faced an earthquake—the great flood of Hellenistic/Roman ideas, a world economy, a military conquest that culminated in the destruction of the Temple, the decimation of Judaea, and the dispersion of the Jews—so, too, we now face an earthquake in the life of the Jewish people.

We have been "conquered," our life-spaces "occupied," by Modernism—including industrialism, nationalism, individualism, corporate capitalism, state socialism, mass democracy, the mass media, total war. Some of this we have liked and might well incorporate into our own tradition, as the Talmud tamed and incorporated aspects of Hellenism. But modernism culminated in three events for which the community and its traditions were utterly unprepared: The Holocaust; the creation of the state of Israel; and in America, a new kind of Diaspora in which Jews have full permission to be both citizens and Jewish. Moreover, our world is one for which the tradition is utterly unprepared because worldwide annihilation of the human race and the biosphere itself are achievable; because instant communication between any two human beings anywhere is possible; because _____ _____ _____ _____ _____

_____ _____ _____ .

Fill in the blanks with almost anything.

What has happened is that powers we previously ascribed to a God outside ourselves have flowered within us: Powers to create, shape, change, destroy. Powers women did not have, powers Jews did not have, powers humans did not have—we now have. God's Own Self has appeared in another Place. And that has changed so much that our stories of how we wrestle God must also change to be truthful to that newness.

What does all this mean in what we might, if we dared, call "God's life-cycle?" Not only in the history of concepts of God, Names of God, but in the biography of the real God, Whose Names change because God's life changes.

The One Who said to Moses at the burning bush, "My Name is 'I Will Be Who I Will Be, I Am Becoming Who I Am Becoming'": What is happening in the life of that God?

## TOWARD A NEW TALMUD

To this question we will return. Meanwhile, what about ourselves? The world in which we live is so utterly different from that in which the Talmud was our portable constitution that it is clear we need a new effort to dis-cover, uncover, new Torah. Not only the content, but even the process of our "Talmud" will have to be different. Not an elite of rabbinic adepts, but the whole community will be part of the discussions that work out our new life-practice.

Not that we will ignore either the content or the process of the Talmud. We will keep drawing on its content in many areas where the very texture of present Jewish culture grows from Talmud. We will draw on all of Torah in the broadest sense: Not only the Bible and the Talmud, but also everything the Kabbalists and the Hassidim, Maimonides and Freud, the secular Zionists and Yiddishists and the new Jewish feminists have said.

All of it can change, and still it is our story.

226

But does it become Torah just because it is our story? Is the Hebron Massacre Torah? Is the Torah's triple rape of Dina Torah?

Yes. And no. All the strands need to be visible, no matter how ugly in my eyes or yours. And we also need the Voice that unifies. That connects. That says the "All" is not yet the "Whole," the Harmony. That insists we weave new strands to repair what is torn, and turn the jagged murderous pieces into bright warning banners.

One aspect of the new Torah that we make in every era is that we take what has become dangerous and destructive, and learn from it instead of using it. That is what we did, for instance, with the lamb of the Passover sacrifice. We spent 2,000 years sacrificing a lamb upon the Altar for Passover, and then we spent the next 2,000 years just setting a bone or a beet on the Seder plate—not even eating lamb for Passover, not even lifting the bone from the plate lest someone think we had used some other altar to sacrifice a lamb. We kept the memory alive, precisely as a midrash—a teaching of why we do not do what we used to do. And so we kept it All, in all its buzzing contradictions,—and yet turned them into a Harmonious Whole.

When I recall the despair of the woman who said the Torah was still raping her, when I think of gay men and women who say they can hardly bear to keep reading Leviticus, when I think of how I myself felt that Purim morning of the Hebron massacre, I realize why we need new Torah at a more personal level.

If we want to keep the Jews Jewish, we need to reach a new starting-place with Torah, as the Talmud was a new starting-place. If we want to keep ourselves Yisrael, wrestling God and Torah, we cannot forever subject ourselves to a version of Torah that torments us. It is one thing to limp away from the Godwrestle; it is another to lie vomiting upon the ground.

Indeed, we are moving, far more quickly and firmly than some believed possible, to shape new midrash that will be so deep and clear that all of us who have been horrified by parts of the ancient text will have a new sense of what Torah is. Again, this has happened before. Long ago, the rabbis told that young Abram had destroyed the idols that his father sold in his shop. For centuries, this story rang so true that generations of Jews thought it was in the Torah. They have scrutinized the Scroll to chase it down. It isn't there. But in the people's minds, it is.

Or take a harsher case. In long passages of Torah, God commands the Jews to eradicate every member of certain nations that lived in the land of Canaan. To the rabbis, this was abhorrent. They dealt with it by simply asserting that these nations had been intermingled by the Assyrian conquest so thoroughly that these nations no longer existed, and the command was a dead letter. Finished.

Once it had become utterly clear that these passages do not control our present actions with other nations, some of our teachers interpreted the stories to be a metaphor of inner spiritual struggle, and gave new life to the text in a different dimension. Turned the All into a Harmony.

Or the command that parents stone to death a rebellious son. First the rabbis looked so carefully at the Torah's description of such a rebellious son that they cleverly restricted the number of such cases to zero. Then they said that not only had there never been such a case, but there never would be. *Never*?! In any conceivable future, never? No! And when one asked, "Why then did the Torah bother to set the rule?" they answered: To give us the pleasure of studying it.

In other words, make healing midrash from what is dangerous, degrading. Take a tiny spark of wisdom, turn it into a glowing presence. Expand on the story of the midwives, uncover the full life-history of Miriam, explore the love life of Jonathan and David, hear the silent voice of the God Who absents Herself from the Scroll of Esther, hear Dina's voice.

I have yet another story to tell of Dina's voice. It is a story of the birthing of new Torah that may come as we plunge deep into the Black Hole of darkside Torah. Years after I had faced the triple rape of Dina, I drew a deep breath—did I dare do this again?—and asked a group of rabbinical students to do a drushodrama with that same story. I asked them to start with its first line: "Dina went out to visit with the daughters of the land."

One woman volunteered to be Dina, others to be the "daughters of the land." Dina stood, stretched, walked over to one of the women, looked lovingly into her face.

"You're beautiful," she said. "I love the compassion, the fire in your eyes. I want to get to know you. Perhaps it is *bashert*, perhaps it is meant to be, that we be lovers."

The other student gasped, blushed, laughed, and responded in a way that advanced the new Torah we had just begun. I thought to myself, "After 4,000 years of Jewish history, there are not many totally new midrashim—but that one probably is!"

When the day comes that a Jewish lesbian can see herself in one of the Torah's heroines, when the day comes that a gay man can take it as much for granted that Jonathan was gay as we take the story of Abraham's smashing his father's idols, when all the voices of the family are speaking through the voice of Torah, then the Torah will be new—and old. As new as it was in days of old. As old, and as new, as the family whose Godwrestling it records.

# PART V

# EARTH AND EARTHLING

# RAINBOW SIGN

What is the relationship between this Jewish family and the two broader families within which it is nestled: The human race and our web of living earth? How should the Jewish people address questions that do not uniquely affect Jews, but arise within the broader planetary life?

One such issue arose late in the 1970s. It was, you might say, the most universal question imaginable: The possible death of the entire human race. Yet for many Jews it seemed to echo their own most terrible, unique experience.

As the Cold War was yet again heating up, Americans began to realize that while their attention had been elsewhere for almost twenty years, the size and deadliness of the world nuclear arsenal had greatly risen. Physicians began talking about "the last epidemic," and scientists about a "nuclear winter" in which a worldwide nuclear war might so reduce photosynthesis throughout the earth that a huge proportion of all living beings would die. The American Catholic bishops warned of profound moral dangers.

Some Jews urged that the organized Jewish leadership also speak out on the nuclear danger. But others argued that this was not a "Jewish issue" because the nuclear arms race, and even a nuclear war, would not uniquely affect Jews. "We have enough to worry about already," they said: "Issues that unite us, like security for Israel and freedom for Soviet Jews. Let Jews who care about this issue join SANE, or the Union of Concerned Scientists. It will only make trouble among us as we argue what position to take."

We who called our work "Jewish renewal" had a different reaction. We had come to care passionately about Torah because Torah addressed all the issues we carried passionately about, from our sexual lives to our money to our music, our very breathing. How could the possible death of everything we cared for—the death of God's Creation—*not* be a Torah issue? *Not* be a Jewish issue?

And there was something else. As Samuel Pisar said in Jerusalem when he chaired the first international gathering of Holocaust survivors, the Holocaust had been a test case, an experiment, in organizing human ingenuity to destroy not just one people, but the entire human race. Who, he said, could bring a deeper understanding of the danger and a deeper commitment to resist it than the Jews?

## A PEOPLE WITH A PURPOSE?

We who were pursuing Jewish renewal saw the Jews as neither an isolated tribe with no stake in the universal destiny, nor a mere accident of history to be cast aside as we left our ghettos and entered the universal arena. Instead, we looked upon the Jewish people as a microcosm of the human macro-community, more like the corner of a hologram than like the corner of a photograph. Tear off a corner of a photograph; study it as long as you like, you will learn hardly anything about the rest of the picture. But if you have a corner of a hologram, you can rebuild the entire picture. All the information is encoded in each part, as the DNA that describes an entire person is present in each cell. As the folk wisdom says, "The Jews are like everyone else, only more so."

"Only more so": What did that mean? From the Torah's earliest description of our people, we felt possessed of a mission. Some of the most troubling passages of Torah—the commands to wipe out the societies of Canaan—are rooted in that sense of mission, the sense that God had called the Jews to create a society of justice and holiness. If we failed to do that, we ourselves would lose the Land. And we were to build this good society not for the sake of the Jews alone, but to transform the world and bring the Messianic days of peace and justice.

Then we did indeed lose the Land, to an empire that acted far less holy than had the Jewish people. We felt helpless. So for thousands of years of Diaspora, the Jewish people put aside the sense of broader purpose. If we had been sent on a military mission to transform the world, we had been militarily defeated. It became an enormous task simply to shape a sacred community within the Jewish people, and preserve it in the nooks and crannies of other civilizations. If the days of Messiah were ever to arrive, God would have to intervene; we could not do the job alone.

But to American Jews in the 1970s, the Jewish people seemed no longer helpless. Miracle of miracles, there was again a self-governing

Jewish community in the Land of Israel. It lived in danger, but it had great strength. A parallel miracle: American Jews were becoming politically powerful in a society where they were free to be both as deeply Jewish as they wished and as fully American as they chose.

And at the same time, the dangers of remaining helpless were now clear. In the modern world, there were no nooks and crannies. Pogroms had been survivable; Holocausts were not. A worldwide "nuclear winter" was not. If the world around the Jewish people were not imbued with holiness, what hope had the Jewish people of living to carry on a holy life?

Were we then caught in a dilemma? On the one hand, we could not conquer the world as the Torah had commanded the Jews to conquer Canaan. On the other hand, if the world remained untransformed we were likely to die. Neither the biblical model nor the Rabbinic model worked any longer. What now?

Something new began to seem possible. Around us we had seen the weak become powerful, not through military conquest but through the use of forceful nonviolent action. Black Americans had transformed the South that way. Soviet Jews were challenging the totalitarian government of a nuclear superpower, with actions as amazing as dancing in the public streets on Simchat Torah. Far from being crushed, they were winning concessions. Could this kind of action point a new direction for the Jewish people? Could we once more see ourselves as a people with a purpose? Could we reshape ourselves as a transgenerational "movement" to work with others to transform a world that otherwise would surely kill us? The Soviet Jews had used the celebration of a Jewish festival to open doors of change. Could we also draw on the wisdom of Torah for a guide to holy action?

The greatest physical danger that we faced was the one we shared with all the other peoples and perhaps all other species: The nuclear peril. So we turned to Torah: Could it speak to this unprecedented question? Instantly, a passage leaped out that we had treated as merely a children's fairy tale: The story of the Flood, of Noah and the Ark and the Rainbow—the only biblical story in which the death of not just the human race but of all life on earth is put at issue. Fairy tale no longer.

How strange: In one of the most archaic levels of the Torah there emerges this story that spoke to the newest, most unprecedented issue of our lives! Or perhaps not quite so strange? Perhaps it was precisely the archaic and archetypal quality of Torah that made it so present in a crisis?

So we began to study the story of the Flood. Since I was now publishing and editing a journal called *Menorah: Sparks of Jewish*

*Renewal* that reached Jewish seekers all across North America, we were able to spark this Torah-study not in one *havurah* alone, but in many clusters of Jewish thought.

## FLOODS OF NEW MIDRASH

The story recounts that violence, corruption, ruin were rampant on the earth. God, seeing that the human imagination was drawn toward evil, determined to destroy all life, except for one human family led by Noah, and one pair of every species. God rained death on every being except those who took refuge with Noah on the Ark. One year later, the waters subsided so that these refugees could emerge. And then God, though explicitly asserting once again that the human imagination is drawn toward evil, took an almost opposite tack: God promised that the cycles of life would never be destroyed again, insisted that new rules of behavior must govern human action in the future, and gave the Rainbow as a sign of this covenant.

As we wrestled with the story, what first leaped out at us was that human acts had propelled God into action. "God" here plays the role of karma: "Whatever you sow, that's what you reap." Old images of a vengeful, punitive God gave way to the concern that we were bringing disaster on our own heads. If all life is, in fact, connected, then walling ourselves off from the weave of life-breath was bound to cut us off from our own breathing.

When we looked at what to *do*, one aspect of the story seemed a not-so-obvious teaching: *Noah is no expert.* He is not an expert on rain, or ships, or animals. He is simply a righteous person. Some of the Rabbinic commentators on the Bible conclude that he is not even extraordinarily righteous. After all, they point out, when God threatened to destroy two cities, Abraham protested; when God threatened to wipe out one people, Moses intervened. Noah, warned that a whole world was in peril, held his tongue. Righteous? Middling righteous, compared to those around him.

Nowadays, some say that to deal with the danger of thermonuclear extinction or global pollution, one must be an expert in nuclear physics or global climate, in military strategy or diplomacy, in biology or economics, in social psychology or ecology. But the Noah story teaches that when all life is in danger, any of us who regard ourselves as simply reasonably decent people—"middling righteous"—are obligated to act.

What must Noah and his family do? They must preserve all life. The first "species preservation act" turns out to be not the one passed by the United States Congress in 1977; it is the command of God to Noah.

If the two-by-two procession of all species onto the Ark bespoke the Species Preservation Act, then the Flood betokened not a single weapons system alone but a flood of new technologies that were endangering the earth: A rain of H-bombs, yes—and also the burning and slashing of great forests, the choking of our air with carbon dioxide and our ozone layer with chlorofluorocarbons, the poisoning of our seas with oil and gasoline.

Indeed, one rabbinic commentary on the story raises the question whether the Torah may view one form of human intervention in the environment as even more dangerous than the nuclear peril. The rabbis usually believed that the universe is built on "measure for measure": God's rewards and punishments fit our action. So the rabbis asked, "Since the purging of the earth came through water, what was being wrongly done through water?" And they answered that before the Flood, all the species were mixing the water of their semen with each other. This water washed away all biological boundaries, confounding the clarity of God's creation; so God sent a Flood of water to wash away all boundaries.

Today we know that few species can mix together and propagate in this way. But we have also invented "genetic recombination," by which indeed the genes of one species can be introduced inside the DNA of another. Should we take the fantasy of the rabbis as a warning to explore this new technology with the greatest care, if at all, lest we bring upon ourselves a global disaster?

## THE FLOOD OF FIRE

But I am leaping ahead of the story of how we wrestled with this story. Let me return to our original question: How do we prevent a thermonuclear war? As we puzzled over the story, we noticed that it never uses the category, the imagery, of "war." Why not?

The human race is used to war. We know, from thousands of years of history, how to live with wars of "us" against "them." All wars have "winners" and "losers." Most of the time, the "winners" are those who have more powerful weapons. So if we are thinking "war," an arms race makes sense. We choose to enter a war depending on whether we can win something important—ideally, on whether it seems "just," reasonably proportioned to decent goals of defense or liberation.

It is hard, within that whole structure of thought, to come to grips with several peculiar questions:

What kind of "war" has no survivors, and therefore no winners or losers?

In what kind of "war" are justice and injustice irrelevant because the human community to which they belong may disappear?

What is a "weapon" with which, after a certain threshold, "more powerful" does not matter?

Perhaps most basic of all: What kind of "war" has no "us" or "them"?

If our basic assumptions about "war" turn into unanswerable questions, perhaps it does not make sense to use the word that invokes all these conventional assumptions. So now we may see in a new light the absence of "war" from the story of the Flood. For the Flood afflicted us all. It cut across all political and geographical boundaries. It did not pit one nation against another. The violence, the corruption, the ruination of the earth took place within every nation, *every* people, perhaps every species. Our own violence, our own corruption, our own ruination overflowed. They rose to Flood stage. Our own behavior led to our destruction, but the disaster was not a war.

If the danger is that my house will be flooded because someone left the water gushing, will I save my house by turning on more water to drown this reckless plumber? No; the flood will just come sooner. By *not* using the language of war, by *not* running an arms race, I am more likely to prevent an all-consuming flood.

Then what word shall we use to shape our actions so we can prevent disaster? As we kept searching in the story, we found an ancient commentary: Long ago, the Rabbis told of Abraham watching the fires that destroyed Sodom and Gomorra. "But, God," said Abraham, "You promised never again to destroy the world through such a Flood. Surely You did not mean to rule out only a Flood of water? Surely You did not mean that You might send a Flood of Fire?"

And God was silent.

Or as the Southern Black song puts it, "God gave Noah the Rainbow Sign: No more water. The fire next time!"

When we tried to put those words, the "Flood of Fire," into contemporary English, the word that rose up for us is also the word that sets us most atremble: "Holocaust." The "All-Burning," for that is what "holocaust" means.

A word, an event, from the Jewish corner of the worldwide hologram. A corner from which we can unfold the whole.

And so we learned from Torah to insist on saying that we faced not thermonuclear war but thermonuclear holocaust. We insisted on saying not "50,000 weapons" or "50,000 H-bombs" when we talked about the worldwide arsenal, but "50,000 instant portable Auschwitzes," each machine capable of doing in thirty minutes what it took Auschwitz thirty months to do.

Soon we realized that our other impending environmental disasters also partake of the nature of a Flood, not of a war. Those who say that we must cut down the Oregon forests to compete with businesses that are burning the Amazon, we must make still more automobiles that fill the air with carbon dioxide to keep ahead of others who are selling automobiles, are thinking in the metaphor of economic war, not that of Flood. If we can change our language, we might change our future.

## TRANSFORMATIONS IN TIME

As we kept peeling layers of the story of the Flood, we realized how obsessed it is with time and dates. It specifies the date when the rain began to fall as "the seventeenth day of the second month." It specifies how long the rain lasted, the date when the waters stopped their rising, the date when dry ground first appeared, the date when the Ark landed. It names the date when the Ark's passengers could disembark and receive the Rainbow Covenant: The "twenty-seventh day of the second month." One lunar year plus eleven days from start to finish: Exactly one solar year.

The exactitude with which these dates are given is still more surprising when we consider that they are the only dates specified in all of Genesis. Indeed, from the Creation until the Exodus from Egypt, the Bible gives no dates except those connected with the Flood. There is no date for the Tower of Babel, or Abraham's departure from the town of Ur, or the Binding of Isaac, or Jacob's wrestle with God, or Joseph's accession to power in Egypt. Only dates for the Flood.

What are we to learn? Although the rabbis of the Talmud debated whether the "second" month was in the spring or fall, they never suggested that the dates be put to practical use. Indeed, these dates have never been used in the life-practice of Jews, or any other religious community. They have not been used as the date of the Exodus is used for Passover or the date of rededication of the Temple for Hanukkah.

Why were Passover and Hanukkah made dates of celebration? Because it was crucial for every generation to reexperience the

Exodus and the Temple's rededication. But the dates of the Flood and the Rainbow never needed to be used—because no generation ever faced the possibility that all life might be destroyed. No generation, that is, until our own.

So some of us decided that, literally to save our lives, we should begin to observe and celebrate the moment of disaster and the moment of renewal: The dates of the Flood and the Rainbow.

Then we faced a practical question: When? The Talmudic rabbis debated over what month was the second month, depending on whether the "first" month comes with the spring equinox and Passover or the fall equinox and Rosh Hashanah. Most of them decided that in regard to the Flood, the Bible meant that the "second month" was in the fall. But one of the most respected rabbis, Joshua, and "all the sages of the other nations" thought it meant the spring.

Such a comment was unusual for the Talmud; rarely did the rabbis turn to "the sages of the other nations" to hear how they might interpret Torah. Yet in the case of the universal Flood, they sought the wisdom of the other nations. Perhaps this was their way of acknowledging that some events both include and transcend all cultural boundaries—and that the danger of universal death is one of these.

Adopting Joshua's view, hundreds of synagogues and other Jewish groups began in the spring of 1982, in the days between the 17th and the 27th of Iyyar, to observe the anniversaries of the Flood and the Rainbow. They prayed, studied Torah, created new rituals to recognize that all life was in danger—and to explore how all life could be preserved. Echoing the Talmud's hint of universal wisdom, many of them invited Christian and Unitarian churches to join with them in the observance.

From this work, congregations recalled how powerful and how necessary it is to move through the yearly festivals, addressing with each festival the question of the preservation of our planet. We rediscovered the *public* power the festivals could carry, if they were carried into public space.

We celebrated a Passover Seder against "the Ultimate Pharaoh," in the Nevada desert where the nuclear Auschwitzes of the future were being tested underground. We gathered in a circle to recite and chant and dance a new version of the Haggadah, preparing to walk onto the forbidden site of the nuclear weapons tests and be arrested. In the midst of the Seder, someone shouted in awe and joy, "Look up!" There we saw, emblazoned in the sky where there had been no rain for many months, a Rainbow. We said the blessing of joy for the One Who "does deeds of Beginning" and "remembers the Covenant." Later, as we were being arrested, someone told me that "Phenomenologically, the desert dust refracts light like raindrops." "Phenomenologically," I answered, "the fact that it happened right now, right here, is a miracle."

We built a sukkah—the fragile, leafy, leaky, hut that celebrates the Jewish harvest festival—at Lafayette Park near the White House and the Soviet Embassy, as a symbol of the fragility of all peoples and the need to make our security not from steel and concrete fallout shelters or "invulnerable" laser shields but from accepting how vulnerable all of us have become.

On the seventh day of Sukkot, we went with willow branches to the banks of a river. On that day for millennia, Jews have danced seven dances around a Torah Scroll. We have beaten willows—the tree that always grows near rivers—on the earth; we have prayed for fructifying rain. In our generation, the tradition has almost died out. But we renewed it, chanting prayers that the rain should be cleansed of acid, the seas of oil slick, the air of methane, the earth of pesticides. We prayed that a healed earth heal its earthlings, that the plagues of cancer subside, that we and the earth learn to nurture each other in joy.

We celebrated the Jewish "Birthday of the Trees" that comes in deepest winter on the fifteenth day of Shvat. We ate the fruits of the Tree of Life; we honored earth, air, water, fire; we planted new trees to give life to the planet.

We learned to draw on the life-giving themes of every holy day, not only for individual spiritual growth, but also for the spiritual growth of the public community.

As we celebrated these rhythms in time, we realized that the Flood story teaches that affirming the rhythmic cycles of life is crucial to preventing the death of life. How did we learn this? When the Flood began, the normal cycles halted. Perhaps they had already been thwarted and ignored, and the Flood came precisely to call forth a conscious understanding that the cycles had stopped. The Bible says that just before the rain began to fall, there were seven days while Noah's family and all their passengers sat waiting in the Ark. The rabbis teach that during those seven days the sun rose in the West and set in the East. In other words, the seven days of Creation were being run backward—and so the sun reversed itself. During the precise solar year that all the animals and humans spent aboard the Ark, the rabbis also say they all refrained from sex—refrained from initiating the life cycle.

When Noah wanted to test out the dry land, he tried to restart the great cycles of night and day, death and life. First he sent out a raven, black as the night, named *arva*, a word similar to *erev*, "evening." Then he sent out a dove, white as the morning, named *yonah*, a word similar to *yom*, "day." The raven, bird of carrion, cleared the earth of the dead carcasses that were the end-product of the last life-cycle before the Flood. The dove brought back for food the olive branch, the first new life that had sprung up after the great disaster.

Noah's effort to renew the cycles won God's response in the Rainbow Covenant. God's promise to renew and preserve life mentions precisely the timely cycles through which life renews itself:

*Never again will I doom the earth...*
*Never again will I destroy all life...*
*So long as the earth endures,*
*Seedtime and harvest,*
*Cold and heat,*
*Summer and winter,*
*Day and night,*
*Shall not cease.*
*...This is the sign that I set*
*For the covenant between Me and you*
*And every living creature with you,*
*For the generations forever:*
*I have set my bow in the clouds.*

What are we to learn from this? In the age of Modernity, the sacred cycles of time have been thwarted. We have let our desire for "productivity" destroy our sense of holy time and holy cycles. We have become so drunk on our new ability to produce goods that we have forgotten to rest, reflect, contemplate, meditate, celebrate.

This hyperproductive mode, in which time is only a raw material of production, has taken us to the brink of hyper-destruction. In a world that discards meditation and celebration as—literally—a waste of time, the H-bomb, destruction of the ozone layer, acid rain, deforestation, global warming are all inevitable. The Flood and the Rainbow remind us that we must renew the cycles and our celebration of them in order to live.

Noah's own name means "the restful one." Only a restful one can save all life.

Perhaps religious communities are especially responsible to say that not only hard work and dire warnings, but also joyful rest and joyful hope are necessary if we are to heal our planet. The Rainbow was an ensign of hope, a flag of new possibility. It was God's reminder that not only human beings but even God must have a symbol of hope, if life is to be renewed.

# THE ARC OF UNITY

What else does the Rainbow teach? The Bible specifies that the Rainbow came on Mt. Ararat. This is surprising and important. Although the Flood was mythically universal—like water in that there was no place to pin it down—it ends at a well-known place with a specific name. Why there?

Because from Ararat, the mountain peak that looms in Turkey high above the Middle East, the Fertile Crescent is a unity. Just as the earth looks like a unity from space, so the "whole known world" looked from Ararat. That was where the human race looked like a single family in all its inner variation: From many colors, one "*adam.*"

Indeed, the Rainbow itself was a heavenly reflection of the great arc of human settlements across the Middle East. And the Rainbow's varied colors remind us that we can only preserve human unity if we accept human diversity. Just as the Flood perched the Ark upon Ararat where the Crescent could appear in its unity, so the same technology that gave us the Bomb and global warming perched the rockets high above us, to give us our first glimpse of ourselves as one great ball of beauty. It is our collective danger that teaches us we are connected.

The great rabbinic commentator Nachmanides wrote that God gave the Rainbow by turning upside-down the bow of war. "See," said God; "My bow can no longer shoot from Heaven. It is now my sign of peace and love and hope."

And in our day, the weapon of ultimate destruction is also connected with the Rainbow. Those who have observed the awesome explosion of an H-bomb have reported how beautiful and terrifying are the flashing myriad colors that appear within the mushroom cloud. All the colors of the rainbow. For the H-bomb and all its technological cousins *are* the Rainbow—shattered.

In the years since the early 1980s when this reexamination of the Flood began, there has been an extraordinarily important change in the world: One of the nuclear super-powers has collapsed, and our fear of the H-bomb has receded from the foreground of our thoughts.

But the H-bomb was only the first, the starkest, of the human technologies that endanger life upon our planet. Now we know more about the other dangers. But this has not meant an automatic healing. Too many feel so spiritually hungry that they hunger to gobble up material goods beyond all use. Too many are frightened that in a world that does not share and celebrate, refusing to join in the gang-rape of the planet will mean a personal disaster for themselves.

So the danger of the Flood of Fire still surrounds us. Those of us who, like Noah, are no experts must begin the building of the Earth as Ark. We must turn away from metaphors of military and economic warfare. We must consciously permeate every aspect of our lives with the effort to preserve life on this planet. All this so that we can fulfill the promise of the Rainbow Covenant. For now it is we who hold the fiery bow of destruction in our hands, aimed at each other. It is our turn to make the Rainbow.

We can learn still more from the story of the Flood. We can learn a method: How to think when one great era is succeeded by another. For the story echoes the wisdom of the era before the Flood, transmuted to make new wisdom afterward.

The Flood story puts this transmuted wisdom into God's own mouth. Before the Flood, God saw that all the urgings of the human heart and mind were bent toward evil, "all the day." Indeed, this is why God decided to blot out all life on earth. After the Flood, something about the new situation—perhaps a planet full of carcasses?—taught God some new conclusions. For in almost the same words, God says, "The urgings of the human heart are evil, from youth onward," and *therefore* God decides never again to doom the earth.

Reinterpreting our older wisdom is the method by which we must learn today. It is not enough to reject the old traditions; nor is it enough to accept them. We must hear them, learn from them, wrestle with them, wring from them their quintessential truth, cast aside old husks of former meaning that are no longer fully truthful—and we must live by our *new* understanding of their ancient wisdom.

When Jews have been at our best in living life, this has been our quintessential method—the midrashic method, the Godwrestling method. But in a time when the Flood threatens and the Rainbow beckons, this process needs to become a path that everyone, not only Jews, can walk. So here is a crucial learning that the Jewish people can offer, from its own corner of the hologram, to all of earth and all its earthlings:

> You can learn from your own wisdom and transform it, without abandoning your own identity. We have done it when in a moment of great crisis we invented Rabbinic Judaism; in the story of the Flood, God does it; each human community can do it. Indeed, you must—if we are all to share in the planet's flowering, not its doom.

Why is this important? Because most human communities would rather die than surrender their identities. They will choose to live and change only if they understand how to do this by renewing their identities.

There is yet another crucial piece of wisdom that we can offer from our corner of the hologram: The wisdom of rhythmic sacred time, celebrating the spirals of the sun and moon and earth as well as the spirals of our history.

The rhythm of reflection and renewal through the midrashic method, and the rhythm of reflection and renewal through Shabbat: These two gifts can bring new life in times of crisis. It is no accident they come together; for they are deeply and forever intertwined.

# CHAPTER 18

# PROCLAIMING JUBILEE THROUGHOUT THE LAND

The Torah does not leave this covenanting vision of restful, rhythmic time to hover in space, glimmering in the evanescent Rainbow. It brings the vision down to earth. The many colors in the one great arc reflect earth's many regions, many climates; and the single earth can only heal if we attend to each particular land and people. Dream globally, you will learn to act locally. Act locally, you will learn to think globally.

Since the Torah is rooted in the Land of Israel and the People of Israel, that is the politics, economics, and ecology it explores in depth. When it does, amazingly enough, it puts forward the vision of a social rhythm—the Jubilee cycle—that has spoken to individuals and peoples thousands of years later and thousands of miles away.

Here the Torah whirls time into its loftiest spiral: The fifty-year rhythm of the Jubilee. The Jubilee passage (Lev. 25 and 26) teaches about time and timelessness, about the rhythms of doing and being, wealth and sharing, work upon the earth and healing with the earth, inward ritual and outward action. In it is the verse (Lev. 25:10) that found an echo in the Liberty Bell: "Proclaim liberty throughout the land, to all the inhabitants thereof."

For several years, as I discovered the Torah, I read and admired this passage in a rather academic way. Then three events in 1975 and 1976 lit up the passage with intensity.

*Take One:* Early on July 4, 1976, people began gathering on the steps of the Jefferson Memorial in Washington, D.C.: A choir of children and teenagers from a Black church. Fiddlers and guitarists wearing knitted yarmulkes. Several dozen sleepy-eyed women and men debarking from a batch of battered trucks, lightweight camping packs upon their backs. An old man in a long white robe, carrying a curved and convoluted ram's horn almost as tall as he was. A band of women setting up the sound equipment for a public address system. Other women putting up an array of glowing banners.

One of the banners read, "Proclaim Jubilee Throughout the Land."

As the number of people grew to about 5,000, the man with the ram's horn climbed to the top of the Memorial stairs. He raised the horn and blew a long and eerie blast. Someone else read from Leviticus:

"You shall count off seven sabbaths of years, seven times seven years....Then you shall make proclamation with the blast of the horn....On the day of atonement you shall make proclamation with the horn throughout all your land. And you shall make holy the fiftieth year, and proclaim liberty throughout the land to all the inhabitants thereof.

"It shall be a jubilee to you, and you—every one of you—shall return to his own ancestral holding, everyone of you, to his family....You shall not sow, nor reap what grows, nor gather the grapes of the unpruned vines....And the land shall not be permanently sold—

"*For the land is Mine. You are strangers and visitors with Me.*"

The energy intensified. People sang. People pledged themselves to work toward sharing wealth and power in America. People spoke with passion about money and justice—a Black woman from Chicago, a rabbi from the Maryland suburbs, an Episcopalian woman who had just been ordained a priest of her Church. The Bible spoke—Isaiah, Jeremiah—and before each passage was heard the voice of the ram's horn. Even the dead spoke: From audiotapes came Phil Ochs, singing about the bells of freedom, and Martin Luther King, Jr., dreaming aloud so that we would awaken. The ram's horn spoke again, and this time a liberty bell rang out with it. The 5,000 moved into a procession, heading for Independence Mall to be joined by thousands more. The mood shifted from service and celebration, to rally and reexamination.

"Liturgy" means "the people's work." That American liturgy for the Bicentennial Fourth of July at Mr. Jefferson's memorial, had actually begun half a world away, in the Land of Israel. Begun there twice—once in its deepest origin in the Bible days 4,000 years ago, which inscribed the line from Leviticus on the Liberty Bell; and again just a year before the liturgy itself.

*Take Two:* One year earlier, I was visiting a kibbutz in the Israeli Negev desert: *Kerem Shalom*, "Vineyard of Peace." I was sitting in a circle, quietly talking with two other visiting American Jews, eight or nine *sabras*, a few kibbutzniks who grew up in Europe or America.

The kibbutzniks were worried—and angry. One of their comrades was in jail for hurting a policeman during a sit-in. Between my sparse Hebrew and their staccato English, I had trouble understanding. I asked them to repeat.

"It happened when the *Gush Emunim*, the Band of the Faithful, were marching onto Palestinian land to set up Jewish settlements. The *Gush Emunim* were breaking the law. But worse, they were making it harder to achieve peace with the Palestinians. They were claiming Jews needed more land so that more Jews could settle in the Land of Israel. They were stirring the blood of many Israelis. We decided we must show how foolish this idea was.

"We decided to act, not just to speak. Their act was stirring; our act must be stirring.

"So we went to the ranch of General Sharon. He is one of their heroes, he wants to annex the Palestinian lands. He is also very rich. He has plenty of land.

"We set up tents on his land, as they had set up tents in the occupied territories. 'Israelis!' we said. 'You need more land? General Sharon has more than he needs, more than any one person needs. We do not need to take Palestinian land, we can share our own land. Come share!'

"We were arrested and dragged away. Our *chaver* kicked a cop when they grabbed him. Now he is going to jail. The *Gush Emunim* does not go to jail. The government criticizes them, but goes along."

I interrupted. "Did you do anything else about Sharon's land?"

"No," they said. "We made our point. That was all we meant to do."

I pressed a little more. Sharing the land, taking back a rich man's land, maybe there were Israelis who would have liked this idea? I had heard so much about the "social gap" between Israeli Jews of Western and Eastern origin, about the poor and downcast Eastern Jews. They voted for the right-wing parties because they got no hope from the Labor government. Maybe this notion of sharing the land would appeal to them?

"You don't understand," the kibbutzniks said. "The real issue we must solve before we can deal with the social gap is the issue of the Palestinians. First peace, then the social gap."

"But...," I muttered, a little embarrassed; after all, it may be my Land, but it is their country. "Maybe you have pressed the Palestinian issue as far as it can go right now. Maybe you should talk about what Israel could be like if there were peace. I have heard you talk about creating an Israeli form of socialism, but you never say what it means. I like this land thing. It reminds me of the Jubilee."

"What?"

"The Jubilee. You know, from the Torah. Maybe it's a Jewish kind of socialism, maybe it's even where socialism comes from. But it's an odd kind of socialism. The Torah doesn't seem to mind if people get rich for awhile. But every fifty years the land must be shared, with every family getting an equal share, family by family, clan by clan. The rich give up their extra land and the poor get back their share. And then there's another odd thing: No one is allowed to work the land at the very moment they get the chance again. Maybe you should call a Jubilee!"

They puzzle out the English, realize what I mean: "Aha, the *yovel*." They grin at me. Torah. Religion. What can you expect from an American Jew?

"No," they say, not so patiently any more. "The primary problem is the Palestinian question. That's what we need to work on."

I keep quiet. It *is* their country. The Jubilee floats to the back of my head.

*Take Three:* A week later, back in Washington. It is late in the summer of 1975, and two sets of people are planning Bicentennial celebrations for the coming year: Officials, who plan fireworks and galas; and populists, modern equivalents of Sam Adams, who see the global corporations as modern equivalents of George the Third.

One group of these new populists, the People's Bicentennial Commission, is meeting at the research center where I work. As they talk about anti-corporate "tea parties" and "economic democracy," a piece of arithmetic leaps out at me: 4 x 50 = 200. The American Bicentennial should really be the fourth American Jubilee, but there has never been even one.

Wait, yes there was—"Hoo-rah, hoo-rah, we bring the Jubilee...Hoo-rah, hoo-rah, the flag that makes you free!...And so we sang the anthem from Atlanta to the sea, As we were marching through Georgia!"

Freeing the slaves, that was our one American Jubilee; yes, that was part of the ancient Jubilee too, all the slaves were to be freed when the Jubilee year came. But in 1865, America never did the other part, never shared the land. That was what "forty acres and a mule" meant: It was the slaves' demand that the land be shared. It was their proposal for a Jubilee.

We never did it, and now look where we are.

I returned to the present with a jerk. The populists want a protest/celebration in Washington on the Bicentennial Fourth of July. They are calling together the labor unions, food co-op organizers, environmental activists, feminists, antiwar people, Blacks, Hispanics, the religious who believe in social justice—to demand the end of the corporate oligarchy and the beginnings of an economic democracy.

They are brainstorming about the early morning of July 4, 1976. Should there be a sunrise service? A memorial service for those who died in the Revolution and those who fought for freedom since then?

I spoke up: What about the Jubilee? The religious traditions not only mourn the dead, they command us to do what the dead had in mind: Free the slaves and share our wealth. They call on us to make a Jubilee!

From that moment to the celebration at Mr. Jefferson's memorial was no straight and simple road. There were many twists and turns and disappointments. And since July 4, 1976, there have been even more disappointments. We have not yet found a way to sound the ram's horn that will call forth "liberty throughout the land, for all the inhabitants thereof."

## WHO OWNS THE EARTH?

Indeed, the years that followed the Bicentennial saw the most sweeping redistribution of wealth in all of American history—but in the opposite direction from what the Torah called for. Far more wealth was concentrated into the hands of far fewer people, leaving the rest of us to become either Overworked or Disemployed (some actually jobless, others working at far lower levels than our ability and education made possible).

Yet, the deeper our disparities in wealth, the more shattered our families and neighborhoods, the more we fear falling off the career ladder, the more despoiled our earth and water, the more I am convinced that the Jubilee has much to teach us.

In 1976, we asked religious officials to join our call for an American Jubilee. One ruefully wrote back that the church laity were not "well enough schooled in the Bible to make the Jubilee alive for them." Another wrote that it seemed like a great idea, but his was the wrong organization: "Our lay trustees are exactly the factory owners whose property would be shared out in the Jubilee. You'd better start somewhere else."

But we also got some unexpected affirmations:

A Black preacher remembered his granddaddy's telling him there was a Jubilee in 1865. He had already organized his own conference on applying the Jubilee to American society.

A rabbi proposed that in honor of the Bicentennial/Jubilee every family in America be offered a small homestead of country land to garden and preserve.

The same rabbi suggested asking groups of ten or a dozen to do "Jubilee dreaming" as a way to work out what kind of community they would like to live in—at the neighborhood or even the continental level.

A Catholic priest told us that in the Holy Years that used to come every fifty years, each diocese forgave the debts owed it by the poorer parishes.

A Reformed Churchman was organizing a church education project for the Bicentennial year, with the Jubilee at its heart.

A Mennonite wrote that when Jesus quoted Isaiah on "the acceptable year of our Lord," he was proclaiming the Jubilee—and was run out of town not for claiming to be Messiah but for demanding that the rich give up their wealth.

This was a new kind of long-distance Godwrestling, not face-to-face like Fabrangen but just as real. And I began to hear the Jubilee in a deeper way, as a great Shabbat.

By now I had been making Shabbat for about four years. I discovered it was not just a set of rules about what I couldn't do, as my neighbor up the street had yelled at me when I was growing up in Baltimore. It was not even just a chance to sleep late, take a nap, rest from my work. After all, I loved my work: Working for justice and peace; healing the fractured human race. Why rest from work like that?

I discovered that was just the point. Even from the best work in the world, I needed rest. Shabbat had brought me a new kind of freedom: Liberation from anxiety, sorrow, guilt that I was not doing even more to heal the wounded world. Shabbat brought not merely sleep, but peacefulness. For on one day of every seven, the world *was* already healed, already perfect. That day was a day of song and neighbors, playful reading and unhurried eating, feeling loved and making love. It was a return to the home of my soul.

I began to see that the Jubilee was about more than redistributing land or money. It was about a longer, deeper Shabbat in which everyone would share. Just as Jewish communities have always known that on Shabbat there must be food for the hungry—otherwise, how could they stop working?—so on this Great Shabbat there must be land for the poor.

And there must also be rest for the land. Odd. Very odd. No reformer or radical I had ever heard of said that if land and wealth were redistributed, the poor should wait a year before beginning to work.

I recalled that the iceskating rink at Rockefeller Center was shut one day a year. Why? Because under common law, if land is totally devoted to public use, the owner may lose legal title to it. Closing the rink for a single day established that its owners were still the owners, with power to control the property. How to assert Divine Ownership of the earth in the face of all the human uses of it? Shut down the rink. Close down the harvest and the sowing-season. The Owner reminds us: All the earth is Mine.

But what does it mean for God to own the earth?

It means that the spiritual and the political, the ritual and the practical, are fused.

How different this is from our "multiple-choice" way of thinking about the world! Tongue in cheek, I began to imagine an exam in Anthropology 101, with a multiple-choice question: Check off the category of cultural behavior (priestly ritual; prophetic pursuit of social justice; governmental economic planning; monkish contemplative meditation) that is exemplified by the following practice:

Rhythmic seven-year event, followed by seven-times-seven year event, initiated by blowing a ram's horn. *Answer: Ritual.*

Redistribution of land. *Answer: Social Justice.*

Moratorium on organized agriculture. *Answer: Economic Planning*

Celebration, study of sacred texts. *Answer: Contemplation, Meditation*

Question 2: If all these practices were the *same* event, under what category would you place them?

That is the Jubilee. Resting, redistributing, and reflecting are profoundly the same act, and that one act is infused with celebration of the Spirit.

The Jubilee tradition says to us: You cannot achieve equality unless you accept that no human really owns the wealth, not the boss, not the proletariat, not even the people as a whole: Only God, Who is Beyond. It says: You cannot achieve spiritual transcendence, you cannot free yourself from "attachment" and addiction to material values, unless you know that everyone needs and must share the wealth. It says: You cannot heal the earth if you are driven by greed, or fear, or envy.

And the Jubilee is not static. It does not imagine that we can achieve a Great Plateau of social peace or spiritual peace, and then just sit there. It speaks of a rhythm, a cycle of change. It does not imagine that the land can be shared and justice achieved once and for all, and it does not imagine that a little change, year after year, can make for real justice. The Jubilee says that in every year the poor must be allowed to glean in the corners of the field, that in every seventh year loans must be forgiven and the poor lifted from the desperation of debt, that for six years of every seven it is all right for some to accumulate wealth and some to lose it, and for the earth to be forced to work under human command—but that once in every generation there must be a great transformation. And that each generation must know it will have to be done again, in the next generation.

This rhythm is not what we have come to know as conservative or liberal or radical. It carries a more subtle sense of human behavior than any one of them.

## RHYTHMS OF REST

And the Jubilee says that there is a connection between the cycle of nature and the cycle of human life. For the Jubilee is rooted in a set of smaller rhythms, the rhythms of earth and sun and moon:

There is first the rhythm of the earth's spin upon its axis. Count seven sunsets, and we dance our way into Shabbat.

And there is the dance of earth and moon. Count seven new moons, and we reach a month of Shabbat. Begin counting with the month the Torah teaches is "the first of months," the month of spring and Passover, and our seventh month is Tishri, the month of holy festivals for every phase of the moon: Rosh Hashanah (the new moon), Yom Kippur (the waxing moon), Sukkot (the full moon) and Sh'mini Atzeret/Simchat Torah (the waning moon). And then if we begin counting again from the Shabbat month of Tishri, we reach the seventh new moon in the spring; Nisan, the month of Passover.

Tishri and Nisan: Months of rest, renewal, sharing—sharing the frail hut of the sukkah in the fall, sharing the flat bread of the matzah in the spring. Months of Shabbat.

And then we count the circlings of the earth around the sun. Count seven autumn equinoxes, and we reach the Sabbatical Year, the year of Shabbat. The year when all debts were to be forgiven and the land was to lie fallow.

Only then, in the year following the seventh seventh year, in the fiftieth year, could the rhythm whirl up the final spiral to the Jubilee.

In each Shabbat, a whiff of the Jubilee to come. In every Jubilee, the delight of a deeper Shabbat.

And how does the cycle feel when the Jubilee itself comes round at last? There stands the land untilled as it stood the year before, the seventh seventh year. Two years in a row untilled! Picture a farming society where twice in a row the land had gone unsown, the trees and vines unpruned. Where the free growth of the soil was for every family to pluck, not for the owners to harvest systematically.

Imagine how strange the land would look: More than a touch of wilderness, a fifth "season" of the year. Nature itself would be transformed along with the society; everyone would have a sense that doing something so basic as sharing the wealth could change something so basic as how the plants grew.

Everyone would learn that the "biggest" action of all was to not act.

Not acting!—How fearful the farmers who tried to live by this teaching! The farmer might fear that waiting two years in a row would bring ruin. But the Torah asserts, and modern science confirms, that letting the land lie fallow is a crucial part of its restoration. What looks like a famine in the short run is necessary to prosperity in the long run.

Perhaps it was shepherds who taught this lesson to farmers. Shepherds knew they must move their flocks from pasture to pasture, to allow each field to recover its nutrient power. Farmers could not move from place to place; for them, rotation in time would take the place of rotation in space. From the wisdom of restfulness in the technological era before us, can we learn the wisdom of restfulness for our own generation?

Let us imagine the farmer who stands on his family plot of land, thinking: Here, right here, is where my grandparents stood fifty years ago, and here, right here, is where my grandchildren will stand fifty years hence. Come what may, in fifty years here my seed will stand, knowing this hill and this wellspring, this rock and this olive tree.

Between the renewed health of my small family and the renewed health of my whole country, land and people, there is a clear unity. For it is only by restoring each family that our country is restored: No king, no priest can accomplish this renewal. Only my family—and every other family.

All this we do not learn from modern secular politics. Today conservatives who demand that the family be strengthened turn furious at the idea of abolishing all wealth and privilege. Radicals who demand that the rich be expropriated are baffled at the ideas that the land be left unproductive or the "regressive" institution of the family be celebrated.

The Jubilee stands beyond the politics of guilt and rage. It does not ask for the rich to give their land away in fear or guilt; it does not ask the wretched of the earth and the prisoners of starvation to rise in rage to take back the land from the swollen rich.

Instead, the Jubilee proclaims a "release," a Shabbat, for everyone. A release for the rich as well as the poor. The rich are released from working, bossing, increasing production—and from others' envy of them. The poor are released from working, from hunger, from humiliation and despair—and from others' pity of them. Both the rich and the poor are seen as fully human, as counterparts to be encountered—not as enemies or victims to be feared or hated.

So the Jubilee Year begins not at Rosh Hashanah when the fiftieth year itself begins, but ten days later—on Yom Kippur, when the community has already purged itself of guilt and rage. Only when the Days of Awe and Turning have already accomplished atonement can the Jubilee be proclaimed. Thus it is both the final healing gift of the people to God to complete the old cycle, and God's first blessing to the people in the new cycle.

But the Jubilee was not based only on recognizing God's image in every human being. It may have appealed to the class interests of a large group of independent small farmers who wanted to prevent the emergence of a permanent, ever-fattening class of large landholders who could lord it over them, on the one hand, and a class of permanent slaves or debtors who would undercut their income, on the other.

## TOWARD A TECHNO-JUBILEE

So let us imagine that the Jubilee could be for us not quite a model but a pointer, a hint. A pointer to what the middling classes of America could say in the search for a decent society—beyond their own greed, beyond their own guilt.

Imagine applying the Jubilee approach to the despair, violence, anomie, alienation of our cities. To drug abuse, the disintegration of families, violence not only on the streets but within families, the abuse of children, the abandonment of old people. What would it say?

That everyone must know *for sure* that neither poverty nor charity, neither despair nor greed, neither envy nor largesse, will last forever; that economic independence and responsibility are coming to everyone.

That there must be hope—not the hope of fantasy, but the hope of sure knowledge.

That in one's own family, neighborhood, community is where cultural roots and economic independence begin.

That individual rest is not enough; whole communities must take their rest together, for that rest to be truly refreshing.

That just as communal rest is necessary for the renewal of work, a rhythm of communal return to the songs, stories, crafts, and foods of communal roots is necessary to healthy cultural growth.

That a rhythmical communal celebration of earth and air and water, plants and animals, is necessary for a healthy return to contact with other human beings.

That we must recreate the rhythms of rest, roots, and nature—to recreate these rhythms in the very midst of the cities where they are now abandoned.

How would we translate such wistful statements into policy and program? When people in 1976 began to "think Jubilee," economic sharing felt most important. When I read the Jubilee passage in 1992 with a group of people at a national convention of Jewish Federations and United Jewish Appeals, the Jubilee's implications for the healing of the earth leaped out at us. We noticed a darker side of the Jubilee tradition (Lev. 26:34-35) that in the more optimistic 1970s we had not even noticed: If the community does *not* let the land rest in the Sabbatical and Jubilee years, "Then shall the land make up for its Shabbat years through time that it is desolate....Through the time that it is desolate, it shall observe the restfulness that it did not rest in the restful-Shabbat years while you were dwelling on it."

Suddenly these Jewish leaders saw encoded in this ancient teaching what they had thought an ultramodern ecological assertion: "It's like the law of gravity. The earth *will* rest, and if we don't get it, if we don't let it rest, and even celebrate by resting too, then the entire planet will 'rest' all right—upon our heads. Sounds like what my eighteen-year-old daughter keeps telling me."

Recently, I have been asking scientists, businesspeople, rabbis, economists with whom I study the Jubilee texts to suspend for a moment their own skepticism over what would be possible to get society to do, and instead just imagine what would be a modern way of carrying out the sabbatical year or the Jubilee. Some interesting ideas have emerged:

From a businessman: "I could set aside one year of every seven when I kept selling my old products but didn't produce any new ones. That would give the whole company a chance to pause and think about where we're going. And it would reduce the strain on the earth a little."

From an engineer: "Suppose every seventh year we stopped all technological research and development, except maybe R & D on mortal diseases. (After all, just as Torah teaches, we're supposed to violate the Shabbat rules in order to save a life.) Suppose the whole society gave us a year off at some reasonable salary, to think and talk about what technology is good for anyway. What we do now is the exact opposite of Shabbat: We're figuring out how to make the earth work harder. Produce more. With a year off, the earth would get to rest a little right away, and we could seek a kind of technology that in the long run would let the earth and human beings rest more deeply."

From a rabbi: "Suppose we brought the idea of Shabbat or even a week-long festival like Sukkot to the public at large: A week-long celebration of communal roots, neighborhood, and playfulness. Maybe the week of the Fourth of July. We would close down not just factories and offices, but gas stations, airplanes, and trains. Even newspapers and TV. Instead of using vacation time to get as far away from our neighbors as possible, we visit. We have street fairs, with music and stories and food and crafts. And neighborhood town meetings where people talk about public issues, protecting the earth, making our neighborhoods alive again, what work is like, why jobs are so hard to get, and what to do about it."

An environmental biologist: "Nowadays we insist on 'environmental impact' assessments before making any major changes in land use. But we don't do this when a corporation is about to introduce a major new product. What if any corporation or agency that was planning to invest more than one billion dollars in producing a new automobile, say, or a new computer, a new weapon—were required to wait for a 'sabbatical' year while its impact on the earth was assessed by independent examiners?"

An economist: "Suppose we had a pool of loan money in every state. Money we could lend to businesses that were owned and run by face-to-face communities: Family businesses where at least 80 percent of the workers were in the family. Co-op grocery stores housed in a synagogue. Bike factories owned by a couple of dozen workers. PTA's, unions, a chapter of the NAACP—they could all start businesses."

"Where would you get the startup capital?"

"Well, if we took the Jubilee seriously, the way they divide up the land every fifty years—for us, I guess we'd put a special tax on, say, any corporation worth more than one billion dollars that has been around more than forty-nine years." He laughs. "Wouldn't be so easy to pass that tax. No wonder it was hard for them to actually do the Jubilee."

A Catholic nun from an urban ministry: "What I like is very earthy," she laughs; "I mean literally. We could work in my neighborhood to develop vegetable gardens and fisheries, maybe even chicken farms. Make us less dependent on the supermarkets. Even canneries, food stores, restaurants."

# THE PULSATING SOCIETY

From all these responses and my own wrestling, I realize that the Torah is envisioning an economy profoundly different from the one we're used to. Ours is based on constant explosive economic growth. But now it's not so clear that the world economy can keep on "growing" in the way we're used to. Put as many Chinese, per capita, in automobiles as there are Americans, and the whole planet would suffocate.

What is the Torah's economic vision? We might call it a "pulsating" rather than an expanding or exploding system. And it may be relevant to us in ways we would not have foreseen, one generation ago. Today, economists are beginning to talk about "sustainable" economies, which can meet their peoples' needs year after year, generation after generation, by restoring the earth to the same degree that they deplete it. Not the same as economic growth.

And the Torah's vision of social justice also differs from our modern notion. At its heart is not equality but "resting," not only from the physical work of tilling the land, but from the political and social work of building institutions and concentrating capital. Even very useful institutions must be periodically dissolved. That way the whole rigid pattern of society—some on top, some on the bottom, some assigned to this role, some to that—all dissolves. People are freed up, the imagination is freed up. How could we win the benefits of that, without bringing on a time of social chaos?

How would we deal with spiritual hunger? We have often encouraged people to buy more goodies, gobble up the world, as a substitute for spiritual nourishment. Our churches, synagogues, schools, families, even our psychotherapists, have gotten sloppy and ineffective in helping us to grow in spiritual depth. If buying new material goods has its limits, will demands for spirituality get stronger? Or, to think of it the other way round, if we need to restrain our material consumption for the planet's sake, do we need to create more spiritual sustenance?

How would we deal with healing the earth? Most official "environmental" programs have focused on cleanup and recycling. There has been very little reexamination of the production end of the process—where destruction is actually likely to begin. The Sabbatical/Jubilee cycle teaches that we must face issues of production if the earth is to be protected.

The more I absorb all this, the more I feel both exhilarated and exhausted. What a task! And what a possibility! Pursuing such changes would renew our roots, redirect our history, and release our creativity. No doubt it would take a great political struggle—since those who hold power rarely give it up or share it without a struggle.

I ask myself, how could we begin?

Suppose that in a particular city for nine days, from a Jewish Shabbat through a Christian Sabbath (from Friday night through Sunday), a group of synagogues and churches held a Jubilee Festival.

Such a Jubilee Festival would address the economic renewal of the city and its neighborhoods by inviting co-ops and worker-managed firms, innovative small businesses, etcetera, to explain their work; by demonstrating equipment for energy conservation and the local generation of solar/renewable energy; by turning empty lots or part of the church or synagogue grounds into communal vegetable gardens; by holding workshops on how tenants can buy apartment houses and turn them into co-ops; by setting up a temporary food co-op and helping people organize a more permanent one.

It would address the spiritual and cultural renewal of the neighborhood through song, dance, storytelling, sharing food.

It would address the political empowerment of the neighborhood by gathering people to discuss in open town meetings some of the major issues of our society—energy, jobs, environment, prices, families.

Where do we find the energy to start?

The Jubilee passages in the Torah teach us: The most effective politics has a powerful ritual element in it, engaging not only material interests but deep emotional, intellectual, and spiritual energies. And when ritual is made fully communal and focused on reality, it becomes precisely politics: Black churches in the South. Soviet Jews dancing and singing, carrying the Torah into the public streets. Gandhi, fasting.

I remember how I began this unexpected journey at the Pesach Seder of 1968, in the midst of an exploding city. What erupted in me was a fusion of "ritual" and "politics." The Jubilee is both.

# CHAPTER 19

# HOW IS THIS YEAR DIFFERENT FROM ALL OTHER YEARS?

For many Jews, the coming of Passover each year marks change in their lives: What elder who used to lead the Seder is too sick to attend? What shy guest has become a spouse, bold and good-humored at the table? What baby-talking child has just learned to chant the Four Questions? What sibling who knew little and cared less about Jewish life has begun to love wrestling with the Haggadah and is testing out some new-learned Hebrew?

For me, Passover has been all this and more. Since my entry into my committed Jewish life-work had come through the Passovers of 1968 and 1969, when a burning city and a Freedom Seder had marked the Pesach poles of bitterness and joy, the festival itself had become for me a kind of Burning Bush: A Voice calling me into my work and vision.

Through the Seder, every year I marked the deep changes in myself and in Jewish and American life. Year after year through the 1970s and 1980s and 1990s, I found joy and hope in the return of the Festival of Freedom. Year by year, I felt myself growing—understanding more deeply as a Godwrestler the meanings of Pesach within myself, in my family, in Judaism, in the politics of America and the world. Year by year, it seemed that scattered bands and momentary gatherings of Jews like me were becoming communities and networks. And year by year, it seemed as if the world were opening its ears more fully to the burning voice of compassion and justice that spoke in the Burning Bush: Caring more deeply for the voiceless earth and for voiceless peoples suffering under governments like Pharaoh. The Berlin Wall fell as the Red Sea had opened. Ishmael and Isaac shook hands on the White House lawn. The slaves of apartheid and their former overseers together brought astounding change, without even a slaughter of the first-born. Earth Day called the whole globe together to hear the voice of spring and heal the wounds of air and trees and water.

But as Passover approached in 1995, it spoke to me in a different voice. It was again the Voice that spoke at the Burning Bush:

*I have seen, yes, seen my people*
*pressed down*
*in the Narrow Space, in Egypt;*
*Their shrieks of pain I have heard*
*as they faced slave-drivers;*
*I have taken their sufferings to heart.*

I kept hearing shrieks of pain in my own country:

The moans of a woman dying of breast cancer—caused by a pesticide poured into earth and air.

The wails of hunger from a baby whose mother had been cut off the welfare rolls.

The sobs of a man whose body was at last surrendering to AIDS.

The coughs of a janitor who caught tuberculosis from a man who could not afford to see a doctor after he got fired and his health insurance stopped.

The tears of a tenth-grade student who had been expelled from school because her father was an undocumented alien.

The shouts of raging quarrel between a suburban professional couple who never got to see each other or their children because they each had to work a twelve-hour day, lest the company give their jobs to someone else.

The last gasps of a thousand dying species of ferns, whales, frogs, owls.

The sad and lonely silences of those with no community, no intimate friends, no sense of a larger Unity in the world.

These outcries were not new in 1995, so why did they seem louder to me? Because in 1995 it seemed that the rulers of America had suddenly become much more like Pharaoh, hardening their hearts against these outcries.

It was not that most Americans were refusing to hear them. Most opinion polls said most Americans did not want the sick or the earth, the children or the old, the disemployed or the overworked, the poor or the lonely, to suffer. Most Americans approved of public action to make sure that all sick people could afford a doctor, that great forests were not destroyed, that the poor had jobs to meet their needs. Yet something had gone wrong in the process by which those grass-roots desires got translated into public action.

What then to do?

The Voice that spoke from the Burning Bush told Moses to awaken the people, to face Pharaoh. Moses responded with fear and skepticism. The Voice spoke out again, taking on a Name of transformation: *Ehyeh Asher Ehyeh*, "I Will Be Who I Will Be," "I Am Becoming Who I Am Becoming."

Indeed, my first reaction to hearing with new clarity the outcry of pain—and the reaction of my friends and communities—was a sense of helplessness, uselessness. Like Moses, we felt tongue-tied. No one of us was ready to be a Prophet alone; we sought not a subservient Aaron to be our mouthpiece, but a community to share the work together.

And we needed to understand more deeply what had happened. Before I could face Pharaoh, I needed to understand who and what were Pharaoh. Why had most people become so helpless? Why had the recent awakening of spirit in so many hundreds of thousands of Americans left us so helpless to help each other?

## ENDANGERED SPECIES, ENDANGERED CULTURES

The shock of facing Pesach in 1995 forced me to reflect on everything we had done since the Pesach of 1968.

Why did a movement for Jewish renewal grow out of the Freedom Seder and the dozen other tiny fellowships of youngish Jews that were getting started at the same time? Because many Jews felt cut off from family, community, and spirituality; ill served by the conventional Jewish structures. Many of us then spent this quarter-century building intimate communities to replace our scattered families, creating prayers and meditations and ceremonies full of life to replace the rote recitals, making the equality of women and gay people real instead of standing at the back of the *shul*, creating progressive funding groups instead of giving money to institutions that seemed brain-dead or worse.

For twenty-five years and more, these Jewish-renewal approaches kept spreading, even into mainstream Jewish institutions. It seemed as if they were increasingly meeting the needs of the Jewish people. It looked as if the problems of Jewish community, intimacy, spirituality, and democracy were being solved.

But now the disease seemed to be outracing the remedy. Why?

In the beginning, many of those who created the *havurot* and the movement for Jewish renewal thought we were being robbed of intimacy, community, democracy, intellectual depth, and spiritual richness by a callous Jewish establishment. Twenty-five years later, it is easier to see that the "Jewish establishment" was just a subset or even just a symptom of a great worldwide earthquake in human relations—the triumph of Hyper-Modernity, a corporate-bureaucratic structure that was undermining all sorts of communal life in the workplace or the neighborhood, leaching all the juice from family life, making citizenship and politics into a high-paid hype for public-relations experts, and turning visions full of meaning into commercial slogans.

All around the globe, governments and corporations were making local communities of all sorts extinct just as they were making many species of plants and animals extinct.

Now we can see that the movement for Jewish renewal was an instinctive effort to protect a small, threatened culture by renewing it under new circumstances: Different, yet still committed to smallness, to intimacy, to community, to an age-old wisdom in all its changing forms, even to that ultimate anachronism—prayer.

Jewish renewal implicitly, in its very being, challenged the machine of global homogenization. Few of us expected the machine of Hyper-Modernity to pose a more direct threat to the process of Jewish renewal. Most of us thought that the growth of our deeper and stronger communities would weaken the machine and allow us to birth a new kind of holistic Judaism and to work with others to birth a new holistic human civilization.

But as the century wanes, it has become apparent that *havurot* and other forms of Jewish renewal have not been able to turn the machine aside. Nor have the analogous groups and approaches that have arisen in non-Jewish communities. By the 1990s, it was clear that the "global economy" has been homogenizing the world faster than the *havurot* and their analogues have been able to decentralize it and rebuild committed communities.

Most basic to this deeper crisis is the emergence of an enormous concentration of top-down power in the hands of a few worldwide corporations, what ancient Jewish tradition might have seen as a global "pharaoh."

Just as the Torah describes some pharaohs as expanding their power out of an open-hearted desire to prevent famine and other pharaohs as expanding their power out of hardhearted, aggressive choice to dominate more people, so it has been for these corporations. Some of the people who own and manage them have deliberately and aggressively expanded their power, leaping across national boundaries and undermining any governments, unions, consumer groups, environmental organizations, or religious and ethnic communities that got in the way. Some owners and managers have felt forced to expand in order to meet the needs and desires of their customers, forced to compete by lowering their costs even when that meant firing their workers and polluting the earth, forced by technological change to become global or die.

## THE DISEMPLOYED AND THE OVERWORKED

In either case, the result is that many grass-roots communities have lost the power to shape their own lives, as both Egyptians and Hebrews lost it to both beneficent and malicious pharaohs in ancient Egypt. These corporations control the mass media, which can now penetrate local cultures and families far more effectively than ever before; they have opposed even meager protections against environmental disaster in order to use "natural resources" more efficiently; they have used computer technology not to share worthwhile work, increase leisure, and strengthen face-to-face community, but to create two new classes of people: The Disemployed* and the Overworked.

The Disemployed are those who in increasing numbers have either been tossed out of their jobs altogether and end up on the streets, in jail, or in jail-like "temporary" shelters, or have been dumped out of well-paid work requiring some skill, into low-paid dead-end menial jobs.

The Overworked are those who out of fear, need, or devotion to a job that too few people have been hired to do, are now working harder, longer, and under greater strain than they or their elder cohorts did.

---

*Why am I saying "disemployed," rather than "unemployed"? One reason is that I am calling "disemployed" both people who end up fully and literally unemployed, and people who get pushed into jobs that are far beneath what their abilities, their skills, and their educations would make possible. A second reason is to remind us that most people do not become "unemployed" by happenstance. They are *dis*employed by someone who makes an active decision.

As Charlie King sings, "What ever happened to the eight-hour day? When did they take it away?" Over the past twenty-five years, hours and stress have multiplied for those who do keep their jobs, and many women have shifted from working at home to working in jobs. Together, these changes have greatly reduced the amount of control that most people have over their own time, the pace of their work, and their ability to focus on their families and their neighborhoods.

## THE GRASS ROOTS WITHER

The fraying of family and community has both weakened the sense of coherent values and culture, and weakened many grass-roots organizations—PTA's, synagogues and churches, public-policy groups—that depend on volunteer time and energy. The sheer exhaustion and tension of this society-wide "speed-up" has been one of the main factors leading toward the crisis in values, culture, and sense of community.

Politics is affected, too. As neighborliness rots away, so do the precincts. The Democratic Party—which once was an amalgam of neighborhood communities, Jewish and Irish and Italian and Black— becomes just another national corporation, built on high-paid media whizzes, hype artists, and big-money fund-raisers.

Under this pressure, a healthy life becomes a vicious cycle:

Economic fear of losing a job fuels overwork, and therefore makes it impossible to spend time at home with family, friends, or neighborhood.

Those who keep their jobs become exhausted, cannot put time into family or religious congregation or neighborhood association or citizenly politics, and collapse into using the mass media to relax.

These media teach that only narrow self-interest matters, that violence is endemic and OK, and that having more property— therefore working still harder—is all that counts, both for security against the ever-present danger of disemployment, and for the sake of prestige and emotional fulfillment where interpersonal communal pleasures have lost their savor.

So people work harder than ever to buy the pretty goodies that never really satisfy their hunger, and to keep from getting fired. They get exhausted. And...

This vicious circle spins into support for right-wing solutions: If my family is dissolving, it must be the fault of those feminists. Put women back in their place. Or maybe it's the fault of runaway fathers: Jail them. If my kids are not growing in the way I'd like, it must be the fault of the public schools—they are only breeding grounds for sex and violence anyway. Starve the schools, and build more prisons. And make the schools control the kids—because I certainly can't. I don't have time.

And if my job is in danger, it may be the fault of those environmentalists and all their regulations, undercutting my company's profits. I look around, and more people are getting sick—cancer, AIDS, these new forms of TB—and if I lose my job I lose my health insurance—so dump those regulations. People count, not owls. (You say it's the pesticides that are causing more cancer, and dropping the regulations will make things worse—maybe even make me very sick in ten years or so? I can't pay attention—I need my job now.)

Meanwhile, those who lose their jobs become hopeless or homeless or violent or drugged—not a new political insurgent energy but politically irrelevant or worse. Indeed, they become good hard reasons for strengthening police and prisons. So in the society as a whole, the polarization between the overworked and the disemployed becomes a larger vicious circle, fueling a politic that gets worse and worse.

## SHARING SHABBAT

What does all this have to do with Passover?

Passover meant liberation from a Pharaoh who was forcing some people into overwork and was ready to kill the surplus useless laborers.

The solution? A journey that was not just geographic. When the Israelites made their way into freedom, it was on the road, even before Sinai, that they worked out one solution. Listen to their muttered conversation:

"My God, that was terrible, that place. How can we make sure it doesn't happen again, under some new boss in our new country?"

"How about this: Let's set aside some time for rest that everybody gets to share—one day of every seven, one year of every seven. And let's make sure everybody has enough land to make a decent income, and if anybody gets in trouble let's make sure they can work for a living on somebody else's land.

"And the fields will get to rest too. That way nobody will be overworked, nobody will get disemployed, and the earth won't be exhausted into the kind of famine that got us into Egypt in the first place."

In other words, Shabbat—the first discovery of the newly freed Israelites, the one that came with manna in the Wilderness. And then, the expanded rhythm of the great Shabbat: Sabbatical years and the Jubilee, which we have already examined. The rhythm that became a vision of the good society, held aloft by a culture that had suffered under Pharaoh and was trying to ensure that its own society would never have a Pharaoh.

Passover calls us, as it called the Israelites, to look past Passover itself toward creating the spiritual community—not only spiritually oriented individuals. That strength freed the Southern Black community to face death, act for life, and win—despite the power of a right wing that had been deeply entrenched for three centuries. That strength has given Passover its staying power for 3,000 years. And yet in modern America, this spiritual community must not be religiously exclusive or discriminatory. Here are some possibilities:

Reducing the work week without reducing income, and at the same time making possible the citizenly use of the new leisure we would gain, would simultaneously provide more jobs for the disemployed and freer time for the overworked. Workers would regain time to strengthen their families, do volunteer work for their communities, and reenter politics at the grass roots.

As part of this program, we could draw on one idea that arose in my discussions of a contemporary Jubilee: The notion of setting aside certain times and resources (perhaps one day a month, plus the week of the Fourth of July) for communal celebration, including social support for neighborhood festivals and family days. Except for emergency services, the whole society would shut down at these times—including the mass media and "vacation" businesses and transportation. This is a way to share work, rest, and some income in society as a whole.

Secondly, just as Passover intertwines the renewal of the earth in spring with the rebirth of human freedom, we need to intertwine issues of the environment and issues of human health.

Conventional environmental efforts are often portrayed as pitting "human" and "non-human" interests and compassion against each other. "Owls" were pitted against "workers," and both lost. This is exactly opposite from what Judaism teaches—what the Hebrew language itself teaches in the words *adamah* (earth) and *adam* (human being, "earthling"). These words show that the earth and the human race are intertwined with each other; in each is something of the other. We need to create a politics that expresses this teaching of the Torah.

We could do this by explicitly connecting healing the earth with healing human bodies. From the standpoint of human health, costs can be reduced only by focusing on prevention more than cure. Prevention means a combination of environmental protection and grass-roots community action on behalf of public-health measures. From the environmental standpoint, the lagging desire to protect the earth could be reenergized by explicitly connecting environmental degradation and the collapse of community with the mounting dangers from cancer, AIDS, and such resurgent diseases as TB and cholera.

Finally, religious communities have said for thousands of years that families are the heart of community, as community is the heart of justice. For thousands of years, "family" had a patriarchal shape based on male domination. Today that shape is not only gone, but for most of us no longer to be desired. Yet we, and most Americans, stand paralyzed between nostalgia for the patriarchal family and disdain for it. We need to create a new vision of family values, sexuality, child-rearing, and education, that draws on the life-experience of children, women, and men.

Schools, as well as families, are crucial arenas where these intimate questions are resolved in people's lives. Drawing on age-old Jewish experience, this means bringing families—elders as well as a younger generation of parents—deeper into the process of educating the next generation. Drawing on Jewish-renewal experiences like our parents-co-op Cheder in Washington, it means explicitly defining such families and schools not as patriarchal and hierarchical but as egalitarian and relational, involving gay as well as heterosexual couples, single parents and non-parents. It means listening to the children as well—as we tried to do in the Cheder. And perhaps above all it means doing the hard day-to-day work of organizing on issues of the schools, as the right wing has recently done so well.

## THE SHAPE OF THINGS TO COME

Supporting public policies that meet public needs is important, but still more important is the form and quality of the way people gather and organize themselves to change the world. Since the neighborhoods—Jewish, Italian, Irish, Black—that used to support political effort in an organic relationship are so much weaker than they were a generation ago, effective political organizers need to create these communities and do their political work in and through them, at the same time.

One crucial truth: The medium is the message and the means become the ends. For communities that draw authentically on Jewish renewal, it is necessary—but not enough—to work for public policies that bear Torah values. It is also necessary to create forms that embody these values, treating organizing as a communal, celebratory, even spiritual act. Remember: It was not pork barrel, patronage-ridden, party-hack politics—and not even good-government reformers or tough-fisted labor organizing—that transformed the South in the last generation. It was fervent Black churches that entered precinct-level party politics as well as sit-in politics.

Precisely because the medium is the message, because political "means" always become the real political "ends," creating local centers of personal, communal, and political healing in the present can also help reshape the future of society. For there is certainly some truth to the "conservative" complaint, now echoed by millions, that bureaucratic government can become divorced from the needs of the people it is intended to serve. The demand for localism and decentralization is fakery when it multiplies the military and leaves giant corporations "free" to poison the earth, disemploy workers, and impose speedups on the whole society. But there is a real need for locally rooted power that can both meet human needs on a face-to-face basis and challenge any institution—whether it is a theoretically "public" government or a theoretically "private" corporation—that becomes oppressive.

What would it mean to create synagogues and *havurot* that could become as effective in the lives of American Jews as the Black Southern churches and ministers of the 1960s were in the lives of their communities?

The Black churches united three key elements of life:

They were centers of celebration and mourning, filled with laughter, prayer, and tears. Joys were shared with a community and with a God Who affirms and undergirds victories. Sufferings were borne with faith in the love of a broader community and a God Who transcends defeats.

They tried to meet the practical needs of the people. Members banded together to feed each other, to visit the sick, to lend each other money in hard times. The churches became centers for learning the skills to build community: Speaking in public and making decisions in committees, planning budgets, managing buildings, running schools, hiring and firing.

After a long history when the churches and their ministers acted as political advocates only privately and cautiously, beginning in the late 1950s more and more of them publicly opposed racial segregation, fought for the right to vote, and used it to secure better schools, streets, and governmental services, as well as taking some initial steps toward economic justice.

For most American Jews, the synagogue or *havurah* is not likely to be the all-encompassing center that the church was for many Black Southerners. But if today's social crisis continues and deepens, the synagogues could become far more important than they have been.

What would need to happen to make them effective centers for addressing a broader spectrum of Jewish concerns in the three areas we have noted—spiritual depth, practical services, and political focus?

We begin with synagogues that most of their members define as limited spiritual centers, focused on a few festivals each year and—far more important—the life-cycle moments of celebrating the birth of children, welcoming the young into adolescence, becoming married, perhaps dealing with serious sickness, and mourning death. Between these events (and often even during them), the spiritual temperature of most congregations is tepid. Congregants facing an emotional or spiritual crisis are more likely to turn to a psychotherapist than to a rabbi.

During the past few decades of Jewish renewal, some mainstream congregations have become more filled with music and dance and the dramatic use of words, more open to using the liturgy and Torah not as frozen crystals of forgotten experience but as keys to open present doors of powerful emotion and intellect. And more rabbis have been learning to do therapeutic counseling. But most synagogues still ignore many of the most important moments in their congregants' lives that are not officially labeled as "Jewish time," and most do not make Shabbat into an experience that speaks to the deeper needs and hopes of most of their members.

## THE TRANSFORMATIVE SYNAGOGUE

To broaden and deepen the synagogue's role as spiritual center would mean creating communal Jewish expressions for such life-moments as learning to drive an automobile, leaving home, beginning one's first full-time serious job, reaching menopause, getting fired or laid off, changing careers, retiring, placing a parent in a nursing home. All these are intense, joyful or painful; few are addressed as moments in communal Jewish time, congregational time, time with God, prayer, Torah.

In the second arena we have noted, how could synagogues and *havurot* meet the practical needs of their members? Many congregations will have as members two kinds of people: Solidly affluent or wealthy lawyers, physicians, and businesspeople; and fraying middle-class professionals who from year to year are either among the Over-worked or the "temporarily Disemployed but not destitute." They will need not soup kitchens or emergency beds, but psychotherapy, job referrals, child care, elder care, support groups for recovering alcohol or gambling addicts, and political involvement. As schools and colleges and health insurance constrict, as corporations sell to their customers and employees more of the services that public institutions used to provide, can we support in our own communities some of the teachers, social workers, psychotherapists, and doctors who are being disemployed?

In regard to the third arena: Few synagogues see themselves as centers of political action or of community organizing, even on issues that directly affect their members. Few have acted to prevent racially exploitative real-estate "blockbusting" and panic sales in their immediate neighborhoods, and to encourage instead a calm and stable process of racial integration. Few have opposed the construction of environmentally dangerous power plants, or insisted on proper regulation of nursing homes, or protected public schools and libraries from censorship, or demanded low tuitions and easily available loans for high-quality colleges and universities—even though their own members might have directly benefited from such efforts. And few rabbis have been trained as community organizers or political activists.

Can synagogues and *havurot* involve the people who are likeliest to be interested in a political vision and action that might address their concerns? These might include students and under-employed younger social workers, teachers, lawyers, and other people-focused professionals with few family involvements, who are fearful of the economic future, hungry for companionship and community, and able to exercise some control over their own time. And they might also include older, retired people with a variety of organizing skills and contacts, who also have some free time and are also hungry for companionship and community.

Such people could organize letter-writing parties, visit corporation executives and members of city councils, school boards, and Congress, register voters, canvass door-to-door, run election campaigns and consumer boycotts, leaflet workplaces. With congregational support, they might be able to start a neighborhood co-op grocery, organize a neighborhood festival, initiate a town meeting. All this work would become emotionally and spiritually fulfilling if it included communal song and prayer.

It might also be useful to explore whether churches, synagogues, mosques, and Buddhist temples, or concerned members within each of these institutions, might work together in these ways. Some might even set up multi-religious centers to enable different religious communities to pursue together a path of social and political action infused with spiritual commitment. Such multi-religious centers might affirm in action, as well as words, a public politics of religious pluralism rather than monolithic, triumphalist religion.

## LIBERATING PESACH

All this is the public program and the path of organizing that we might remember and apply from the great tradition of the liberating Pesach, the Jewish journey into new forms of community and freedom. What about Pesach itself, the festival on which we gather to remember and reenact our freedom?

I think the time has come once more to renew the celebration of Passover. On the one hand, we are facing a top-down, pyramidal system of pharaonic power with a much more worldwide grasp than we have known before. On the other hand, for many people the Seder itself has once more become a time of joyful community and purposeful vision, a fusion of personal growth and public concern. As a group of friends and family sit around the table, they embody the ends in the means, the vision in the reality. And they can talk about what to do.

In the Haggadah, two passages begin, "In every generation..."

In every generation, someone arises to destroy our freedom.

In every generation, we ourselves must go forth from slavery to freedom.

At either or both of these places, those who share the Seder can pause and say to each other what outcries of pain they hear, what has arisen to starve the hungry, poison the earth, ignore the sick, demonize the stranger, force some workers into overworking and others into disemployment. Then they could talk about what they might do, singly or together, to face the pharaohs of our day; even some actions they might take that very week, the week of freedom, or during the seven weeks between Passover and the coming of the Torah at Mount Sinai.

This might happen at any Seder of friends and family. It might also happen at new waves of Freedom Seders, held during the latter days of Passover or even in the days before the festival begins, in which Jews would gather in broader communities—sponsored by synagogues, *havurot,* or other Jewish organizations. Such Freedom Seders might also bring together Jews with those from other communities of faith to share in a public covenant toward strengthening grass-roots communities of compassion and justice.

If Jews and other religiously rooted progressives do not take initiatives along these lines, the sense of American civic spirit and community will probably continue to erode, and our society will become even more deeply divided into those exhausted in despair, those consumed by rage, and those embittered by fear and frustration. That is a recipe for right-wing panaceas: Prescribing prayer, abandoning the middle class, punishing the poor, demonizing the stranger. Not good for the Jews, or anyone else.

# PART VI

# TOWARD UNITY

# CHAPTER 20

# ONE "I"

I find myself standing at the foot of Sinai.

As I look toward the holy mountain, I see an enormous mirror. More than enormous: Infinite.

In it I see my self, and the whole Jewish people: Thousands who have just trekked out of slavery; ancient Sarah laughing with her husband Abraham; my grandfather Pop, his yellow mustache shaking as he tells a bawdy story; some whose clothing I have never seen in history books.

And I see Egypt, Mother Egypt. And Babylon. And Rome. And India, and the Americas, and snowy plains of ice, and rolling oceans.

The intricate web of human settlements, languages, cultures, dances; a hundred thousand foods, herbs, drinks of nourishment and ecstasy, the shimmering touch of hands and thighs and lips in delicate connection.

And the glaring sun. Spinning planets. Whole whirling galaxies.

My blood cells. One tiny red corpuscle. An atom of oxygen within it. Weightless positrons, dancing in nothing.

All the while I see, I also hear. Echo: The infinite mirror, echoing a sound, a word: *Anokhi*, I.

From all around me and from within myself, an overwhelming single word:

*Anokhi,*

"I!"

It comes like a drumbeat, again again: *Anokhi.*

This is my "I," my own self, but there is no "my," no possessing, no being possessed.

The "I" is the "I" that I am. I speak it, rolling from my throat, I affirm it, I. *Anokhi.*

And the "I" is also the entire people. I speak *Anokhi* as one voice

275

of all the people. Again again again again, *Anokhi*. I.

At every moment—there is only one moment—there is "I" the person, "I" the people.

One I.

And, still in the same moment, the entire universe becomes *Anokhi*, "I."

My "I" is caught up in the "I" of the universe, the "I" of the universe is caught up in my "I."

This "I" is all there is; there is no "Thou," no "Other," no verb, no predicate. No past, no future, no present, no tense. Only the subject is the sentence, only "I."

I see the wilderness, I am the wilderness, the shimmering heat waves rising from its surface are my I, the spiral twirls of history, the woven tapestries of art and custom, the patterned laws of science: World upon world, infinity upon infinity, all I.

I see myself, part of an unfathomable Whole, not facing it but integrated in it.

For an instant I am infinitesimal, a tiny rhythmic breathing conscious cell in some vast breathing conscious Ultrahuman.

For an instant, I am infinite, containing in one enormous self all the worlds of fact and meaning.

These instants are themselves a single instant, infinitely unfolding: They last for just a flashing moment, it stretches out for all eternity.

All time, all space whirls like a Moebius strip through a vast expanse curved in an unspeakable dimension—while it holds but one surface and one edge.

I tremble, topple, fall to ground that disappears beneath while its textures enter every inch of blazing, open skin.

I am the shaking earth, all my skin is quivering, unending one-great-quivering-shudder.

Stop stop how can I stop forget how can forget, I need forget, how can forget

I see too deep, I stand too big, I must forget, how to forget?

Our body quivers; I taste the world, the world is tasting me, is touching all my skin, and inside too: Inside our mouths, my belly, every opening filled and every limb outreaching to fill whatever is empty in the world.

Back and forth, I am/we are All All There Is—*Anokhi*, "I"—and Everything is all there is, we/I am part of everything and less than nothing,

*Anokhi* I a cell of great *Anokhi* of the world come conscious.

I stand inside God's skull, behind the face; I look out through God's eyes, my face in Face, I see myself, ourself. *Anokhi*.

And reeling, stunned, I fall, roll, stumble away from the Mirror in the Mountain, I close all eyes and shriek to see that I can still see Everything.

I close our ears, I hear the Voice still ringing in my bones, I back away and try to blot it out, forget. To not be "I" or "we" or any one.

And gradually I become a separate "thou." Gradually I can/we can/you can/they can begin to hear the "I" expand, contract, become—

"I YHWH *your* God Who brought *you* out..."

I disentangle our selves, distinguish between the voice in their throats and the voice in my ears. Gradually they/I distinguish me/us/themselves from the ground beneath, distinguish the pain in tightly clenched fists from pleasure in their open mouth, the breath within them from the wind around them,

*Na'aseh,* "*We will do*...we/All There Is/will do," there is no Other.

*Nishma,* "*We will hear*...the Other speak to us."

I

I-Thou.

I connect Thou, Thou connect I.

Connect.

An artery channels streams of blood, just I; but now organic unity is gone. "Connect" is necessary.

Gradually: Connections and commandments. "You shall keep Shabbat." "You shall not kill."

From organic into what is organized; replace harmonious wholeness with a plan, a patterning. Gradually distinguish what they are doing from what they should be doing.

Ruefully I linger, trying to remember the *Anokhi* and trying to forget it, relieved I have been able to escape and joyful I will never be able to escape, already wishing to recreate the moment and frightened that the moment will recur without my wishing, still tingling, touching the impossible I have just done, laughing, tasting an apple, rolling on my tongue each drop of juice as if I had just returned to Eden.

## THINKING ABOUT ANOKHI

*Anokhi* is not Ego. Within the experience of *Anokhi* lie the dangers of inflating the ego and of annihilating it. How do we avoid these dangers while enriching the ego with *Anokhi*-sense?

Thinking about the *Anokhi* experience is one way of healing it, healing from it, and healing through it.

For the moment of *Anokhi* there is no distinction between the "mystical" and "secular." One Consciousness suffuses/gives life to/ becomes the life of all the infinite worlds/Is "God"/Is world.

In Mirrored Sinai, there is not God on the one side and the secular, the world, on the other. There is no way to leap out of the world to have a "mystical" experience—because the world is all there is, there is no "out" of it. There is no way to turn away from God by turning toward the "secular" world. For God is all there is, there is no "away" from God.

Fully to experience the secular world is itself the mystical experience.

From this utter wholeness the Israelites fled. They could not bear to live in I, *Anokhi* , so they sent Moses into the Mountain's heart to live It.

And most modern Jews, most modern human beings, still flee— into seeing "I" counterposed to "Thou," "God" counterposed to "the world." Once this separation, this duality, had been established, it became one of the great tasks of the Jewish people to hold both ends of the rope, so as neither to "ascend" into the utterly spiritual nor "descend" into the purely material.

How do we hold both ends of the rope while remembering it is a single rope?

## THE BREATH OF LIFE

A second experience:

In the fall of 1982, I was teaching a course on Martin Buber at Swarthmore College. I had decided to make the course a conversation "with" Buber, rather than "about" him. Perhaps all studies of ideas should be shaped into conversations with the thinkers; this felt especially appropriate with Buber, the preeminent philosopher of dialogue, conversation, I-Thou.

So the class and I were reading passages of Buber as if it were Torah or Talmud: We read some Buber aloud in class, responded as if he were in the room, and listened to his answer.

We were reading *Moses*, Buber's remarkable theological biography of the greatest of the Prophets. In one passage of *Moses*, Buber looks at the Torah story of the seventy elders who, with Moses and Aaron, went up the mountain, "saw the God of Israel, under Whose feet there was the likeness of a pavement of sapphire, like the sky itself in purity." "They saw The God, and they ate and drank."

What, says Buber, is going on? He answers that the elders

...have presumably wandered through clinging, hanging mist before

278

dawn; and at the very moment they reach their goal, the swaying darkness tears asunder (as I myself happened to witness once) and dissolves except for one cloud already transparent with the hue of the still unrisen sun. The sapphire proximity of the heavens overwhelms the aged shepherds of the Delta, who have never before tasted, who have never been given the slightest idea, of what is shown in the play of early light over the summits of the mountains. And this precisely is...[what the elders perceive] as that which lies under the feet of their enthroned Melek [King]....The bodily function of eating the covenantal meal must link itself with the continuous consciousness of the Divine Presence....As the sun rises higher the primal blue grows paler; but the heart of the hallowed eaters of the hallowed food remains full of the primal blue...

As we discussed this passionate piece of scholarship, we focused on the connection Buber had made between the world and the Divine. To see God, the shepherds had turned *toward* the world, not away from it. They had seen the world more fully, more deeply, more newly than ever before: Seen a sky they had never looked at. "They saw The God and they ate and drank." Ate and drank what? God's Own Self?

In this atmosphere, with the distance between God and the world almost vanishing, we turned to Buber's next chapter, "The Words on the Tablets," in which he looks at the Ten Words that came from Sinai. And I turned inward, and toward the students, and toward Buber himself—no longer toward the pages of his book. I started speaking my thoughts aloud, half meditating, half conversing with my students and with Buber:

"Professor Buber, you skip the first two words on the Tablets. The first is *Anokhi*, 'I.' The second is this strange non-word, 'YHWH.' God's Name. That is the word we are not supposed to pronounce, not allowed to pronounce.

"What does it mean to pronounce it, anyway? You've just been teaching us to connect the world and God, the blue sky and Heaven's Throne, eating and drinking and seeing God—not to keep them in separate boxes. Why should we keep this name so utterly separate and not dare to pronounce it?

"What we've done all these years was to say 'Adonai,' 'Lord,' whenever we saw 'YHWH.' That's what my Grandmom taught me to do when I was learning Hebrew. Sometimes I've seen the vowels for 'Adonai' written beneath the letters 'YHWH.' Some Christians saw those vowels and figured the real pronunciation was 'YaHoVaiH,' so they said the name was 'Jehovah.' Wrong.

"Now the academic Bible scholars understand that 'Jehovah' was an error. But they figure the Israelites had a name for God just like the other peoples, a friendly name like Marduk and Osiris and Ashtoreth. So they've decided it's 'Yahweh,' and they use it casually—as in 'The Hebrews' favorite God was Yahweh.' They ignore the dialogue between God and Moses at the Burning Bush, where it's clear the Name is strange beyond eerie, not like a name at all.

"So they're all wrong. And still, we're not allowed to pronounce it.

"All right. I've been a troublemaker all my life. If those elders could see God and have lunch, I might as well try to pronounce the name. No vowels?"

So I took a deep breath and said aloud to my students: "Yyyyyhhhhwwwwhhhh.

"Huh?" I said. "Let's try that again. Yyyyyhhhhwwwwhhhh.

"Sounds like just a breath. Just feels like breathing, too.

"No wonder we can't pronounce it. There is no way to pronounce it. It's just breathing!

"Of course, of course!" I said, now practically babbling. "Any word we would make with our lips and tongues, it would be an idol, it would be 'the work of our hands.' Not God's. But breathing, just breathing! You might say that's the word that has no words, the word that includes all words, the word God puts into our mouths to speak it!

"And what does it say in the prayerbook? 'The breath of all that's living praises your Name.' Not 'You,' but 'Your Name.' Of course, of course! The breath of all alive will bless Your Name because the breath of all alive, it is Your Name. The breath is in us and beyond us, intimate and transcendent. We are all breathing each other into being!"

Dazed, I turned back to the students, who have been listening with their mouths open, barely breathing. Slowly we explore what all this means, how it connects with Buber, how he understands the Name.

## SPARKS IN AMBER

I keep thinking and thinking: If it is all that simple and that profound, if God is breathing, if the Breath of Life is God, why do we need all this apparatus? Bibles and prayerbooks, rabbis and rituals—what is the point?

I get the paradox. Look at the sentence in the prayerbook that now speaks so intimately, so powerfully, to me. Some rabbi got it, long ago. He was stumbling his ordinary way through his ordinary life, just as I was, and he got it. He said, "*Nishmat kol chai*, the breath of all alive"—and somebody put it in the prayerbook lest this wonderful insight be lost. It was a wonder, so it must be kept where future

280

generations could find it.

But once it was in the book, it moldered. For generations, Jews chanted the sentences at 90 miles an hour. They did not pause to breathe before they chanted, let alone to think about the meaning of these words, let alone to meditate on how their own breath was itself the Name of the Breath of Life.

Choose not to preserve such an insight in "the tradition," and it is utterly lost until someone discovers it independently. Choose to preserve it in "the tradition," and it becomes part of the dead past: "The tradition," a closed book even when the book is open.

It is the paradox of all religion. God, even God, especially God, can be made into an idol.

Flies caught in amber look still alive; but they are dead. How do we preserve in an electric field of amber sparks of holy truth that will crackle full of energy whenever we unlock the golden amber?

If there is any way out of this paradox, it is easy to say and hard to do: Always be fully conscious that "the tradition" is made up of moments of power, insight, transformation. Leave space and time to ask what is going on in each tale, each prayer. Put ourselves in the place of the one who wrote it down, the one who decided to put it in some crucial book. Why, why? If I had just written that, what hot shiver would have just gone through me?

The question I raised out of my experience at Mirrored Sinai was: How do we keep ourselves aware that "God" and "the world" are two aspects of the same reality?

The story of my Buber class offers two answers. One is the answer of process, sheer immediate experience. In that realm, the distinction between sacred transformation and secular study really did vanish. All I was doing was teaching a college class. I have done it a thousand times when nothing special happened. This time I opened up fully to my own inklings of truth, to my students (I was not embarrassed to follow my half-formed thoughts aloud), and to Buber. As Buber himself wrote, open the I-Thou relationship between human beings and at once its trajectory is Infinite. God is simply the Eternal I-Thou.

At another level, there is the content of our learning: The Breath as an image, a metaphor, for God. The Breath is both within us and beyond us. If it were absent from either place, we would die. It is just one breath, interchangeable and ever-changing. Yet it moves in a rhythm from within to beyond. The God Who is beyond and the God Who is within: One God.

Most contemporary Jews have a sense that Judaism evolves. They, we, understand that at different periods of our history, we have had different "pictures" of God. Even within the Bible, there is a clear though bumpy road of change in imagery of God, from the transcendent intervening God of the Creation stories who speaks the world into being and the One of Exodus Who stage-manages the downfall of Pharaoh, to the God Who speaks through the Prophets to urge and beg the people to act, and on to the wholly immanent God of the Song of Songs, who neither acts nor speaks as a Being separate from the earth and its earthlings.

For the Rabbis of the Talmud, God is encoded in their collective decisions—even more subsumed into the earth plane than was the Voice Who transfixed the Prophets. Indeed, the Rabbis refuse to hear that Voice when it tries to speak, and thus it becomes inaudible.

In our own time, God becomes even more fully infused in the enormously creative and destructive acts and doings of the human race, not just its words.

Is this path of changing images simply the human path of reconceiving God? Or are these images trying to convey a deeper truth, that the God-principle of the universe is Itself changing? *Is it possible, is it valuable, is it truthful, to imagine God's Own Self living through a life-cycle—a life-spiral?*

## THE BIOGRAPHY OF GOD

In order to explore the biography of God, we can begin with one strand of the mystical Kabbalah. There is an extraordinary mythic tale of the Creation:

Beyond all time, before there was a before, all is God. Unboundaried holiness. God contracts inward, does a *tzimtzum*, in order to permit a world to emerge. But as God withdraws, like olive oil being poured out of a sacred but non-existent flask, there is left behind a thin film of God in the ethereal bottle. That thin film of God is the only material available to give thought and form to this world. Folded and re-folded, it becomes the seed and substance of the world.

So there emerges a World that is really God-wrapped-in-robes-of-God, a world that is the limited and immanent aspect of God. To keep this World from dissolving into the other aspect of God, the Unutterable Infinitude of Holiness, there must be the thinnest of boundaries between God-Transcendent and God-Immanent. In that boundary, as it were, God must be absent. This is the Void.

Already we have described a life-decision on God's part, a decision to change God's Self by letting a residue of God become the world.

And what is to happen on our side of the boundary?

On our side, the task is for the world to unwrap the disguising robes, uncover its naked truth, that it is also God. To grow up. To become fully conscious.

In this tale, the history of earth is the story of an awakening consciousness of the truth that we are God. From seething volcanoes to a bio-soupy sea, from the self-absorbed amoeba to the hives of bees affirming that in many there is One, from ferns and flounders to the long-delayed maturing of a human baby—there is Divinity Emerging.

Within human history, the process continues. Here (if not before) the flow of increasing God-consciousness branches into two currents: The imbuing of the human race with more Power, and with more Love. The single *Anokhi*/I branches into what Buber called I-It, and what he called I-Thou. For God is both a maker, a doer, a definer of It, and a lover, a connector, a relater with Thou. Each of these pours into human history, and each becomes a context and a cause for the other to pour forth.

The Divine I-It pours in: Human beings make fire. The Divine I-Thou pours in: They learn to become families and clans.

Sinai and the Talmud were moments of I-Thou Divinity Emerging. Hellenism and Modernity were moments of I-It Divinity Emerging.

Feminism and ecology bring a new step in I-Thou Divinity Emerging. This is partly because both of them take seriously the life-experience of many species and of half the human race—whose lives have mostly been ignored by "official" thought and institutions. But arising from that insistence is perhaps an even more important way in which feminism and ecology lift all human consciousness: They teach a relational, woven, interconnected sense of truth and wisdom, not a notion of wisdom from On High. In that way they strengthen those currents of human consciousness that sense God in the process of the earth and human society.

In each moment of rising consciousness, God becomes more present in the world that already *is* God—but has not yet been fully conscious of it.

From this perspective, evolutionary science—whether in cosmology, biology, or human history—looks profoundly different. Once it was seen as purely secular, corroding any possibility of a spiritual outlook on the world. Seen as the unfolding of God's Presence in the world, it becomes instead a richly evocative invitation to a spiritual path.

How does this effort to imagine a God of many changing Images square with the God of the philosophers, including such Jewish philosophers as Maimonides, who saw God as necessarily unchanging, "I Am What I Am"? That aspect of God—Unutterable, Infinite, and therefore Unchanging—is also true. That is God on the other side of the Void.

# THE MADNESS OF GOD

The more deeply we experience ourselves as part of God and God as part of us, the more deeply we have to face a painful issue: What in ourselves is crazy and cruel? What aspect of the God Who fills heaven and earth is cruel and crazy? The more fully we feel the world as God wrapped in robes of God, the more we feel that the Holocaust was then a part of God. How could this be? How could we live with such a sense of ourselves and God?

We refuse to live with a God Who is mad.

We refuse to live with a God Who is *not* mad and yet creates a world in which the Holocaust can happen.

How do we live with this primal contradiction?

There is a Hassidic tale:

The Prime Minister says to the King: "The grain supply for next year is contaminated. Eating it will make our people mad. But there is just enough healthy grain stored from this year for the two of us to keep alive next year, and not go crazy. Shall we eat this healthy grain?"

The King replies: "We must not isolate ourselves from our people by saving the healthy grain for ourselves. We must share their pain. We too must eat the grain that drives people mad, but we must mark our foreheads so that when I look at you and you at me, we shall remember that we both are mad."

Read God for the king; the world and humankind for the prime minister.

This means: Imagine a God Who is sometimes mad, yet preserves just enough sanity to seek an end to that madness. Seeks desperately, imploringly, for us to love each other so as to make the world—to make God—sane again. Seeks after each outbreak of madness to scream, "See! Hear! *Sh'ma*! Stop me before I kill again! Only you can do it!"

During the moments of sanity, when we recall the meaning of the marks upon each other's foreheads, we can learn from the moments of madness.

The Holocaust was part of God's madness. Now we have a chance, only a chance, to learn from the Holocaust what we need to do to prevent an earthwide holocaust.

The Holocaust did not come into the world as part of God's plan for education: It is not part of God's sanity. But once it has happened, the best we/God can do is to learn from it. And act upon our learning.

If this is the direction we must go, why bother with God-language at all? Why not say simply that we humans struggle our way toward decency, or don't? Because God-language preserves the sense that we are one, One. That our madness is always self-destructive because it is our own vitals we are tearing at. That just as there is no "away" to throw our garbage, there is no "other" to oppress or murder.

Since this wholeness is actually the fact, God is always present— embodied in that fact of wholeness. But sometimes we do not act as if we are conscious of this truth, and then we are not witnessing to God's Presence, and God is present only in a shadowy way. When we are so conscious of wholeness that we nurture all the parts of us in- stead of destroying them, then we are fully conscious of God, and God is most fully Present.

For me, that is the meaning of the Jewish morning blessing, "Blessed is the One Who impels light and creates darkness, makes harmonious wholeness (*shalom*) and creates the All." This blessing deliberately misquotes Isaiah, who said that God "impels light and creates dark- ness, makes wholeness and creates the *evil*."

Most commentators say that the rabbis who rewrote the passage thought that people would not be able, morning after morning, to bless the God who creates evil; so they softened the words. But I think the rabbis also saw a fuller truth: That the "All" that is not "*shalom*" is itself the source and the place of evil. God creates the All that we see in all its buzzing confusion before us. When we see only the con- fusion, when we cannot see that it is All connected, that it is one and stems from the One, then we act in such a way as to leave it only an All, a place of evil, and not a Harmonious Whole, not *shalom*.

Only connect! Why? Because we are already connected.

The mark upon God's forehead reminds us that the All is really one, connected, and that it is madness to forget this.

This mark is also the mark that God put on Cain's forehead after he murdered Abel. Then others, seeing Cain face to face, could see the mark and recall that he was mad, that he had become a murderer because he had failed to see the Unity.

*What we did not know before this Hassidic tale was that God had placed this mark as well upon the Godhead.*

But when and where did God place this mark upon us and upon the Godhead? If this mark is intended to remind us that we and God are mad and must restore our sanity, what is this mark of conscious- ness?

The Book of Job is Cain's mark upon the Godhead.

For Job speaks of a God sublimely mad, violently mad, Who ex- plains that Madness to a human being. A God Who deliberately sends evil upon a decent human being—and then explains to that suffering human that there is no way to explain. A God who takes the trouble to explain that God cannot be explained, does not need or want to be explained. This God is clearly one Who woke up that morning to notice on the Godhead's forehead the Mark of Cain.

In Job there are no easy answers:

Job's friends think that God is just, and therefore Job must have done evil; God says this is not so.

Job says that he is just, and therefore God must have done evil; God says this is not so.

What God appeals to is not proof, not reason, not justification, but Mystery.

And then not only Mystery: God invokes not images of justice or mercy or community, but images of birth and death, earth and cosmos. Images of the spiral of transformative time, in which what is true and just at one moment is no longer true and just at another.

## LOVE BEYOND GOOD AND EVIL

These images hint that social space, the space Job is appealing to, happens within a larger cosmic time; that all our ethics of justice, mercy, community, though they are true enough, emerge within the time of stars and glacial ages and meteor collisions.

And on the grand scale, social time, historic time, is also a spiral in which every ethical and political understanding dies and gives birth, so that no one who lives within it can master it. There are moments in the spiral of historic time when the world is "beyond good and evil" because the old sense of good and evil, the existing conventional and normal and reasonable ethics, are exhausted.

Why does this happen? Because more raw life-force, amoral energy, the aspect of God or Reality that creates not Wholeness but Allness, including evil, has entered the arena—more God-force than anyone knows how to deal with.

The twentieth century has been such a moment. More raw knowledge, force, power, possibility has come into human hands than anyone has known how to deal with.

At such moments, there is the danger of immense evil, of "*sinat chinam*" or "causeless hatred," as the rabbis said when they explained why the Second Temple was destroyed.

The moment of raw cosmic energy beyond good and evil is the moment Purim hints at, when the rabbis taught that Jews should get so drunk as not to know the difference between "blessed Mordechai" and "cursed Haman." The moment for storms of tears and gusts of laughter that recognize how limited our sense of ethics is when floods of raw new life-force enter the world.

At such a moment, there is a kind of "Shabbat," a pause, a catching of the breath, on ethics. Normal ethics are suspended, and an ethic of "I don't know" goes into effect.

As we have seen—in real life, not merely the pages of a book—such a moment can result in murder.

Since ethical understanding is suspended, must we stand silent before immense evil like a mass murder or a Holocaust?

No. Job did not stand silent. Like him, we must both rage against and celebrate the Mystery, not allow it to degenerate into murder. The Mystery carries within itself another possibility besides the one of causeless hatred: There is the possibility of "*ahavat chinam*," "causeless love." Love that is given by God's grace to us even though we have done too little to deserve it.

What does it mean to put *ahavat chinam* into action, in our lives? It means the nonviolence of Gandhi and Martin Luther King—a kind of unreasonable good that is not in the normal ethics because it does not reward the good and punish the evil. For nonviolence is the practice in which even those who deserve evil are met with unreasonable love.

Is this loving ethic the message of the Book of Job? Not in any simple sense. Job himself is not simply loving, simply patient. The picture of the "patient" Job is built upon a deliberate misconstrual that gave us "Though He [God] slay me, yet will I trust in Him." This is not what the written text of the book has Job saying (though it is what the rabbinic commentators said should be read aloud): Rather, as Stephen Mitchell's superb translation has it,

"He may kill me, but I won't stop;
I will speak the truth, to his face."

Job loves God, but not in a patient and accepting way. Job rages at God, demands that God stand trial. When God confesses that on the Godhead is the mark of Cain, when God confesses that God is sometimes but not always just, that God is sometimes raw mad cosmic energy, Job must decide: Do I love this explosive, uncontrolled eruption of raw Life-energy, or do I hate it?

And Job concludes, in pain and rage and awe, that he can love this raw Life-energy: Better such an unreasonable love than the deadly, deadening hatred that will curdle all his life.

We only get to Job's open-mouthed wonder at the Inexplicable God by going through Job's open-throated shriek at the Unjust God. We get to the new place only by wrestling with the old one. Only by living on the knife-edge. This is what it means to be named "*Yisrael*," the "Godwrestling" people.

And of course, like our forebear Wrestler Jacob, when we wrestle God we are always wrestling with the God within us, with ourselves.

As Jacob stood *alone* at the river's edge and looked into himself to see the Person with whom he had to wrestle, so we, each one of us, must look into that Face with Whom we wrestle. —And see our Self.

When we do this, no human being who looks deeply into her or his own heart can shrug away the God of *Job*. For there too we see the great *Anokhi*, "I."

Just as we look into the Sinai Mirror and see an I of Wholeness, Harmony, so we look fiercely at the God of *Job* and see the Cain mark on the forehead that reminds us we too are mad, we too...

We too are sometimes only All, not always Whole.

CHAPTER 21

# THE EMBODIMENT OF GOD

If God is increasingly embodied in the world, increasingly immanent, how do we pray? If we are ourselves an aspect of God, how do we speak to what is not Other but an aspect of our selves?

We must "embody" our connection with the God who is embodied. We who are the heirs of "word-Judaism," the Judaism of the rabbis who taught us to get in touch with the mind of God through words of prayer and Torah, must remind ourselves that we are also the heirs of "body-Judaism," the Judaism of the priests who brought offerings of food from the body of the land to turn it into savory smoke for the mouth and nostrils of that God.

I am not suggesting that we return to the Judaism of the Bible and the Temple, but that we open ourselves up once more to learn more deeply from it. I am suggesting that we learn to synthesize the body and the word, and bring them together in a more holistic Judaism of the whole person, the whole community, the whole earth. I am suggesting that we learn new forms of prayer.

If this seems frightening—are we to abandon our own identity?— let us remember that we have done this before. The Bible describes how Hannah, aching to birth a child, comes to the Shrine to beg this gift of God. She does what is normative in body-Judaism: She brings a goat as an offering. But she also murmurs words of prayer. This is so far from normal that the priest rebukes her: "Are you drunk?!"

The rabbis of the Talmud take this marginal moment, Hannah's prayer, and make it the model of what prayer ought to be. Indeed, for all the centuries of Rabbinic Judaism, a specific passage of softly murmured words of prayer has been called "*HaTefillah*," *The* Prayer, and has become in every traditional synagogue the most sacred way of connecting with God. Imagine how deep the transformation it took in society and personality to turn what was intolerable in the Judaism of priests into what was crucial for the Judaism of rabbis! Yet this transformation was accomplished without shattering the threads of memory and identity that connect us today not only to Hannah and her story but also to the priest who accosted her.

So we today can imagine that we may have to change our ways of touching God a great deal, and that we can do so without losing ourselves.

*How* do we go about embodying God as we address the God Who is embodied in the world, in our selves? There are two different times or aspects for our doing this. There are inwardly or communally directed times when we are conscious of bringing our consciousness into God's Presence; and there are outwardly or publicly directed times when we are acting to shape the world that is God's Presence. To the former we must bring much more of our selves than the words we have become accustomed to calling "prayer." To the second, we must bring a prayerful consciousness of God's presence that has not traditionally been part of "social action."

## FACE TO FACE WITH GOD

On the side of what we usually call "prayer," the communities of Jewish renewal have begun to make important changes. The first changes came not from thoughts of word and mind, but from an act of body: If you *davven* in a circle, where is God?

Not somewhere else. Not in the Ark, across many rows of behatted heads and past an empty gulf of no man's land. Not in Jerusalem, thousands of miles away. Not high above, reigning in royal splendor.

As we *davven* in a circle, God begins to appear in the faces round the circle—and in the vibrations between—and in our own hearts and minds.

Jewish renewal communities have developed some powerful ways of recognizing this Presence:

The song the Kabbalists created to welcome Shabbat says in its chorus, "*P'nai Shabbat n'kabbalah,*" "We will receive the presence of Shabbat." Literally, this phrase means, "We will receive the *faces* of Shabbat." So we may ask people to let their work-tense faces receive the face that Shabbat wears: Take off their glasses, let their hands stroke their foreheads, smooth away frowns, loosen the jaw muscles, rub the eyes. All this while they sing or hum the song, until they feel their face has entered *Shabbat* space.

Some *havurot* have begun to pause at the moment of *Barchu*, when traditionally an amalgam of individual davenners becomes annealed into a community. We look around the circle of the davenners, pausing at each face to say, "This is the face of God." "And this is the face of God." "And this." "And this." We look deep into the closed and angry faces, the crinkling humorous ones, the calm and peaceful faces and the closed, withdrawn ones, into worried frowns and anxious glances, into tear-filled eyes and smiles of welcome. As we do this, we see the faces open, change, deepen—not dropping whatever had been there before, simply enfolding it in a deeper vision.

Do this often enough, and you begin to believe it: My face and your face *are* the face of God. Believe it long enough, and you begin to act it out: You nourish every neighbor, for each is a face of God.

A more complex and subtle way of facing God through the Psalms has been explored by Rabbi Zalman Schachter-Shalomi, an extraordinary davvener who is also one of the most creative choreographers of new forms of davvening. Schachter-Shalomi brought his own profound mystical sensibility first into a deep learning with the Lubavitcher Hassidim, and then into the much wider world of Sufi dancers, Zen sitters, Buddhist meditators, feminist seekers, and transpersonal psychologists. Convinced that for a new era of Jews God must be sensed as directly present, he saw that since the Psalms are addressed directly to God, they offer an important opportunity to embody God in the community of davveners. Rabbi Jeff Roth brought to this insight his own work with Martin Buber's call for dialogue, and what emerged was what Roth and Schachter-Shalomi called "dialogical davvening" with the Psalms.

This meant that pairs of people read a psalm in dialogue within the *minyan*: One person reads the first verse of the psalm silently, absorbs it, and decides how to express something close to this thought in her or his own words. Then s/he will face the "spark of God" in the other partner to say the new thought to the God Who lives in the partner's face. The second partner pays full attention to what the first one says, and then turns back to the printed page to absorb the second verse of the psalm and do the same work of midrashic transmutation—taking into account both what s/he has already heard, and what the text says. They continue to go back and forth, speaking to God in each other, until the psalm is completed.

Becoming God and facing God in this way brings the psalm alive. The movement of thought and feeling that is characteristic of most psalms becomes far more intelligible than what emerges from a more-or-less rote reading. In addition, by addressing a human partner as God and being addressed as God, many participants find themselves spiritually moved in new ways.

What is the secret behind the power of such practices? We are taking what seem to be poetic metaphors about the face, and turning them into physical reality. The process is a kind of three-dimensional midrash, turning words into actions.

## EVERY BONE, EVERY BREATH

Similarly with the breath: Early in Fabrangen's history, we noticed a prayer that begins *Elohai neshamah*, "God of breath," then continues with a paragraph full of words with a strong "-ahh" ending. Every word, a strong breath out. Most congregations race right through their recitation of this paragraph, taking it all at one breath like any other. We learned to pause, breathe deep at almost every word, make the paragraph itself into a breathing exercise.

As that prayer ends and the air goes bubbling through our bodies, we do the morning blessings. As the prayerbook itself says, "All my bones will praise You." Yet most Jews let their bodies sit locked into place during prayers, let the holy breath become shallow and weak. Since in the morning blessings we praise the God who opens our eyes, stretches our muscles, strengthens our footsteps, this is an important moment to let every bone and muscle praise the Breath of Life. Indeed, originally these prayers were chanted as people arose from bed, when the bodily actions themselves were connected with the words. Nowadays, since the morning prayers are often said in the congregation, many *havurot* and some more formal congregations encourage the people to stand, stretch, turn, walk, make a kind of dance of the acts of morning waking.

So the prayers become not only ways to praise the God who gets our bodies going in the morning, but also ways to *get* our bodies going in the morning. The praise and the act are suffused with each other: We embody God.

The davvening leader may ask each person in the circle to create a gesture on the spot that expresses each of the morning blessings, and then everyone imitates this gesture. These gestures may be repeated— first one, then two, then three, and so on until the congregation has, in effect, created a unique dance for that one morning.

We take the spirit-breath and send it racing through our bodies, stretching every muscle, opening every eye, passing energy to lips and tongue and throat. Every breath *is* a praise of God's Name, and every breath sings the words and melodies that *express* the praise of God.

These approaches appeared in the early years of the process of Jewish renewal. Twenty years later, some of us are bringing deeper knowledge and experience of meditative breathing and movement to our prayer. We have learned to voice the letters "YHWH" not with the traditional "*Adonai*, Lord," but with "*Yahh*," said like a breath, and to address God not as King (*Melech ha-Olam*), but as "Breath of Life, *Ruach ha-Olam*," or "Life of all the Worlds, *Chai ha'Olamim.*"

One adept, Shefa Gold, has developed an entirely new form of prayer, deeply rooted in the traditional service, that uses chanting to focus the breath and to fuse breath, melody, and verbal meaning into a unity. She has looked beneath the fleshed-out, opulently clothed order of prayer we have inherited; has stripped it down to its skeleton of purpose; has from the traditional text chosen a few phrases that crystallize the meaning in each of the crucial elements , and has turned these crystalline phrases into melodic chants. Thus she may take the section of the service that precedes the *Sh'ma*—several pages long— and instead of murmuring every word, as in a traditional service, lead the congregation into a powerful chant of half a dozen words that she has set to melody. That chant may go on for five or ten minutes, over and over, as the congregation deepens first its understanding of the prayer, and finally its presence *within* the prayer.

Through these chants, the breath enters deeply into the body, is carried by the blood to every nerve and muscle. The Breath of Life becomes a divine presence in every cell.

One Shabbat evening, a dancer taught Fabrangen to "dance" the different rhythms of our workdays and of Shabbat. First we relived and "gave away" the work week by acting out in stylized movement how we answer the telephone, take out the garbage, type a letter, argue in meetings. Then we turned toward Shabbat, to the rhythms of the stately cedar trees in the "psalm of the Shabbat day" that we sing each Friday night, to the rhythms of ambling and laughing and being with each other.

On another Shabbat, we formed a procession. We circled through the room, chanting sometimes in a quiet undertone and sometimes in an ecstasy of shouting. Our procession danced its way up the slopes of Sinai, recalling how Moses took the seventy elders there to eat and drink with God. At the peak of the *Amidah*, at the peak of Sinai, we found ourselves clustered close together, touching each other with our eyes closed, murmuring the blessings almost in each other's ears.

Another time we turned a psalm into mime and dance. We took the psalm about the idols who have hands but touch not, feet but walk not, eyes but see not, a mouth but breathe not—and whose makers become, like them, deadened to the world. We read the psalm together, talked it through, until we felt we understood the story in and behind it. Then we mimed the idols who were stone-deaf and the idolators who turned to stone. We danced the Israelites dancing with their unpredictable Living God. We learned the psalm from inside, from our lungs and muscles rather than just our ears and minds.

Some among us have learned how to "sign" prayers with arms and hands until they become a visual dance. We have experimented with body movements keyed to particular thoughts in particular prayers, movements that we might learn to use with variations week after week, just as we learn to chant prayers in changing tones and rhythms week by week. One Jewish-renewal dancer, Yehudit Goldfarb of the Oakland-Berkeley region, developed dance-gestures to represent the shapes of the Hebrew letters. These "*Otiot Chayyot*" or "Living Letters" became ways to spell out Hebrew words in delicate and graceful dance that looks a good deal like Tai Chi.

One of the deepest and most evocative of these new ways of embodying prayer was developed by Rabbi Schachter-Shalomi. For years, Hassidim had taken the Simchat Torah festival, with its seven circle-dances with the Torah Scroll, as an important time to draw deeply on a Kabbalistic tradition about seven aspects of God. In that tradition, God emanated Divinity into the world not through one undifferentiated flash, but in seven distinct *S'phirot*, dimensions of Divinity that were symbolized by seven different parts of the body: The right and left arms, the heart, the right and left legs, the male genitals, and the female genitals. (The mystics noted the existence of three higher *S'phirot*, symbolized by parts of the head, but saw these as mostly inaccessible to humans.)

These *S'phirot* are different in quality from each other: *Chesed*, overflowing unboundaried outpouring love, differs from *Gevurah*, rigorous boundary-making, and each differs from their synthesis, *Tiferet* or *Rachamim*—the intense and focused love borne by and in and of the womb, shining in overpowering beauty. Among Hassidim, the seven Simchat Torah dances mentally recalled the different *S'phirot*. But they danced all seven dances in a single way, tinged with *Gevurah*: Bodies locked, all seven dances identical, rarely ecstatic or improvised.

Schachter-Shalomi taught Jewish-renewal communities to create distinctive dances for the different *S'phirot*—unrestrained and giddy for *Chesed*, focused and rigorous for *Gevurah*, and so on. Suddenly, the *S'phirot* became embodied, available to celebrants as aspects of their own selves. People learned to explore which of the *S'phirot* within themselves were weak and needed practice toward the healing of the *neshama* (breathing-soul).

And thus the embodiment of God's aspects and emanations in the human body opened a path toward experiencing the manifestation of God's aspects in a person's character structure and behavior. The great *Anokhi*, "I," did indeed appear in the "I" of a human being.

## EMBODYING TORAH

When we pray we speak *to* God; when we read and learn Torah we are opening ourselves to *hear* God. In a community that hears the speaker and the listener, God and the world, as deeply intertwined, what does it mean to embody Torah—the listening—just as we embody prayer—the speaking?

I have already described the use of "drushodrama" with the stories of Dina and the Binding of Abraham: People take on particular parts in a Bible story and act out the untold parts of the tale. For decades, Jewish renewal *havurot* and teachers used this approach; then Peter Pitzele, a professional psychodramatist, brought it to a new level of expertise and power. Taught by him, congregational rabbis have begun to incorporate it in their work as a new, more engaging kind of "sermon."

Other forms of embodiment of Torah have also emerged. The *aliyot* in which people are called up to the Torah as various passages are read have been given new life by Phyllis Berman, among others. Whoever is leading the Torah service will choose a few parts of the weekly portion that address a continuing Godwrestle likely to be urgent among some congregants. (For example, the Torah passage where the Israelites stand between Pharaoh's chariots and the Red Sea may evoke a frightening moment of choice between uncertain futures.) The leader will invite all congregants who feel the Torah passage is speaking to this issue in their lives to join in that *aliyah*. After the Torah passage has been read and translated, the leader asks God's blessing in a specifically directed way to meet the special needs of those who came up for each *aliyah*. This practice has made the archetypal nature of the Torah apparent to many who had never before understood how it might speak to their own lives.

One nationally known dancer and choreographer, Liz Lerman, taught an approach to interpretation of Torah that engaged the body and the emotions in strenuous new ways. Addressing the weekly portion about the rebellious Korach, for example, she asked everyone who had just heard the Torah to pick one of the active forces in the story: Korach, the mouth of the earth that opened to swallow him up, Aaron, the almond tree that sprouted from Aaron's rod, God. Each "character" began to chant aloud its name and to act out its being through dance and gesture, not conversation. Whenever the player wanted to change characters, s/he did. The story was turned into a dream, as logical order vanished and psychological fluidity took over. Time and order whirled and shifted, and the dream coalesced around a new center as the dancers whirled around each other. As the dance continued, new meaning emerged from the dreaming of the reconfigured tale.

All these methods were midrash in a new key, turning poetic metaphors into bodily acts. Not that such physical midrash was utterly unheard-of among Jews. For example, Jeremiah wore a yoke upon his shoulders to make physically explicit his warning that the people faced the yoke of slavery to Babylon. What was new was the use of such approaches not only by a few Prophets or Kabbalistic adepts, but by much larger circles of the Jewish people.

## THE OPEN-ENDED PRAYERBOOK

How best to preserve and broaden this new life-giving liveliness? Participants in Jewish renewal have faced a classic quandary. It is the same one faced by the rabbis who long ago discovered that "the breath of all alive blesses Your Name." They decided to write this insight into "the tradition" so as to keep it available for others, and so accepted the risk that its very availability might freeze and stultify the process of opening up anew to the Breath of Life. We, after many doubts and debates—did we really want to create another prayerbook so that its readers could find it easier to forget what they were reading?—decided to create something between blank space and a book. We sought to shape an anthology that would provoke its readers to become writers.

Poets and scholars and liturgists and prophets joined with Rabbi Schachter-Shalomi in creating *Or Chadash (New Light)*, a guide to Shabbat-morning prayer. It follows the traditional pattern of a service, and at each step provides a enormous range of alternatives: Traditional Hebrew, and Hebrew with the verbs for God and human beings made feminine; transliteration and translation; English poetic renderings; guides to the use of body language, dance, and dialogue; guides for meditations and visualizations; brief descriptions of new ways to read the Torah and to learn together. We decided that even in its physical form, the anthology would signal that it was open to the renewal of itself; so we bound it as a three-ring binder notebook, easy to enlarge, shorten, or revise.

In creating the text, discussing how in our era to speak with God, we came to feel ourselves living inside the section of the Talmud called *B'rakhot*, "Blessings," where the Rabbis worked out the prayers that Jews then used for almost two millennia. We felt the fear and exhilaration, the joyful chutzpah intertwined with baffled humility, that they, too, must have experienced.

## POLITICS AS PART OF PRAYER

What about the other side of embodying God—the question of how to act in the public sphere with prayerful concern?

Far less has been done to enrich the sacred repertoire of *tikkun olam*, the healing of the world, than to enrich more classic forms of prayer. Most of the work in making *tikkun olam* a consciously sacred practice has addressed the protection of the earth from the dangers of nuclear holocaust, global warming, or other major catastrophes—probably because these questions address the Unity of the interrelated web of life more obviously than do many other public issues.

Two comments of Rabbenu Abraham Joshua Heschel:

The first he said at a conference on liturgical renewal:

"Prayer is meaningless unless it is subversive, unless it seeks to overthrow and to ruin the pyramids of callousness, hatred, opportunism and falsehood. The liturgical movement must become a revolutionary movement, seeking to overthrow the forces that continue to destroy the promise, the hope, the vision."

And the second he said when he came back home from taking part in a civil rights march in Selma, Alabama, alongside Martin Luther King, Catholic nuns, Protestant church leaders, and secular civil rights activists:

"I felt that my feet were praying."

These are the two sides of the question:

Is it possible to shape liturgies that subvert the injustice, war, tyranny, and exploitation of the earth around us while also subverting the callousness, hatred, opportunism, and falsehood within us?

Is it possible to shape public "political" acts in such a way that we are praying? So far, efforts at these fusions have included—

Using at the base of the U.S. Capitol building during the Gulf War a basically traditional liturgy for the calling of a *taanit tzibbur*, a public fast in time of such calamities as war, not to take a political position on the war itself but to call for a heartfelt reexamination of what to do. The ceremony included draping the Sefer Torah in sackcloth and ashes, blowing the shofar, and reading from Torah, Prophets, and modern Jewish poets.

Celebrating Hoshana Rabbah, the beating of willows on the earth and the chanting of prayers for the protection of the Earth from plague and famine, on the banks of a river endangered by pollution.

In these events, the medium and the message fused: As one participant said, "If earth is spirit, politics is prayer." And it became clear in
such actions that the Divine intervention the prayers were imploring
would have to include human action. God was no longer totally separate from human beings.

## PROBLEMS WITH THE EMBODIMENT OF GOD

Some object that the new prayers, practices, and symbols of God's
immanence are "not Jewish," either because they are just too new
and break with accepted Jewish practice, or because they echo other
traditions too much—especially that they seem too pantheistic or
panentheistic, too Buddhist, or even too incarnational and therefore
too Christian.

But these images are not so new as many assume. In Kabbalah and
Hassidism especially, Jews have explored such ideas and used such
metaphors before. In ways that are unexpected but reasonable, they
fuse Mordechai Kaplan's "transnaturalist" Reconstructionism with
images from the days of Hassidic upheaval in the 18th century, and
both with one undoubtedly new element—feminist spirituality.

If the Jewish people and Judaism are going through a transformation as profound as the one that shaped and was shaped by the Talmud, it would be neither surprising nor outrageous for Jews to seek
new "names" and ways of connecting with God. As for those who
dismiss such ways of thinking as historicism that itself denigrates the
Eternal, some Jewish-renewal people answer that it is God that has
veiled Itself from our access in the old ways, God Who is working in
the world to bring about these changes, and therefore God Who is
calling us to create new forms of contact.

It is not surprising that the new forms might remind some people
of other traditions, because God is after all One and Universal. Although there are and will continue to be many differences in the ways
Jews approach that One God from the ways Christians, Buddhists,
and Native Americans do, there are also likely to be some similarities
as different communities try to approach the One Truth.

There is one more concern—perhaps the most important: That a
God "embodied" in the universe is less likely to demand of us a con-
stant transcendence of the present state of things. If whatever is, is
Divine, then who will need to change it?

But the notion of *tikkun olam* in Kabbalah is not so static. Even
those who said God, Israel, and Torah were One did not think
we could forget about doing the *mitzvot* that would repair the shattered vessel. They simply said that God, Torah, and Israel were all

shattered, all needed healing.

From this standpoint, there are "lower" and "fuller" versions of immanence. Although it is true that whatever exists is Divinity, it may be Divinity in its reduced and shattered state. It remains our task through conscious action to lift this Divinity from merely being All *(ha'kol)* to its fuller level of conscious Harmony *(shalom)*.

In this way, God's Body—of which we are all part—becomes most fully God's Body only when we seek to know and act as part of it.

# CHAPTER 22

# SPIRALING TOWARD MESSIAH

For thousands of years, whenever Jews have sought to turn the buzzing contradictions of the All into the harmony of Wholeness, *Shalom*, we have recalled our wistful hope to bring *Mashiach*, the Anointed One, Messiah. Imagine a whole planet massaged with warm and fragrant oil: *Anointed*.

We have had many would-be Messiahs. Perhaps we should view them not as "false" Messiahs so much as experiments, each a specialist in testing out one aspect of Messiah. If the test is whether any of these experiments can transform the world, beat all swords into plowshares, then none has yet succeeded. But maybe it is in the nature of such experiments never to succeed, but always and only to point us more accurately in the correct direction on the endless journey.

From this perspective, one of the earliest important experiments was Jesus. He (or his followers) focused on the perfected single human individual as the *Anokhi* who could be Messiah. Others looked toward a more communal and more social task. Bar Kochba hoped to free the Jewish people by expelling the Roman conquerors with military force. Shabtai Tzvi wanted to free the Jewish people from many of its traditional rules and strictures.

The most recent experiment, Menachem Schneerson of Lubavitch, took exactly the opposite tack, hoping to liberate all Jews not *from* the most traditional path of Jewish life but *into* it, liberating them through joy in the very generation after their worst torture.

It is hard enough to bring the Jubilee; is there any point in pursuing the still grander vision of Messiah?

There are two answers to this question. One arises from visceral hope and flaming desire; the other, from analysis of history.

I remember that one day on the fruitful farm in Pennsylvania where we first experimented with creating a kibbutz, when I was new to the

Jewish renewing of myself, when together we were glimpsing the first glow of a Judaism renewed and transformed, when Americans were hoping actually to build a society without racial oppression or the subordination of women—in that moment, I remember musing aloud about Messiah:

"I will be very angry if I die before *Mashiach* comes. Imagine missing such a festival of joy, the great parade and carnival in one! Here swords beaten into plowshares, there a great Jubilee of sharing wealth and sharing prayer, men and women at peace, parents and children at peace. Who could bear to miss it?"

And in the decades since, what Messiah has come to us? Only a Rebbe who kept women at the back of the *shul*; who opposed the glimmers of peace between Israel and the Palestinians; who defined so narrowly what Judaism was that he tried to keep away those who flocked to join the Jewish people, if they entered through a doorway different from his own; who defined so narrowly what Hassidism was that he could not keep in his community two of the most creative Jews of their generation, Shlomo Carlebach and Zalman Schachter-Shalomi.

Not my Messiah. So now I more than half expect to die without *Mashiach*, my anger softened into irony. Or perhaps my anger will still come to life? Perhaps upon my deathbed after all I will have the strength and ecstasy to shriek my anger against the failure of every level of *Anokhi*, my self included, for this deep failure? Or perhaps...perhaps...the seeds we have sown this quarter-century still may grow into strong Trees of Life, still may fruit with the olives of the Anointing Oil—still, yet? For after all, *Ani ma'amin,* with a wholehearted faithfulness I still believe, I still believe, despite all this we see, though s/he delay beyond belief I still believe.

## MASTERY OR MYSTERY

From the heart, I believe; from the head, I insist. For we *need* the Messianic transformation. The human race and the earth, *Adam* and *Adamah*, are now caught up in the greatest crisis of our history. It is hard for us to absorb how basic this crisis is. The quickest way to say it is that we stand on the verge of mastering our own DNA, and thereby bringing under conscious control our own biological evolution. We will be the only species ever to do so.

This and other new technologies of mastery are Godlike powers.

The Torah asserts that in the very moment of God's greatest Creativity, God needed to put self-limitations on the Divine Power, needed to pause and make nothing, needed to catch the Divine Breath and make Shabbat.

To human beings, that says: If you have Godlike powers, you must have a Godlike willingness to limit yourself. To make Shabbat. To limit mastery with Mystery.

The great Shabbat of all Shabbats, in Jewish tradition, is not the Jubilee but the Messianic Age. That is when the opposites will be unified: The opposites that went awry at the beginning, when the Tree of Knowing Good and Evil and the Tree of Life were sundered into two. It is when, the mystics said, we will know deeply that there was always, is always, but "one tree in the center of the Garden."

"Unifying opposites" is where this book began. But how do we get there? What should our journey look like?

The two Trees that are truly one Tree are the I-It and the I-Thou that at root are aspects of the one I, *Anokhi*. The Tree of making distinctions grows into the practice of objectifying and analyzing what we need to know in order to eat. The Tree of flowing life grows into the process of relating, loving, creating the communities that nourish us. Without either, we would die.

They enter the world in bursts of energy. I have already suggested that Hellenism was a burst of God as I-It into the human community. To absorb and shape this new power of Doing and Knowing, the human communities needed to receive and shape new patterns of God as I-Thou, Being and Relating. Rabbinic Judaism, Christianity, and Islam emerged as these responses.

The I-It and I-Thou processes intertwine with each other. Together, they shape history into a double spiral.

Why a spiral? Why not see each of these relationships as growing in a straight line of historical development?

The growth of human technology, I-It, seems at first glance to follow a straightforward trajectory: It goes from the fist to the stone to the spear to the arrow to the bullet to the bomb to the missile tipped with hydrogen. From the foot to the canoe to the horse cart to the steam locomotive to the airplane to the Jupiter rocket. From voice to papyrus to printing press to telephone to radio to Internet. Straight lines!

And the I-Thou mode: Does this not also grow in a straight line? From the bond of mother-child to clan to neighborhood to language-group to human race to the web of species in the planetary ecosystem: The expanding bond of love?

Why then do I see the two modes moving in a spiral?

Because they are intertwined, dancing with and around each other. Because I see how the widening circle of I-Thou curves the forward-marching of I-It.

Let me put this spiral on a map of time.

As I have already said, both the I-It and I-Thou processes are aspects of God pouring into the world through human history. They are the Messianic process, and they are necessary to reach the Messianic Age.

The I-It process is embodied in the efforts of one or another part of humanity—a class, a nation, a sex—to dominate others and subdue the earth—and the efforts of the oppressed and the natural world to resist and overcome.

In any given geographic or social space, this relentless march threatens to gobble up the world. Shepherds seek to feed better the most visible people they love, their parents and children. So they breed better sheep. The flocks increase, they devour the grass and the bushes and trees. The shepherds see that the land will be used up in one generation. Unless the shepherds transform their sense of community to love the great-grandchildren whom they cannot see and the grass they did not know was part of the "family," their world will be stricken.

The growing circle of I-Thou comes to give a turn, a *t'shuvah*, to the forward march of technology and power. The shepherds pause, they reflect, they make love—they "make" love, they create more love than there was before. Love expands. By expanding, it saves the world.

In the new and broader world, the improvement of technology can be used to heal, to create, to give life. It is not bottled up to suffocate and smother in its own offdroppings.

And this release does not move in only one direction, where I-Thou saves I-It from its own destructiveness. I-It also makes it possible to broaden the circle of love and community. Once upon a time, it took papyrus for us to include in the community those who were beyond the sound of a voice. Today, we see that the Internet and airplanes make it possible for people we might never have known to become our partners in I-Thou.

So the I-It gives a curve outward to the I-Thou, just as the I-Thou gives a curve upward to the I-It. And that is why this process comes into the world as a spiral.

Once the I-It spiral has reached the point of "total control" over human beings and the planet, there is a danger of massive disaster or even death to human civilization and many species. Whether the process ends with this denouement or another depends on whether the human race achieves another turn of the I-Thou spiral.

This final turn of the I-Thou spiral is that we "turn" to face a Thou so deep that we can achieve an I-Thou among all humans and from humanity to other species and the entire planet as a living organism.

And this is what our seers and prophets meant when they spoke of a Messianic Age.

## FIVE KEYS TO MESSIANIC TIME

What would it take for us to move our history around the next curve of the spiral? What are the key aspects of the Messianic process? For these, I look to the Prophetic images of Messianic time, and to the Genesis story of the departure from Eden. Together, these stories and prophecies point out five great processes that were crucial to Messiah-time.

Genesis specifies these five steps from Eden to "normal" history:

1. The beginning of enmity between humankind and nature.

2. The beginning of rigid sex roles, the subjugation of women, and changes in the nature of sexuality and birth.

3. The beginning of the necessity of hard labor to eat.

4. The beginning of exile: You can't go home again.

5. The beginning of violence: Cain kills Abel.

So the Messianic Days would require the reversal of these five:

1. Achieving harmony between humanity and nature.

2. Achieving equality of women and men and the transformation of sex roles, sexuality, and reproduction and birth.

3. Achieving a decent livelihood without exhausting overwork or servility.

4. Ending the exile: We (the Jewish people and other peoples) can go home again.

5. Abolishing war and other forms of massive violence.

Indeed, the Prophets describe four of these five as criteria for the Days of Messiah: Harmony between humanity and nature, prosperity without toil, the end of exile, and the abolition of war.

Although most of the Prophets ignore the transformation of sex roles and sexuality, Hosea (2:18-25) longs for the day when a husband will be not a "boss" *(baal)* but a "man" *(ish),* like Adam in the Garden, and when God too will no longer be a Boss, when betrothals on earth and between God and Human will be in righteousness and justice, goodness and lovingkindness, and faithfulness. For the fullest celebration of a transformed relationship between women and men and a transformed outlook on sex, we must turn to the Song of Songs, with its midrashic overtones of a higher Eden.

The Prophets applied the notion of ending exile "from Eden"— that is, ending exile as a broad human and existential experience— with intense particularity and detail to how in the Days of Messiah, after great turmoil, the Jewish people would return to the Land of Israel. Their outlook on this fourth event is unique in its addressing of one people rather than all Humanity.

They expected the time immediately preceding the Days of Messiah to be dreadful—the worst days of human history, the war of Gog and Magog. Examining the five Messianic categories in this light, we can see that all five are, at this moment of history, at a crucial threshold between disaster and transformation:

1. The delicate web of *Adam* and *Adamah* is threatened; but the I-Thou science of ecology can now for the first time describe and explain the whole weave of this relationship.

2. The basic assumptions about human sexuality, sex roles, procreation, and genetics that have defined most of history are being questioned. From the subordinated half of the human race, women, has risen a new social philosophy that focuses on relationship and community.

3. The technology has been achieved that could support life for all humans without onerous toil. Yet its fruits are so distributed that the distance between enormous wealth and abject misery is greater than ever before, and this new technology is

set up in such ways that few people carry through a job of work from start to finish, and most do work that is "alienated"—that is, disconnected from any product that they use. Thus, at the same moment, the liberation of all from toil and the subjugation of all to alienated work are both made possible.

4. The Jewish people has suffered the most horrendous destruction since the defeat of Bar Kochba. Yet for the first time since then, a sizable proportion has assembled in the Land of Israel.

5. Peoples and cultures that before never knew each other existed now have the means both to destroy each other—and the whole human race—and to communicate with each other. Total war and universal peaceful relationships are both possible.

## MOVING ON THE SPIRAL

Where would the energy come from to make these five aspects of the Messianic transformation move forward another curve of the I-Thou strand in the spiral?

From the traditional "Left opposition" of labor unions and socialists? They have become very weak. Perhaps as a cause and a symptom of their weakness, they have focused almost as much on the I-It dimension (economic production and consumption) as have the corporations. Most unions are so rigidly organized on national lines that it is hard to create a sense of community where it is most needed, between workers in long-prosperous industrial nations and workers in the neo-industrial Third World. Yet even in these old-form unions, there is still at least the memory of solidarity and community that might become the seed of a new I-Thouing.

From a new kind of opposition? In recent decades new sensibilities and organizations have emerged precisely in response to the dangers of an overpowering modernity. Feminists and environmentalists appeal to a sense of broader, deeper community in exactly the ways necessary to complete another turn on the I-Thou spiral.

Religious communities might, as in the past, become sources for a deepening of the I-Thou relationship, and the broadening of a sense of community. But they can hardly do that as long as they restrict "community" to their own membership. To fulfill their own best visions of themselves, they would have to renew the sense that all human beings and the earth are an intertwined community.

In the last generation, there has indeed been a resurgence in many religious traditions, as Modernity has begun to look not only successful but dangerous. But the religious resurgence has gone in two different directions: Restoration and renewal. *Restoring* as much of the pre-Modern past as possible; or *renewing* the ancient traditions in new forms.

On the one hand, an effort to put women back in their pre-Modern place; on the other, openness to religious change based on the full involvement of women.

On the one hand, circling the wagons against other faiths or cultures; on the other, openness to honoring and learning from the spiritual paths of others.

On the one hand, belief that only human beings bear God's Image, so that reverence for the earth is paganism; on the other, a realization that human beings are both part of God's earth and God's stewards of the earth.

This division between restoration and renewal is taking place within each religious tradition and community.

Today we face the question whether we can create spiritually rooted movements that embody *both* the I-It economic-political concerns of justice and power, and the I-Thou concerns of community and a sense of purpose.

What is now the path that a Judaism reinvigorated by the Messianic vision could decide to walk?

At the beginning of the Jewish journey, God said to Abraham, "*Lekh lekha.*" The usual translation is something like "Go forth." More literal would be, "Walk toward you." But no translation quite works, for the two Hebrew words that mean "Walk!" and "Toward yourself" are identical to the eye and almost identical to the ear. The echo, the pun, is deliberate. We might come close in English as "Outward bound/Unbind inward." In other words, "Go beyond yourself in order to find your innermost being." Outward and in, outward and in: An ever-deepening spiral.

Ever since, we have been walking toward Messiah in this strange looping spiral. The root of *lekh*, "walk," expands to make *halakhah*, literally the walking-way; more broadly, the path of Jewish life. Although the code of Jewish law is called *halakhah*, the word itself teaches that the practice and process of life are not static. They never get settled because truth is unsettling; we are always on the move because our Teacher is always learning something new.

To achieve another turning in the I-Thou spiral, we need to make *halakhah* that is pointed toward Messiah.

One of the most salient facts of Jewish history of the last three centuries is the breakdown of the halakhic process. The breakdown began with the outburst of Messianic hope in 1666 around Shabtai Tzvi. The breakdown was no accident, and only partly a mistake. For if history was making still another turn toward the Messianic moment, it is not surprising that people sensed a shortcoming in the content and process of *halakhah*. If God has brought us to this point, a point at which transformations in sexuality, work, conflict, and ecological relationships have already begun, large numbers of the Jewish people would be bound to feel these currents of transformation from without and whispers of the Voice from within, and therefore be struggling to live in new ways, not encompassed by the old *halakhah*.

Their first response was to throw off the old *halakhah*, as many did after Shabtai Tzvi, with first the Reform movement, then secularist Jewish movements, and then various versions of assimilation into the modern world. Only later would people begin to search toward a new content for *halakhah* and a new process for arriving at it that would reach toward the Messianic Age.

## TOWARD A NEW HALAKHAH

How are we to begin to know this path? First of all, the tradition teaches that the most important form of social action is to try to create in the present a model, a foretaste, of the future toward which the world is striving. Thus Moses acts out in his own person, in miniature, the history of the people: He plunges into Egypt, then he rebels, then he flees, then he receives Revelation. Thus Shabbat is explained as a foretaste of the Messianic Age, and we are taught that if the whole Jewish people can observe two Shabbats, Messiah will come. More darkly, Jeremiah "acts out" the Captivity in advance, by wearing a yoke upon his shoulders. And, in the fullest and deepest version of the practice, the Jews as a whole are to become a holy people in order to enact in the present what should become possible in the future for all the peoples of the earth.

From this Teaching, it would make sense for a Messianically-oriented *halakhah* to be based on looking toward the Messianic lineaments of the Eden story, the Prophets, and the Song of Songs. From these we could discern what *halakhah* we should now live by.

This has not been the typical halakhic method until now; for in Rabbinic Judaism, *halakhah* has been deduced or at least approved only by reference to the Five Books, not the Prophets or the Song of Songs. To shape a new Jewish life-path by reorienting ourselves to these more visionary texts would in some ways be a radical departure. Yet in other ways it would be deeply conservative, giving practical weight to elements of our ancient wisdom that are now treated *only* as visionary. In the mode of *lekh lekha*, we would both go outward and return within.

By doing this we are doing something like what the tradition does when it says, not that on Shabbat there is a new *halakhah,* but that the *halakhah* directs us to behave differently on Shabbat from the way we behave on the workdays. There is not a new *halakhah* for the Messianic Age, but our whole halakhic process teaches us to behave differently as the Great Shabbat approaches.

How do we begin "foretasting" and "modeling" the days of Messiah? Small communities begin acting on their understanding of a Messianically-oriented *halakhah*. If they have well chosen what practices will enhance life in our era, other communities will use them as models to emulate (but not necessarily to imitate).

Second, the tradition teaches that the whole Jewish nation is to become holy, a nation of priests; or as Moses said, "Would that all my people were prophets!" The *halakhah* of previous history has been developed not by the whole people but by a small elite: Only adults, only male adults, only heterosexual male adults, only heterosexual male adults who had received long, complex training in an elaborate verbal tradition. So we should be working out ways for a Messianically-oriented *halakhah* to be developed through discussion by old and young, learned and unlearned, women and men, gay and heterosexual (and all the "curved" identities—neither "bent" nor "straight"—that characterize most human beings).

Third, we should explore Abraham Joshua Heschel's insight that a special Jewish contribution to the theory of liberation is the focus on liberating time. Most theories of social transformation—especially the secularized messianism of Marxism—have focused on the liberation of space, territory, geography. But their own history has shown that liberating space alone imposes sharp limits on what liberation is. Maybe that is why Sinai had to include the time-liberating message of Shabbat.

So perhaps a Messianically-oriented *halakhah* should learn how to move into the Messianic Age by liberating chunks of time rather than space. Turning the "weekend" into the Shabbat, turning summer "vacation" (vacancy and emptiness) into Elul, a month of study and spiritual growth. Choosing some piece of time that is comparatively well insulated from the devouring society around, and working within that segment of time to develop a Messianic life-path that works well for that particular piece of time. And then, once that time span is redeemed, moving to free a new, somewhat more precarious piece of time.

Keeping these three overall approaches in mind—creating models of the future in the present; involving the whole community in the process; and liberating time—we might then begin to imagine how communities could begin to walk a Messianically-oriented *halakhah*. By wrestling with the parts of Revelation most focused on Messiah, could we discern what questions we would have to ask in the five arenas of Messianic change?

*In regard to violence*: In a Messianically-oriented *halakhah*, is war forbidden? How should Messianic forerunners address not only soldiering but such grayer areas as weapons-relevant research and paying taxes for military forces? What about the more covert violence behind the police and courts? Could Messianic forerunners replace resorting to official courts with resolving conflicts through mediation and arbitration, through consultation with an advisory *beit chesed* (house of lovingkindness)?

*In regard to "earth and earthling"*: Eden was "home" to all of life. Adam was to eat of the herbs and fruits, but evidently not of animal life. In the Days of Messiah, says Hosea, God will make a "covenant on behalf of Israel with the wild beasts, the birds of the air, and the things that creep on the earth."

So in a Messianically-oriented *halakhah*, should we eat no meat? Should we live by "eco-kosher" rules for consuming paper, oil, electric power?

*In regard to work*: In Eden, Adam was to work the garden (but not in toil or pain) and could freely eat of its trees; and in the Days of Messiah, says Isaiah, "They shall build houses and dwell in them, they shall plant vineyards and enjoy their fruit. They shall not build for others to dwell in, or plant for others to enjoy."

In a Messianic Path, are the kibbutz and other forms of workers' ownership and self-management to be preferred? Should we seek new technologies and easily available sources of renewable energy so that small groups of workers can "build houses and dwell in them," instead of depending entirely on a remote chain of economic life?

*In regard to sexuality, women and men, the family*: We have seen how the ancestresses of Messiah point toward, and the heroine of the Song of Songs exemplifies, a liberated womanhood. Do we need new sexual ethics and liturgies for marriages, for long-term committed relationships, for more experimental and uncommitted relationships? How should single people and people who do not have biological children participate in intergenerational obligations like raising children? What would be the best relationships between sex and love or deep friendship?

*In regard to peoplehood and land*: Eden was "home" to the whole human race. To the Prophets, the Days of Messiah meant that the Jewish people can again shape its own destiny in and create a holy relationship with the Land of Israel. Today, what is a Messianically-oriented relationship between Israel and the Palestinian people, in regard to the Land of Abraham? And what are the obligations of Jews in other lands they live in, when issues arise of the self-determination of peoples or of the rights of the stranger within the gates?

All these halakhic questions (*shylas,* as the tradition called them) are couched in the territory of one of the five arenas of Messianic transformation. But in fact transformation probably will not come through a change about violence here, a change about sexuality there. It may come more fully in the emergence of whole new communities, as the kibbutz was a coherent new community, a mutation. How do we create them?

## VISIONS ON THE WAY

Let me put forward three visions—one that could be fulfilled soon, one perhaps a Jubilee generation hence, and another that might require yet one more Jubilee cycle:

Groups might begin by both liberating and making sacred summertime as a time for communal growth toward a Messianic *halakhah.* After a year of planning, sharing, studying, meeting each other in a serious way, such a group might then come together for four weeks or so of communal work, politics, celebration, and study. Simply by living and working together, they would create a situation in which halakhic answers would necessarily be developed to the specific questions of daily living.

Provisionally, a vision: Within one Jubilee cycle—fifty years from now—thousands of face to face Jewish communities have sprung up in many countries to experiment with living one or another version of a Messianically-oriented *halakhah.* These communities have revivified the Jewish festivals to celebrate the cycles of joy and sadness in their lives. They are in vital touch with each other, as a transnational Jewish movement. In all these places this Jewish ferment is learning from and teaching the ferment of other cultures and peoples. The new communities are carefully but vigorously challenging aspects of the larger society that are deadly toward the human race and the earth.

Provisionally, an even further vision: Within two Jubilee cycles, a century from now, these grassroots communities have banded together to create free Jewish commonwealths (not states), in North America and Russia. Together with communities of other holy peoplehoods, they have become so strong that the great super-states have been radically decentralized, war has been abolished, extremes of wealth and poverty ended, and restoration of the planetary environment is well advanced.

Harder to describe, but spiritually important: That the women and men of these communities have achieved a new spiritual synthesis of the Tree of Knowledge and the Tree of Life, analysis and fluidity, structure and spontaneity; and human beings have achieved a more open, loving, and comradely relationship with the Infinite and Living God.

Will this, then, be the end of human conflict and striving? No. The Days of Messiah are a new level, not the end, of human history and the God-human interaction. Since the God with Whom the Messianic human community will have a new relation is indeed living, unpredictable, and infinite, surely even in Messiah-time there will emerge new needs of the human spirit that are now unimaginable to us.

The Prophet Elijah—the one who never died, the one who will return to announce the coming of Messiah—faced the Jewish people three thousand years ago with an image of the choice between Baal and God: A bird, hopping on both twigs of a diverging branch, comes finally to the point where the two twigs separate so far that it can no longer walk on both at once. It must choose. So Elijah said to Israel, and Israel chose God.

What Elijah did not say was that when the divergence of the branches becomes unbearable, the bird can fly off the tree in some new direction.

The human race has always walked on both branches at once, choosing a little life and a little death. But now the branches diverge too far, and we are beyond the point where we can walk both twigs at once. Now we must choose between widespread death for ourselves and the other beings with whom we share the earth, or a life renewed and transformed. A Messianic life.

# CHAPTER 23

# CONNECTING: FROM THE WRESTLE TO A DANCE

In a traditional prayer service, just before the davenners reach the *Sh'ma*, the affirmation of God's Unity, they gather together the *tzitzit* from the four corners of the prayer shawl and hold them in a unity. After the *Sh'ma*, they turn their eyes to the *tzitzit* and focus their attention on these symbols of connection, finally kissing them several times before releasing them. Then they stand for the murmured prayer in which all become one with the One.

It is time for me to gather together the threads of my dialogue with you from the four corners of this book, and weave them into the great web of Unity. The God Who is *Anokhi* and the God with Whom we wrestle, the brothers and the mothers, the Godwrestling people and the struggling species of which it is a microcosm, the earth and all its earthlings: How do we come together?

We are taught that these *tzitzit* we hold, these threads that reach out to each other, are symbols of the *mitzvot*, that if we look clearly at these knotted fringes that connect us we will remember to do all the *mitzvot*. We will remember that we are connected with each other, with all the other communities and beings of the earth; and that we must not only know we are connected but *act* that way.

What are the *mitzvot*? In traditional Jewish lore, they are understood as commands that come from the Divine Commander, Lord and King of the universe. Some Jews think these commands came once and are immutable; others think the Commander occasionally changes the decrees He issues—yes, as Commander He is surely "He"—and that the Jewish community can with great care discern these changes. Still others think there really are no commands from a Supernal Commander, that what we call the *mitzvot* are merely folkways, and that the individual must consult the still, small voice of his or her own conscience to know what to do. And others say that precisely because there are really no *mitzvot* from Above, it is whole communities that actually embody the holy process of connection. So, they say, it is communities, not lonely individuals, that must together work out how to live.

## THE BONDS WITHIN ANOKHI

For me, none of these approaches is fully adequate. Plunged into the midst of the *Anokhi*, the Infinite and Infinitesimal *I*, I find there no commands. Instead I find an organic Unity that is simultaneously within me and beyond me. I find the One Great Body, in which the heart sends blood bearing oxygen to the brain, and the brain sends electrical impulses through the nerves to the heart. Together they keep each other alive.

Yet we think of the electric impulses as a "command," and the blood as only a "substance." We think that the brain is in charge. Why? I think because we have been taught to honor what is "up," "higher," and to treat the more rarefied forms of reality as more sacred than the more substantive forms—electrons more to be honored than fluid blood (and earthy flesh still lower in the scale). But in the Bible's metaphors, the heart was the seat of the mind, and in the blood was the life-breath.

Instead of elevating one organ above the others, we could celebrate precisely the web of connection, the process of connection, the unity of connections. We could celebrate the *da'at* that is simultaneously "knowing" and "love-making." We could take joy in experiencing a relationship in which "command" and "connection" are the same thing, one in which the blood might just as well be said to "command" the brain and the nerve impulses to "connect" the brain and heart.

And so, living within *Anokhi*, we understand the *mitzvot* not as commandments but as connections.

Seeing *mitzvot* as connections opens us up to a sense of the world in which God is not Commander but the Web of Connections that makes a Unity of the universe. These connections exist at two levels: Potential and actual. The connections are already there as an underlying reality, and they are strengthened, given vividness and life, when human beings act on them.

Every act of *mitzvah*-doing strengthens the Unity, makes God more fully real. This is similar to how a Hassidic rebbe read the text, "I am God, and you are My witnesses," to mean, "If you are not my witnesses, then I am not God." That is, I assume, "Not fully God." By doing *mitzvot*, we witness; by acting, we make God fully God.

Now there arises a troubling question: Can *mitzvot* change? Could it be that at one point in human development a certain way of behaving is a *mitzvah*, a way of affirming and enlivening a deep connection in the world, and that at another time in history the same action would scratch sidewise against reality, would tear things apart rather than heal them?

For example: At one configuration of the Divine Process, bringing sacrifices of food, including animals, to the Holy Temple was a *mitzvah*. It strengthened connections between human earthlings and the earth, between the Jewish people and God. But later, to do such sacrifices ran crosswise against the flow of life; it broke connections rather than strengthened them.

Similarly, we might say that at one period of human history, the *mechitzah* (the barrier between men and women at prayer) may have been the best available way of enhancing some crucial connections. Perhaps it was a way of balancing the energies of "doing" and "relating," I-It and I-Thou, at a time when the "doing" energies were held mostly by men and the "relating" energies mostly by women.

By the same token, could this pattern change so that the best way to balance these energies would come to be not balancing them between a group of all men and a group of all women, but balancing them *within* each man and woman, and so to get rid of the *mechitzah*? Could the context of an act that used to be a *mitzvah* change so that this very act shatters, rather than repairs, connections? And could the *mitzvah* underneath, which is the balancing and connection of I-It and I-Thou, then be most effectively fulfilled by abolishing the *mechitzah*?

I am saying Yes, *mitzvot do* change. This is because God changes, the shape of the Web of Connections changes. The God Who is *Ehyeh Asher Ehyeh*, "I Will Be Who I Will Be," "I Am Becoming What I Am Becoming"—*that* God changes. No doubt there are aspects of God that do not change; the Unutterable Infinite *Eyn Sof* may not change; but to *that* aspect of God, the *mitzvot* are irrelevant. At the moment of fullest *Anokhi*, as I experienced, history both did and did not exist: I could see flow and history, the whirling of galaxies and empires and blood cells and neutrons, and in the very same glance I could see that all the whirls of change were present in one fused moment of eternity. All the pasts, all futures, and all presents; all souls—the dead, the living, and the yet unborn, were There, *Anokhi*. It was not that all change had been abolished into stasis; it was that all change was simultaneously visible.

So the *mitzvot* change—and yet they are Divine and Eternal.

This approach to *mitzvot* thinks of them, feels them, not merely as "nice" folkways but as profound and Divine in their origin and their intention. This approach invites and requires us not only to act in accord with the *mitzvot*, but also to fully use our intellects and emotions and spiritual openness to God's Will, so as to shape and define what the *mitzvot* are in our own time. This approach requires us both to apprehend ourselves as Infinitesimal elements within *Anokhi*, and to experience ourselves as *Anokhi* Myself.

## GIVING LIFE TO MITZVAH

If we apply the Kabbalistic metaphor of the Four Worlds of reality, what this approach does is to infuse our actual action in doing the *mitzvot* (the world of *Asiyah*) with thought (the world of *Briyah*), feeling (the world of *Yetzirah*), and open-being (the world of *Atzilut*). Thus within each *mitzvah* the Four Worlds are united, and God is made One in a way that is not achieved if the *mitzvah* is only done, without being rethought, refelt, reopened, and redone.

So now, when human beings are more fully Godlike than ever before, more fully part of *Anokhi*, this way of understanding the *mitzvot* may be—or be becoming—itself the highest *mitzvah*, because it demands that we be whole as we do every *mitzvah*.

Or perhaps a better way of thinking about this is not to assert that only this way of doing a *mitzvah* is a *mitzvah* (thereby implying that any other way of doing a *mitzvah* is an *aveirah*, a violation of God's will) but to suggest that this way of doing a *mitzvah* is a *m'chayeh* (a "life-enhancer"), a way of filling the act with a higher, deeper life. And that in our generation, we are called whenever possible to affirm and strengthen connection in the world by doing not only a *mitzvah* but a *m'chayeh*.

For me, introducing the notion of *m'chayeh* into the *mitzvah* process accomplishes something broader: It helps me move away from the assumption that all action is On/Off, Black/White, Good/Bad. If I assert that there are at least three levels of action—doing a *mitzvah*, which carries out a needed connection; doing a *sh'virah* ("shattering") which breaks it; doing a *m'chayeh*, which gives it added life—then I am seeing a continuum of action, a spectrum of action, rather than simple dichotomies.

On that basis, it's a *mitzvah* to do a *mitzvah stamm*—just like that—and it's a *m'chayeh* to do a *mitzvah* in all Four of the Worlds.

If our hearts are filled with love, our minds with accurate planning, our hands with steadiness and strength, our souls with

318

openness, then any act we do will be a *mitzvah*, will strengthen the great Web of all connections, will make God more fully God. And any act of connection-making that we do will enliven life.

It is a *mitzvah* for each of us to face the dark and terrible shadows within her/his own heart, and make sure they do not harm and terrify another being; it is a *m'chayeh* to search out the sacred root of their fearfulness, integrate it into our whole self, and so to clarify our hearts that they can serve the One in truthfulness.

It is a *mitzvah* for us to live in peace with all our brothers and sisters, and a *m'chayeh* to weave their stories and our own into a great Torah of wisdom.

It is a *mitzvah* to tolerate the different strands of Jewish peoplehood, and a *m'chayeh* to draw from each its own deep *mitzvah* to enhance the new life-giving pattern of the Jewish people.

It is a *mitzvah* to make sure the poor and the outcast get fed, and a *m'chayeh* to make sure that all have the power to help shape the future and make their own prosperity.

It is a *mitzvah* to protect each living species and each pattern of the chemistry of earth, and a *m'chayeh* to understand their intertwining and celebrate the wholeness of all life.

It is a *mitzvah* to dedicate our lives to shaping integrity within our selves, or to nurturing love within a family, or to making peace and justice in society, or to protecting the planetary life-web; it is a *m'chayeh* to shape our lives so that we do *all* these.

It is a *mitzvah* to expect Messiah in our own lifetimes, to wait with utter faithfulness, and a *m'chayeh* not just to wait but to walk each present moment in a path of life that comes ever closer to the Messianic pattern.

To experience *Anokhi*, I, in Its/My fullness, is to shatter all expectations and assumptions, to connect us with the All and with the Whole, and to fill all the deadly, deadening places in the world with life.

We have lived long enough in the era when we understood the process of Creation as Division: Dividing light from darkness, land from sea, plant from animal, human from earth, man from woman. In that world, every relationship between the separated beings has been a wrestle—close, intimate, and yet a struggle.

Let us enter the era when we can affirm these distinctions—and yet Create a world by Connecting. The era when across each separation, our beings can see more clearly what connects us, can take our differences as part of the delightful music of the universe.

Let us move from the Wrestle to a Dance.

# NEW TEXTS

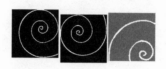

# THE COVENANT OF THE FIRE
# AND THE RAINBOW

During the summer of 1993, I spent several days teaching "eco-Judaism" to high-school students at a leading Jewish camp. When I left, I felt utterly dissatisfied with myself: I had been an ineffective teacher of the generation closest to my concerns, regarding the questions closest to my heart. Back at Elat Chayyim, a Jewish-renewal retreat center, I tried to rethink, re-feel; but I felt mostly stuck in sadness and depression. On Thursday morning, Rabbi Zalman Schachter-Shalomi asked me to read in English, "in the way you do that brings it to life," the Prophetic reading for the coming Shabbat service. I agreed, thinking that this at least I knew how to get right.

That midnight I awoke possessed of a teaching, its words and rhythms gleaming like the Rainbow that arched across its phrases. I wrote them down. I went to Reb Zalman to say that I would like to read the *Haftarah* that had come to me, rather than the one the Rabbis had assigned for the day. He agreed. When I read it for the community on Shabbat morning, it was clear to me and everyone that its energy was flaming through me but not from me.

*[Blessed are You, the Breath of Life, Who makes of every human throat a shofar for the breathing of Your truth.]*

You, My people, burnt in fire,
still staring blinded
by the flame and smoke
that rose from Auschwitz and from Hiroshima;

You, My people,
Battered by the earthquakes
of a planet in convulsion;

You, My people,
Drowning in the flood of words and images
That beckon you to eat and eat,
to drink and drink,
to fill and overfill
your bellies

at the tables of
the gods of wealth and power;

You, My people,
Drowning in the flood of words and images
That—poured unceasing on your eyes and ears—
drown out My words of Torah,
My visions of the earth made whole;

Be comforted:

I have for you a mission full of joy.
I call you to a task of celebration.

I call you to make from fire not an all-consuming blaze
But the light in which all beings see each other fully.
All different,
All bearing One Spark.
I call you to light a flame to see more clearly
That the earth and all who live as part of it
Are not for burning:
A flame to see
The rainbow
in the many-colored faces
of all life.

I call you:
I, the Breath of Life,
Within you and beyond,
Among you and beyond,
That One Who breathes from redwood into grizzly,
That One Who breathes from human into swampgrass,
That One Who breathes the great pulsations of the galaxies.
In every breath you breathe Me,

In every breath I breathe you.
I call you—
In every croak of every frog I call you,
In every rustle of each leaf,
        each life,
I call you,
In the wailings of the wounded earth
I call you.

I call you to a peoplehood renewed:
I call you to reweave the fabric of your folk
and so to join in healing
the weave of life upon your planet.
I call you to a journey of seven generations.

For seven generations past,
the earth has not been able to make Shabbos.

And so in your own generation
You tremble on the verge of Flood.
Your air is filled with poison.
The rain, the seas, with poison.
The earth hides arsenals of poisonous fire,
Seeds of light surcharged with fatal darkness.
The ice is melting,
The seas are rising,
The air is dark with smoke and rising heat.

And so—I call you to carry to all peoples
the teaching that for seven generations
the earth and all her earthlings learn to rest.

I call you once again
To speak for Me,
To speak for Me because I have no voice,
To speak the Name of the One who has no Name,
To speak for all the Voiceless of the planet.

Who speaks for the redwood and the rock,
the lion and the beetle?

My Breath I blow through you into a voicing:
Speak for the redwood and the rock,
the lion and the beetle.

I call you to a task of joy:
For seven generations,
this is what I call for you to do:

To make once more the seasons of your joy
into celebrations of the seasons of the earth;
To welcome with your candles the dark of moon and sun,

To bless with careful chewing
    the fruits of every tree
For when you meet to bless
    the rising juice of life
      in every tree trunk—
I am the Tree of Life.

To live seven days in the open, windy huts,
And call out truth to all who live beside you—
You are part of the weave and breath of life,
You cannot make walls to wall it out.

I call you to a covenant between the generations:
That when you gather for a blessing of your children
as they take on the tasks of new tomorrows,
You say to them, they say to you,
That you are all My prophet
Come to turn the hearts of parents
and of children toward each other,
Lest my earth be smashed in utter desolation.

I call you
To eat what
I
call
kosher:
Food that springs from an earth you do not poison,
Oil that flows from an earth you do not drain,
Paper that comes from an earth you do not slash,
Air that comes from an earth you do not choke.

I call you to speak
to all the peoples,
all the rulers.

I call you to walk forth before all nations,
    to pour out water that is free of poison
      and call them all to clean and clarify the rains of winter.

I call you to beat your willows on the earth
    and shout its healing to all peoples.

I call on you to call on all the peoples
to cleanse My Breath, My air,
from all the gases
that turn My earth into a furnace.

I call you to light the colors of the Rainbow,
To raise once more before all eyes
That banner of the covenant between Me,
and all the children of Noah and Naamah,
and all that lives and breathes upon the Earth—
So that
never again,
all the days of the earth, shall
      sowing and harvest,
      cold and heat,
      summer and winter,
      day and night
      ever cease!

I call you to love the Breath of Life—
      For love is the fire
      That blazes in the Rainbow.

I call you so to live for seven generations
As in the days when you went forth from slavery;
So in these seven generations
The earth will bring forth manna,
The bread of joy and freedom—
and all earth can sing together
Songs of Shabbos.

*[Blessed are You, the Breath of Life, Who makes of every human
throat a channel for the breathing of Your truth.]*

# II

# NISHMAT

When God speaks to us through Torah, say our sages, echo the learning back to God through prayer. As we wrestled with the Breath of
Life to write the prayerbook *Or Chadash*, this came as my reflection
of the Torah we were learning:

You Whose very Name—
YyyyHhhhWwwwHhhh—
Is the Breath of Life,
The breathing of all life
Gives joy and blessing to Your Name.

As lovers lie within each other's arms,
Whispering each the other's name
Into the other's ear,
So we lie in Your arms,
Breathing with each breath
Your Name, Your Truth, Your Unity.

You alone,
Your Breath of Life alone,
Guides us,
Frees us,
Transforms us,
Heals us,
Nurtures us,
Teaches us.

First, last,
Future, past,
Inward, outward,
Beyond, between,
You are the breathing that gives life to all the worlds.
And we do the breathing that gives life to all the worlds.

As we breathe out what the trees breathe in,
And the trees breathe out what we breathe in,
So we breathe each other into life,
We and You.

YyyyHhhhWwwwHhhh.

# LEARNINGS

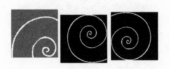

# LEARNINGS

Some teachings, like the Torah itself, are encoded in ink on paper, black fire on white fire. Others are encoded in DNA, alive and breathing in four or five or six dimensions of humanity.

Across the quarter-century that shaped this book, only a few people were my teachers at the beginning and are my teachers still. Max and Esther Ticktin have walked a life-path filled with kindness, devotion, intelligence, and Torah. My brother Howard Waskow and my children David Waskow and Shoshana Elkin Waskow appear at many points in this book not only because we shared our lives but because they shared their wisdom with me. As I wrote, they insisted that I reflect in words and actions on my own previous "editions" of my life.

At the very beginning, Michael Tabor translated the Freedom Seder from the pages of a book into the songs and wine and matzah of a live community. Harold White opened up for me not only the delights of ancient midrash, but the astonishing truth that I was doing the same work. Rob Agus and David Shneyer brought the Fabrangen into being, and with it the wonderful discussions on Shabbat that whispered this book into my heart and mind. To all those Fabrangeners who remember those discussions differently, I say: You are right—and so am I.

Ever since I began to learn from Zalman Schachter-Shalomi, I have been unfolding the implications of his dance with God. He has been the rarest kind of rebbe—for he creates not clones of himself but independent leaders, among them some of our most life-giving teachers, artists, composers, writers, and davveners.

Beyond these, I hesitate to name my teachers, for there have been not a few adepts alone, but a myriad of comrades, friends, sometimes even a person who has taught a crucial insight in one glowing moment and then flown like a comet from my vision. And yet:

During my years in Washington, there were Shlomo Carlebach, Irene Elkin, Cherie Koller Fox, Everett Fox, Debbie Friedman, Everett Gendler, Lynn Gottlieb, Arthur Green, Rachel Hammer, William Kavesh, Liz Lerman, Michael Masch, Diane Levenberg, Jeff Oboler, Rosalie Riechman, Joel Rosenberg, Gerry Serotta, Nessa Spitzer, Toba Spitzer, Rivka Nurit Stone, Michael Strassfeld, Sharon Strassfeld, Burt Weiss, and Chava Weissler.

During my years in Philadelphia, there were Barbara Breitman, Jeffrey Dekro, Ari Elon, Shefa Gold, Leonard Gordon, Julie Greenberg, Shaya Isenberg, Mordechai Liebling, Mitch Marcus, Susan Marcus, Marcia Prager, Jeff Roth, Chaim Rothstein, Susan Saxe, Bahira Sugarman, Brian Walt, Rivkah Walton, and Sheila Weinberg.

That there could be no Jewish renewal without feminist Judaism I knew in my bones, perhaps from my mother. I learned it in the brain from Martha Ackelsberg, Phyllis Berman, Barbara Breitman, Esther Broner, Laura Geller, Mary Gendler, Susannah Heschel, Joanna Katz, Liz Koltun, Judith Plaskow, and Sheila Weinberg.

When I wrote the first version of this book, I needed to mention several who had been my teachers or models and had died: Paul Goodman, Abraham Joshua Heschel, Paul Jacobs, Harry Koenick, and my grandfather Samuel M. Waskow. Since then others have joined them: My grandmother Rose Honigman Osnowitz Gertz, my mother and father Hannah Osnowitz Waskow and Henry B. Waskow, Shlomo Carlebach, Paul Lichterman, Rita Poretsky, Ira Silverman, and Anne Sara Weiss. May all their names be lit brightly in that one Great Name in which all names are written.

For almost a quarter of my life, Phyllis Ocean Berman and I have with intense and loving energy and with calm restfulness learned together the Torah that the words of this book try to express. Phyllis has also worked with me to shape these words so that they would more fully embody the dance of loving Torah. Only she, my editor Arthur Magida, and my publisher Stuart Matlins have read the whole of my manuscript. From them all I have had extraordinarily wise and thoughtful criticism.

For deft and creative work in giving the book its physical reality, I thank Sandra Korinchak and Glenn Suokko.

And so we come back to ink and paper:

**The Bible:** Everett Fox's translations of Genesis and Exodus (*In the Beginning* and *Now These Are the Names*), with more to come; Marcia Falk's *Song of Songs*; Stephen Mitchell's *The Book of JOB*; *Five Megillot and Jonah* and the five-volume *JPS Torah Commentary*, both from the Jewish Publication Society.

**The Rabbis:** *Pesikta de Rav Kahane*; *Midrash Rabbah* (Soncino); the El Am translation of some sections of the Talmud Bavli; the Steinsaltz translation of some parts of the Talmud Bavli; Daniel Boyarin, *Carnal Israel*; Rami Shapiro, transl., *Wisdom of the Jewish Sages* [Pirke Avot].

**Kabbalah and Hassidism:** Daniel Chanan Matt, *Zohar*, and Isaiah Tishby, *Wisdom of the Zohar*; Menahem Nahum of Chernobyl, *Upright Practices & The Light of the Eyes* (transl. by Arthur Green);

Arthur Green, *Tormented Master*; Nehemiah Polen, *Holy Fire*; Moshe Idel, *Golem*.

**Twentieth Century:** Martin Buber, *I and Thou, Moses, Paths in Utopia*, and many others; Abraham Joshua Heschel, *The Sabbath* and many others; Andre Neher, *Exile of the Word*; Emanuel Levinas, *Nine Talmudic Readings*; Franz Kafka, *Parables and Paradoxes*; Jerome Rothenberg and others, *A Big Jewish Book*; Arthur A. Cohen, *In the Days of Simon Stern*; Arthur A. Cohen and Paul Mendes-Flohr, eds., *Contemporary Jewish Religious Thought*.

**Jewish-renewal approaches:** Michael Strassfeld, Sharon Strassfeld, and Richard Siegel, eds., *The Jewish Catalogs*; Lawrence Kushner, *Honey from the Rock, The River of Light*, and *God Was in this Place and I, i Did Not Know*; Lawrence Kushner and Kerry Olitzky, *Sparks beneath the Surface*; Esther Broner, *A Weave of Women* and *The Telling*; Marge Piercy, *He, She and It*; Michael Lerner, *Jewish Renewal*; Rodger Kamenetz, *The Jew in the Lotus*; Judith A. Kates and Gail Twersky Reimer, eds., *Reading Ruth*; Tony Kushner, *Angels in America*; Ari Elon, *Alma Di*; Judith Plaskow, *Standing Again at Sinai*; Liz Koltun, ed., *The Jewish Woman*; Susannah Heschel, ed., *On Being a Jewish Feminist*; Rami Shapiro, *Embracing Esau*; Arthur Green, *Seek My Face, Speak My Name*; Peter Pitzele, *Our Fathers' Wells* and *Scripture Windows: Theory and Practice of Biblical Psychodrama*.

**Prayer and Liturgy:** Zalman Schachter-Shalomi, *Paradigm Shift*; Shohama Harris Wiener and Jonathan Omer-Man, eds., *Worlds of Jewish Prayer*; *Or Chadash* (P'nai Or Religious Fellowship/ALEPH: Alliance for Jewish Renewal); Marcia Falk, *A Book of Blessings*; Shefa Gold, "Chants Encounters," "Tzuri: My Rock," "Abundance," and other audiotapes.

If this book has stirred in you further questions or thoughts about Godwrestling and Jewish renewal, please write me at ALEPH: Alliance for Jewish Renewal, 6711 Lincoln Drive, Philadelphia, PA 19119. ALEPH is an international network of congregations and *havurot*; writers, singers, artists, and teachers; activists and meditators; veterans and newcomers—who are all exploring Jewish renewal. I edit its journal *New Menorah* (subscription, with ALEPH membership, $36 a year), and I welcome you to join in as *New Menorah* deals with these questions. I would be delighted to keep wrestling and dancing with you who read this book.

Traditionally, when together we complete a time of learning Torah, we say the blessing Kaddish d'Rabbanan. Please join me:

*For the people Yisrael*
*and all who wrestle with God,*
*for our teachers the rabbis*
*and for all our teachers,*
*for their students—ourselves, myself—*
*and for the students of their students,*
*those whom we go forth to teach,*
*for all who search deeply into Torah in its places*
*and all who aim their hearts and minds toward wisdom every-*
    *where,*
*may there be*
*peace in our hearts*
*and a peaceful world around us,*
*abundant love and kindness,*
*an honorable and sufficient livelihood*
*that flows from working in harmony with earth,*
*and the sense that all these blessings come not from our isolated*
    *efforts*
*but from our efforts as threads of the great weave of life*
*that is the One.*

—Arthur Ocean Waskow,
on the full moon of Tammuz,
July 14, 1995

# ABOUT THE AUTHOR

Arthur Ocean Waskow and his wife Phyllis Ocean Berman decided to share a new middle name when they got married. They live in a lively integrated Philadelphia neighborhood, Mount Airy, among trees, streams, and a Toonerville Trolley. Waskow has two grown children of his own and is "associate parent" for two others. He is a Pathfinder of ALEPH: Alliance for Jewish Renewal, an international network with headquarters in Philadelphia.

Since 1969, Waskow has been one of the leading creators of theory, practice, and institutions for Jewish renewal. He founded the journal *New Menorah* and The Shalom Center, helped found the Fabrangen Cheder and the National Havurah Committee, wrote such classics of Jewish renewal as *The Freedom Seder, Godwrestling, Seasons of Our Joy,* and *Down-to-Earth Judaism,* and taught at the Reconstructionist Rabbinical College, Swarthmore College, and Temple University. In the fall of 1995, Waskow was ordained a Rabbi by a committee of one Hassidic, one Reform, and one Conservative rabbi, and a Jewish feminist theologian.

Waskow has often worked closely with other members of his family. When his children David and Shoshana were young, they wrote together a book of tales of the Creation, *Before There Was a Before.* With his brother Howard he wrote *Becoming Brothers,* a "wrestle in two voices" about their process of conflict and reconciliation. He and Phyllis, who is also a leader of Jewish renewal and is the founding director of a unique school for adult immigrants and refugees from all around the world, often join to speak, teach new forms of prayer, tell stories from their book *Tales of Tikkun,* and lead retreats and workshops in many Jewish, interreligious, and college settings.

Waskow was born in Baltimore in 1933. He studied United States history at Johns Hopkins University and the University of Wisconsin. He worked as a legislative assistant for a U.S. Congressman, and through the 1960s, as one of the founding Fellows of the Institute for Policy Studies, wrote several books on military strategy, disarmament, nonviolence, and social change, and was active in opposing the Vietnam War. He co-authored "A Call to Resist Illegitimate Authority" and was elected by the citizens of the District of Columbia to the 1968 Democratic National Convention.

# About JEWISH LIGHTS Publishing

People of all faiths and backgrounds yearn for books that attract, engage, educate and spiritually inspire.

Our principal goal is to stimulate thought and help all people learn about who the Jewish People are, where they come from, and what the future can be made to hold. While people of our diverse Jewish heritage are the primary audience, our books speak to people in the Christian world as well and will broaden their understanding of Judaism and the roots of their own faith.

We bring to you authors who are at the forefront of spiritual thought and experience. While each has something different to say, they all say it in a voice that you can hear.

Our books are designed to welcome you and then to engage, stimulate and inspire. We judge our success not only by whether or not our books are beautiful and commercially successful, but by whether or not they make a difference in your life.

We at Jewish Lights take great care to produce beautiful books that present meaningful spiritual content in a form that reflects the art of making high quality books. Therefore, we want to acknowledge those who contributed to the production of this book.

PRODUCTION
Maria O'Donnell

EDITORIAL & PROOFREADING
Jennifer Goneau

COVER DESIGN
Maria O'Donnell

COVER PRINTING
Phoenix Color Corp., Taunton, Massachusetts

PRINTING AND BINDING
Quebecor Book Press, Brattleboro, Vermont

# New from Jewish Lights

## "WHO IS A JEW?"
### Conversations, Not Conclusions
by *Meryl Hyman*

Who is "Jewish enough" to be considered a Jew? And by whom?

Meryl Hyman courageously takes on this timely and controversial question to give readers the perspective necessary to draw their own conclusions. With the skill of a seasoned journalist, she weaves her own life experiences into this complex and controversial story. Profound personal questions of identity are explored in conversations with Jew and non-Jew in the U.S., Israel and England. *"Who Is a Jew?"* is a book for those who seek to understand the issue, and for those who think they already do.

6" x 9", 272 pp. HC, ISBN 1-879045-76-1 **$23.95**

---

## THE JEWISH GARDENING COOKBOOK
### Growing Plants and Cooking for Holidays & Festivals
by *Michael Brown*

Through gardening and cooking for holiday and festival use, we can recover and discover many exciting aspects of Judaism to nourish both the mind and the spirit. Whether you garden in an herb garden, on a city apartment windowsill or patio, or on an acre, with the fruits and vegetables of your own gardening labors, the traditional repasts of Jewish holidays and celebrations can be understood in many new ways!

Gives easy-to-follow instructions for raising foods that have been harvested since ancient times. Provides carefully selected, tasty and easy-to-prepare recipes using these traditional foodstuffs for holidays, festivals, and life cycle events. Clearly illustrated with more than 30 fine botanical illustrations. For beginner and professional alike.

6" x 9", 208 pp (est). HC, ISBN 1-58023-004-0 **$21.95**

---

## WANDERING STARS
### An Anthology of Jewish Fantasy & Science Fiction
Edited by *Jack Dann; with an Introduction by Isaac Asimov*

*Jewish* science fiction and fantasy? Yes!

Here is the distinguished list of contributors to *Wandering Stars*, originally published in 1974 and the only book of its kind, anywhere: Bernard Malamud, Isaac Bashevis Singer, Isaac Asimov, Robert Silverberg, Harlan Ellison, Pamela Sargent, Avram Davidson, Geo. Alec Effinger, Horace L. Gold, Robert Sheckley, William Tenn and Carol Carr. Pure enjoyment. We laughed out loud reading it. A 25th Anniversary Classic Reprint.

"It is delightful and deep, hilarious and sad." —*James Morrow, author*, Towing Jehovah

6" x 9", 272 pp. Quality Paperback, ISBN 1-58023-005-9 **$16.95**

---

## THE ENNEAGRAM AND KABBALAH
### Reading Your Soul
by *Rabbi Howard A. Addison*

What do the Enneagram and *Kabbalah* have in common? Together, can they provide a powerful tool for self-knowledge, critique, and transformation?

How can we distinguish between acquired personality traits and the essential self hidden underneath?

6" x 9", 160 pp (est.), Quality Paperback Original, ISBN 1-58023-001-6 **$15.95**

# *Spirituality*

## HOW TO BE A PERFECT STRANGER, In 2 Volumes
### A Guide to Etiquette in Other People's Religious Ceremonies
Edited by *Stuart M. Matlins & Arthur J. Magida*

BEST REFERENCE BOOK OF THE YEAR

*"A book that belongs in every living room, library and office!"*

•AWARD WINNER•

Explains the rituals and celebrations of America's major religions/denominations, helping an interested guest to feel comfortable, participate to the fullest extent possible, and avoid violating anyone's religious principles. Answers practical questions from the perspective of *any* other faith.

### VOL. 1: America's Largest Faiths

VOL. 1 COVERS: Assemblies of God • Baptist • Buddhist • Christian Science • Churches of Christ • Disciples of Christ • Episcopalian • Greek Orthodox • Hindu • Islam • Jehovah's Witnesses • Jewish • Lutheran • Methodist • Mormon • Presbyterian • Quaker • Roman Catholic • Seventh-day Adventist • United Church of Christ

6" x 9", 432 pp. Hardcover, ISBN 1-879045-39-7 **$24.95**

### VOL. 2: Other Faiths in America

VOL. 2 COVERS: African American Methodist Churches • Baha'i • Christian and Missionary Alliance • Christian Congregation • Church of the Brethren • Church of the Nazarene • Evangelical Free Church of America • International Church of the Foursquare Gospel • International Pentecostal Holiness Church • Mennonite/Amish • Native American • Orthodox Churches • Pentecostal Church of God • Reformed Church of America • Sikh • Unitarian Universalist • Wesleyan

6" x 9", 416 pp. HC, ISBN 1-879045-63-X **$24.95**

---

## GOD & THE BIG BANG
### Discovering Harmony Between Science & Spirituality
by *Daniel C. Matt*

Mysticism and science: What do they have in common? How can one enlighten the other? By drawing on modern cosmology and ancient Kabbalah, Matt shows how science and religion can together enrich our spiritual awareness and help us recover a sense of wonder and find our place in the universe.

"This poetic new book...helps us to understand the human meaning of creation."
—*Joel Primack, leading cosmologist, Professor of Physics, University of California, Santa Cruz*

•AWARD WINNER•

6" x 9", 216 pp. Quality Paperback, ISBN 1-879045-89-3 **$16.95** HC, ISBN-48-6 **$21.95**

---

## MINDING THE TEMPLE OF THE SOUL
### Balancing Body, Mind, & Spirit through Traditional Jewish Prayer, Movement, & Meditation
by *Tamar Frankiel* and *Judy Greenfeld*

This new spiritual approach to physical health introduces readers to a spiritual tradition that affirms the body and enables them to reconceive their bodies in a more positive light. Relying on Kabbalistic teachings and other Jewish traditions, it shows us how to be more responsible for our own psychological and physical health. Focuses on the discipline of prayer, simple Tai Chi–like exercises and body positions, and guides the reader throughout, step-by-step, with diagrams, sketches and meditations.

7"x 10", 184 pp. Quality Paperback Original, illus., ISBN 1-879045-64-8 **$16.95**

**Audiotape of the Blessings, Movements & Meditations** (60-min. cassette) **$9.95**
**Videotape of the Movements & Meditations** (46-min. VHS) **$20.00**

# Spirituality

## MY PEOPLE'S PRAYER BOOK
### Traditional Prayers, Modern Commentaries
### Vol. 1—The Sh'ma and Its Blessings
Edited by *Rabbi Lawrence A. Hoffman*

Provides a diverse and exciting commentary to the traditional liturgy, written by 10 of today's most respected scholars and teachers from all perspectives of the Jewish world.

This groundbreaking first of seven volumes examines the oldest and best-known of Jewish prayers. Often the first prayer memorized by children and the last prayer recited on a deathbed, the *Sh'ma* frames a Jewish life.

"This book engages the mind and heart....It challenges one's assumptions at whatever level of understanding one brings to the text."
*—Jewish Herald-Voice*

7" x 10", 168 pp. HC, ISBN 1-879045-79-6 **$19.95**

## FINDING JOY
### A Practical Spiritual Guide to Happiness
by *Dannel I. Schwartz* with *Mark Hass*

Searching for happiness in our modern world of stress and struggle is common; *finding* it is more unusual. This guide explores and explains how to find joy through a time-honored, creative—and surprisingly practical—approach based on the teachings of Jewish mysticism and Kabbalah.

"Lovely, simple introduction to Kabbalah....a singular contribution...."
*—American Library Association's* Booklist

•AWARD WINNER•         6" x 9", 192 pp. HC, ISBN 1-879045-53-2 **$19.95**

## THE DEATH OF DEATH
### Resurrection and Immortality in Jewish Thought
by *Neil Gillman*

Noted theologian Neil Gillman explores the original and compelling argument that Judaism, a religion often thought to pay little attention to the afterlife, not only offers us rich ideas on the subject—but delivers a deathblow to death itself. By exploring Jewish thought about death and the afterlife, this fascinating work presents us with challenging new ideas about our lives.

"Enables us to recover our tradition's understanding of the afterlife and breaks through the silence of modern Jewish thought on immortality.... A work of major •AWARD WINNER• significance."
*—Rabbi Sheldon Zimmerman, President, Hebrew Union College–Jewish Institute of Religion*

6" x 9", 336 pp., HC, ISBN 1-879045-61-3 **$23.95**

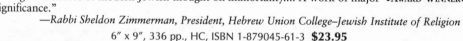

## THE EMPTY CHAIR: FINDING HOPE & JOY
### Timeless Wisdom from a Hasidic Master,
### Rebbe Nachman of Breslov
*Adapted by Moshe Mykoff and the Breslov Research Institute*

A "little treasure" of aphorisms and advice for living joyously and spiritually today, written 200 years ago, but startlingly fresh in meaning and use. Challenges and helps us to move from stress and sadness to hope and joy.

Teacher, guide and spiritual master—Rebbe Nachman provides vital words of inspiration and wisdom for life today for people of any faith, or of no faith.

•AWARD WINNER•

"For anyone of any faith, this is a book of healing and wholeness, of being alive!"
*— Bookviews*

4" x 6", 128 pp., 2-color text, Deluxe Paperback, ISBN 1-879045-67-2 **$9.95**

# *Spirituality*

## MEDITATION FROM THE HEART OF JUDAISM
### Today's Teachers Share Their Practices, Techniques, and Faith
Edited by *Avram Davis*

A "how-to" guide for both beginning and experienced meditators, it will help you start meditating or help you enhance your practice.

Twenty-two masters of meditation explain why and how they meditate. *A detailed compendium of the experts' "Best Practices"* offers practical advice and starting points.

> "A treasury of meditative insights and techniques....Each page is a meditative experience that brings you closer to God."
> —*Rabbi Shoni Labowitz, author of* Miraculous Living: A Guided Journey in Kabbalah through the Ten Gates of the Tree of Life

6" x 9", 256 pp. Hardcover, ISBN 1-879045-77-X **$21.95**

## SELF, STRUGGLE & CHANGE
### Family Conflict Stories in Genesis and Their Healing Insights for Our Lives
by *Norman J. Cohen*

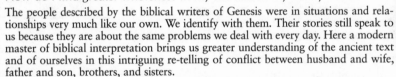

*How do I find greater wholeness in my life and in my family's life?*

The people described by the biblical writers of Genesis were in situations and relationships very much like our own. We identify with them. Their stories still speak to us because they are about the same problems we deal with every day. Here a modern master of biblical interpretation brings us greater understanding of the ancient text and of ourselves in this intriguing re-telling of conflict between husband and wife, father and son, brothers, and sisters.

"Delightfully written...rare erudition, sensitivity and insight."    —*Elie Wiesel*

6" x 9", 224 pp. Quality Paperback, ISBN 1-879045-66-4 **$16.95**; HC, ISBN-19-2 **$21.95**

## ECOLOGY & THE JEWISH SPIRIT
### Where Nature & the Sacred Meet
Edited and with Introductions by *Ellen Bernstein*

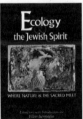

*What is nature's place in our spiritual lives?*

A focus on nature is part of the fabric of Jewish thought. Here, experts bring us a richer understanding of the long-neglected themes of nature that are woven through the biblical creation story, ancient texts, traditional law, the holiday cycles, prayer, *mitzvot* (good deeds), and community.

For people of all faiths, all backgrounds, this book helps us to make nature a sacred, spiritual part of our own lives.

"A great resource for anyone seeking to explore the connection between their faith and caring for God's good creation, our environment."
—*Paul Gorman, Executive Director, National Religious Partnership for the Environment*

6" x 9", 288 pp. HC, ISBN 1-879045-88-5 **$23.95**

## ISRAEL—A SPIRITUAL TRAVEL GUIDE
### A Companion for the Modern Jewish Pilgrim
by *Rabbi Lawrence A. Hoffman*

*Be spiritually prepared for your journey to Israel.*

A Jewish spiritual travel guide to Israel, helping today's pilgrim tap into the deep spiritual meaning of the ancient—and modern—sites of the Holy Land. Combines in quick reference format ancient blessings, medieval prayers, biblical and historical references, and modern poetry. The only guidebook that helps readers to prepare spiritually for the occasion. More than a guide book: It is a spiritual map.

"To add spiritual dimension to your journey, pack this extraordinary new guidebook to Israel. I'll be bringing it on my next visit."
—*Gabe Levenson, travel columnist for* The New York Jewish Week

4 3/4" x 10 1/8", 192 pp. (est.) Quality Paperback Original, ISBN 1-879045-56-7 **$18.95**

# Spirituality—The Kushner Series

## INVISIBLE LINES OF CONNECTION
### Sacred Stories of the Ordinary
by *Lawrence Kushner*

Through his everyday encounters with family, friends, colleagues and strangers, Kushner takes us deeply into our lives, finding flashes of spiritual insight in the process. This is a book where literature meets spirituality, where the sacred meets the ordinary, and, above all, where people of all faiths, all backgrounds can meet one another and themselves.

•AWARD WINNER•

"Does something both more and different than instruct—it inspirits. Wonderful stories, from the best storyteller I know."
— *David Mamet*

5 1/2" x 8 1/2", 160 pp. Quality Paperback, ISBN 1-879045-98-2 **$15.95**  HC, -52-4 **$21.95**

## HONEY FROM THE ROCK
### An Easy Introduction to Jewish Mysticism
by *Lawrence Kushner*

"Quite simply the easiest introduction to Jewish mysticism you can read."

An introduction to the ten gates of Jewish mysticism and how it applies to daily life.

"Captures the flavor and spark of Jewish mysticism. . . . Read it and be rewarded." —*Elie Wiesel*

6" x 9", 168 pp. Quality Paperback, ISBN 1-879045-02-8 **$14.95**

## THE BOOK OF WORDS
### Talking Spiritual Life, Living Spiritual Talk
by *Lawrence Kushner*

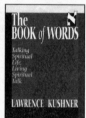

In the incomparable manner of his extraordinary *The Book of Letters*, Kushner now lifts up and shakes the dust off primary religious words we use to describe the spiritual dimension of life. For each word Kushner offers us a startling, moving and insightful explication, and pointed readings from classical Jewish sources that further illuminate the concept. He concludes with a short exercise that helps unite the spirit of the word with our actions in the world.

"This is a powerful and holy book."
—*M. Scott Peck, M.D., author of* The Road Less Traveled *and other books*

"What a delightful wholeness of intellectual vigor and meditative playfulness, and all in a tone of gentleness that speaks to this gentile."
—*Rt. Rev. Krister Stendahl, formerly Dean, Harvard Divinity School/Bishop of Stockholm*

6" x 9", 152 pp. HC, beautiful two-color text, ISBN 1-879045-35-4 **$21.95**

## THE BOOK OF LETTERS
### A Mystical Hebrew Alphabet
by *Rabbi Lawrence Kushner*

In calligraphy by the author. Folktales about and exploration of the mystical meanings of the Hebrew Alphabet. Open the old prayerbook-like pages of *The Book of Letters* and you will enter a special world of sacred tradition and religious feeling. Rabbi Kushner draws from ancient Judaic sources, weaving talmudic commentary, Hasidic folktales, and kabbalistic mysteries around the letters.

"A book which is in love with Jewish letters."
— *Isaac Bashevis Singer* (לֹ)

•AWARD WINNER•

• **Popular Hardcover Edition** 6"x 9", 80 pp. HC, two colors, inspiring new Foreword. ISBN 1-879045-00-1  **$24.95**

• **Deluxe Gift Edition** 9"x 12", 80 pp. HC, four-color text, ornamentation, in a beautiful slipcase. ISBN 1-879045-01-X  **$79.95**

• **Collector's Limited Edition** 9"x 12", 80 pp. HC, gold-embossed pages, hand-assembled slipcase. With silkscreened print. **Limited to 500 signed and numbered copies.** ISBN 1-879045-04-4  **$349.00**

*To see a sample page at no obligation, call us*

# *Spirituality*

## GOD WAS IN THIS PLACE & I, i DID NOT KNOW
### Finding Self, Spirituality & Ultimate Meaning
*by Lawrence Kushner*

Who am I? Who is God? Kushner creates inspiring interpretations of Jacob's dream in Genesis, opening a window into Jewish spirituality for people of all faiths and backgrounds.

In this fascinating blend of scholarship, imagination, psychology and history, seven Jewish spiritual masters ask and answer fundamental questions of human experience.

"Rich and intriguing."
—*M. Scott Peck, M.D., author of* The Road Less Traveled *and other books*

6" x 9", 192 pp. Quality Paperback, ISBN 1-879045-33-8 **$16.95**

---

## THE RIVER OF LIGHT
### Spirituality, Judaism, Consciousness
*by Lawrence Kushner*

THE RIVER *of* LIGHT
Spirituality, Judaism, Consciousness
LAWRENCE KUSHNER

A "manual" for all spiritual travelers who would attempt a spiritual journey in our times. Taking us step by step, Kushner allows us to discover the meaning of our own quest: "to allow the river of light—the deepest currents of consciousness—to rise to the surface and animate our lives."

"Philosophy and mystical fantasy....Anybody—Jewish, Christian, or otherwise...will find this book an intriguing experience."
—*Kirkus Reviews*

6" x 9", 180 pp. Quality Paperback, ISBN 1-879045-03-6 **$14.95**

---

## GODWRESTLING—ROUND 2
### Ancient Wisdom, Future Paths
*by Arthur Waskow*

BEST RELIGION BOOK OF THE YEAR

This 20th-anniversary sequel to a seminal book of the Jewish renewal movement deals with spirituality in relation to personal growth, marriage, ecology, feminism, politics, and more. Including new chapters on recent issues and concerns, Waskow outlines original ways to merge "religious" life and "personal" life in our society today.

•AWARD WINNER•

"A delicious read and a soaring meditation."
—*Rabbi Zalman M. Schachter-Shalomi*

"Vivid as a novel, sharp, eccentric, loud....An important book for anyone who wants to bring Judaism alive."
—*Marge Piercy*

6" x 9", 352 pp. Quality Paperback, ISBN 1-879045-72-9 **$18.95** HC, ISBN-45-1 **$23.95**

---

## BEING GOD'S PARTNER
### How to Find the Hidden Link Between Spirituality and Your Work
*by Jeffrey K. Salkin* Introduction by *Norman Lear*

Being God's Partner
How to Find the Hidden Link Between Spirituality and Your Work
Jeffrey K. Salkin

Will challenge people of every denomination to reconcile the cares of work and soul. A groundbreaking book about spirituality and the work world, from a Jewish perspective. Helps the reader find God in the ethical striving and search for meaning in the professions and in business and offers practical suggestions for balancing your professional life and spiritual self.

"This engaging meditation on the spirituality of work is grounded in Judaism but is relevant well beyond the boundaries of that tradition."
—*Booklist (American Library Association)*

6" x 9", 192 pp. Quality Paperback, ISBN 1-879045-65-6 **$16.95** HC, ISBN-37-0 **$19.95**

# Healing/Recovery/Wellness

## Experts Praise *Twelve Jewish Steps to Recovery*

"Recommended reading for people of all denominations."
—*Rabbi Abraham J. Twerski, M.D.*

### TWELVE JEWISH STEPS TO RECOVERY
### A Personal Guide to Turning from Alcoholism & Other Addictions...Drugs, Food, Gambling, Sex...
by *Rabbi Kerry M. Olitzky & Stuart A. Copans, M.D.*
Preface by *Abraham J. Twerski, M.D.;* Intro. by *Rabbi Sheldon Zimmerman;* "Getting Help" by *JACS Foundation*

A Jewish perspective on the Twelve Steps of addiction recovery programs with consolation, inspiration and motivation for recovery. It draws from traditional sources and quotes from what recovering Jewish people say about their experiences with addictions of all kinds. Inspiring illustrations of the twelve gates of the Old City of Jerusalem introduce each step.

6" x 9", 136 pp. Quality Paperback, ISBN 1-879045-09-5 **$13.95**

---

### *Recovery from Codependence: A Jewish Twelve Steps Guide to Healing Your Soul*
by Rabbi Kerry M. Olitzky

6" x 9", 160 pp. Quality Paperback Original, ISBN 1-879045-32-X **$13.95**   HC, ISBN-27-3 **$21.95**

### *Renewed Each Day: Daily Twelve Step Recovery Meditations Based on the Bible*
by Rabbi Kerry M. Olitzky & Aaron Z.

6" x 9", Quality Paperback Original,   **V. I**, 224 pp. **$14.95**   **V. II**, 280 pp. **$16.95**
**Two-Volume Set** ISBN 1-879045-21-4   **$27.90**

### *One Hundred Blessings Every Day: Daily Twelve Step Recovery Affirmations, Exercises for Personal Growth & Renewal Reflecting Seasons of the Jewish Year*
by Rabbi Kerry M. Olitzky

4 1/2" x 6 1/2", 432 pp. Quality Paperback Original, ISBN 1-879045-30-3   **$14.95**

---

### HEALING OF SOUL, HEALING OF BODY
### Spiritual Leaders Unfold the Strength and Solace in Psalms
Edited by *Rabbi Simkha Y. Weintraub, CSW, for The Jewish Healing Center*

A source of solace for those who are facing illness, as well as those who care for them. The ten Psalms which form the core of this healing resource were originally selected 200 years ago by Rabbi Nachman of Breslov as a "complete remedy." Today, for anyone coping with illness, they continue to provide a wellspring of strength. Each Psalm is newly translated, making it clear and accessible, and each one is introduced by an eminent rabbi, men and women reflecting different movements and backgrounds. To all who are living with the pain and uncertainty of illness, this spiritual resource offers an anchor of spiritual comfort.

"Will bring comfort to anyone fortunate enough to read it. This gentle book is a luminous gem of wisdom."
—*Larry Dossey, M.D., author of* Healing Words: The Power of Prayer & the Practice of Medicine

6" x 9", 128 pp. Quality Paperback Original, illus., 2-color text, ISBN 1-879045-31-1   **$14.95**

# Theology/Philosophy

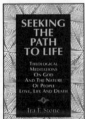

•AWARD WINNER•

## A LIVING COVENANT
### The Innovative Spirit in Traditional Judaism
by *David Hartman*

*WINNER,*
*National Jewish*
*Book Award*

The Judaic tradition is often seen as being more concerned with uncritical obedience to law than with individual freedom and responsibility. Hartman challenges this approach by revealing a Judaism grounded in a covenant—a relational framework—informed by the metaphor of marital love rather than that of parent-child dependency.

"Jews and non-Jews, liberals and traditionalists will see classic Judaism anew in these pages."
— *Dr. Eugene B. Borowitz, Hebrew Union College–Jewish Institute of Religion*
6" x 9", 368 pp. Quality Paperback, ISBN 1-58023-011-3 **$18.95**

## THE SPIRIT OF RENEWAL
### Finding Faith after the Holocaust
by *Edward Feld*

Trying to understand the Holocaust and addressing the question of faith after the Holocaust, Rabbi Feld explores three key cycles of destruction and recovery in Jewish history, each of which radically reshaped Jewish understanding of God, people, and the world.

"A profound meditation on Jewish history [and the Holocaust]....Christians, as well as many others, need to share in this story."
— *The Rt. Rev. Frederick H. Borsch, Ph.D., Episcopal Bishop of L.A.*
6" x 9", 224 pp. Quality Paperback, ISBN 1-879045-40-0 **$16.95**

•AWARD WINNER•

## SEEKING THE PATH TO LIFE
### Theological Meditations On God
### and the Nature of People, Love, Life and Death
by *Rabbi Ira F. Stone*

For people who never thought they would read a book of theology—let alone understand it, enjoy it, savor it and have it affect the way they think about their lives. In 45 intense meditations, each a page or two in length, Stone takes us on explorations of the most basic human struggles: Life and death, love and anger, peace and war, covenant and exile.

•AWARD WINNER• "A bold book....The reader of any faith will be inspired...."
— *The Rev. Carla V. Berkedal, Episcopal Priest*
6" x 9", 132 pp. Quality Paperback, ISBN 1-879045-47-8 **$14.95** HC, ISBN-17-6 **$19.95**

CLASSICS BY ABRAHAM JOSHUA HESCHEL

*The Earth Is the Lord's: The Inner World of the Jew in Eastern Europe*
5 1/2" x 8", 112 pp, Quality Paperback, ISBN 1-879045-42-7 **$13.95**

*Israel: An Echo of Eternity* with new Introduction by Susannah Heschel
5 1/2" x 8", 272 pp, Quality Paperback, ISBN 1-879045-70-2 **$18.95**

*A Passion for Truth: Despair and Hope in Hasidism*
5 1/2" x 8", 352 pp, Quality Paperback, ISBN 1-879045-41-9 **$18.95**

THEOLOGY & PHILOSOPHY...Other books—Classic Reprints

*Aspects of Rabbinic Theology* by Solomon Schechter, with a new Introduction by Neil Gillman 6" x 9", 440 pp, Quality Paperback, ISBN 1-879045-24-9 **$18.95**

*The Last Trial: On the Legends and Lore of the Command to Abraham to Offer Isaac as a Sacrifice* by Shalom Spiegel, with a new Introduction by Judah Goldin
6" x 9", 208 pp, Quality Paperback, ISBN 1-879045-29-X **$17.95**

*Judaism and Modern Man: An Interpretation of Jewish Religion* by Will Herberg; new Introduction by Neil Gillman 5.5" x 8.5", 336 pp, Quality Paperback, ISBN 1-879045-87-7 **$18.95**

*Tormented Master: The Life and Spiritual Quest of Rabbi Nahman of Bratslav* by Arthur Green 6" x 9", 408 pp, Quality Paperback, ISBN 1-879045-11-7 **$18.95**

*Your Word Is Fire* Ed. and trans. with a new Introduction by Arthur Green and Barry W. Holtz 6" x 9", 152 pp, Quality Paperback, ISBN 1-879045-25-7 **$14.95**

# Life Cycle

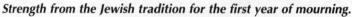

## GRIEF IN OUR SEASONS
### A Mourner's Kaddish Companion
by *Rabbi Kerry M. Olitzky*

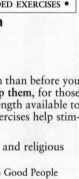

**Strength from the Jewish tradition for the first year of mourning.**

Provides a wise and inspiring selection of sacred Jewish writings and a simple, powerful ancient ritual for mourners to read each day, to help hold the memory of their loved ones in their hearts. It offers a comforting, step-by-step daily link to saying *Kaddish*.

"A hopeful, compassionate guide along the journey from grief to rebirth from mourning to a new morning."
—*Rabbi Levi Meier, Ph.D., Chaplain, Cedars–Sinai Medical Center, Los Angeles*

4 1/2" x 6 1/2", 448 pp., Quality Paperback Original, ISBN 1-879045-55-9 **$15.95**

---

## MOURNING & MITZVAH    • WITH OVER 60 GUIDED EXERCISES •
### A Guided Journal for Walking the Mourner's Path Through Grief to Healing
by *Anne Brener, L.C.S.W.*; Foreword by *Rabbi Jack Riemer*; Introduction by *Rabbi William Cutter*

"Fully engaging in mourning means you will be a different person than before you began." **For those who mourn a death, for those who would help them,** for those who face a loss of any kind, Brener teaches us the power and strength available to us in the fully experienced mourning process. Guided writing exercises help stimulate the processes of both conscious and unconscious healing.

"A stunning book! It offers an exploration in depth of the place where psychology and religious ritual intersect, and the name of that place is Truth."
—*Rabbi Harold Kushner, author of* When Bad Things Happen to Good People

7 1/2" x 9", 288 pp. Quality Paperback Original, ISBN 1-879045-23-0 **$19.95**

---

## A TIME TO MOURN, A TIME TO COMFORT
### A Guide to Jewish Bereavement and Comfort
by *Dr. Ron Wolfson*

A guide to meeting the needs of those who mourn and those who seek to provide comfort in times of sadness. While this book is written from a layperson's point of view, it also includes the specifics for funeral preparations and practical guidance for preparing the home and family to sit *shiva*.

"A sensitive and perceptive guide to Jewish tradition. Both those who mourn and those who comfort will find it a map to accompany them through the whirlwind."
—*Deborah E. Lipstadt, Emory University*

7" x 9", 320 pp. Quality Paperback, ISBN 1-879045-96-6 **$16.95**

---

## WHEN A GRANDPARENT DIES
### A Kid's Own Remembering Workbook for Dealing with Shiva and the Year Beyond
by *Nechama Liss-Levinson, Ph.D.*

Drawing insights from both psychology and Jewish tradition, this workbook helps children participate in the process of mourning, offering guided exercises, rituals, and places to write, draw, list, create and express their feelings.

"Will bring support, guidance, and understanding for countless children, teachers, and health professionals."
—*Rabbi Earl A. Grollman, D.D., author of* Talking about Death

8" x 10", 48 pp. HC, illus., 2-color text, ISBN 1-879045-44-3 **$15.95**

# Life Cycle

## A HEART OF WISDOM
### Making the Jewish Journey from Midlife Through the Elder Years
Edited by *Susan Berrin*

We are all growing older. *A Heart of Wisdom* shows us how to understand our own process of aging—and the aging of those we care about—from a Jewish perspective, from midlife through the elder years.

How does Jewish tradition influence our own aging? How does living, thinking and worshipping as a Jew affect us as we age? How can Jewish tradition help us retain our dignity as we age? Offers insights and enlightenment from Jewish tradition.

"A thoughtfully orchestrated collection of pieces that deal candidly and compassionately with a period of growing concern to us all: midlife through old age."
—*Chaim Potok*

6" x 9", 384 pp. HC, ISBN 1-879045-73-7 **$24.95**

---

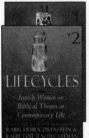

## LIFECYCLES
### V. 1: Jewish Women on Life Passages & Personal Milestones
Edited and with Introductions by *Rabbi Debra Orenstein*
### V. 2: Jewish Women on Biblical Themes in Contemporary Life
Edited and with Introductions by
*Rabbi Debra Orenstein* and *Rabbi Jane Rachel Litman*

This unique multivolume collaboration brings together over one hundred women writers, rabbis, and scholars to create the first comprehensive work on Jewish life cycle that fully includes women's perspectives.

•AWARD WINNER•

"Nothing is missing from this marvelous collection. You will turn to it for rituals and inspiration, prayer and poetry, comfort and community. *Lifecycles* is a gift to the Jewish woman in America."
—*Letty Cottin Pogrebin, author of* Deborah, Golda, and Me:
Being Female and Jewish in America

**V. 1:** 6" x 9", 480 pp. HC, ISBN 1-879045-14-1, **$24.95**; **V. 2:** 6" x 9", 464 pp. HC, ISBN 1-879045-15-X, **$24.95**

---

LIFE CYCLE— The Art of Jewish Living Series for Holiday Observance
by Dr. Ron Wolfson

*Hanukkah*—7" x 9", 192 pp. Quality Paperback, ISBN 1-879045-97-4 **$16.95**

*The Shabbat Seder*—7" x 9", 272 pp. Quality Paperback, ISBN 1-879045-90-7 **$16.95**; Booklet of Blessings **$5.00**; Audiocassette of Blessings **$6.00**; Teacher's Guide **$4.95**

*The Passover Seder*—7" x 9", 336 pp. Quality Paperback, ISBN 1-879045-93-1 **$16.95**; Passover Workbook, **$6.95**; Audiocassette of Blessings, **$6.00**; Teacher's Guide, **$4.95**

---

LIFE CYCLE...Other Books

***Bar/Bat Mitzvah Basics: A Practical Family Guide to Coming of Age Together***
Ed. by Cantor Helen Leneman  6" x 9", 240 pp. Quality Paperback, ISBN 1-879045-54-0 **$16.95**

***Embracing the Covenant: Converts to Judaism Talk About Why & How***
Ed. and with Intros. by Rabbi Allan L. Berkowitz and Patti Moskovitz
6" x 9", 192 pp. Quality Paperback, ISBN 1-879045-50-8 **$15.95**

***The New Jewish Baby Book: Names, Ceremonies, Customs—A Guide for Today's Families*** by Anita Diamant  6" x 9", 328 pp. Quality Paperback, ISBN 1-879045-28-1 **$16.95**

***Putting God on the Guest List, 2nd Ed.: How to Reclaim the Spiritual Meaning of Your Child's Bar or Bat Mitzvah*** by Rabbi Jeffrey K. Salkin  6" x 9", 224 pp. Quality Paperback, ISBN 1-897045-59-1 **$16.95**; HC, ISBN 1-879045-58-3 **$24.95**

***So That Your Values Live On: Ethical Wills & How to Prepare Them***
Ed. by Rabbi Jack Riemer & Professor Nathaniel Stampfer
6" x 9", 272 pp. Quality Paperback, ISBN 1-879045-34-6 **$17.95**

# Children's Spirituality

## A PRAYER FOR THE EARTH
### The Story of Naamah, Noah's Wife

**For ages 4 and up**

by *Sandy Eisenberg Sasso*
Full-color illustrations by *Bethanne Andersen*

NONDENOMINATIONAL, NONSECTARIAN

This new story, based on an ancient text, opens readers' religious imaginations to new ideas about the well-known story of the Flood. When God tells Noah to bring the animals of the world onto the ark, God *also* calls on Naamah, Noah's wife, to save each plant on Earth.

> "A lovely tale....Children of all ages should be drawn to this parable for our times."
> —*Tomie dePaola, artist/author of books for children*

**•AWARD WINNER•**

9" x 12", 32 pp. HC, Full-color illus., ISBN 1-879045-60-5 **$16.95**

---

## THE 11TH COMMANDMENT
### Wisdom from Our Children

**For all ages**

by The Children of America

MULTICULTURAL, NONDENOMINATIONAL, NONSECTARIAN

"If there were an Eleventh Commandment, what would it be?"

Children of many religious denominations across America answer this question— in their own drawings and words—in *The 11th Commandment*.

> "Wonderful....This unusual book provides both food for thought and insight into the hopes and fears of today's young."
> —*American Library Association's* Booklist

8" x 10", 48 pp. HC, Full-color illus., ISBN 1-879045-46-X **$16.95**

---

## SHARING BLESSINGS
### Children's Stories for Exploring the Spirit of the Jewish Holidays

**For ages 6 and up**

by *Rahel Musleah* and *Rabbi Michael Klayman*
Full-color illustrations by *Mary O'Keefe Young*

**What is the spiritual message of each of the Jewish holidays?
How do we teach it to our children?**

Many books tell children about the historical significance and customs of the holidays. Now, through engaging, creative stories about one family's spiritual preparation, *Sharing Blessings* explores ways to get into the *spirit* of 13 different holidays.

> "A beguiling introduction to important Jewish values by way of the holidays."
> —*Rabbi Harold Kushner, author of* When Bad Things Happen to Good People *and* How Good Do We Have to Be?

7" x 10", 64 pp. HC, Full-color illus., ISBN 1-879045-71-0 **$18.95**

---

## THE BOOK OF MIRACLES
### A Young Person's Guide to Jewish Spiritual Awareness

**For ages 9–13**

by *Lawrence Kushner*

**With a Special 10th Anniversary Introduction and all new illustrations by the author.**

From the miracle at the Red Sea to the miracle of waking up this morning, this intriguing book introduces kids to a way of everyday spiritual thinking to last a lifetime. Kushner, whose award-winning books have brought spirituality to life for countless adults, now shows young people how to use Judaism as a foundation on which to build their lives.

6" x 9", 96 pp. HC, 2-color illus., ISBN 1-879045-78-8 **$16.95**

# *Children's Spirituality*

**For ages 8 and up**

## BUT GOD REMEMBERED
### Stories of Women from Creation to the Promised Land
by *Sandy Eisenberg Sasso*
Full-color illustrations by *Bethanne Andersen*

NONDENOMINATIONAL, NONSECTARIAN

A fascinating collection of four different stories of women only briefly mentioned in biblical tradition and religious texts, but never before explored. Award-winning author Sasso brings to life the intriguing stories of Lilith, Serach, Bityah, and the Daughters of Z, courageous and strong women from ancient tradition. All teach important values through their faith and actions.

•AWARD WINNER•

"Exquisite....a book of beauty, strength and spirituality."
—*Association of Bible Teachers*

9" x 12", 32 pp. HC, Full-color illus., ISBN 1-879045-43-5 **$16.95**

---

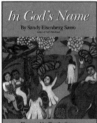

## IN GOD'S NAME
by *Sandy Eisenberg Sasso*
Full-color illustrations by *Phoebe Stone*

**For ages 4 and up**

MULTICULTURAL, NONDENOMINATIONAL, NONSECTARIAN

Like an ancient myth in its poetic text and vibrant illustrations, this modern fable about the search for God's name celebrates the diversity and, at the same time, the unity of all the people of the world. Each seeker claims he or she alone knows the answer. Finally, they come together and learn what God's name really is, sharing the ultimate harmony of belief in one God by people of all faiths, all backgrounds.

•AWARD WINNER• "I got goose bumps when I read *In God's Name*, its language and illustrations are that moving. This is a book children will love and the whole family will cherish for its beauty and power."
—*Francine Klagsbrun, author of* Mixed Feelings: Love, Hate, Rivalry, and Reconciliation among Brothers and Sisters

"What a lovely, healing book!"
—*Madeleine L'Engle*

> Selected by
> Parent Council, Ltd.™

9" x 12", 32 pp. HC, Full color illus., ISBN 1-879045-26-5 **$16.95**

---

**For ages 4 and up**

## GOD'S PAINTBRUSH
by *Sandy Eisenberg Sasso*
Full-color illustrations by *Annette Compton*

MULTICULTURAL, NONDENOMINATIONAL, NONSECTARIAN

Invites children of all faiths and backgrounds to encounter God openly in their own lives. Wonderfully interactive, provides questions adult and child can explore together at the end of each episode.

"An excellent way to honor the imaginative breadth and depth of the spiritual life of the young."
—*Dr. Robert Coles, Harvard University*

•AWARD WINNER•

11" x 8 1/2", 32 pp. HC, Full-color illus., ISBN 1-879045-22-2 **$16.95**

## *Also Available!*
**Teacher's Guide: A Guide for Jewish & Christian Educators and Parents**
8 1/2" x 11", 32 pp. PB, ISBN 1-879045-57-5 **$6.95**

# AVAILABLE FROM BETTER BOOKSTORES. TRY YOUR BOOKSTORE FIRST.

## *Order Information*

| # of Copies | Book Title / ISBN (Last 3 digits) | $ Amount |
|---|---|---|
| _____ | _____ | _____ |
| _____ | _____ | _____ |
| _____ | _____ | _____ |
| _____ | _____ | _____ |
| _____ | _____ | _____ |
| _____ | _____ | _____ |
| _____ | _____ | _____ |
| _____ | _____ | _____ |
| _____ | _____ | _____ |
| _____ | _____ | _____ |
| _____ | _____ | _____ |
| _____ | _____ | _____ |
| _____ | _____ | _____ |

For shipping/handling, add $3.50 for the first book, $2.00 each
add'l book (to a max of $15.00)   **$ S/H** _____

**TOTAL** _____

Check enclosed for $_____ *payable to:* JEWISH LIGHTS Publishing

Charge my credit card:     ❒ MasterCard     ❒ Visa

Credit Card #_____Expires _____

Signature _____Phone (_____)_____

Your Name _____

Street_____

City / State / Zip _____

**Ship To:**

Name _____

Street_____

City / State / Zip _____

*Phone, fax or mail to:* **JEWISH LIGHTS Publishing**
Sunset Farm Offices, Route 4 • P.O. Box 237 • Woodstock, Vermont 05091
Tel (802) 457-4000   Fax (802) 457-4004   www.jewishlights.com
***Credit card orders*** **(800) 962-4544** (9AM–5PM ET Monday–Friday)
*Generous discounts on quantity orders. SATISFACTION GUARANTEED. Prices subject to change.*